PERSIAN FIRE

Also by Tom Holland

RUBICON

PERSIAN FIRE

*The First World Empire and
the Battle for the West*

Tom Holland

DOUBLEDAY

New York   London   Toronto   Sydney   Auckland

For Jamie and Caroline

PUBLISHED BY DOUBLEDAY
a division of Random House, Inc.

DOUBLEDAY and the portrayal of an anchor with a dolphin are
registered trademarks of Random House, Inc.

Persian Fire was originally published in Great Britain in 2005 by Little,
Brown, a division of Time Warner Books UK. The Doubleday edition is
published by arrangement with Little, Brown.

Cataloging-in-Publication Data is on file with the Library of Congress

ISBN-13: 978-0-385-51311-1
ISBN-10: 0-385-51311-9

PRINTED IN THE UNITED STATES OF AMERICA

1 3 5 7 9 10 8 6 4 2

First Edition in the United States

Contents

Acknowledgments

I have been wanting to write a book on the Persian Wars since I was very young, and I owe an immense debt of gratitude to all those who have given me the opportunity to devote three years of my life to its study. To Patrick Walsh, best of friends and agents. To my editors, Richard Beswick and Steve Guise. To Gerry Howard, Dan Israel, Ricardo Artola and Joan Eloi Roca Martinez, for all their encouragement from abroad. To Louise Allen-Jones and Elizabeth van Lear, for their support from nearer home. To Amélie Kuhrt and Paul Cartledge, for sharing their incomparable scholarship so generously, and saving me from more errors than I care to count. To the staff of the library of the Society for the Promotion of Hellenic Studies, for their perfect blend of efficiency and courtesy. To Maike Bohn, for going out with Michael Cullen, and thereby introducing me to a travel writer with a limitless knowledge of Greece. To Philip, Francis and Barbaro Noel-Baker, for happy months in Euboea. To Jonathan Tite, for arranging a perfect day on a motorboat around Salamis. To Nick and Sarah Longman, for their hospitality in Athens. To my father, for his companionship on expeditions over Thermopylae. To Michael Lowry and Deniz Gurtin, for their hospitality in Bodrum. To Elahe Tabari, for her help at Persepolis. To Audrey and Becky Gordon, for everything they have done to keep the enemies of good art from the hall. To Caroline and Jamie Muir, without whose friendship, support and good humor I would still be writing this book, and to whom it is dedicated. To my beloved family, Sadie, Katy and Eliza, for enduring my long stretches of scholastic seclusion with such forbearance, and for touring dusty ruins across Greece, Iran and Turkey with such jollity, and giving me some of the happiest times of my life. οὐ μὲν γὰρ τοῦ γε κρεῖσσον καὶ ἄρειον.

List of Maps

Note on Proper Names

In the interests of accessibility, it has been my policy throughout this book to use the familiar Latinate form of a proper name rather than the Greek or Persian original: Darius, for instance, rather than Dareios or Daryush.

Preface

In the summer of 2001 a friend of mine was appointed the head of a school history department. Among the many decisions he had to take before the start of the new term in September, one was particularly pressing. For as long as anyone could remember, students in their final year had been obliged to study a special paper devoted to the rise of Hitler. Now, with my friend's promotion, the winds of change were set to blow. Hitler, he suggested to his new colleagues, should be toppled and replaced with a very different topic of study: the Crusades. Howls of anguish greeted this radical proposal. What, my friend's colleagues demanded, was the point of studying a period so alien and remote from contemporary concerns? When my friend countered by suggesting that history students might benefit from studying a topic that did not relate exclusively to twentieth-century dictators, the indignation only swelled. Totalitarianism, the other teachers argued, was a living theme, in a way that the Crusades could never be. The hatreds of Islam and Christendom, of East and West – where was the possible relevance in these?

The answer, of course, came a few weeks later, on September 11, when nineteen hijackers incinerated themselves and thousands of others in the cause of some decidedly medieval grievances. The Crusades, in the opinion of Osama bin Laden at any rate, had never ended. "It should not be hidden from you," he had warned the Muslim world back in 1996, "that the people of Islam have always suffered from aggression, iniquity and injustice imposed on them by the Zionist–Crusaders alliance."[1] Menacingly proficient at exploiting the modern world of air flight and mass communications he may be, but bin Laden has long interpreted the present in the light of the Middle Ages. In his manifestos, past and present tend to merge as though one: blood-curdling abuse of the crimes of America or Israel will mingle with demands for the restoration of Muslim rule to Spain or of the medieval Caliphate. No wonder that when President Bush chose in an unguarded moment to describe his administration's war on terrorism as a "crusade" his advisers begged him never to use the fateful word again.

That an American president might be less *au fait* with the subtleties of medieval history than a Saudi fanatic is hardly surprising, of course. "Why do they hate us?" In the days and weeks that followed September 11, President Bush was not the only one to wrestle with that question. Newspapers everywhere were filled with pundits attempting to explain Muslim resentment of the West, whether by tracing its origins back to the vagaries of recent American foreign policy, or further, to the carve-up of the Middle East by the European colonial powers, or even—following the bin Laden analysis back to its starting point—to the Crusades themselves. Here, in the notion that the first great crisis of the twenty-first century could possibly have emerged from a swirl of confused and ancient hatreds, lay a pointed irony. Globalization was supposed to have brought about the end of history, yet it appeared instead to be rousing any number of unwelcome phantoms from their ancestral resting places. For decades, the East against which the West had defined itself was communist; nowadays, as it always used to be, long before the Russian Revolution, it is Islamic. The war in Iraq; the rise of anti-immigrant, and specifically anti-Muslim, feeling across Europe; the question of whether Turkey should be allowed into the EU; all these have combined with the attacks of September 11 to foster an agonized consciousness of the fault-line that divides the Christian West from the Islamic East.

That civilizations are doomed to clash in the new century, as both al-Qaeda terrorists and Harvard academics have variously argued, remains, as yet, a controversial thesis. What cannot be disputed, however, is the degree to which different cultures, in Europe and the Muslim world at any rate, are currently being obliged to examine the very foundations of their identities. "The difference of East and West," thought Edward Gibbon, "is arbitrary and shifts round the globe."[2] Yet that it exists—that East is East, and West is West—is easily history's most abiding assumption. Older by far than the Crusades, older than Islam, older than Christianity, its pedigree is so venerable that it reaches back almost two and a half thousand years. "Why do they hate us?" It was with this question that history itself was born—for it was in the conflict between East and West that the world's first historian, back in the fifth century BC, discovered his life-work's theme.

His name was Herodotus. As a Greek from what is now the Turkish resort of Bodrum, but was then known as Halicarnassus, he had grown up on the very margin of Asia. Why, he wondered, did the peoples of East and West find it so hard to live in peace? The answer appeared, superficially, a simple one. Asiatics, Herodotus reported, saw Europe as a place irreconcilably alien. "And so it is they believe that Greeks will always be their enemies."[3] But why this fracture had opened in the first place was, Herodotus acknowledged, a puzzle. Perhaps the kidnapping of a princess or two by Greek pirates had been to blame? Or the burning of Troy? "That, at any rate, is what many nations of Asia argue—but who can say for sure if they are right?"[4] As Herodotus well knew, the world was an infinite place, and one man's truth might easily be another's lie. Yet if the origins of the conflict between East and West appeared lost in myth, then not so its effects. These had been made all too recently and tragically clear. Difference had bred suspicion—and suspicion had bred war.

Indeed, a war like no other. In 480 BC, some forty years before Herodotus began his history, Xerxes, the King of Persia, had led an invasion of Greece. Military adventures of this kind had long been a specialization of the Persians. For decades, victory—rapid, spectacular victory—had appeared to be their birthright. Their aura of invincibility reflected the unprecedented scale and speed of their conquests. Once, they had been nothing, just an obscure mountain tribe confined to the plains and mountains of what is now southern Iran. Then, in the space of a single generation, they had swept across the Middle East, shattering ancient kingdoms, storming famous cities, amassing an empire which stretched from India to the shores of the Aegean. As a result of those conquests, Xerxes had ruled as the most powerful man on the planet. The resources available to him were so stupefying as to appear virtually limitless. Europe was not to witness another invasion force to rival his until 1944, and the summer of D-Day.

Set against this unprecedented juggernaut, the Greeks had appeared few in numbers and hopelessly divided. Greece itself was little more than a geographical expression: not a country but a patchwork of quarrelsome and often violently chauvinistic city-states. True, the Greeks regarded themselves as a single people, united by language, religion and custom; but what the various cities often seemed to have most in common was an addiction to fighting one another. The Persians, during the early years of their rise to power, had found it a simple matter to subdue the Greeks who lived in what is now western Turkey—including those of Herodotus' home town—and absorb them into their empire. Even the two principal powers of mainland Greece, the nascent democracy of Athens and the sternly militarized state of Sparta, had seemed ill equipped to put up a more effective fight. With the Persian king resolved to pacify once and for all the fractious and peculiar people on the western fringe of his great empire, the result had looked to be a foregone conclusion.

Yet, astonishingly, against the largest expeditionary force ever assembled, the mainland Greeks had managed to hold out. The invaders had been turned back. Greece had remained free. The story of how they had taken on a superpower and defeated it appeared to the Greeks themselves the most extraordinary of all time. How precisely had they done it? And why? And what had caused the invasion to be launched against them in the first place? Questions such as these, not lacking in urgency even four decades later, prompted Herodotus into a wholly novel style of investigation. For the first time, a chronicler set himself to trace the origins of a conflict not to a past so remote as to be utterly fabulous, nor to the whims and wishes of some god, nor to a people's claim to a manifest destiny, but rather to explanations that he could verify personally. Committed to transcribing only living informants or eyewitness accounts, Herodotus toured the world—the first anthropologist, the first investigative reporter, the first foreign correspondent.[5] The fruit of his tireless curiosity was not merely a narrative, but a sweeping analysis of an entire age: capacious, various, tolerant. Herodotus himself described what he had engaged in as "inquiries"—"*historia.*" "And I set them down here," he declared, in the first sentence of the first work of history ever written, "so that the memory of the past may be preserved by recording the extraordinary deeds of Greek and foreigner alike—and above all, to show how it was that they came to go to war."[6]

Historians always like to argue for the significance of their material, of course. In Herodotus' case, his claims have had two and a half millennia to be put to the test. During that time, their founding presumption—that the great war between Greek and Persian was of an unexampled momentousness—has been resoundingly affirmed. John Stuart Mill claimed that "the battle of Marathon, even as an event in English history, is more important than the battle of Hastings."[7] Hegel, in the more expansive tones that one would expect of a German philosopher, declared that "the interest of the whole world's history hung trembling in the balance."[8] And so it surely did. Any account of odds heroically defied is exciting—but how much more tense it becomes when the odds are incalculably, incomparably high. There was much more at stake during the course of the Persian attempts to subdue the Greek mainland than the independence of what Xerxes had regarded as a ragbag of terrorist states. As subjects of a foreign king, the Athenians would never have had the opportunity to develop their unique democratic culture. Much that made Greek civilization distinctive would have been aborted. The legacy inherited by Rome and passed on to modern Europe would have been immeasurably impoverished. Not only would the West have lost its first struggle for independence and survival, but it is unlikely, had the Greeks succumbed to Xerxes' invasion, that there would ever have been such an entity as "the West" at all.

No wonder, then, that the story of the Persian Wars should serve as the founding myth of European civilization; as the archetype of the triumph of freedom over slavery, and of rugged civic virtue over enervated despotism. Certainly, as the word "Christendom" began to lose its resonance in the aftermath of the Reformation, so the heroics of Marathon and Salamis began to strike many idealists as an altogether more edifying exemplification of Western virtues than the Crusades. More principled, after all, to defend than to invade; better to fight for liberty than in the cause of fanaticism. One episode above all, the doomed defense of the pass of Thermopylae by a tiny Greek holding force—"four thousand against three million,"[9] as Herodotus had it—took on the particular force of myth. Teeming hordes of Asiatics, driven forward into battle by the whip; a Spartan king, Leonidas, resolved to do or die; an exemplary death, as he and three hundred of his countrymen were wiped out making a suicidal last stand:* the story had it all. As early as the sixteenth century AD, the great French essayist Michel de Montaigne could argue that although other battles fought by the Greeks were "the fairest sister-victories which the Sun has ever seen, yet they would never dare to compare their combined glory with the glorious defeat of King Leonidas and his men at the defile of Thermopylae."[10] Two and a half centuries later, Lord Byron, appalled that the Greece of his own day should be languishing as a province under the rule of the Turkish Sultan, knew exactly where to look in the history books to find the most heart-swelling call to arms.

> *Earth! render back from out thy breast*
> *A remnant of our Spartan dead!*
> *Of the three hundred grant but three,*
> *To make a new Thermopylae!*[11]

---

*To be strictly accurate, only 298 of the Spartans that Leonidas took with him to Thermopylae died there in battle. See p. 341.

Putting his money where his mouth was, Byron would subsequently emulate the example of Leonidas by dying in the glorious cause of Greek liberty himself. The glamour of his end, the first true celebrity death of the modern age, only added to the luster of Leonidas, and helped ensure that Thermopylae, for generations afterward, would serve as the model of a martyrdom for liberty. Why, the novelist William Golding asked himself during a visit to the pass in the early 1960s, did he feel so oddly stirred, despite the fact that Sparta herself had been such a "dull, cruel city"?

> It is not just that the human spirit reacts directly and beyond all arguments to a story of sacrifice and courage, as a wine glass must vibrate to the sound of the violin. It is also because, way back and at the hundredth remove, that company stood in the right line of history. A little of Leonidas lies in the fact that I can go where I like and write what I like. He contributed to set us free.[12]

Moving words, and true—and yet it is sobering to reflect that Golding's encomium might well have served to enthuse Adolf Hitler. To the Nazis, as it had been to Montaigne, Thermopylae was easily the most glorious episode in Greek history. The three hundred who defended the pass were regarded by Hitler as representatives of a true master race, one bred and raised for war, and so authentically Nordic that even the Spartans' broth, according to one of the Führer's more speculative pronouncements, derived from Schleswig-Holstein. In January 1943, with the Battle of Stalingrad at its height, Hitler explicitly compared the German 6th Army to the Spartan three hundred—and later, when its general surrendered, raged that the heroism of his soldiers had been "nullified by one single characterless weakling."[13] Denied a Leonidas, Hitler fumed, the Wehrmacht had been frustrated of a perfect chance to make its own new Thermopylae.

That the Nazis—as much as Montaigne, Byron or Golding—could feel such a passionate sense of identification with the example of the three hundred suggests that any portrayal of the Spartans as defenders of liberty does not perhaps tell the whole story. As is so often the case, the truth is both messier and more intriguing than the myth. Had Xerxes succeeded in conquering Greece, and occupying Sparta, then it would indeed have spelled the end of that proud city's freedom—for all the Persian king's subjects were ranked as his slaves. Yet even slavery can be a matter of degree: what would have been regarded as a fate worse than death by the Spartans themselves might well have proved a blessed relief to their neighbors. Sparta's greatness, as Hitler was well aware, rested upon the merciless exploitation of her neighbors, a demonstration of how to treat *Untermenschen* that the Nazis would brutally emulate in Poland and occupied Russia. The Persian monarchy, brilliantly subtle in the exploitation of its subjects' rivalries, would certainly have granted, with an imperious show of graciousness, emancipation and patronage to Sparta's neighbors. To people who had suffered under Spartan oppression for generations, Xerxes' rule might almost have felt like liberty.

A momentous, indeed a history-shaping paradox: that annexation by a foreign power might perhaps, under certain circumstances, be welcomed. Xerxes was certainly, as the Greeks accused him of being, a despot, an Iranian who ruled as heir to the millennia-old traditions of ancient Iraq, of Akkad, Assyria and Babylon, kingdoms that had always taken it for granted that a monarch should rule and conquer as a strong man. Mercilessness and repression: these had invariably been the keynotes of the Iraqi imperial style. The empire of the Persians, however, although certainly founded amid "the tearing down of walls, the tumult of cavalry charges, and the overthrow of cities,"[14] had also, as it expanded, developed a subtler response to the challenges of dominion. By guaranteeing peace and order to the dutifully submissive, and by giving a masterly demonstration of how best to divide and rule, a succession of Persian kings had won for themselves and their people the largest empire ever seen. Indeed, it was their epochal achievement to demonstrate to future ages the very possibility of a multi-ethnic, multi-cultural, world-spanning state. As such, the influence of their example on the grand sweep of history would be infinitely more long term than the aberrant and fleeting experiment that was the democracy of Athens. The political model established by the Persian kings would inspire empire after empire, even into the Muslim era: the caliphs, would-be rulers of the world, were precisely echoing, albeit in piously Islamic idiom, the pretensions of Xerxes. Indeed, in a sense, the political model established by the ancient monarchy of Persia was one that would persist in the Middle East until 1922, and the deposition of the last ruling caliph, the Turkish Sultan.* It is the stated goal of Osama bin Laden, of course, to see the Caliphate resurrected to its prerogative of global rule.

Granted, the influence of ancient Persia, certainly in comparison with that of Greece, has always been indirect, occluded, underground. In 1891, a young British Member of Parliament, George Nathaniel Curzon, visited the site of Xerxes' palace, which had been left charred and abandoned since being torched, 150 years after Thermopylae, by a vengeful Alexander the Great. "To us," Curzon wrote, in soaring Byronic mode, "it is instinct with the solemn lesson of the ages; it takes its place in the chapter of things that have ceased to be; and its mute stones find a voice, and address us with the ineffable pathos of ruin."[15] Seven years later, the by-now Baron Curzon of Kedleston was appointed Viceroy of India. As such, he ruled as the heir of the Mughals—who had themselves been proud to wear the title, not of kings, but of viceroys to the kings of Persia. The British Raj, governed by the products of self-consciously Spartan boarding schools, was also thoroughly imbued with "that picturesque wealth of pomp and circumstance which the East alone can give"[16]—and which ultimately derived from the vanished flummery of Xerxes' palaces. It might have flattered the British Empire to imagine itself the heir of Athens; but it owed a certain debt of obligation to the mortal enemy of Athens, too.

Persia was Persia, in other words, and Greece was Greece—and sometimes the twain did meet. They might have been combatants in the primal clash of civilizations, but the ripples of their influence,

---

*The Caliphate itself was abolished two years later, in 1924.

spilling out across the millennia to the present day, can sometimes serve to complicate the division between East and West rather than to clarify it. Had the Athenians lost the Battle of Marathon, and suffered the obliteration of their city, for instance, then there would have been no Plato—and without Plato, and the colossal shadow he cast on all subsequent theologies, it is unlikely that there would have been an Islam to inspire bin Laden. Conversely, when President Bush speaks of "an axis of evil," his vision of a world divided between rival forces of light and darkness is one that derives ultimately from Zoroaster, the ancient prophet of Iran. Although the defeat of Xerxes was certainly decisive in giving to the Greeks, and therefore to all Europeans, a sense of their own distinctiveness, the impact of Persia and Greece upon history cannot entirely be confined within rigid notions of East and West. Monotheism and the notion of a universal state, democracy and totalitarianism: all can trace their origins back to the period of the Persian Wars. Justifiably it has been described as the axis of world history.

And yet, by and large, how little it is read about today. Peter Green, whose wonderful book *The Year of Salamis*, published over thirty years ago, was the last full-length account written for a non-academic audience, marveled, in his customarily witty fashion, at the shortage of overviews of the subject.

> Bearing in mind the fact that the Greek victory in the Persian Wars is routinely described as a fundamental turning point in European history (advocates of this view don't quite argue that today, had things gone the other way, mosques and minarets would dominate Europe, but you can sense the unspoken thought in the air), this omission seems all the more inexplicable.[17]

Perhaps Green has not been to Rotterdam or Malmö recently; and yet the fact that nowadays mosques and minarets are to be seen even in Athens, long the only EU capital without a Muslim place of worship, hardly detracts from the sense of perplexity he is expressing. If anything it gives it added force. The Persian Wars may be ancient history, but they are also, in a way that they never were during the twentieth century, contemporary history, too.

What Green describes as inexplicable, however, is not entirely so. For all its momentousness, its sweep, and its drama, the story of the Persian Wars is not an easy one to piece together. The indisputable truth that they were the first conflict in history that we can reconstruct in detail does not mean that Herodotus tells us everything about them; far from it, regrettably. Yes, historians can attempt to cover some of the gaps by stitching together shreds and patches garnered from other classical authors; but this is a repair job to be attempted only with the utmost caution. Many sources derive from centuries—even millennia—after the events that they are purporting to describe, while many were written not as "inquiries" but as poetry or drama. Iris Murdoch, in her novel *The Nice and the Good*, observed of early Greek history that it "sets a special challenge to the disciplined mind. It is a game with very few pieces, where the skill of the player lies in complicating the rules."[18] Historians of archaic Greece, who rarely feature in novels, love to quote this passage: for the task that they have set themselves, to reconstruct a vanished world from often meager scraps of evidence, does indeed resemble, at a certain level, a game. We can never know for sure what happened at a battle such as Salamis, when the sources on which any interpretation must depend manage to be simultaneously contradictory and full of holes: one might as well look to complete a half-broken Rubik's Cube. No matter how often the facts are studied, twisted, and rearranged, it is impossible to square them all; a definitive solution can never be found. Yet even Salamis, notoriously hard to make sense of though it is, can appear prodigally rich in detail in comparison with, say, the early history of Sparta. That particular topic, one eminent scholar has baldly confessed, "is a puzzle to challenge the best of thinkers."[19] A second has described it as requiring "intellectual gymnastics."[20] A third, even more up front, simply titled a book *The Spartan Mirage*.[21]

But at least the sources for Greek history, no matter how patchy, derive from the Greeks themselves. The Persians, with one key exception, did not write anything at all that we can identify as an account of real events. Tablets inscribed by imperial bureaucrats do survive, together with royal proclamations chiseled on palace walls, and, of course, the ruins of the astounding palaces themselves. Otherwise, if we are going to attempt to make any sense of the Persians and their empire, we must rely, to an alarming degree, upon the writings of others. These, coming as they do mainly from the Greeks—a people variously invaded, occupied and pillaged by the imperial armies—tend not to be wildly keen on giving a balanced portrait of the Persian character and achievement. Herodotus, ever curious, ever open-minded, is the exception that proves the rule. "*Philobarbaros*"—"barbarian lover"—one indignant patriot labeled him:[22] the closest to the phrase "bleeding-heart liberal" that ancient Greek approached. Yet even Herodotus, writing about remote and peculiar peoples whose languages he did not speak, has to be excused the occasional inaccuracy, the occasional prejudice, the occasional tendency to treat early Persian history as a fairy tale. None of which does much to make the modern historian's task any easier.

Three obvious responses to the challenge present themselves. The first is to accept Greek prejudices at face value, and portray the Persians as effete cowards who somehow, inexplicably, conquered the world. The second is to condemn everything that the Greeks wrote about Persia as an expression of racism, Eurocentrism, and a whole host of other thought crimes to boot. The third, and most productive, is to explore the degree to which Greek misinterpretations of their great enemy reflected the truth, however distorted, of how the Persians lived and saw their world. It is this approach that has been adopted by a formidable band of scholars over the past thirty years, and the results have been spectacular: a whole empire brought back to life, redeemed out of oblivion, rendered so solid that it has become, in the words of one historian, "something you can stub your toe on."[23] As a display of resurrectionism, it is worthy to stand beside the opening of Tutankhamen's tomb.

And yet the Persians remain shrouded in obscurity. Perhaps this is hardly surprising. There have been no golden death masks to give a face to their rediscovery—only scholarly tomes and journals. The study of Persia, even more than that of Greece, depends on the minutest sifting of the available evidence, the closest analysis of the sources, the most delicate weighing of inferences and alternatives. This is a field in which almost every detail can be debated, and certain themes—the religion of the Persian kings, most notoriously—are bogs so treacherous that even the most eminent scholars have been known to blanch at the prospect of venturing into them.

Fools rush in where angels fear to tread; but I hope, even so, that my attempt to build a bridge between the worlds of academic and general readership does not end up appearing as vainglorious as did the two-mile pontoon which Xerxes built from Asia to Europe, to the horrified derision of the Greeks. Readers should certainly be warned that many of the details out of which this book's narrative has been constructed are ambiguous and ferociously disputed—and that the sudden appearance of a number in the text, hovering like a fly over a dunghill, generally indicates that qualification is being offered in an endnote. Yet while it is true that we can never definitively reconstruct a period so remote from ourselves, even more striking than our ignorance, perhaps, is the fact that the attempt can be made at all. I have sought with this book to provide something more than merely a narrative, for it has been my ambition, following in the footsteps of Herodotus himself, to paint a panorama of the entire world that went to war—East as well as West. The reader will be taken to Assyria, Persia and Babylon before Greece; will read of the rise of the first global monarchy before that of Spartan militarism or the democracy of Athens; and only halfway through the book will embark on the account of the Persian Wars themselves. That a story traditionally told from one side may now be glimpsed, albeit opaquely, from the other as well, is justification enough, I hope, for attempting to piece together, out of the many scattered and ambiguous fragments of evidence, a new account of those wars, of why they were fought, and by whom. It is, after all, an epic as powerful and extraordinary as any to be found in ancient literature; and one that is, despite all the many imponderables, not myth but the very stuff of history.

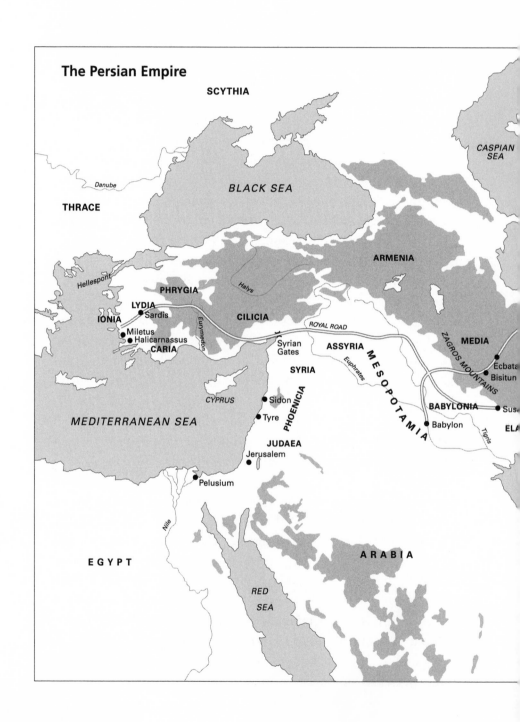

The Persian Empire

SCYTHIA

CASPIAN SEA

Danube

BLACK SEA

THRACE

ARMENIA

Hellespont

Halys

PHRYGIA

LYDIA

CILICIA

ROYAL ROAD

MEDIA

IONIA

Sardis

ZAGROS MOUNTAINS

Ecbata

Bisitun

Miletus

Halicarnassus

Eurymedon

CARIA

Syrian Gates

ASSYRIA

MESOPOTAMIA

Euphrates

SYRIA

Susa

BABYLONIA

CYPRUS

Sidon

PHOENICIA

Babylon

ELA

MEDITERRANEAN SEA

Tyre

Tigris

JUDAEA

Jerusalem

Pelusium

Nile

ARABIA

EGYPT

RED SEA

ARAL
SEA

Jaxartes

Cyropolis●

SOGDIANA

KHORASAN HIGHWAY

BACTRIA

HINDU KUSH

GANDHARA

Indus

PERSIA

●Pasargadae
●Persepolis

ARACHOSIA

INDIA

CARMANIA

PERSIAN
GULF

N

1000 meters

0

0

500 km

250 miles

Greece and the Aegean

MACEDONIA

Myrcinus

Mt. Olympus

TEMPE

Mt. Ath

AEGEAN SEA

MAGNESIA

Sciathos

THESSALY

EUBOEA

MOUNT
OETA
Thermopylae
DORIS
Delphi ● MOUNT
PARNASSUS
Chalcis
● Eretria

BOEOTIA
Plataea ● Thebes

ATTICA
Megara ● Athens

Corinth ●

PELOPONNESE
● Olympia

Salamis

● Argos

Aegina

● Tegea
Troezen ●

MESSENIA
Sparta ●

LACEDAEMON

N

1000 meters

0   100 km
0   50 miles

THRACE

CHERSONESE

●Abydos

Hellespont

●Troy

AEGEAN SEA

●Phocaea

●Sardis

LYDIA

Samos

IONIA

Miletus ●

Delos

CARIA

Naxos

●Halicarnassus

Listen now to a further point: no mortal thing
Has a beginning, nor does it end in death and obliteration;
There is only a mixing and then a separating of what was mixed,
But by mortal men these processes are named "beginnings."

Empedocles

1

THE KHORASAN HIGHWAY

Woe to the Bloody City

The gods, having scorned to mold a world that was level, had preferred instead to divide it into two. So it seemed to those who lived in the Zagros, the great chain of peaks which separates the Fertile Crescent from the upland plateau of Iran. Yet these mountains, though savage, were not impassable. One road did snake across them: the most famous in the world, the Khorasan Highway, which led from the limits of the East to the West, and joined the rising to the setting of the sun. In places, as it climbed through the Zagros Mountains, winding along river beds, or threading between jagged pinnacles and ravines, it might be little more than a foot-path—but even that, to those who used it, was a miracle enough. Only a beneficent deity, it was assumed, could ever have fashioned such a wonder. Who, and when, no one really knew for sure,* but it was certainly very ancient—perhaps, some said, as old as time itself. Over the millennia, the Khorasan Highway had been followed by any number of travelers: nomads, caravans—and the armies of conquering kings.

---

*Although the Greeks plumped for Semiramis, a Syrian warrior-goddess who was also supposed to have founded Babylon.

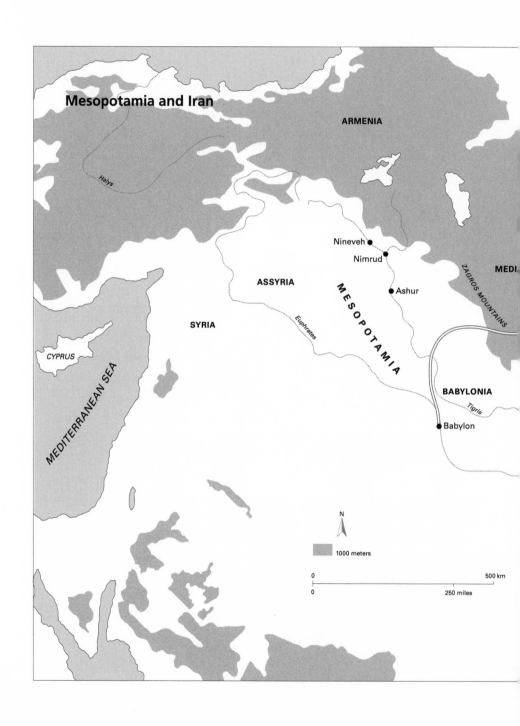

Mesopotamia and Iran

ARMENIA

Halys

Nineveh
Nimrud

MEDI.

ASSYRIA

M E S O P O T A M I A

Ashur

ZAGROS MOUNTAINS

SYRIA

Euphrates

CYPRUS

MEDITERRANEAN SEA

BABYLONIA

Tigris

Babylon

N

1000 meters

0   500 km
0   250 miles

CASPIAN SEA

BACTRIA

KHORASAN HIGHWAY

Ecbatana

Bisitun

Sikyavautish

Susa

PERSIA

ELAM

Persian
Gates

Pasargadae

Persepolis

CARMANIA

PERSIAN
GULF

One empire, in particular, for centuries synonymous with cruel and remorseless invincibility, had sent repeated expeditions into the mountains, dyeing the peaks, in its own ferocious vaunt, "like wool, crimson with blood."[1] The Assyrians, inhabitants of what is now northern Iraq, were city-dwellers, a people of the flat, alluvial plains; but to their kings, warlords who had spread terror and extermination as far as Egypt, the Zagros was less a barrier than a challenge. Themselves the patrons of a proud and brilliant civilization, sumptuous with palaces, gardens and canals, the kings of Assyria had always seen it as their duty to flatten resistance in the wilds beyond their frontiers. This, the wilds being what they were, had proved a calling without limit. Not even with their incomparable war machine could the Assyrians pacify all the mountain tribes—for there were some living in the Zagros who clung to the peaks like birds, or lurked in the depths of thick forests, so backward that they subsisted entirely on acorns, savages hardly worthy of the royal attention. These too, however, with regular incursions, could be taught to dread the name of Assyria, and provide her with the human plunder on which her greatness had come increasingly to depend. Again and again, punitive expeditions would return from the mountains to their native plains, to the sacred cities of Ashur, Nimrud and Nineveh, while in their wake, naked and tethered, followed stumbling lines of captives. Increasingly, the Assyrians had fallen into the habit of moving entire populations, shunting them around their empire, transplanting one defeated enemy into the lands of another, there to live in the houses of the similarly transported, to clear weeds from the rubble, or cultivate the abandoned, smoke-blackened fields.

These tactics had in the end had due effect. By the late eighth century BC, the reaches of the Khorasan Highway had been formally absorbed into the empire and placed under the rule of an Assyrian governor. "Grovelling they came to me, for the protection of their lives," boasted Assyria's greatest king, Sargon II. "Knowing that otherwise I would destroy their walls, they fell and kissed my feet."[2]

Not that captives were the only source of wealth to be found in the Zagros. Wild and forested though the mountains were, and often bitter the climate, the valleys were famous for their clover-rich pasture. Over the centuries, and in increasing numbers, these had been attracting tribes who called themselves "Arya"—"Aryans": horse-taming nomads from the plateau to the east.[3] Even once settled, these immigrants had preserved many of their ancestors' instincts, filling the valleys of their new homeland with great herds of long-horned cattle, and preferring, wherever possible, to live in the saddle. The Assyrians, no horse-breeders themselves, would speak in wondering terms of the stud farms of the Zagros, with their "numberless steeds."[4] It was relatively easy for the Assyrian army to cherry-pick these as tribute, for the finest horses, by universal consent, were those bred by the Medes, a loose confederation of Aryan tribes settled conveniently along the Khorasan Highway itself. No wonder the Assyrians came to prize the region. Their mastery of Media,[5] as well as enabling them to control the world's most important trade route, permitted their armies to develop a new and lethal quality of speed. By the eighth century BC, cavalry had become vital to the ability of Assyria to maintain her military supremacy. The tribute of horses from the mountains had become the lifeblood of her greatness. The richest silver mine could not have been more precious to her than the stud farms of the Zagros.

And yet, in Assyria's supremacy lay the seeds of its own downfall. The mountains were a mishmash of different peoples, Aryans and aboriginals alike, with even the Medes themselves ruled by a quarrelsome multitude of petty chieftains. Foreign occupation, however, by imposing a unitary authority upon the region, had begun to encourage the fractious tribes to cohere. By the 670s BC, menaced by the shadowy leader of a formal Median union, the Assyrians' hold on the Zagros started to slip alarmingly. Tribute dried up as its collection became ever more challenging. Open revolts blazed and spread. Over the following decades, the scribes of the Assyrian kings, employed to keep a record of the victories of their masters, ceased to make mention of Media at all.

This silence veiled an ominous development. In 615 BC, a king who claimed sovereignty over all the clan chiefs of the Medes, Cyaxares by name, joined an alliance of the empire's other rebellious subjects and led his troops from their fastnesses against the Assyrians' eastern flank. The effect of this sudden eruption of the mountain men was devastating. After only three years of campaigning, the inconceivable occurred: Nineveh, greatest of all the strongholds of Assyrian might, was stormed and razed. To the amazement—and joy—of the empire's subject peoples, "the bloody city" was pulverized beneath the hooves of the Median cavalry. "Horsemen charging, flashing sword and glittering spear, hosts of slain, heaps of corpses, dead bodies without end—they stumble over the bodies!"[6]

Four years later, and all traces of the Assyrian colossus, which for so long had kept the Near East in its shadow, lay obliterated. To the victors, naturally, had fallen the spoils. Media, precipitately elevated to the rank of great power, seized a huge northern swath of the defeated empire. Her kings, no longer small-time chieftains, could now indulge themselves in the occupations proper to their newly won status—throwing their weight around and scrapping with other great powers. In 610 BC, the Medes swept into northern Syria, burning and looting as they went. In 585, they went to war with the Lydians, a people based in the west of what is now Turkey, and only a solar eclipse, manifesting itself over the battlefield, finally persuaded the two sides to draw back. By the terms of a hurriedly patched-up treaty, the Halys, a river flowing midway between Media and Lydia, was established as the boundary between the rival empires, and for the next thirty years, throughout the Near East, peace, and the balance of power, were maintained.[7]

Not that the new king of Media, Astyages, had any intention of hanging up his saddle. Undistracted now by war with other major empires, he turned his attention instead to the wilds north and east of his kingdom, far distant from the cockpit of the Fertile Crescent. Leading an expedition into the badlands of Armenia and what is now Azerbaijan, he was following in the footsteps of the Assyrian kings, teaching the savages beyond his frontiers to fear his royal name.[8] In other ways, too, the traditions of the great monarchies of the Near East, so alien to those of his own people, still semi-tribal and nomadic as they were, appear to have whetted the ambitions of the Median king. After all, a ruler of Astyages' stature, no less powerful than the King of Lydia or the Pharaoh of Egypt, could hardly be expected to rule his empire from a tent. What the monarchs of more ancient lands had always taken for granted—a palace, a treasury, a mighty capital— Astyages, naturally, had to have as well: proofs of his magnificence raised in gold and blocks of stone.

Travelers who made the final ascent through the mountains along the Khorasan Highway would see, guarding the approaches to the Iranian plateau ahead of them, a vision which could have been conjured from some fabulous epic: a palace set within seven gleaming walls, each one painted a different color, and on the two innermost circuits, bolted to their battlements, plates of silver and gold. This was Ecbatana, stronghold of the kings of Media, and already, barely a century after its foundation, the crossroads of the world.[9] Commanding the trade of East and West, it also opened up to its master the whole range of the Zagros, and beyond. Here, for the Median clan chiefs, in particular, was a thoroughly alarming development. The surest guarantee of their freedom from royal meddling, and of the continued factionalism of the kingdom itself, had always been the inaccessibility of their private fiefdoms—but increasingly they found themselves subordinated to the reach of Astyages' court. At one time, before the building of the polychrome palace walls, Ecbatana had been an open field, a free meeting place for the tribes, a function preserved in the meaning of its name: "assembly point." But now those days were gone, and the Medes, who had fought so long to liberate themselves from the despots of Nineveh, found themselves the subjects of a despot nearer to home.

No wonder that later generations would preserve a memory of Astyages as an ogre. No wonder, either, that when they sought to explain their loss of freedom, the Medes would identify Ecbatana as both a symbol of their slavery, and a cause.[10]

King of the World

Astyages, it was said, even amid all the proofs of his greatness, was haunted by prophecies of doom: strange dreams tormented him, warning him of his downfall and the ruin of his kingdom. Such was the value ascribed by the Medes to visions of this kind that a whole class, the Magi, existed to divine what their meaning might be. Skilled in all the arts of keeping darkness at bay, these ritual experts provided vital reassurance to their countrymen, for it was a principle of the Medes, a devout and ethical people, that there was shadow lurking beyond even the brightest light. All the world, it seemed to the Magi, bore witness to this truth. A fire might be tended so that it burned eternally, but there was nowhere, not beside the coolest spring, nor even on the highest mountain peak, where the purity of its flame might not be menaced by pollution. Creation bred darkness as well as the daylight. Scorpions and spiders, lizards, snakes and ants, all crept and seethed, the visible excrescences of a universal shadow. Just as it was the duty of a Magus to kill such creatures wherever he found them, so shadows had to be guarded against when they darkened people's dreams—and especially the nightmares of a king. "For they say that the air is full of spectres, which flow by exhalation, and penetrate into the sight of those with piercing vision."[11] Greatness, like fire, had to be tended with care.

That a kingdom as powerful as Media, less than a century after its first rise to independence and greatness, might once again be prostrated and subjected to foreign domination must, to many, have seemed implausible. But this, as the Medes themselves had good cause to know, had always been the baneful rhythm of the region's power play: great empires rising, great empires falling. No one kingdom, not even Assyria, had ever crushed all who might wish to see it destroyed. In the Near East, predators lurked everywhere, sniffing the air for weakness, awaiting their opportunity to strike. Ancient states would vanish, new ones take their place, and the chroniclers, in recording the ruin of celebrated kingdoms, might find themselves describing strange and previously unknown peoples.

Many of these, just like the Medes themselves, were Aryans—
nomads who had left little trace of their migrations upon the records
of the time. In 843 BC, for instance, the Assyrians had campaigned in
the mountains north of their kingdom against a tribe they called the
"Parsua"; two centuries later, a people with a very similar name had
established themselves far to the south, on the ruins of the venerable
kingdom of Anshan, between the lower reaches of the Zagros and
the sweltering coastlands of the Gulf. No chronicler, however, could
know for sure if they were one and the same.[12] Only by putting down
roots, and by absorbing something of the culture of the people they
had displaced, had the newcomers finally been able to intrude upon
the consciousness of their more sedentary neighbors. These, reluctant to change the habit of centuries, had continued to refer to the
region as they had always done; but the invaders, when they spoke of
their new homeland, had naturally preferred to call it after themselves. So it was that what had once been Anshan came gradually to be
known by a quite different name: Paarsa, Persia, the land of the
Persians.[13]

In 559 BC, while Astyages still ruled in Media, a young man came to
the throne of this upstart kingdom. His name was Cyrus, and his
attributes included a hook nose, immense ambition and quite limitless
ability. From even before his birth, it appeared, he had been marked
out for greatness; for it was he—if the stories are to be believed—
who had been prophesied as the bane of Median greatness. Astyages
was supposed to have seen it all in a dream: a vision of his daughter,
Mandane, urinating, the golden stream flowing without cease, until at
last the whole of Media had been drowned. When the king had
reported this the next morning, his Magian dream-readers had turned
pale and warned him that any son of Mandane would be destined to
imperil the Median throne. Hurriedly, Astyages had married off his
daughter to a vassal, a Persian, the prince of a backward and inconse-
quential kingdom, hoping in that way to defeat the omen's malice.
But after Mandane had fallen pregnant, Astyages had dreamed a
second time: now he saw a vine emerging from between his daughter's

9

legs, nor did it stop growing until all Asia was in its shade. Panic-stricken, Astyages had waited for his grandson to be born, and then immediately given orders that the boy be put to death. As invariably happens in such stories, the orders had been defied. The baby had been abandoned on a mountainside, to be discovered and brought up by a shepherd; or perhaps, some said, a bandit; or maybe even a bitch, her teats conveniently swollen with milk. Whatever its precise details, the miraculous nature of such an upbringing had clearly betokened a godlike future for the foundling—and so, of course, it had proved. Cyrus had survived and prospered. Once he had grown to a splendid manhood, his natural nobility of character had served to win him the Persian throne. Thus it was that all the wiles of Astyages had been foiled—and the empire of the Medes been doomed.

Or so the legends had it. It is the nature of great men to attract tall stories, and it may be that the early proofs of Cyrus' destiny were not quite so manifest as the Persians would later claim.[14] Even so—and irrespective of whether there had truly been prophecies—his potential was evidently sufficient to alarm Astyages: for the Median king, overlord of the Zagros, and wary of high-flying vassals, decided, after six years of watching his grandson on the Persian throne, that Cyrus was altogether too able and dangerous to be left in place for long. Accordingly, in 553 BC, he mustered his fearsome horsemen and struck south. Heavily outnumbered, the Persians resisted ferociously. When it appeared that surrender was imminent, even their women took to the battlefield, to encourage Cyrus and his warriors to fight on. For three years, the conflict convulsed the Zagros—and then, suddenly, in 550 BC, it was over. Even the gods, it appeared, were taken by surprise. They began appearing in the dreams of neighboring kings to broadcast the startling news. "Cyrus scattered the large armies of the Medes with his small army. And he captured Astyages, King of the Medes. And he took him to his country as captive."[15] Not since the downfall of Assyria had there been an upset on such a scale.

How had it come about? Yes, Cyrus had proved himself a steely and indomitable opponent. As had his Persian subjects, a people so toughened by poverty that they had uncomplainingly endured the sternest hardships—even, notoriously, to the extent of wearing leather trousers. Yet Astyages, with all the resources of a mighty empire behind him, would surely still have triumphed—had he not been grievously stabbed in the back. The story of his betrayal was a strange one—and, as the years passed, the retellings of it grew ever more fantastical and grotesque. The bare essentials were not in doubt. Harpagus, commander of the Median army, and most prominent of the clan chiefs, had deserted to Cyrus, leading a rebellion in mid-battle, and taking Astyages captive. But why such treachery? Because—so the story went—Harpagus, a close kinsman of Astyages, had simultaneously been bound by the most terrible ties of obligation to the King of Persia. It was Harpagus, according to the Medes, who had been charged with the murder of the infant Cyrus, a task which—dissembling—he had claimed to have carried out. Years later, when the truth had at last emerged, Astyages was rumored to have wreaked a bloody revenge, butchering Harpagus' son, jointing the corpse, and then serving it dressed as mutton to the unsuspecting father. Harpagus himself, having consumed his own child, had swallowed the insult too, and remained a loyal, if chastened, servant of his king. Or so he had pretended. His act had certainly been convincing, for when the war against the Persians broke out, Astyages had appointed Harpagus to the supreme command. Not the cleverest piece of man-management, perhaps—and, in reality, so foolish as to be palpably absurd.

So how had this tall story ever come to be believed? Maybe—somewhere within the shadow play of implausibility and rumor—a faint hint of the truth could still be glimpsed? The family relationship between Astyages and Cyrus had mirrored the close ties, of culture as well as blood, which had always bound the Persians to the Medes. Both peoples, after all, were Aryan; and, to an Aryan, it was only the "*anairya*"—the non-Aryan—who was foreign. Indeed, any of Astyages' courtiers who were suffering from nostalgia had only to look south for a glimpse of the good old days. Like their Median cousins, the Persians were at heart a nomadic people, and their country, "rich with good horses, rich with good men,"[16] had remained as much a confederation of different clans as a state. "King of Anshan" though he was, Cyrus had also claimed his throne by virtue of his status as his people's greatest chieftain—for he was head of the Achaemenids, the leading family of the Pasargadae, the leading Persian tribe. Master both of the stiff rituals of a Near Eastern court and of assemblies of wild horsemen wheeling beneath the open sky, of ancient cities and of the hills and plains, of the Persians' future and of the memories and customs of their past, Cyrus was adept at playing all these roles, and more. As a result, Persia had largely avoided the tensions that afflicted Media: between a king impatient with the traditional tribal structures of his people and a nobility still defined by them. The Median clan chiefs, suffering from the authoritarian ambitions of Astyages, had taken note. Over time, the contrast between their own king and Cyrus must have struck them as ever more pronounced. It was almost certainly this which had persuaded Harpagus to take his fateful step. "So it was that the Persians, who had once been the slaves of the Medes, became their masters,"[17] and Cyrus, marching into Ecbatana, reaped the due rewards of his forbearance, acuity and charm.

Nor, even after this first great victory, did the subtlety of his balancing act fail. The kings of Assyria, honing the traditional rights of conquest to a peak of savagery, had prescribed unspeakable cruelties for defeated enemies, but Cyrus, prompted by calculation and—no doubt—by temperament as well, preferred the course of mercy. Having lured important swaths of the Median aristocracy into his camp, he resisted the temptation to treat their countrymen as slaves. Even Astyages, rather than being flayed, fed to animals or impaled, was pensioned off into princely retirement. True, the treasury was emptied and its contents carted away to Anshan, but Ecbatana was otherwise spared the fate of Nineveh. Cyrus had no intention of destroying the most strategically sited city in the Zagros. The most pleasant, too—for if, in winter, the cold was savage, with blizzards blocking off the passes, in summer, while the lowlands of Persia burned, Ecbatana was a paradise of greenness, the mountain peaks behind it still capped with cooling snow, the slopes below the walls terraced with orchards and gardens, the air bright and crystal clear. Not only did the city remain the capital of Media, but it became, during the broiling summer months, the effective capital of Cyrus' whole empire. No wonder that the Medes were able to feel, if not exactly the equals of their conquerors, then at least associates in the great adventure of their new king's reign.

And that adventure, as events were soon exhilaratingly to prove, had only just begun. The downfall of a king as great as Astyages had sent shock waves throughout the whole Near East. Not only the Median Empire but the decades-old international status quo had been left in rubble. Suddenly, it seemed, there was everything to play for, and neighboring great powers, still barely able to take the Persians seriously, began to wonder what pickings might be on offer for themselves. In 547 BC, Croesus, the King of Lydia, led a huge army over the River Halys to find out. Cyrus, having descended from the Zagros, advanced hurriedly to meet him, the ruined cities of Assyria standing sentinel as he passed by, nothing now but dust-blown and jumbled heaps of mud, mute witnesses to the precariousness of power. Yet such a lesson might serve an ambitious man as inspiration as well as warning, and Cyrus, even though it was by now late in the campaigning season, pressed on urgently, eager to engage Croesus. As before, when the Lydians had met with the Medes, an indecisive battle was fought; but this time there was no eclipse, and no end to the war. Instead, with winter drawing on, Croesus withdrew to his capital, Sardis, never imagining that Cyrus would dare to follow him, for the city was so far to the west that the Aegean lay only three days' journey beyond it—a tremendous distance from the Median frontier. But the Persians did not retreat. Instead, braving the bitter cold, they shadowed Croesus, never alerting him to their presence, allowing him time to dismiss his allies, lurking and waiting for his conscripts to melt away. Then, with Sardis denuded, Cyrus struck. Frantically, Croesus cobbled together what few troops remained. A desperate battle, with the Lydians staking everything on a final cavalry charge—and then the storming of

Sardis, and the capture of Croesus himself. Far off in the Fertile Crescent, the details were recorded with a terseness that hardly hinted at their seismic effect: "[Cyrus] defeated the King [of Lydia], seized his possessions, and stationed his own garrison there."[18] Over the Lydian Empire itself, the news of Croesus' downfall burst with such a thunderclap that the priestess of one temple was said to have sprouted a beard from the shock. As well she might have done, for in the space of just six years, the Persians, so small in numbers, once so backward and obscure, had made their kingdom the greatest power in the world.

Not that the victory had been theirs alone. The Median cavalry, perfectly equipped for a winter campaign with their sheepskin coats and their tough mountain horses, had more than played their part. Median generals, too. Of all the advice given to Cyrus during the campaign, the best had come from Harpagus, who had suggested, just before the final Lydian cavalry charge, that the baggage camels be placed at the forefront of the Persian battle line. Cyrus had duly given the order, the Lydians' horses, startled by the unfamiliar stench, had swerved and bolted, and the battle had been won. Perhaps it was not surprising, then, that Cyrus, buoyed by this victory, sought to conciliate the Lydians just as he had previously wooed the Medes, *anairya* though his new subjects were. Croesus, like Astyages, was spared execution, and welcomed into his conqueror's entourage; his fabulously well-stocked treasury was kept at Sardis; even the gathering of tribute was entrusted to native grandees. The Lydians, however, startled by this magnanimity, interpreted it as weakness; and no sooner had Cyrus left for Ecbatana than the very aristocrats whom he had most trusted, those in charge of the treasury, were rising in revolt. It was a fatal miscalculation. Cyrus, menaced by what he justly regarded as the basest treachery and ingratitude, responded with furious expedition. Fresh troops, with fresh orders, were sent speeding from Ecbatana. There was to be no clemency now. Instead, the Persians were commanded to demonstrate their mastery of more traditional methods of pacification: cities were to be ravaged, rebel leaders executed, their followers enslaved. And all was done as the King of Persia had instructed.

Yet Cyrus, even as he showed his capacity for repression, had not abandoned the fundamentals of his imperial policy. The Medes, if no longer the Lydians, were still to be offered a form of partnership in his dazzling new order. Accordingly, Harpagus, first and most valued of all Cyrus' foreign servants, was sent west, to take command of the Persian forces. Reaping opportunities that would never have come his way had he remained loyal to Astyages, the clan chief from the Zagros arrived in Lydia sporting the splendid title of "Generalissimo of the Sea."[19] Living up to this office with savage efficiency, he had no sooner finished off the Lydians than he was looking to plant his standards along the extremities of Asia, right on the shore of the "bitter sea,"[20] the Aegean itself. There, dotted along the coastline, and enticingly prosperous, were the gleaming cities of a people known to the Persians as the "Yauna"—the Ionians.* Emigrants centuries previously from Greece, the men of Ionia remained as determinedly and defiantly Greek as any of their countrymen back in the motherland across the Aegean. Too quarrelsome to present a united front, they certainly proved easy meat for Harpagus. City by city, he brutally subdued them all. Indeed, so menacing was his reputation that many Ionians, rather than submit to Persian rule, opted for flight across the sea, emigrating to Sicily or the Italian peninsula. One city, Phocaea, evacuated its entire population, "women, children, moveable property, everything, in fact . . . leaving the Persians to take possession of nothing but an empty shell."[21] A dark shadow had been cast over the Ionian imagination, and the memory of Harpagus' coming would long serve to blacken even the most intimate moments of joy:

---

*Variations of the word "Ionian" were used as a generic term for "Greek" throughout the Near East. See, for instance, Genesis 10.2, where one of the sons of Japheth is called "Javan." The Greeks themselves counted the island cities of Chios and Samos as Ionian, so, in total, there were reckoned to be twelve cities of Ionia.

In winter, as you lie on a soft couch by the fire,
Full of good food, munching on nuts and drinking sweet wine,
Then you must ask questions such as these:
"Where do you come from? Tell me, what is your age?
How old were you when the Mede came?"[22]

Not, it might be noted, "How old were you when the Persian came?"—for such was the impact of Harpagus upon the Ionians that it left them perplexed, even as they submitted to their new masters, as to who precisely these were. Ever after, when referring to the Persians, the Greeks would invariably say, "the Medes." Such confusion was hardly surprising. What were the ethnic complexities of the Zagros to a people so far distant from them? That cities on the western sea should find themselves subject to a people they had barely heard of suggested the dawn of a new and unsettling age. The world seemed suddenly shrunken. Never before had one man's reach extended quite so far. Cyrus, however, far from glorying in his achievements, remained restless and anxious for more. For all the scale of his victories in Lydia, he dreaded the danger that he imagined lurking in his rear. Back from Sardis, he turned his gaze toward the eastern horizon. Ignore what lay beyond that and even the most brilliant conqueror might find that his greatness had been raised on shifting sand. No kingdom could reckon itself wholly secure while it still feared the depredations of migrant tribes and the thunder of hoofbeats across the plains of Iran. Who better to appreciate that than a Persian, himself a descendant of nomads?

So it was that Cyrus, disdaining to stamp out the revolt in Lydia in person, had instead taken the opposite route from Ecbatana, following the Khorasan Highway as it wound ever east.[23] This, for Persians and Medes alike, was to journey back into their past, toward the legendary homelands of their ancestors, "rich in pastures and waters . . . the abode of cattle,"[24] where everything seemed on a more heroic scale, the plains much vaster, the mountains touching the sky. Fighting his way into the uplands, gazing at last toward the Hindu Kush, Cyrus would have been able to watch the dawning of the sun over the peaks of Central Asia—"the undying, swift-horsed sun; who, foremost in a golden array, takes hold of the beautiful summits, and from them looks over the abode of the Aryans with a beneficent eye."[25] This same "abode of the Aryans," long after the Persians had emigrated from it, had remained the fiefdom of swaggering noblemen, backward in comparison to their cousins in the Zagros, perhaps, but rich, and hulking, and addicted to war. Once Cyrus had succeeded in forcing their submission, they were to provide him with formidable new resources of manpower and wealth. The badlands would never entirely lose their turbid character, for their new master, chameleon-like as ever, was careful to portray himself as the heir of the region's traditions, leaving the local noblemen to continue in their rambunctious ways—but in the cause, henceforward, of the Persian king. Loose though it was, the order imposed by Cyrus was subtly calibrated to meet his needs: not only troops and gold, but a buffer zone. The establishment of an immense arc of provinces, stretching from the Hindu Kush to the Aral Sea, served to fence off the approaches to Persia where they had always been most vulnerable, in the northeast, which previously had lain wide open to incursions from the steppes of Central Asia. Gandhara, Bactria and Sogdiana: these lands, once breeding grounds of menace and instability, were now transformed into bulwarks of Persian might.

And bulwarks of much besides. Savages, as all civilized peoples were agreed, belonged exactly where Cyrus was pinning them, in the remote bleakness of the rim of the world. What might happen otherwise was still the stuff of nightmares. The Medes, for instance, preserved lurid folktales of how their empire, at the very peak of its might, had been subjected to the slant-eyed Saka, a notoriously brutal people, cruel and untamed like the steppes from which they came, who had held on to Media for twenty-eight years. There was great alarm, then, when Cyrus, advancing from Sogdiana into what is now Kazakhstan, found himself confronted by these same demons from the Median past, readily distinguishable by their high pointed caps and their alarming facility with axes. A leader of the Saka, captured by Cyrus and treated with notable chivalry, duly submitted to the invaders, and his people, taking service with the Persian king, soon established themselves as the most ferocious of the imperial troops. But this had been only a single tribe. Beyond its homeland lay further plains, bandit-haunted and drear, their immensity mocking all human ambition—even that of the greatest conqueror ever known. How far they stretched no one could say for sure, nor what might be found at their extremities: griffins, some claimed; and tribes of men with goats' feet; and frozen wastes, where the inhabitants hibernated for six months every year; and beyond them, surrounding the world, the great River Rangha, as wide as the most immense sea.[26] Cyrus, crossing the monotony of the steppelands, certainly had no intention of pushing that far; and when at length he found a broad river obstructing his path, he rested on its bank, and there, amid mudflats and the buzzing of mosquitoes, called a halt, at last, to his advance. The river itself, the Jaxartes, was shallow and island-dotted, affording only the barest of natural frontiers; so Cyrus, making good the deficiencies of nature, ordered the construction of seven frontier towns, naming the greatest one after himself—"Cyropolis."[27] Henceforward, like a slave, the featureless savagery of the steppes was to wear the mark of the Persian king.

This branding of his identity upon the land of the Saka proclaimed an imperious dual message. No more would the untamed war-bands beyond the Jaxartes be permitted to raid southward; and no more would those behind it have to fear for their security. Cyrus' strategy had always been to menace his enemies and to reassure his slaves—and by 540 BC, with the eastern frontier stabilized, he felt ready to put it to its ultimate test. Returning to the Zagros, he fixed his predatory gaze on that supreme goal of every conqueror's ambition, the wealthy flatlands of what is now southern Iraq, stretching from Assyria to the Persian Gulf, the stage for splendid cities since the very dawn of time. No man could truly be hailed as the master of the world until he had subdued its ancient heartland—as Cyrus, the arriviste, was all too well aware. Yet he would also have known that its inhabitants were no backward frontiersmen, untutored in the propaganda of despots. Indeed, it was they who regarded the Persians as savages. Cyrus, a man who specialized in overturning hostile preconceptions, chose to meet this new challenge head on. Launching his invasion of enemy territory, he claimed to be defending it; leading an immense army, he affected to be an avatar of peace. And everywhere, strongholds met him with an opening of their gates.

In truth, Persian firepower being what it was, this had been the only sane policy for the defenders to adopt. The one army which sought to defy the invasion had been summarily obliterated; for Cyrus, as he had shown in Lydia, was not averse to the occasional atrocity when he felt that it might serve a salutary purpose. Yet his preference, by and large, was to live up to the high-flying claims of his propaganda. His regime once established, there were no more pogroms. Executions were kept to the barest minimum. His diktats were couched in a moderate and gracious tone. To cities crowded with ancient temples, and scented with incense, Cyrus presented himself as a model of "righteousness and justice," and his "universal lordship" as a payback from the gods.[28] But which gods, precisely? Coolly, Cyrus posed as the favorite of them all. Assorted priesthoods duly scrabbled to hail him as their own, and assorted peoples as the heir to their customs and concerns—the perfect gilding on his mastery of the world. A glorious thing, for the clan chief of the upstart Achaemenids, to be the patron of ancient cities such as Ur and Uruk. Not even in their records, although they reached back to the dawn of time, could be found another man who had risen quite so fast, so far.

To many, inevitably, there appeared something fearsome, even monstrous, about this prodigy. When Cyrus at last fell in battle he was seventy, his appetite for conquest still unassuaged, for his death had come north of the Jaxartes, far beyond the limits he had once set on his own ambitions.[29] In her triumph, the queen of the tribe which had killed him was said to have decapitated his corpse, and dropped the head into a blood-filled wineskin, so that the old man's thirst might glut itself at last. This was to cast Cyrus as a spirit of the kind that haunted the imaginings of the Near East, a demon of the night, eternally hungry for human flesh. Among those who had submitted to him, however, a quite different tradition would be preserved. Cyrus, the man who had convulsed the world, would be remembered with an almost unqualified admiration, for his exceptional nobility of character, and as the architect of a universal peace. For centuries afterward, even among its bitterest enemies, the glow of its founder's memory would suffuse the empire of the Persians. "He eclipsed all other monarchs, either before him, or since." Such was the verdict of Xenophon, an Athenian, writing almost two centuries after Cyrus' death. "No matter whom he conquered, he would inspire in them a deep longing to please him, and to bask in his good opinion. They found themselves longing to be guided by his rulings—his, and no one else's."[30] An astonishing verdict, it might be thought—and yet Cyrus had indeed seduced as well as forced himself on the world, persuading a host of different peoples that he understood them, respected them and desired their love. No empire had ever before been raised on such foundations. No conqueror had ever before displayed such clemency, such restraint.

This had been the genius of Cyrus—and his reward had been dominion on a scale beyond all dreams.

O Brother, Where Art Thou?

He died in the summer of 529 BC. His corpse, redeemed from the tribe that had killed him, was brought back to Persia, where an immense stone tomb stood waiting to receive it. This had been raised, according to legend, on the location of the decisive defeat of Astyages, and was just one of a number of structures which Cyrus had sponsored in the area. Less a city than an assemblage of palaces, pavilions and gardens, the site certainly bore ample witness to the scale of the Persians' greatness—but it also suggested just how disorientating and precipitous their rise had been. Beyond the masonry, herds of livestock still roamed the bleakness of the open hills and plains. Winds gusting across the featureless landscape coated gilded doorways and columns with dust. Even the palace complex itself, despite being built of stone, conveyed in its layout more than a hint of camps and tents. Not for nothing was the site known as Pasargadae: the name of Cyrus' tribe. It was hardly a paradox, after all, that a nomad too might have his roots.

Now, with Cyrus dead, maneuverings among the clans and tribes of Persia would affect millions. Could a successor hope to take Cyrus' place, or was the empire of the Persians, suddenly deprived of its founder's charisma, doomed to vanish as rapidly as it had emerged? As the chronicles of countless vanished empires bore witness, the death of a king was a moment ripe with peril for even the greatest monarchy. Cyrus, with a dynast's natural enthusiasm for progeniture, had fathered three daughters and—more significantly—two sons; but this guaranteed nothing. To a great empire as to a nomad's clan, a superfluity of heirs might prove quite as perilous as none.

Farsighted as ever, though, Cyrus had understood the danger and sought to insure against it, carefully providing for the hopes of both his sons. Before his death, he had appointed the elder, Cambyses, crown prince, and the younger, Bardiya, governor of Bactria. This was the largest and most important of the eastern provinces, and even though denied a *kidaris*, the fluted tiara of royal power, Bardiya had been exempted from paying tribute, a privilege properly befitting a king. Whether his resentment of his brother had been mollified by such an honor, or whether it had only piqued his taste for royal status, time would have to tell. Either way, due notice had been given to the world of Cyrus' plans for its future: Cambyses was to sit on the throne of the Persians, and Bardiya was to be his lieutenant. No one else was to have a sniff of power. Just to press this point home, a scandalous match was arranged between Cambyses and his two elder sisters, Atossa and Rhoxsane, a spectacle of incest without precedent in the traditions of Persia, but which set a satisfying block on the ambitions of any rival noble house.[31] After all, who worthier of Cyrus' daughters than Cyrus' son? The bloodline of the great conqueror had become—like a spring watched over by the Magi or the flames of a sacred fire—something precious, to be tended and preserved from all pollution.

Even as Cyrus' corpse was laid to rest in a sarcophagus of gold, inside a tomb carefully oriented toward the rising sun, amid the prayers and lamentations of its Magian attendants, Cambyses moved to claim his birthright. The monarchy of the world was now his. True, as he took his place upon his father's throne, a few eyes may have turned toward his brother; but Bardiya, confirmed in the governorship of his great fiefdom in the east, gave no sign of any treacherous intent. Cyrus' last will and testament proved to have been most cunningly constructed. Both brothers had much to gain by interlocking their interests. It might have been thought that Cambyses would have sought, as his priority, to avenge his father's death—but that would have required him to lead a massive army into the eastern provinces, and provoke his brother's open resentment. Equally, it might have been thought that Bardiya, possessed of a menacing power base, would have sought to force further privileges from Cambyses—but that would have been to risk the open fury of the new king. Whether tacitly or not, the two brothers formed a compact. Bardiya was to be left undisturbed in his province, but he would guard his brother's back;[32] Cambyses, every bit as ambitious for conquest as his father, would turn his armies not against the impoverished tribesmen who had killed Cyrus but toward a kingdom at the opposite end of his frontiers, rich in gold and gargantuan temples, the one great power still surviving from the old world order, and that the most timeless and celebrated of all. He would wage war on Egypt.

Such a campaign, of course, could not be rushed. The might of the pharaohs may have been much diminished from its ancient splendor, having grown dependent upon the support of shiftless mercenaries, and been leeched of income by over-mighty temple priests, but it still posed a formidable challenge. Cambyses spent four years preparing for the invasion. The subject nations of the empire were leaned upon to provide tribute and levies. Ships were built or commandeered, and a Persian king, for the first time in his country's history, became the master of a great and powerful navy. Intelligence was gathered and carefully analyzed. When the Persians finally met the Egyptians in battle, it is said that they did so with cats pinned to their shields, reducing their opponents' archers, for whom the animals were sacred, to a state of outraged paralysis.[33] Victory was duly won. Pelusium, the gateway to Egypt, was stormed, and the bodies of the defeated left scattered across the sands; a century later, their bones could still be seen. Nor, of course, was Cambyses' army the only prong of his assault. All the while, the battle fleet was gliding along the coast. With navy and army shadowing each other in a perfectly coordinated amphibious operation, the Persians advanced to seize their golden prize. Resistance was brutally crushed. Egypt submitted. Her people hailed as pharaoh the "Great Chief of the Foreign Lands."

But the speed of Cambyses' victory had been delusive. A land so ancient and mysterious was not easily absorbed into anyone's empire. True, some measures were easily taken: the income from one town, for instance, was channeled to keep the Persian sister-queens in shoes.[34] Others, however, soon began to suck Cambyses into the sinking sands. Change in Egypt had never been a straightforward matter, and it so happened that the most pressing challenge, to tame and tax the priesthood, was also the most intractable. Cambyses, brutal in a way that native pharaohs had never dared to be, did succeed in forcing requisitions from the bloated estates of the temples, but the effort took him four years and naturally won him the eternal enmity of the priests. No effort was spared by them to blacken his name, and Cambyses would ever after be remembered in Egypt as a lunatic, much given to murder and to gibbering mockery of the gods. Sometimes he was even accused of combining both pastimes, as when he was supposed to have spitted a bull worshipped by the Egyptians as divine.

Lies, all lies. Far from having jeered at the sacred beast, as the black propaganda would have it, Cambyses had actually behaved with exemplary propriety, ordering the dead bull embalmed and reverently laid

to rest. Just as Cyrus had done, he sought to show himself scrupulously respectful of foreign gods, no matter how outlandish. After all,
as pharaoh, he had become a son of Ra himself. To a man only one
generation away from wearing leather trousers, the grandiosity of
Egyptian traditions, aureate like no other, must have provided scope
for considerable reflection. Too much scope, perhaps: for while the
Egyptian priesthood came to regard Cambyses as an oppressive
maniac, so too, and far more fatefully, did the Persian clan chiefs.
Cyrus, even as he conquered the world, had never forgotten his roots,
and as a result he had been loved, and called the "father" of his
people—but Cambyses would be remembered by the Persians in a
very different way, as "cruel and haughty," and they would label him
a "despot."[35] As evidence, spectacular stories of his savagery would be
adduced: how he had used his cupbearer for target practice, and shot
him dead; how he had buried twelve noblemen alive and upside-
down. More smears? Perhaps—and yet surely reflecting memories of
a genuine crisis, one with which the Medes in Cambyses' entourage
would have been only too familiar, of a king intolerant of any hint of
opposition, and resolved to break the will of the chiefs of rival clans.
Many of these, having gone on the Egyptian adventure, had been kept
securely by Cambyses' side, where they could serve their king as
hostages as well as lieutenants. Not all were in Egypt, however. Despite
the absence of the court, Persia remained the surest fount of royal
power. Whoever could master the heartland might also master the
empire beyond. Cambyses' long absence in Egypt served to make this
an increasingly suggestive calculation. Treason began to be muttered
in the clan lands of the Persians.

Three decades previously, the Median chiefs, in their desperation to
topple Astyages, had been reduced to countenancing a foreigner as
king; but the Persian nobility, even as they chafed under the imperi-
ousness of Cambyses, had a more acceptable alternative to hand.
Bardiya was not only the son of Cyrus the Great, but also—and just as
importantly—proficient in all the qualities that the Persians most
admired in a king. His physical strength had won him the nickname

"Tanyoxarces," or "Mighty-frame," and his skill with the bow—the Persians' weapon of choice—was legendary.[36] That he had remained the master of the troublesome eastern marches for almost a decade was ample evidence of his talents as a warlord. In other ways, too, Bardiya had proved himself his father's son. Like Cyrus, it appears, he could conciliate as well as fight. Sensitive to the resentments of the Persian aristocracy, he was also solicitous of the subject peoples, who were increasingly weighed down by the exactions of Cambyses. Whispering it to those who mattered, Bardiya began to moot a startling measure: perhaps, for three years, the subjects of the Persian people might be exempted from providing tribute and further levies to the king? Not that Cambyses would ever agree to that, of course. But a new king? A new king might agree . . .

Such sedition could hardly be kept quiet for long. Spies were everywhere. Cambyses, his African conquests by now secured, woke abruptly to the menace at his rear. Despite all his great achievements, which had seen him extend the supremacy of the Persian people far into the Libyan desert and even into the land of the fabled Ethiopians, "the tallest and best-looking of all men in the world,"[37] he had been too long away from home. By early 522 BC, having set out at last on the long road back to Persia, Cambyses found himself in a desperate race against time. Although he still had his crack troops with him—and much of the nobility as well—events were slipping out of his control. On March 11, Bardiya openly laid claim to the throne. A month later, he was being hailed as king throughout the eastern provinces.[38] Would the empire of the Persian people, raised up to such splendor by Cyrus, now be shattered on the ambitions of his rival sons, break into separate halves, or maybe crumble away entirely? There seemed no escape from the looming fratricide.

And then accident—or something very like an accident—intervened.[39] Cambyses, as he leaped onto his horse to continue his advance through Syria, was said to have wounded himself in the thigh with his sword. Gangrene set in. Within days he was dead. A startling misadventure—and most convenient in its timing, if true. The obvious beneficiary, of course, was Bardiya, now left as Cyrus' only surviving male heir, and therefore king by right as well as might. All had been foreseen by the Magi, who had glimpsed, in the spectacle of a headless baby born to Rhoxsane, the extinction of Cambyses' line, although the Egyptian priests, more malicious and inventive, would whisper that Cambyses had brought the horror on himself—for he was said to have kicked his sister-bride in the stomach, killing not only the fetus but the queen. Now, in Cambyses' childlessness, there seemed a welcome chance of peace—and Bardiya moved quickly to seize it. In July, he was formally invested by the Magi, dressed in the robes of his father and the royal *kidaris*. At the same time, he married Atossa, Cambyses' surviving sister-bride. Succession and bloodline: both now seemed secured. Who else was there, after all, to challenge Bardiya for the monarchy of the world?

But while the new king, confident of his supremacy, withdrew for the summer to the cool of Ecbatana, conspiracy and rumor still swirled across the baking lowland plains.[40] Whether accident or not, the death of Cambyses presented a fearsome temptation to others aside from Bardiya. On the trunk road which led from Syria to the Zagros, the royal army now stood leaderless. But for how long? The highest-ranking officers, scions of great families, had returned from the African adventure battle-hardened and intimate with the workings of power, often beyond their years. Cambyses' "lance-bearer," for instance, a distant cousin of the king by the name of Darius, was a mere twenty-eight. Rank, in the Persian court, was measured by proximity to the royal person, so the young Darius' title, far from implying menial status, had been a splendid and prestigious honorific. It marked him out publicly as a major player at court, and left him privy to the most sensitive royal secrets. In the weeks leading up to Cambyses' death, he could not have been better placed to sift intelligence on the coup.

To sift—and to analyze. For Darius could see, with the pitiless eye of a born politician, that Bardiya's position might not be as strong as it had originally appeared. The clan chiefs' loyalty was divided and unsure. A manifesto of tribute reform, however welcome to the subject nations, was unlikely to prove popular with the Persian ruling class. Bardiya, if his coffers were not to be emptied, would have to recoup the loss of revenue somehow. Since he had no wish to commit political suicide, the new king could hardly put the squeeze on his own supporters; but with much of the nobility far away in Syria, and in Cambyses' camp, an alternative source of income appeared ready to hand. The orders duly went out. The estates of those regarded as Bardiya's opponents, their "pastures and herds, their slaves and houses,"[41] all were confiscated. This windfall, however, urgently needed though it was, came at a fearful cost. The split in the nobility was confirmed. In the eyes of many Persians, Bardiya had branded himself "a disgrace to his country, and to his ancient throne."[42] One king that summer had already passed away; now plans were hurriedly made for the disposal of a second.

The conspirators were seven in total. All were of the highest rank. Among them was Darius, the young lance-bearer of Cambyses—and an Achaemenid. Not that membership in Persia's foremost clan necessarily guaranteed him leadership of the plotters, for it was shared by a second conspirator, a wealthy grandee by the name of Otanes, who also appears to have had an eye on the throne. Furthermore, according to a later tradition, it was Otanes who had first organized the conspiracy—with Darius invited to join only as an after-thought. But this version does not quite add up. For a supposed late-comer, Darius was acknowledged as the conspiracy's linchpin with remarkable speed. His status, right from the beginning, appears to have been preeminent. Linked by blood to Cyrus, he also stood at the heart of the web that bound together the seven conspirators. One of them, Gobryas, was both his father-in-law *and* the husband of his sister: marriage ties could hardly have bound the two any tighter. Darius' brother, Artaphernes, a man of rare daring and intelligence, was also, although not one of the seven chief conspirators, ready to move on whatever was decided. More than a hint, then, of a family affair. Wherever one looks, Darius seems to loom as the ringleader of the plot.

27

Why, then, the insistence that he had not been in on it from the start? How might he have benefited from this apparent distortion of the time frame? What, to put it bluntly, might he have had to cover up? One obvious and fateful answer suggests itself—regicide. After all, who better placed than a king's lance-bearer to plot the murder of a king? Such an act of treachery would have been regarded even by Cambyses' enemies as beyond the pale. While Darius would soon prove himself as bold as he was ruthless, he was never one to flaunt his crimes. As a result, the truth of his guilt or otherwise is forever lost to us.[43] Yet if Darius' involvement in the death of Cambyses must be reckoned, not proven, his role in spurring forward the plot against Bardiya is far more certain. When Otanes, urging a course of prudence, suggested the recruitment of more conspirators, and playing for time, Darius argued for immediate action. They should rely, he insisted, not on force of numbers, but on speed and surprise. To waver would be to lose their advantage. The greater their daring, the greater their chances of success.

With his brother, Artaphernes, and a majority of the seven backing him, Darius had his way. His calculations had been precise. A rare opportunity was indeed now opening. As the conspirators and their train, following the Khorasan Highway, closed in on the foothills of the Zagros, they would have felt the violent heat of summer on the plains starting to diminish. Autumn was on its way. Soon, the king would be descending from the mountains. If the assassination squad could ambush him on open ground, somewhere on the road between Ecbatana and the heartland of royal power in Persia, then he might be dispatched with relative ease. Practiced horsemen all—for there had never been a Persian nobleman not raised in the saddle—the seven conspirators and their accomplices rode at a scorching pace, desperate not to lose their chance. By September, they had arrived at the borders of Media. Ahead of them lay the Khorasan Highway, twisting through the mountains up to Ecbatana. And descending it, approaching them, somewhere, was Bardiya.

News of his progress would have been easily come by. The road was always busy. Merchants, profiting from the consolidation of Persian authority, had begun to throng the great highway in growing numbers, businessmen from the wealthy trading cities of the lowlands, their talk an exotic babel, their laden pack animals clopping in tow.[44] Those coming from Ecbatana would have been able to assure the conspirators that the king had indeed left his summer capital, that he was on the move, that he was not far ahead of them. Then, with Bardiya drawing ever nearer, the traffic on the road would have grown even more varied, the king's lackeys and outriders increasingly in evidence, their costumes rich, their beards and hair elaborately curled, their peacock extravagance alerting travelers to the approach of their master, the King of Persia, the King of the World.

Nevertheless, amid all the clamor and clarions and color, traces of a far more ancient order still abided. By late September, as the conspirators pressed along the northern edge of Nisaea, the most fertile of the Zagros valleys, they would have been able to mark the most dramatic of these. Away from the courtiers and caravans on the highway, covering the clover-rich pastureland, there spread a spectacle familiar to numberless generations; indeed, a reminder of ways more primordial than Media itself. Horses, white horses, covered the plain—as many as 160,000 of them, it was said. These were the same breed that had been paid in tribute to the Assyrians almost two centuries before, "the best, and the largest"[45] in the world, for not even the fabulous kingdoms of India—where, as was well known, every animal grew to a prodigious size—had anything to compare. Once the Medes had been nomads, and now they were the subjects of a foreign monarchy; but riding across the Nisaean plain, abreast of the shimmering herds, they knew themselves supreme as the tamers of horses still. A splendid consolation to them in their slavery: for the white horses, so strong and swift and beautiful, were regarded by the peoples of the Zagros as creatures sacred, bound by mysterious ties of communion to the divine, and to their king.

Even the conquering Persians acknowledged this. At Pasargadae, a horse from Nisaea would be sacrificed every month before the hallowed tomb of Cyrus himself. Perhaps that was why Bardiya, turning off the Khorasan Highway and pausing in his descent toward the lowlands, lingered in the presence of the herd. Whether he sought legitimization, or a sign from the heavens, or perhaps just the reading of bad dreams, he would have found in Nisaea ready experts on hand. Magi, interpreters of all that was mysterious, were the guardians of the sacred horses too. Did Bardiya summon these masters of ritual to his presence and ask them what his future might hold? Perhaps. What is certain, however, is that on September 29, 522 BC, a man calling himself Bardiya was in Nisaea, in a fort named Sikyavautish—and that it was there that Darius finally tracked him down.

What happened next would be retold by all those who traced their lineage from the seven leaders of the assassination squad. Many versions must have been elaborated over the years. All agreed, however, that Bardiya was taken wholly by surprise. It seems that the conspirators and their followers, coolly riding up to the gates of the fortress, baldly announced that they had come to see the king. The guards, overawed by the rank of the new arrivals, scurried to let them in. Only in the courtyard, as they approached the royal quarters, did anyone think to challenge them—but by then it was too late. The assassins, overpowering the courtiers in their path, burst into Bardiya's chamber. The king, it is said, was with a concubine. Desperately, he sought to stave off his attackers with the leg of a broken stool, but to no avail. It is also said that it was Darius' brother, "faithful Artaphernes," who finally plunged the dagger home.[46]

And Bardiya, the son of Cyrus, King of the Persians, slumped dead to the ground.

Double Vision

Or did he? No sooner had the assassins completed their bloody work than they themselves were promoting a quite different tale. The corpse of the murdered man may not have been exposed to public view, but a great deal else was now revealed, to universal amazement.

The story told by the conspirators was staggering. The man they had slain, they claimed, was not Bardiya, the son of Cyrus, at all. That Bardiya was already long dead. Cambyses, jealous and savage, had ordered his execution years before. Had it not been for the acumen of Darius and his fellow patriots, who had stumbled upon the secret, and their courage in daring to expose it, the Persian people might never have learned of the monstrous scam.

All of which begged a rather obvious question. If the man assassi-nated at Sikyavautish had not been the son of Cyrus—and the rightful king—then who had he been? Here the revelations took an even more sinister turn. That an impostor had taken on the role of a prince of the royal blood was alarming enough, but that he had played it for years unsuspected even by his family and household could only be evidence of the blackest necromancy. Surely, then, a Magus, one who had been schooled in the mastery of the supernatural, was the likeliest suspect? Could it have been merely a coincidence that the impostor had been surprised in Nisaea, on the plain of the sacred horses, well known as a haunt of the Magi? It seemed not—for Bardiya's doppelgänger, the conspirators hurriedly announced, had indeed been a Magus, "Gaumata by name."[47] An obscure and low-born villain he may have been, and yet so potent had his sorcery proved itself, and so audacious his plot, that he had almost won the empire by his fraud.

Sensationalist retellings would tease out the full implications of this scandal and adorn them further. For all his powers, it appeared that the Magus had forgotten to conceal one crucial detail: his ears, for some unspecified crime, had long before been cut off by Cyrus. A daughter of Otanes named Phaidime, a wife of Bardiya who had never suspected that he might have been killed and replaced by a double, had brushed the side of her husband's head one evening while he slept, and uncovered the appalling truth. Telling her father of her discovery, she had thereby set in train the dramatic sequence of events which had culminated in the murder of the impostor. Such, at any rate, was the story which years later would be told across the empire. And there was nobody, by then, left to dispute it.

31

Even on the night of the assassination, if there had been anyone in Nisaea to query the conspirators' self-justification, or to point out some of its more glaring implausibilities, or to ask why the corpse of the supposed impostor had been disposed of with such speed, he would have known better than to speak his mind. With blood still being washed from the fittings of Sikyavautish, it was hardly the time for quibbles. The conspirators were in no mood to tolerate dissent. The warning given by Darius could not have been more stentorian: "Thou who shalt be king hereafter, protect thyself vigorously from the Lie; the man who shall be a follower of the Lie, him do thou punish well!"[48] Here, from a master political strategist, was a dazzling sleight-of-hand. It would serve to place not the assassins but their accusers on the defensive. Skeptics were to be anathematized as the enemies of truth.

And this, for any Persian, was a feared and dreadful fate. It was an article of faith to Darius' countrymen that they were the most honest people in the world. Three things were taught them, it was said: "to ride, to fire a bow and to tell the truth."[49] Darius, by threatening those who might doubt his story of the Magus' crimes, was not just shoring up a rickety case; his claims were altogether more soaring. Only a Persian could have made them—for only a Persian could understand what truth really meant. He knew, as more benighted peoples did not, that the universe without truth would be undone and lost to perpetual night. More than an abstraction, more even than an ideal, it formed instead the very fabric of existence.

This was why, in the beginning, when Ahura Mazda, greatest of the gods, had summoned time and creation into being, he had engendered Arta, who was Truth, to give order to the universe. Without Arta, it would have lacked form or beauty, and the great cycles of existence set in motion by Lord Mazda could not have brought life into the world. Even so, the work of Truth was never done. Just as fire, when it rises to the heavens, is accompanied by black smoke, so Arta, the Persians knew, was shadowed by Drauga, the Lie. Two orders—one of perfection, the other of falsehood, each the image of the other— were coiled in a conflict as ancient as time. What should mortals do, then, but take the side of Arta against Drauga, Truth against the Lie, lest the universe itself should totter and fail? "The wretch who weaves deceit will bring death into his country":[50] so it had been anciently proclaimed. How much more deadly the peril, then, if a "wretch" had somehow seized his country's throne. The Magus, by taking on the image of Bardiya, and impersonating the rightful king, had handed to Drauga the scepter of the world. Darius and his fellows, by riding to Sikyavautish, had toppled an evil infinitely more threatening than a mere impostor. Far from staging a squalid putsch, they had been engaged in nothing less than the redemption of the cosmos.

And now, with Gaumata justly toppled and dispatched, the throne which he had tainted stood empty. The insignia of royal power—a robe, a bow and a shield—waited in Sikyavautish for the rightful claimant. Who that might be, however, and how he was to be recognized, remained, on the evening of the assassination, a mystery. Only the most garbled account of what followed has survived. The conspirators, it was said, rode out by night into the open plain. At an agreed point, they reined in their horses and awaited the coming of dawn. When the sun's first rays appeared above the rugged line of mountains to the east, it was Darius' horse who neighed to them in greeting. At once, his companions slipped from their saddles and fell to their knees in homage. The Greeks, when they repeated this story, would claim that it had been agreed among the conspirators that "the one whose horse was first to neigh after dawn should have the throne"[51]—and they added, furthermore, that Darius had cheated. His groom, it was said, had dabbled his fingers inside a mare's vulva beforehand, and then, just as the sun rose, placed them beside the nose of Darius' horse. But this was scurrilous nonsense, and typical of the Greeks. How like them to distort the holy rites of Truth!

For it is evident, even from the unsatisfactory version that we have, that Darius' accession was marked by potent and awful ritual. The conspirators gathered in the chill of that September night not because they wished to discover who the next king might be, but because they already knew. Otanes, Darius' only conceivable rival, had already bowed to the inevitable and discounted himself as a candidate for the throne: the noblemen riding across the plain of Nisaea were celebrating a fait accompli. Blessed by the neighing of the sacred white horses, and by the mountain dawn, Darius could know himself doubly the champion of Arta. As the first rays illuminated the plain, so night, the order of Drauga, menacing and indistinct, began to fade before the brilliant light of the sun. "So can I recognize you as strong and holy, O Mazda, when by the hand in which you hold the twin destinies of the Liar and of the Righteous Man, and by the glow of your fire whose power is the Truth, the might of Good Thought shall come to me."[52] And now, that late September dawn, the might of Good Thought had indeed come to Nisaea, for the Liar was dead, and the Righteous Man was king.

Or so it pleased Darius to claim. Yet the imagery, although it would suffuse his propaganda, was not his own. If it bore witness to the reverence for Arta found among all the Aryans, then it drew as well on the teachings of a far more rigorous dualism. "The twin destinies of the Liar and of the Righteous Man": not Darius' words but those of that most fabled of visionaries, Zoroaster, the prophet of the Aryans, the man who had first revealed to a startled world that it was the battleground in a relentless war between good and evil. Here, in this war, was the great death struggle of things—for the Prophet, continuing with his novel doctrines, had taught that the cycles of the cosmos would not keep revolving forever, as had always been assumed, but move instead toward a mighty end, a universal apocalypse in which Truth would annihilate all falsehoods, and establish on their ruin an eternal reign of peace. Presiding over this final and decisive victory would be the Lord of Life, Wisdom and Light, Ahura Mazda himself— not, as other Iranians had always believed, one among a multitude of divinities, but the supreme, the all-powerful, the only uncreated god. From him, like fire leaping from beacon to beacon, all goodness proceeded: six great emanations of his own eternal light, the Amesha Spentas, holy and immortal;[53] a broader pantheon of beneficent spirits; the world in its many beauties; plants and animals (and, in particular, because it spent its days preying upon insects, those swarming spawn of the dark side, the hedgehog); the faithful and ever-righteous dog; and finally, noblest of all creations, man himself. "Unblock your ears, then, to hear the Good News—gaze at the bright flames with clear-seeing thought!" the Prophet had proclaimed, alerting humanity to the great decision that confronted it. "You have the choice as to which faith you will follow, everyone, person by person, with that freedom all are granted in the mighty test of life."[54] Choose wrong, and the path of the Lie, and of chaos, would be opened; choose right, and the path of order, tranquillity and hope.

Was Darius the first usurper to appreciate just how amenable to his purposes this great religion of peace and justice might prove to be? We shall never know for sure. The early history of Zoroaster and his doctrines was a puzzle even to his own followers. That the Prophet had been the only baby to laugh, rather than cry, at his birth; that he had been granted his first vision of Ahura Mazda at the age of thirty, as he emerged from a river; that he had finally succumbed, aged seventy-seven, to an assassin's knife: these few scraps of his biography had been preserved by the devout. But as to when he had lived, and where, wildly divergent opinions were held: some dated Zoroaster to the dawn of time, others only to the reign of King Astyages;[55] some held that he had been raised in Bactria, others on the steppes. What everyone agreed, however, was that he had been neither a Mede nor a Persian—and that the knowledge of his teachings had first come to the Zagros from the East.[56]

But to what effect? The empire founded by Cyrus was certainly no theocracy; it was never, in any real sense, "Zoroastrian" at all. The Persians continued to worship their ancient gods, to honor mountains and flowing streams, and to sacrifice horses before the tombs of their kings. But if the Achaemenid court remained pagan in much of its practice, it was also, in its dominant sensibility, not entirely removed from Zoroaster's teachings. As in the eastern kingdoms of Iran, where the monotheism of the Prophet had taken its strongest hold, so also in the west, Ahura Mazda had long been worshipped as supreme. Between the native paganism of the Persians and the teachings of Zoroaster there appears to have been, not rivalry, but rather synergy, and even fusion. Both were the expressions of a single religious impulse, one that had been evolving over centuries, and was still, as the Persians conquered the world, in a state of flux. In particular, between the Magi, who had long been adepts of the most occult and sacred knowledge, and the priests of Zoroaster, there were numerous correspondences. It was not even clear which order had first proclaimed eternal war against insects and reptiles, had first worn white robes as the mark of their status, or had first exposed the corpses of their fellows to be consumed by birds and dogs (a fate otherwise regarded among the Persians as so terrible that it was reserved for regicides). So too with the worship of the Good Lord, Ahura Mazda himself, influence had long been percolating both ways. Far from dividing the Medes and Persians from their cousins in the East, their "Mazdaism" appears to have served them as a source of unity.

A bond certainly appreciated by Cyrus. Looking to dramatize his unprecedented dominion over the various Iranian peoples, he had consciously adopted certain customs from their ancient heartlands. In the nursery of his own tribe, at Pasargadae, far distant from Bactria or Sogdiana, he had ordered the building of three startling new structures: fire-holders made of stone, their tops hollowed out into deep, wide bowls, in which white-hot ashes could be kept forever burning.[57] Fire had long been sacred to all the Iranians, but to no one more than to Zoroaster himself, who had taught that its flames were the very symbol of righteousness and truth. Daily prayer before fire had been laid upon his followers as a sacred duty, and Cyrus, in the course of his eastern conquests, would surely have witnessed the spectacle of such worship for himself. There can be no doubt that it was from Zoroaster that the Persians "derived the rule against burning dead bodies or defiling fire in any way," for a Lydian scholar, in the earliest reference to the Prophet recorded by an *anairya*, commented as much.[58] The fire-holders built by Cyrus, their flames rising into the azure of the Persian sky, would certainly have blazed out the new doctrine high and clear—but they would also have served to broadcast a very different lesson. Cyrus had hit upon the perfect image of his power. How better to represent royal greatness than to associate it with fire? Even those otherwise ignorant of the customs of the Iranians might readily appreciate such a notion. Soon enough, throughout the empire, similar sanctuaries began to appear, their flames guarded by the Magi, only ever to be extinguished on the death of the reigning monarch, symbols both of Arta and of the rule of Persia's king.

And now Darius, his hands wet with royal blood, was moving to make this identification of the two orders, celestial and mortal, even more explicit. As he would never cease to acknowledge, everything he was, everything he had achieved, was due to the favor of Ahura Mazda: "He bore me aid, the other gods too, because I was not faithless, I was not a follower of the Lie, I was not false in my actions."[59] Darius was surely protesting too much. But as a regicide and usurper, he had little choice. With his claim to the throne so tenuous, he could hardly rely on it to justify his coup. Other legitimization had to be concocted—and fast. This was why, far more than Cyrus or his sons had ever felt the need to do, Darius insisted on his role as the chosen one of God.

Who precisely God might be, however, whether the Ahura Mazda of his ancestors' pantheon, or the one supreme being proclaimed by Zoroaster, the new king was content to leave unclear. Ambiguity had its uses. Above all, it was essential that Darius show his respect for the traditions of his own people—and it so happened that his situation on the Nisaean plain provided the perfect stage. Some fifteen miles north of Sikyavautish, rising high and somber from the midst of a level plain, loomed the twin peaks of Bisitun, "the place of the gods," the most sacred mountain in the whole Zagros range.[60] Here, near the scene of his ambushing of Bardiya, Darius could offer sacrifice just as the Persians and the Medes had always done, in the sanctity of the pure and open air. Yet the murder itself, the stern and epic quality of its execution, and the configuration of the assassins, would have conjured up associations for the followers of Zoroaster just as ripe with potential for Darius' propaganda. Six, according to the teachings of the Prophet, were the Amesha

Spentas, the Beneficent Immortals who proceeded from Ahura Mazda—and six were the accomplices of Darius in his war against the Lie. That men might ponder this coincidence—or symmetry—could serve only to buttress the new king's cause. Darius might not have been the son of Cyrus, but he could pose as something infinitely more impressive: the proxy of the Good Lord, Ahura Mazda himself.

This seamless identification of his own power with that of a universal god was a development full of moment for the future. Usurpers had been claiming divine sanction for their actions since time immemorial, but never such as Ahura Mazda could provide. Already, with the daring and creativity that were the trademarks of his style, Darius was moving with deadly speed to take advantage of this fact. Out of murder and usurpation, he would manufacture a rare legitimacy for himself. Out of weakness, he would forge a strength such as no monarch had ever possessed before.

Dizzying as this startling ambition was, however, so too was the yawning of a waiting abyss. The chosen one of Ahura Mazda could not afford to stumble: just one slip, and Darius would have failed. Already, as he and the other conspirators nursed their strength in Media, disturbing news was coming through to them of the empire's reaction to their coup. In Elam, an ancient kingdom on the borders of Persia, open revolt had broken out. In Babylon,* the great metropolis which was the largest and wealthiest city in the world, a pretender was reported to have emerged to claim its long-vacant throne. Suddenly, it seemed that the empire of the Persians, rather than bringing the universal peace of Arta to mankind, might dissolve, lost to chaos and the reach of a lengthening shadow. For Darius, the self-proclaimed champion of light, the ultimate test was looming. Not only his own future but that of the whole Near East was at stake.

Ahead of him waited the road to Babylon.

---

*Located just south of modern-day Baghdad.

2

BABYLON

Stairway to Heaven

Without dirt, there could never have been cities or great kings. So claimed the people of Babylon, who knew full well that their civilization had been fashioned out of mud. Back in the beginning, when all the earth had been ocean, Lord Marduk, king of the gods, had built a raft of reeds, covered it with dust, mingled it with water to form a primordial slime and out of this raised a home for himself, the Esagila, the first building in the world. This could still be seen eons later, standing in the heart of Babylon—but it had needed no temple to make the Babylonians appreciate what could be done with earth and water. They knew it in their bones. "I will take blood," Marduk had announced, in the earliest days of the world, "and I will sculpt flesh, and I will form the first man."[1] As good as his word, he had duly mixed dust with the gore of a slaughtered rival, and fashioned humanity out of the sticky compound. Here, in the primal act of man's creation, had been set a pattern for all time. The crops in a field, the bricks in a city wall: what would these have been without mud? Hemmed in as they were by the bleakness of mountain and desert, the Babylonians could gaze at their land, and know they were the most fortunate of people, blessed not by one but by two mighty rivers, prodigious evidence of the favor of the gods. The fertility of their estates, the towering splendor of their buildings, the easy passage of their merchants to the sea; all were gifts of the Euphrates and the Tigris. Well might Greek travelers have described the mud steppes as "Mesopotamia," the "Land Between the Rivers"; for without water all the wealth of Babylon would have been as nothing but dry dust.

As it was, the city ranked as the jewel in the King of Persia's crown. Lose it, and he might lose everything—as the Babylonians themselves were well aware. Never lacking self-regard, they were perfectly accustomed to view their city as the fulcrum of great events. For centuries, their ambitions had shaken the Near East. Of all the many foes of Assyria, Babylon had been the most obdurate, and had led, with the Medes, the revolt that had destroyed the hated empire. Over its wreckage the Babylonians had then raised their own dominion, imposing upon their neighbors, and by the same amiable methods once employed by the Assyrians, "an iron yoke of servitude."[2] As Jeremiah, in far-off Judah, had wailed, "Their quiver is like an open tomb, they are all mighty men. They shall eat up your harvest and your food; they shall eat up your sons and your daughters; they shall eat up your flocks and your herds; they shall eat up your vines and your fig trees; your fortified cities in which you trust they shall destroy with the sword."[3] And all had come to pass just as the prophet had foreseen. In 586 BC, Jerusalem had been taken and left a blackened pile of rubble, and the hapless Judaeans hauled off into exile. There, weeping by the rivers of Babylon, they had been kept company by the transplants of other nations from across the Near East—for Mesopotamia, populous and fertile though she was, had long since left behind self-sufficiency. Only by feasting, vampire-like, on far-off lands had she been able to maintain herself, satisfying her monstrous appetites with foreign peoples as well as products. Immigrants, whether slaves and exiles or mercenaries and merchants, thronged the streets of Babylon—history's first truly multicultural city. Even after the loss of her independence to Cyrus, she had remained the Near East's supreme melting pot, her streets filled with a thousand different tongues, the roaring of exotic animals and the flashing of strange birds, the golds and scarlets and mother-of-pearl of the ends of the earth. What, in comparison, were the backwoods of Persia? The homeland of an empire, maybe—but hardly the heartbeat of the world.

It was scarcely surprising, then, that the Babylonians should have regarded Persian rule as merely—the gods willing—a temporary aberration. Cyrus, with his customary imperious magnanimity, had disdained to eliminate the defeated royal family; and even though the last king, Nabonidus, had been an old man when his city fell, on his death he had left no lack of thrusting heirs. One of these, taking advantage of the chaos unleashed by Bardiya's murder, emerged in early October to proclaim himself Nebuchadnezzar III. Here, for all those who had suffered from the Babylonians' attentions in the past, was a name of ominous portent: for the second Nebuchadnezzar had been Babylon's greatest ruler, the conqueror of Jerusalem and much more besides, a shatterer of cities and a breaker of proud nations, his memory preserved among those he had defeated as something fabulous, golden and deadly. But if the name of the new king would have sent shivers throughout the Near East, its effect on the Babylonians themselves would surely have been to set them dreaming. Their world must have seemed to be returning to its former balance. Universal dominion, pilfered from Mesopotamia by Persian bandits, could now be restored to where it belonged. As was only right, a Nebuchadnezzar would once again reign supreme.

Darius, ever alert to the possibilities of propaganda, knew better than to take these sentiments lightly. Which was why, even though the rebellion in Elam had cut him off from his heartland, he headed not for Persia but directly for Mesopotamia. Descending at his usual break-neck speed from the mountains, he was following the same road that Cyrus had taken seventeen years previously—and, just as Cyrus had done, he found the way wide open at first. A huge phallus, raised out of stones, stood by the wayside, marking the border of the Land of the Two Rivers; ahead of him, flat and unbroken, stretched a monotony of alluvium. Only the occasional peasant, stooping to plant barley, would have intruded upon the emptiness, and every so often a broken line of palms. These, marking the courses of ditches and canals, would have been far less abundant than they were further south, around the Euphrates; for the Tigris, in contrast to its sister river, had impressively steep banks, and—inconveniently for farmers—flowed so fast that its name in Persian meant "the arrow."

Yet what rendered it unsuitable for the purposes of irrigation made it ideal as a line of defense: easily the most formidable that Mesopotamia possessed amid the general featurelessness of the landscape. To strengthen it against the menace of invasion from Media, and to plug the open flatlands that lay between the Tigris and the Euphrates, a great stretch of fortifications had been constructed, eight meters wide and ten meters high, their crenellations proudly visible across the drear of the plains. Even sixty years after its construction, this "Median Wall" still bore witness to the monarch who had raised it, Nebuchadnezzar II, whose greatness had been the dread of the world. Nor, indeed, could a more fitting location for such a display of royal power have been imagined. Akkad, the region through which the Median Wall ran, was numinous with memories of a fateful innovation. Here, millennia before Nebuchadnezzar, an intoxicating dream had come to a man named Sargon, one never since forgotten, so that the kings of Babylon had been honored to name themselves the kings of Akkad. Such a title, in contrast to some other Mesopotamian appellations—"King of the Four Quarters of the Earth," say, or "King of the Universe"—might have appeared modest; but it had served to link the kings of Babylon to the origins of empire. Provincial though Akkad had long become, its ancient grandeur lost to the wind, it had once been the seat of a global monarchy—for it was in Akkad, back in the 2200s BC, that the concept of world conquest had first been conceived.

Sargon, the obscure adventurer who had emerged as though from nowhere to nurture this proud ambition, to extinguish the independence of neighboring city-states and to rule supreme over the "totality of the lands under heaven,"[4] had always remained the model of a Mesopotamian strongman. Almost two thousand years after his foundation of Akkad, he remained the cynosure of great kings. Indeed, in the decades before the Persian conquest, the obsession with him had become a veritable craze. At Susa, the capital of Elam, a victory memorial originally inscribed by Sargon's grandson had been lovingly dusted down and put on prominent display; in Akkad itself, when a statue of the great man was excavated, Nabonidus had come rushing in high excitement to inspect it, and to supervise its restoration. Museums had sprung up everywhere: at Ur, for instance, the antiquities collection maintained by Nabonidus' daughter, Princess En-nigaldi-Nanna, had been carefully labeled and put on display for the edification of the public. Meanwhile, in Babylon itself, scholars pored over great libraries of archives, tracing ancient documents, recycling archaic phrases, looking to the distant past to legitimize the needs and whims of their masters. The people of Mesopotamia, living as they did amid the lumber of millennia, had always been profoundly respectful of antiquity. Rather than feeling oppressed by it, they recycled it, cannibalized it, and turned it to their advantage.

Confronted by this menacing venerability, the Persians might have been expected to respond to it very differently: with suspicion, and even fear. It was not just that their own history, by comparison, was the merest blink of an eye. The turning of the ages of the world, scrupulously recorded in king lists and star charts, meant knowledge for those who tracked it—and knowledge meant power. Babylon was famed as a metropolis of sorcerers. Throughout Mesopotamia, a great network of observatories had been established, enabling astrologers to trace the warnings of the heavens, and speedily to dispatch news of them back to their intelligence chiefs in Babylon. This ability to read the future and to map the patterns cast on statecraft by the stars had always been a potent weapon of the Babylonian kings. When combined with the elaborate and unfathomable rituals for which their city was also famous, its myriad ziggurats and temples, and the supposedly primordial foundations on which its monuments had been raised, their layout dating back to the beginning of time, their bricks touched with the fingerprints of the gods, Babylon could hardly fail to overwhelm.

And yet Cyrus, back in 539 BC, when he had first arrived in the city as its conqueror, had not been remotely intimidated. Indeed, he had shown himself far more sensitive to the alien and complex traditions of Mesopotamia, and to the potential they might offer his regime, than Nabonidus had ever done. The last king of Babylon, fascinated though he was by antiquity, had eventually pushed his researches too far. Not content with hero-worshipping Sargon, he had also extolled the kings of Assyria, naming them his "royal ancestors"[5] and adopting their ancient titles. This, in a city which one Assyrian king had sought to obliterate from the face of the earth, had been tactless, to say the least. Even more offensive to Babylonian sensibilities, however, and ultimately fatal to Nabonidus' cause, had been his putting Marduk's nose out of joint.

For a god more prickly with regard to his dignity it would have been hard to imagine. No mortal, not even the greatest monarch, could afford to offend him. This was why, every new year, the king was expected to visit the Esagila, the city's greatest temple, to have his cheeks slapped and his ears yanked in a grand ritual of humiliation before the admonitory gaze of Marduk's golden statue. If tears were brought to the king's eyes, then so much the better, for that would indicate that the god was well pleased; if, however, the king did not turn up at all, then it would presage certain disaster for his realm. Nabonidus' behavior, to the Babylonians' way of thinking, had been particularly egregious. Not only had he absented himself from Babylon, and therefore the Esagila, for ten whole years, but he had rubbed salt in the wounds by promoting the cult of a venerable moon god, Sin, in Marduk's place. Admittedly, he had unearthed good antiquarian reasons for doing so—for just as Babylon, far from being the most ancient city in the world, as her citizens liked to boast, had in fact been a relatively late foundation, so Marduk, its patron, had been an equally late promotion to the throne of the gods. By sponsoring the worship of Sin, Nabonidus had hoped to provide for his far-flung empire a less obviously chauvinistic focus of loyalty than the domineering Marduk. By doing so, however, he had laid himself fatally open to Cyrus' propaganda. "Marduk," it was claimed, "scanned all the countries of the world, looking for a righteous ruler,"[6] and he had found one in the King of Persia. Cyrus, welcomed into Babylon by his new subjects, had duly damned Nabonidus as a heretic, while cheerfully promoting himself as Marduk's chosen one. The city's ancient rituals had been permitted to continue undisturbed; cult statues, appropriated by Nabonidus for safe-keeping, had been returned to their proper shrines; in the first months of Persian rule, Cambyses, acting as proxy for his father, had even reported to the Esagila for the ritual New Year slapping.

And Marduk had been gratified. Order had been maintained in the Land of the Two Rivers. Yes, the Persians were upstarts, and yes, it was disconcerting for the citizens of the world's greatest city to be ruled as though they were mere provincials; but Cyrus and Cambyses had given the Babylonians peace. No greater virtue could be ascribed to a king. The priests of Marduk, confirmed in both their primacy and in their extensive property-holdings across Mesopotamia, were not the only natives to have collaborated enthusiastically with foreign rule. Big business had also flourished. Inflation, galloping out of control under Nabonidus, had been stabilized; trade routes, no longer blocked by Persian sanctions, had filled with caravans again. For merchants and financiers, the absorption of Mesopotamia into a world empire had opened up unprecedented opportunities. Sentimental notions of loyalty to the old regime could hardly be expected to stand in the way of profit. The Egibis, for instance, a dynasty of bankers who had been operating as agents to the native kings of Babylon for decades, had no sooner witnessed the downfall of Nabonidus than they were smoothly accommodating themselves to the new order, dating their commercial documents from the accession year of Cyrus, and looking to expand into Iran. Within a couple of years, they had opened offices in Ecbatana and throughout Persia, diversifying enthusiastically into fields as varied as the slave trade and the hawking of marriage contracts. Then, suddenly, caught short by the revolt in Mesopotamia, the Egibis found themselves facing meltdown. By the late autumn of 522 BC, their headquarters in Babylon had lost contact with the regional branches. Two of the family's brothers were cut off in Persia. The bank's debts began to mount. As far as the Egibis were concerned, their city's rebellion promised not liberation but disaster. The sooner it was quelled, and stability restored to the markets, the better.

Of course, the fact that the rule of the Persians had collapsed into murder and factionalism was, for most Babylonians, a justification in itself for their revolt. Just as Marduk had been offended by Nabonidus, so now, self-evidently, he was bending his frown upon the warring house of Cyrus. Yet this assumption, even though it threatened Darius' claim to the throne, also presented him with a dazzling opportunity. The chosen one of Ahura Mazda, why should he not prove himself the favorite of the supreme god of Babylon, too? Was it likely, after all, that Marduk, having overthrown the heretical Nabonidus, should now bless his son? What better chance for Darius to establish his credentials as monarch of the world than to crush a revolt in Babylon? No wonder that he drove so hard toward the city. Already, by early December, Persian outriders had reached the Median Wall. Next, turning its flank, Darius led his army over the Tigris, his soldiers clinging to horses, camels and inflated animal skins. On December 13, 522 BC he met the army of Nebuchadnezzar III in battle, and routed it. Six days later, with a second victory, Darius completed his annihilation of the Babylonian forces. Nebuchadnezzar, turning tail with what was left of his cavalry, fled back to his capital. Not one of those who stayed behind to surrender was spared. The road to Babylon stood wide open.

Darius, not hesitating, took it. Ahead of him, blotting out the horizon, was a monstrous haze of smoke and dust, the exhalation of a metropolis without rival on the planet. An unprecedented quarter of a million people lived in Babylon, crowded into the narrow, twisting streets; yet, cramped though the city was, a dense agglomeration of brick, bodies and dung, it had still required the longest urban fortifications ever built to enclose just a portion of its sprawl. Stupendous, like everything else in

Babylon, the walls enclosed three full square miles, had eight colossal decorated gates, and were protected, where the Euphrates did not provide a natural barrier, by moats, "great floods of destroying waters like the great waves of the sea." A fittingly grand enceinte for the theater of the world's fantasies: "Babylon, the city of opulence; Babylon, the city whose people are glutted with wealth; Babylon, the city of celebrations, rejoicing and endless dance."[7] Even through the darkest back alleys, it was said, Ishtar, the goddess of love, might be seen gliding, visiting her favorites in taverns and on the open streets, so that all the city, mingling festival with erotic adventure, appeared to glimmer with desire. Well might Babylon, to the Judaean exiles, have appeared a stew of licentiousness, and to those in distant countries, it was a superhuman and magical place. The city walls, it was confidently asserted, stretched for fifty-six miles, and had a hundred gates of bronze. In its streets, so it was whispered, prostitution was regarded as a sacred duty, and daughters would be joyously pimped by their own fathers. Not so much a city, Babylon was rather a veritable world unto itself. Indeed, "such was the immensity of her scale that Cyrus," it was claimed, "had been able to seize control of the outskirts without anyone in the center even being aware of his arrival, so that the Babylonians, who were celebrating a festival, had continued dancing, and indulging themselves. And so it was that the city had fallen for the first time."[8]

But the second? The stories that told of Cyrus' capture of Babylon, for all their implausibilities, still hinted at a certain strategic truth: any army breaking into the city might indeed find itself swallowed up by the vastness. Darius' soldiers, as they saw the walls of Babylon looming toward them through the smog, must have felt a quickening of their hearts; for nothing, not even the temples of Egypt, would have prepared them for the gargantuan scale of such a place. But it is doubtful that their general felt any lurch of doubt. Darius knew, for his intelligence agents would have told him as much, that Babylon was ripe for the plucking. The city, impregnable though it might have appeared, was in truth far too riven by division to be defended. If it was, as those who marveled at it claimed, a mirror of the world, then the reflection that it offered was one of social and ethnic hatred. It was not only priests and businessmen who were eager to collaborate with the Persian king. Babylon was also filled with the descendants of deportees, scattered throughout the suburbs. Few of these were willing to die in the cause of a Nebuchadnezzar. The cosmopolitanism of the great city, once the mark and buttress of its imperial might, now threatened it with anarchy. The Babylonians were bound to shrink from such a prospect, even at the cost of surrender to an alien master. Chaos, in Mesopotamia, had always been the ultimate nightmare. Men knew that in the beginning all the world had been under the sway of demons, uncontrollable and savage, until the gods, taking pity on mankind, had established order by giving them a king. Without a monarch, civilization itself would cease to hold; the demons would surely return. "To have authority, and possession, and strength, these are princely divine properties." So it had been anciently asserted, in a remote age when even Sargon and his empire lay in the future. "You should submit to the strong man; you should humble yourself before the man who wields power."[9] Not, perhaps, the most heroic of maxims, but practical, and sanctified by the habits of millennia. The Babylonians, seeing the Persian king ride victorious toward them, duly scrambled to prostrate themselves. Once again, as they had done to Cyrus, they opened up their gates.

Darius, passing through the brilliant glazed blue of the main gateway, took easy possession of the city. No getting sucked into the urban labyrinth for him. Symmetry as well as chaos were to be found in Babylon. Just as the gods had structured the formlessness of human society by gifting it the sacred institution of monarchy, so, across the seething ferment of the world's largest city, there had been laid an imperious grid of boulevards. Now, down the grandest of these, the Processional Way, Darius made his entry into Babylon.

"May-The-Arrogant-Not-Flourish," the Babylonians called the street, in memory of past triumphs; and to ride down its length as its master was to lay claim to the city's very proudest dreams. Display, in

Babylon, was the essence of kingship. Far from empty pomp, it was seen as the blazing of a god-given order, one which could be imagined as rippling like a lightning charge throughout the city, suffusing mortal flesh and bone, and dust and limestone and brick. The architecture of the Processional Way gave stirring illustration to this metaphor. At the boulevard's far end, abutting it, and placing even the Esagila in shadow, was the most staggering of all Babylon's monuments, an immense stepped tower, formed out of seventeen million bricks, and looming almost a hundred meters high: the Etemenanki, or "House that is the Frontier between the Heavens and the Earth." Here, as the name of the temple implied, there dwelt a profound mystery, located, with portentous symbolism, in the precise center of the city. But the Etemenanki was not its only incarnation. So too, in the opinion of the Babylonians, was the mortal person of their king; for he, according to the age-old traditions of Mesopotamia, was both the beating heart of society and a man set utterly apart. That this was no paradox could be illustrated by a simple visit to the Processional Way. Beside the city's main gates, open to the gaze of all who entered Babylon, there stood an immense palace, as visible, in its own way, as the Etemenanki at the opposite end of the boulevard; and yet such was the polychrome gorgeousness of its brick-work, inlaid as it was with gold and silver, and lapis lazuli, and ivory, and cedar, that those who viewed it could hardly help but lower their eyes to the ground. Opulence of such an order was not merely an expression of royal power, but was calculated, very precisely, to reinforce it. All were to feel submission and prostration in their souls.

Mesopotamia, by virtue of its glamor, had always exerted a powerful influence over its neighbors, and the kings of Anshan, among many others, had long looked to Babylon as a model of how best to be royal. Darius, settling himself into the great royal palace on the Processional Way, was laying claim to the same rich inheritance: King of Persia, he would rule as King of Babylon; and, yes, as King of Akkad too. Proud of his background though he was, "an Achaemenid, and a Persian, the son of a Persian,"[10] Darius did not scorn to adorn himself in the plundered robes of a Mesopotamian "King of Lands." Far more than Cyrus or Cambyses, he had good cause to try them on for size. As a usurper, he needed every scrap of legitimacy that he could find.

Having won Babylon, Darius was alert to all the city could teach. For a man of his penetrating intelligence, the city must have appeared as an immense illustration of what kingship might truly be, enshrined within ritual, and luxury, and stone. The lessons that he was absorbing in Babylon promised to be valuable, and they would need to be—for as Darius lingered in the city, grim news began to reach him. His victory in Mesopotamia had failed to deliver a knockout blow to his other enemies. Rebellion was rife, and growing, throughout the dominions he aspired to master. Insurrection and war were reported everywhere.

For Darius, all the world was still at stake.

The End of History

"Every king on earth," Cyrus had once boasted, "brought me heavy tribute, and kissed my feet where I sat in Babylon."[11] Darius' own sojourn in the city, which brought him only tidings of rebellion, was marked by none of the ostentatious gestures of clemency so beloved of his predecessor. Rather, beleaguered as he was, his preference was for carefully targeted acts of savagery and retribution. So it was that the hapless Nebuchadnezzar, captured on the downfall of his capital, was denied even the right to his celebrated name. Darius, pulling a favorite trick, accused him of being an impostor, and had him arraigned as "Nidintu-Bel." Just as the corpse of "Gaumata" had been disposed of with suspicious haste, now Nidintu-Bel, rather than being paraded down the Processional Way, was hurriedly and discreetly impaled. Forty-nine of the supposed impostor's lieutenants perished alongside him—his closest intimates, no doubt.* Dead men, after all, could tell no tales.

---

* It is impossible to know the truth about the identity of "Nidintu-Bel," but the circumstantial evidence suggests that he probably was of royal blood.

Yet the suspicions of those who lurked beyond Darius' reach, and their continued defiance, were not so easily allayed. That winter, the capture of Babylon notwithstanding, it appeared as though the new king's scattered and outnumbered forces might be overwhelmed. Even Persia itself had risen in revolt. Fatal though Bardiya's division of the aristocracy into rival factions had proved to be, it had at least ensured that the cause associated with his name would survive his murder— for those noblemen who had profited from the dead king's policies could hardly bank on the favor of his assassin. Urgently, they had banded together in opposition to the coup. Promoting one of their own, Vahyazdata, as king, they took a leaf out of Darius' book and announced that their man was in fact Bardiya himself. To add to the superfluity of pretenders, rebels throughout Asia were similarly emerging from the shadows, laying claim to the bloodlines of long-toppled monarchs, and to the glories of vanished empires. Ancient ambitions, briefly stifled by Persian rule, began to blaze back into life. Most threateningly of all, a nobleman by the name of Phraortes seized control of Ecbatana. Making common cause with rebels in the eastern half of the empire, many of whom hurried to acknowledge him as their overlord, he proclaimed the golden days of Media reborn.

There was more to this defiance of Darius than mere nostalgia for a vanished dynasty. Phraortes was quick to boast of his descent from Astyages, but he was also heir to the same resentments that had helped destroy the Medes' last king. The Median nobility—and the Persian too, if they wished to preserve any independence—had no choice but to oust the usurper; for Darius, decisive, brutal and charismatic, was patently not a man to indulge the pretensions of anyone save himself. Here, for the clan chiefs, was a truly agonizing choice: either forgo the opportunities of global empire, but enjoy once again the smaller-scale pleasures of factionalism, or remain masters of the world, but as vassals of a universal king. This, even amid what might have seemed its death agony, was the measure of Persian greatness: that all "the heavens and the earth and the sea and the dry land"[12] could be shaken, and yet the great convulsion, at its heart, be a civil war.

Everywhere the deadliest fighting was between men who only months previously had been comrades in arms. Vahyazdata's forces, striking eastward from Persia to seize the adjacent province, found themselves blocked by its governor, who had chosen to throw in his lot with Darius; in the north, where rebels had risen in support of Phraortes, Darius' loyalists were led not by a Persian but by one of Phraortes' own countrymen, a Mede; meanwhile, in Media itself, amid sub-zero temperatures and snowdrifts, clan chief fought with clan chief for control of the Khorasan Highway. By January, Phraortes' forces were pushing hard: advancing almost to the Nisaean plain, they threatened to break through into Mesopotamia, just as Darius himself had done barely two months before. Here loomed the great fulcrum of the crisis: Darius, knowing that he could not afford to lose Babylon, yet also frantically orchestrating a war on numerous fronts, dispatched a small army under Hydarnes, one of the seven original conspirators, to hold the highway at all costs. Hydarnes, his future by now irrevocably hitched to Darius' star, obediently retraced his steps into the frozen Zagros, and there, with grim resolution, positioned his troops to block the descent of the rebellious Medes. Although battle was duly joined, the result was a stand-off: no significant damage was inflicted on Phraortes' army, but neither was it able to continue its advance. Hydarnes, entrenching himself before the sacred cliff face of Bisitun, stood garrison and waited for his master.

Finally, by April, with a great victory reported against Vahyazdata, and the crushing of the rebellion in the north, Darius was ready to commit himself to the Median campaign. Leading his reserves up from Babylon, he joined with Hydarnes, and then, in a bloody and decisive battle, routed Phraortes, captured him, and loaded him with chains. Darius, having neglected to expose either Gaumata or Nidintu-Bel to public obloquy, now more than made amends. Indeed, the fate of Phraortes could not have been more gruesomely exemplary. His nose, tongue and ears were cut off; then for good measure, he was blinded in one eye. While other prominent rebels were flayed and their skins then stuffed with straw, their master was chained before the gates of the royal palace in Ecbatana, "where everyone could see him."[13] Only once his countrymen had been given sufficient opportunity to gawp at his humiliation was Phraortes, the would-be King of Media, impaled.

All done for the particular edification of the clan chiefs, of course. Certainly, the twisted corpse rotting on the spike above Ecbatana would have weighed as heavily on the nobility's minds as its stench would have hung in the summer air. Two months later, and the Persian aristocracy were graced with the same lesson. Vahyazdata, brought to battle and defeated a second time, was duly impaled; his closest lieutenants, sentenced to the same excruciating fate, writhed upon an immense forest of stakes. Darius, stern-faced and implacable, surveyed the scene. No more pretenders would come forward now claiming to be Bardiya. The murdered king, at last, lay in his grave. Smoothly, Darius moved to annex his dependants to himself. The various female offshoots of the royal family—the sisters, wives and daughters of the man he had displaced—were swept into the marital bed. Among these was the already twice-widowed Atossa, who now, for the first time, became the queen of a man who was not her brother. What her emotions must have been as she slept with Bardiya's murderer one can only imagine. Certainly, she is reported not to have been Darius' favorite wife. That title went to her younger sister, Artystone—the second of Cyrus' daughters to have given the new king a marriage link to the past.

Not that Darius, having waded through blood to seize the *kidaris*, was the man to rely merely on a harem to cement his claim. Even as he staked his exclusive rights to the bloodline of Cyrus, he was loudly broadcasting the primacy of his own: "I am Darius, King of Kings, King of Persia, King of Lands, the son of Hystaspes, grandson of Arsames, an Achaemenid."[14] So, with a sonorous roll, it was splendidly proclaimed. "There were eight of my family who were kings before me. I am the ninth. Nine times in succession have we been kings."[15] Which was stretching the truth to breaking point, of course. What of Cambyses, what of Cyrus, what of the legitimate royal line? What, indeed, of Darius' father, Hystaspes, who was still very much, albeit somewhat embarrassingly, alive? Darius, now that he had the world in his hands, could afford to sweep aside such minor inconveniences. What mattered, after all, was not what an inner circle of courtiers and clan chiefs might know, but what the empire—and posterity—might be made to understand.

Besides, the fabrications only veiled a deeper truth. By the summer of 521 BC, although there were still smoldering bushfires in Elam and Mesopotamia, Darius' triumph was not in dispute: he had secured the throne for himself and saved the world for the Persian people. Who but a man strong in the favor of Ahura Mazda, just as Darius had always proclaimed himself to be, could have achieved such startling things? A notable symmetry had framed the arc of his exertions—certain evidence of a guidance more than mortal. It was surely no coincidence, for instance, that Bisitun, holiest of mountains, had witnessed both the execution of Gaumata and the defeat of Phraortes—the two decisive turning points in Darius' progress to the throne. The new king, looking to immortalize his campaign against the Lie, duly chose to do so at the scene of these stirring events. Already, even before his victory in Persia, masons had been set to work at Bisitun. For the first time ever, "cut like the pages of a book on the blood-colored rock,"[16] the Persian language was to be transcribed into written form. The story of how Darius had rescued the world from evil was far too important to be trusted to the recitations of the Magi alone. Only solid stone could serve such an epic as its shrine. "So it was chiselled, and read out in my presence. And then the inscription was copied and dispatched to every province."[17] No one in the empire was to be ignorant of Darius' deeds.

And yet the king, even as he proclaimed his achievements to the far ends of the earth, was already seeking to distance himself from the swirl of revolt and war. His intentions could be seen illustrated on the cliff face of Bisitun itself, carved in immense relief next to the blocks of cuneiform. There loomed a giant Darius, crushing a prostrate Gaumata beneath his foot, while in front of him, dwarfish and tethered, stretched a line of liar-kings. On the face of the conqueror, however, there was no wrinkled lip, no sneer of cold command, only serenity, dignity, majesty and calm; as though the triumphs celebrated in the relief were, to their hero, simply ripples upon an order outside time. Here was a radical departure from the norms of royal self-promotion. When the Assyrian kings had portrayed themselves trampling their foes, they had done so in the most extravagant and blood-spattered detail, amid the advance of siege engines, the flight of the defeated, piles of loot and severed heads. There were no such specifics at Bisitun. What mattered to Darius was not the battle, but that the battle had been won; not the bloodshed but that the blood had dried, and an age of peace had dawned. Yes, the victory over the liar-kings had been a great and terrible one, and because it had proved the truth of what he had always insisted, that he was indeed the champion of Ahura Mazda, the new king had ordered its details to be recorded and proclaimed. Never again, however, would he permit himself to be shown enclosed within mere events. As universal monarch, he was now above such things. Just as Lord Mazda dwelt beyond the rhythms of the world, so had his proxy, the King of Persia, transcended space and time. History, in effect, had been brought to a glorious close. The Persians' empire was both its end and its summation—for what could a dominion be that contained within it all the limits of the horizon, if not the bulwark of a truly cosmic order? Such a monarchy, now that Darius had redeemed it from the Lie, might be expected to endure for all eternity: infinite, unshakable, the watchtower of the Truth.

Except, of course, that history still persisted in its flow. In 520 BC, even as Darius' masons were hard at work at Bisitun, the ever-fractious Elamites rose again in revolt. Darius, infuriated, promptly anathematized them in new and startling terms. "Those Elamites were faithless," he thundered. "They failed to worship Ahura Mazda."[18] This, the condemnation of a people for their neglect of a religion not their own, was something wholly remarkable. Until that moment, Darius, following the subtle policy of Cyrus, had always been assiduous in his attention to foreign gods. Now he was delivering to the subject nations of the world a stern and novel warning. Should a people persist in rebellion against the order of Ahura Mazda, they might expect to be regarded not merely as adherents of the Lie but as the worshippers of "*daivas*"—false gods and demons. Conversely, those sent to war against them might expect "divine blessings—both in their lives, and after death."[19] Glory on earth and an eternity in heaven: these were the assurances given by Darius to his men. The manifesto proved an inspiring one. When Gobryas, Darius' father-in-law, led an army into Elam, he was able to crush the revolt there with a peremptory, almost dismissive, speed. Never again would the Elamites dare to challenge the awful might of the Persian king. Such was the effect of the world's first holy war.

For there had been, in this otherwise obscure and unmemorable campaign, the hint of something fateful. Darius, testing the potential of his religion to its limits, had promoted a dramatic innovation. Contained within it were the seeds of some radical notions: that foreign foes might be crushed as infidels; that warriors might be promised paradise; that conquest in the name of a god might become a moral duty. Not that Darius, even as he ordered the invasion of Elam, had ever aimed to impose his religion at the point of a sword; such an idea was wholly alien to the spirit of the times. Nevertheless, a new age was dawning— and Darius was its midwife. His vision of empire as a fusion of cosmic, moral and political order was to prove stunningly fruitful: the foundation stone not only of his own rule but of the very concept of a universal order. The dominion raised by Cyrus, having been preserved from dissolution, was now, in effect, to be founded a second time—and a global monarchy, secured anew, was to spell a global peace.

For, earth-shaking though Darius' usurpation had proved to be, it had never been his intention to turn the whole world upside-down. Just the opposite. The ancient kingdoms of the Near East, having had their last hour of rebellion, were now finished as international players; yet Darius, the man responsible for their quietus, still indulged their specters. Brutal though the Persians could be when required, violent revolution was hardly their ideal. The new king, even as he set about constructing his new order, fitted and adorned it with the cladding of the past. A pharaoh still reigned in Egypt; a king of Babylon in Mesopotamia; a self-proclaimed heir of the house of Astyages in Media. Darius was all these things, and more. "King of Kings":[20] such was the title he most gloried in, less because he viewed foreign kingdoms as his fiefdoms—although he did—but rather because it gratified him to pose as the quintessence of royalty. All the monarchies there had ever been were to be regarded as enshrined within his person. He was the Great King.

And there was no one left undiminished. Even his former peers, even those possessed of the most famous and honored names in Persia, even the six other conspirators, all were ranked merely as "*bandaka*"— as servitors of the king. The nobility, decimated by civil war, and intimidated by Darius' battle-hardened armies, no longer dared dispute the pretensions of royal power. Darius himself, who had not passed the first months of his reign in Babylon for nothing, moved swiftly to drive this home. At Susa, capital of the defeated Elamites, orders were given to flatten much of the old town and construct an immense new royal city, one raised in contempt of the site itself; for it was built not upon natural contours but on an artificially leveled surface, an immense foundation block of gravel and baked brick. Darius, not content with building one new capital from scratch, then began scouting round virgin sites in Persia itself, looking to found a second and even greater one. He settled upon a location some twenty miles south of Pasargadae, a city which, although Darius continued to honor it, was too associated with Cyrus ever to serve him as his own. Darius wanted a stage that was his and his alone; and he had fixed upon a site already lit up by his glory. This was the Mount of Mercy, a name not without irony, for it was at its foot that Vahyazdata and the rebel nobles had been impaled. Now, abutting the slope of the mountain, Darius ordered the construction of a gigantic terrace, a platform with perfect views on to the killing field below, "beautiful and impervious"[21]—a fitting base for the capital of the world.

Darius named it "Paarsa," as though all the expanse of Persia were to be shrunk and maintained within its walls. And so, in a sense, it was. The king's appetite for centralization was insatiable. The city which the Greeks would much later call Persepolis was built as nerve center, powerhouse and showcase. Not only Persia but the realms of the vast dominion beyond it were to be unified into one immense administrative unit, focused, as was only natural, upon the figure of the king himself. Darius had not spent the first years of his reign shoring up the empire for nothing; and he was resolved never again to see it threatened by collapse. With his habitual energy, he threw himself into the most overwhelming task of administration that any monarch had ever faced: nothing less than to set the world upon a sound financial footing. This was the same challenge that had destroyed both Cambyses and Bardiya; but Darius' talents, once again, were to prove the equal of his ambition. The financial crisis that had racked the empire in the last year of Cambyses' reign was briskly resolved: the ramshackle system of tribute that had prevailed under Cyrus and his sons was streamlined and reformed; levies in every province, to the far ends of the known world, were carefully fixed. It was an unprecedented achievement, and one destined to endure for almost two centuries as the bedrock of Persian power. Even more than his generalship or his genius for propaganda, it was Darius' punctilious mastery of fiscal policy that pulled the empire back from the brink. If the rising splendors of Persepolis and Susa spoke loudly of his dominance, then so too, as they glided among the building works, loaded down with parchments, tablets and tables of figures, did the bureaucrats who staffed the royal palaces. The Persian nobles, sneering behind Darius' back, may have mocked their king as a "shopkeeper,"[22]—but the empire, and Persia's greatness, would have been nothing without accounts.

A truth illustrated by the very fabric of the palaces themselves—for tribute receipts to the Great King were not merely the stuff of dusty archives, but of splendid and sacred drama. During his months in Babylon, Darius would have seen how much of that city's greatness, from the fittings of its palaces to the many languages on its streets, bore witness to the scale of its vanished empire. It was only proper, then, that Susa and Persepolis, as the capitals of a dominion incalculably more extensive than that of Babylon, should have lavished on them "materials brought from afar."[23] Here, as it was designed to be, glimmered a comprehensive trumping of the magnificence of every king who had gone before. If furnishings could be reckoned the measure of greatness, then Darius, with his *grands projets*, had hit unprecedented heights. "The gold was brought from Sardis, and from Bactria, and fashioned by craftsmen here, and the precious stones that were used here, lapis lazuli and carnelian, these were brought from Sogdiana." So visitors to Susa were grandly informed. "The silver and ebony was brought from India, and the friezes on the walls, they were brought from Ionia, and the ivory that was carved here, that came from Ethiopia, and India, and Arachosia."[24] And so on and on, in rolling tones of house-pride, the record of tribute or labor drawn from twenty-three territories of the empire. Never before had the details of tax returns made for quite such a dazzling show.

And what of the Babylonians, whose city had previously been the capital of the world? Their allotted task was to dig foundations and bake mud bricks. Not the most glamorous responsibilities, it might be thought; but Darius, when he came to enumerate the various subject peoples who had contributed to Susa, put the men of Babylon at the head of the list. "That the earth was dug out, and the rubble packed down, and the sun-dried bricks were moulded, this was due to the Babylonians—they performed these tasks."[25] The symbolism was profound, and—Darius being Darius—no doubt deliberate. As he would well have known, it was the practice in Mesopotamia never to clear away the rubble of toppled monuments, but always to seal it before raising new structures on top of the ruins. A temple, for instance, even though it might tower into the heavens, would be founded on the detritus of the past. And so it was with the palaces of the Great King.

Resting on massive terraces of Babylonian brickwork, and adorned with the luxuries and treasures of the world, Susa and Persepolis might not have been the dwelling homes of gods, but they still enshrined an imperiously spiritual vision. Where Babylon seethed with an energy that derived from its own awesome size, the capitals of the Persian monarch, modeled according to their founder's every whim, held up splendid mirrors to the harmonies of order. This is not to say that they were wholly lacking in metropolitan character: already, even before the foundation of Persepolis, that ubiquitous banking family, the Egibis, had opened an office in the area, soon to be followed by other merchants and financiers; bureaucrats swarmed everywhere; craftsmen and laborers, transported from all corners of the world, brought their own hint of babel to the streets. But Persepolis and Susa were not, in the febrile sense that Babylon was, cosmopolitan; nor had it ever been part of Darius' ambitions that they should be so. It did not require the Great King to emerge from his palace into a stinking mass of humanity for him to flaunt and represent his sway. The detail of a tax payment, safely logged inside an archive; the glinting on a palace door of rare and precious metals, quarried from an incalculably distant mountain range; the portrayal on a frieze of some humble tributary—an Arab, or an Ethiopian, or a Gandharan—his submission forever frozen by the pattern of the design; all these spoke with perfect clarity of the timeless nature of Persian power. Significant as the bloody practicalities of imperial rule were to Darius, so also was their shadow, his sacral vision of a universal state, one in which all his vast dominion had been imposed for the conquered's good. The covenant embodied by Persian rule could not have been made any clearer: harmony in exchange for humility; protection for abasement; the blessings of a world order for obedience and submission. This was, of course, in comparison to the propaganda of the great empires of Mesopotamia, notably lacking in a relish for slaughter—but it did serve very effectively to justify global conquest without limit.

For the logic was glaring. If it was the destiny of the Persian people to bring peace to a bleeding world, then those who defied them were clearly the agents of anarchy and darkness. Tools of the Lie as they were, they menaced not merely Darius' empire but the cosmos that it mirrored. Even the earth and sky, on occasions, might manifest their revulsion for the foes of the Great King. In 519 BC, one year after the suppression of the Elamites' revolt, a fresh uprising broke out on the empire's northern frontier, among those inveterate rebels, the Saka. Darius, leading an army against them, was betrayed by his guide, and found himself lost and parched amid the bleak steppes. With no water for miles, nor any hint of rain, the king had little choice but to take desperate measures: climbing to the summit of a hill, he duly divested himself of his robes and *kidaris*, and thrust his scepter in the ground. As dawn broke, purging the shadows of darkness from the earth, the King of Kings raised his voice in his prayer. His appeals were answered: rain began to fall from the sky; the earth was refreshed by water. Darius, gathering the accoutrements of royalty, then led his army to victory over the rebels. For the Persians, the adventure could hardly have had a more inspiring theme: it taught that there was nowhere so remote that it could not be ordered and tamed. "From this side of the ocean to the far side of the ocean, and from this side of the parched land to the far side of the parched land,"[26] Darius ruled it all.

Admittedly, unprecedented though the Great King's reach was, it did not yet quite embrace every limit of the world. Beyond the Jaxartes, the steppelands of Asia still stretched unconquered to the remote, encircling River Rangha; in Africa, a Persian army, dispatched westward by Cambyses, had been swallowed whole by a desert storm;* in Europe, across the sea from the cities of Ionia, an entire strange continent, as yet barely even explored, was waiting to be penetrated and subdued. But the time of these remote and savage lands would surely come. There could be no holding back the armies of the Great King. Order would be brought to the final strongholds of the Lie. No sooner had Darius returned from defeating the Saka than he was looking to make fresh conquests. In 518 BC, gazing eastward, he dispatched a naval squadron to reconnoiter the mysterious lands along the Indus. Invasion swiftly followed; the Punjab was subdued; a tribute of gold dust, elephants and

---

* According to Herodotus, at any rate, who admittedly is not the most reliable of sources when it comes to the details of Cambyses' reign. It is only fair to record that all attempts to discover the skeletons of Cambyses' lost army, where they are presumed to lie beneath the sands of the Libyan desert, have ended in failure.

similar wonders was imposed. Even the great river itself was placed symbolically under the yoke: its waters were brought to Darius in an immense jar, and placed in his treasury, there to join the waters of other rivers, likewise held captive to the greater glory of the King.[27]

It was true that there lay still further lands beyond the Indus, as yet independent of Persian rule; but even these, though not formally constituted into a province, might still be blessed by the favor of the king. All that petitioners had to do was to deliver to him a tribute of earth and water, and then, in return, they might be warmed by the light of his attention. Solemn and awe-inspiring ritual accompanied the presentation of these gifts. Supplicants, swearing their oath of loyalty to Persia, would have to do so prostrate on the scattered soil of their own land. In this way the Great King symbolized that the works of nature, as well as man, had been absorbed into his order—the better for everyone. The supplicants themselves, withdrawing from the dreadful presence of the king, could have no possible doubts as to the significance of the gesture they had performed. They had taken a step from which there could be no retreat. They had become a part, however humble, of the empire of the world.

It did not take the armies of the Great King, then, to expand the limits of Persian power. Westward as well as eastward they continued their advance; over sea as well as land. Around the time of the conquest of the Punjab, Otanes, Darius' one-time rival for the throne, had been cruising the eastern waters of the Aegean. The island of Samos had been formally absorbed into the empire; neighboring islands, as they looked to forestall the Persian fleet, began to contemplate making gifts of earth and water to the ambassadors of the King. Here, for Darius, was a development of much promise. With the rich plains of the Indus pacified, his attentions could now be turned to the opposite end of his dominion. Two continents had already submitted to his supremacy—why should not a third?

The gaze of the Great King, inexorably, began to fix itself on the West.

3

SPARTA

"Who Are the Spartans?"

Back in the early years of the Persian rise to greatness, while Cyrus was still in Lydia, he had found himself unexpectedly visited by a delegation from across the Aegean Sea. The ambassadors were Greek, but quite different from the Greeks of Asia, whose cities, prosperous and tempting, Cyrus was plotting at that very moment to crush and make his own. The strangers wore their hair long; they sported distinctive red cloaks; they spoke not with the subtlety and sense of propriety that conventionally marked an ambassador's language, but brusquely, bluntly, rudely. The message they gave the greatest king on earth was simple: Cyrus should leave the cities of the Ionians well alone; if he did not, then he would have to answer to those who had sent them—the Spartans. Evidently, the strangers felt that the mere mention of this name was sufficient to chill the blood, for they added nothing more. Cyrus, turning from them, was obliged to summon a nearby Ionian attendant. "Tell me," he demanded, all bemusement, "who are the Spartans?"[1]

A startling question for any Greek to have to answer. How could an Asiatic *not* have heard of the Spartans? Nothing could better have illustrated the remote and alien quality of the Persians than the fact that they were ignorant of history's most notorious woman. Helen of Sparta, hundreds of years before, had brought ruin to Asia as well as Greece. Her abduction from the home of her husband, King Menelaus, to the fabled city of Troy had made all the world bleed. For ten long years, the heroes of East and West had butchered each other in the dust of the Trojan plain. Only with the annihilation of what, in the opinion of the Greeks, had been Asia's greatest city, the slaughter of its men and the enslavement of its women, had the terrible war at last been brought to an end. To the descendants of the victors, there had been, in the sheer scale of the destruction, something sobering and fearful: after all, "an immense expeditionary force had been assembled, Asia invaded and Trojan power wiped out, merely for the sake of a single Spartan woman."[2] No wonder that many Greeks, and particularly those who actually lived on the margins of Asia, imagined the whole vastness of the East to be sullen still with resentment, brooding on ancient wrongs. Perched precariously as they were on the edge of the great continent, the Ionians had good cause to fear the vengeful shadows of the Trojan dead.

To the Spartans themselves, however, the memory of their city's most famous daughter was precious. Menelaus, it was said, searching for Helen amid the final massacre of the Trojans, had been planning to add her to the piles of corpses, a fitting punishment for all the slaughter she had caused—but when at last he had found his wife, rather than kill her, he had instead dropped his sword, struck dumb by the perfection of her naked breasts, and swept her up into his arms. Both had returned to Sparta, and their tomb could still be seen on a promontory south of the city, its immense stone blocks raised on earth as red as Menelaus' hair. Helen herself, "that radiance of women,"[3] had been altogether more aureate than her husband: not only had she been a blonde, but even her spindle had been fashioned out of gold. Had Cyrus known that the Spartans worshipped at the shrine of such a woman, sensual and pleasure-loving, he would no doubt have been confirmed in his contempt for their ridiculous pretensions. Certainly, their ambassadors, long-haired and scarlet-cloaked as they were, would have appeared apt devotees of Helen; for Cyrus would have had sufficient opportunity to learn that the wearing of long hair, among the Greeks, was generally regarded as evidence of effeminacy, and the use of expensive vermilion as a mark of wild extravagance. The Persians, unsurprisingly, chose to scorn the Spartan threats. Surely they could have little to fear from such a luxury-loving race?

Appearances, of course, could be deceptive; but it was true that once, in the earliest years of their history, the Spartans had indeed been notorious for their materialism and greed. "Acquisitiveness will be their ruin" had been a common prediction.[4] Sparta, in the eighth and seventh centuries BC, had served as a model of everything that other Greeks hoped to avoid: her elite was brutal and rapacious; its land-hunger was obscene; the impoverishment of the average citizen, leeched of his patrimony and often even of his freedom, was something shocking. Appalled foreign analysts, observing the toxic quality of Sparta's class hatreds, had no hesitation in judging her "the worst-governed state in Greece."[5] And this at a time when competition was hardly lacking; for everywhere in the Greek world, by the seventh century BC, the gap between rich and poor, the few and the many, had begun to widen alarmingly, so that the ideal of good governance, "*eunomia*" as it was called, seemed a distant dream, and all was instability.

Social convulsions were not unknown elsewhere in the world, as the clan chiefs of Media or Persia could have vouched. Among the Greeks, however, the yearning for *eunomia* had a peculiar urgency. In their search for it, they were, in a sense, alone. There was certainly no equivalent in their poor and backward land of the millennia-old traditions of the monarchies of the East. Unlike the clansmen of the Zagros, they were far removed from the wellsprings of civilization. With no ready models of bureaucracy or centralization to hand, the Greek world had early on fragmented into a multitude of competing city-states, each with its distinctive brand of constitutional crisis. Racked by chronic social tensions though they were, however, the Greeks were not entirely oblivious to the freedom that provincialism gave them: to experiment, innovate and forge their own distinctive paths. "Better a small city perched on a rock," it could be argued, "so long as it is well governed, than all the splendors of idiotic Nineveh."[6] Certainly, compared to the rugged landscape across which Greek cities were dotted, the bland alluvium of Mesopotamia might indeed appear just a little effete. In Greece, the mountains which hemmed in the lowlands, cutting many a state off from state, to say nothing of the reach of the broader world beyond, afforded a rough-hewn autonomy as well as isolation.

The Spartans, certainly, had profited from the location of their city. That they had been left free to indulge their taste for class warfare had owed almost everything to geography. Lacedaemon, the territory in the remote reaches of southern Greece which their city dominated, was framed all around by formidable natural bulwarks: to the east and south, the sea; to the north, gray, forbidding hills; to the west, savage and immense, the mountain of Taygetos, its five claw-like peaks streaked with snow even in the heat of summer. Behind such frontiers a city might easily bring itself to the point of ruin, and still remain undisturbed.

But behind such frontiers it might equally evolve and metamorphose. The Spartans, like the Persians, had originally been a tribal monarchy, with a state that had its roots in an ancient nomadic past. Sparta itself, despite its venerable name, was little more than an agglomeration of four villages, founded on what had previously been an almost virgin site. Certainly it owed nothing to the original Sparta, the Sparta of Helen and Menelaus. Impressively though the couple's tomb loomed over the Lacedaemonian plain, the shrine bore witness not to continuity but to the very opposite: a brutal rupture with the past. Hillocks of buried rubble surrounded it, all that remained of a long-abandoned palace, perhaps one that had been occupied by Helen and Menelaus themselves; and yet, around 1200 BC, it and all the other great buildings of Lacedaemon had been sacked and burned to the ground. Why, and by whom, had rapidly been forgotten: the ruin had been too total for the memory to be preserved. Centuries had passed.

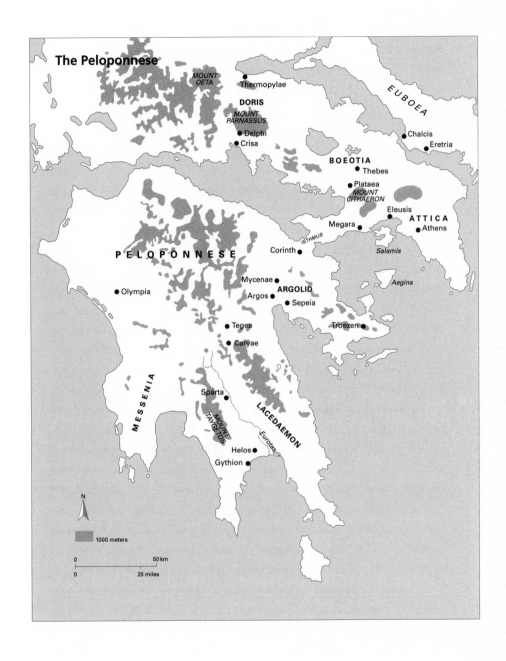

The Peloponnese

MOUNT
OETA

• Thermopylae

DORIS

MOUNT
PARNASSUS

• Delphi

• Crisa

EUBOEA

• Chalcis

• Eretria

BOEOTIA

• Thebes

• Plataea

MOUNT
CITHAERON

Eleusis •

• Megara

ATTICA

• Athens

P E L O P O N N E S E

ISTHMUS

Corinth •

Salamis

• Olympia

Mycenae •

Argos •

ARGOLID

• Sepeia

Aegina

• Tegea

Troezen •

• Caryae

MESSENIA

Sparta •

LACEDAEMON

MOUNT
TAYGETOS

Eurotas

Helos •

Gythion •

N

1000 meters

0   50 km

0   25 miles

Gradually, the void left by the collapse of Menelaus' kingdom had been filled by newcomers from the north, wandering tribes who would be known much later as the Dorians, in proud contradistinction to the vanquished native Greeks.[7] Yet the Dorians too were Greek, and far from oblivious to their adopted homeland's golden past. Indeed, it would be said of them that there was no nation more devoted "to tales of the age of heroes, of the ancient beginnings of cities, and of anything that related to far-off times."[8] The settlers, intrigued by Lacedaemon's pedigree, began to appropriate it to themselves. Around 700 BC, for instance, roughly when the Medes and Persians were putting down their own roots in the distant Zagros, the fortuitous identification of Helen's tomb was first made. Even more sensationally, the Spartan elite also began to manufacture an ancestry for itself that stretched far beyond the reign of Menelaus, back to the greatest hero of them all, Heracles, slayer of monsters and son of Zeus, the king of the gods. What had been an invasion by the Dorians' distant ancestors could now be presented as a return; what had been won by conquest as a patrimony. The leading Spartans called themselves "Heraclids"—and they laid claim, as the heirs of Heracles, not only to Lacedaemon but to the dominion of much of Greece.

All of which, of course, was profoundly alarming for their neighbors. By 700 BC, the Spartans had already achieved the startling feat of crossing the most intimidating of their natural frontiers, the Taygetos range, and launching a war of annexation in the land of Messenia that lay beyond it to the west. The "broad dancing-grounds" to be found there, "good for ploughing, good for growing fruit,"[9] were more fertile even than those of Lacedaemon, and although the Messenians too could lay claim to Dorian ancestry, the Spartans savagely demonstrated their disdain for any possible ties of kinship by the brutality of their assault, and by the implacability of their resolve. A territory as extensive as Messenia was not easily subdued, but the Spartans, keeping grimly to their objective, had continued for decades to wash its fields and groves with blood. The Messenians' submission, when it came at last, was total. Victory had taken their conquerors more than a century to force.

1. A relief from Nineveh, showing the Assyrian army on a mountain campaign; cavalry predominates. The tribute of horses from Media was vital to Assyria's efforts to stay ahead in the Near Eastern arms race. *(The Art Archive/Musée du Louvre, Paris/Dagli Orti)*

2. The head of a king found among the ruins of Ecbatana. If not a fake, then this is almost certainly a representation of Astyages, the dream-haunted last King of Media.

3. The tomb of Cyrus the Great at Pasargadae. "Mortal!" an inscription on it is said once to have read. "I am Cyrus, who founded the dominion of the Persians, and was King of Asia. Do not begrudge me then my monument!" *(Bridgeman Art Library)*

4. A coin illustrating a fire altar. The blaze of fire was profoundly sacred to the Persians, and served as an empire-wide symbol of the power of the Great King. *(Ancient Art & Architecture)*

5. Bisitun as it appears today, with the main Iran-Iraq road in the foreground. It was ten miles to the south of the sacred mountain that Darius and his assassination squad murdered Bardiya, on the Khorasan Highway that ran below it that he defeated the rebel king of Media, and on its cliff face that he memorialized his great victory over the Lie. *(Tom Holland)*

6. Darius triumphant, as represented on the cliff face of Bisitun. A prostrate Gaumata grovels beneath his foot. The nine liar kings who dared to challenge him are shown tethered by their necks: Nidintu-Bel, the rebel king of Babylon, is second from the left; Phraortes, the rebel king of Media, third from the left; Vahyazdata, the rebel king of Persia, sixth from the left. The rebel king of the Saka, wearing his distinctive pointed cap, brings up the rear. *(R. Woods)*

7. The face of the most terrifying state in Greece. A Spartan warrior, long-haired and swathed in a cloak, peers out through the eye slits of his helmet. *(Wadsworth Atheneum Museum of Art, Hartford, CT; gift of J. Pierpont Morgan)*

8. A mask from the temple of Artemis Orthia in Sparta. The masks hung upon the walls, some of them of young men or soldiers, but many more, like this one, withered and grotesque. In their ugliness lay a reminder to every Spartan of the failure it was his lifelong duty to avoid. *(British School at Athens)*

9. Athena "Polias"—"The Guardian of the City." The original icon of the warrior goddess, jealously preserved by the Boutad clan on the Acropolis, was the oldest and most sacred statue in the whole of Athens. *(Acropolis Museum)*

10. By the sixth century BC, the Athenian aristocracy were rousing themselves from their traditional provincialism. The interior of this Attic drinking cup shows revelers adorned in the turbans and long robes that were characteristic of the international party set. *(Ashmolean Museum)*

11. Harmodius and Aristogiton. Following the establishment of democracy in Athens, a bronze of the tyrannicides—of which this is a Roman copy—was the only public portrait to be seen in the whole of the city. A squalid crime of passion had been transfigured into a heroic blow struck for liberty. *(Museo Archeologico Nazionale, Naples/Bridgeman Art Library)*

12. The site of the great city of Sardis. The splendors that made it the capital of the Persian West have long since vanished, but the imposing acropolis still rises steep and jagged above the plain. *(Tom Holland)*

13. Ionians bringing the Great King tribute, as shown on a relief at Persepolis. Above them, instantly recognizable in their pointed hats, are the ambassadors of the Saka. *(The Art Archive/Dagli Orti)*

14. A bronze weight in the shape of a duck, found in the Treasury at Persepolis. Ducks, just like any other user of the imperial road system, would be issued with ration chits by the ever-punctilious Persian bureaucracy. *(Oriental Institute Museum, University of Chicago)*

15. Darius and his court, as imagined by a Greek painter of the fourth century BC. A century after Marathon, Darius remained the archetype of royal power. *(Museum of Naples)*

Such an enslavement of one Greek people by another was wholly without precedent. It established the Spartans not only as the richest people in Greece, but as a prodigy, a mutant race, unnerving and unique. As far as the Spartans themselves were concerned, this aura of mystery was merely their due. Where else in a world long since decayed from the golden age of heroes could a bloodline be traced back to the king of the gods himself? Brutally pragmatic in the ends to which they put their superstitions, the Spartans believed in them devoutly all the same. They knew themselves shadowed, in everything they did, by the whims of the divine. Offend the gods, and all might be lost; attend to their wishes, and Sparta's greatness would surely be secured. So it was that she had been able, in the end, to subdue Messenia. And so it was, in the teeth of that interminable campaign, that she had also been able to redeem herself from an even greater crisis, a near-fatal social meltdown, and emerge from it, astonishingly, as the model of *eunomia*.

This choice—between reform or ruin—was one that the Heraclids had long sought to postpone. The conquest of Messenia, however, far from putting off the hour of reckoning, had served only to hasten it. Victory, although it brought Sparta great wealth, had done little to ease the miseries of the poor. Indeed, by concentrating even greater resources in the hands of the aristocracy, it had threatened to exacerbate them. Perhaps, had the circumstances of the Spartan upper classes corresponded to those of their counterparts in far-off Media, they could have afforded to ignore the impoverishment of their fellow citizens, their cries for redistribution of land, and all their "seditions against the realm."[10] But Sparta was not Media—and a great revolution in military affairs, one that had begun to surge and swell across the whole of Greece, was at that very moment threatening to sink the Heraclids.

For it was not cavalry—prancing, expensive, indelibly upper class—that had won Messenia for Sparta. Rather, the victory had gone to plodding foot soldiers, citizens of farming stock, men who may not have had the resources to afford horses but who could still supply themselves with arms and armor; and in particular with *hopla*, circular shields of a radically new design, a meter high and wide, and faced with bronze across their wood. A line of *hoplon*-holders— "hoplites"—advancing in a phalanx, protected as well, perhaps, by bronze helmets and cuirasses, and bristling with spears, was potentially a devastating offensive weapon; and the Spartans, in the course of the Messenian War, had been given every opportunity to experiment with this radical and lethal new form of warfare. Yet it was not easily waged. A particular breed of man was required to make it succeed. Every *hoplon*, if it were to serve its purpose, had to offer protection to its neighbor as well as its holder—so that the line of a phalanx, as it advanced toward an enemy, risked being cut to pieces on any show of social division.

"Keep together," exhorted a Spartan battle hymn, "hold the line, do not give in to alarm, or disgraceful rout."[11] A cry for discipline aimed at hoplites of every class. What, after all, would be the fate of even the most blue-blooded Heraclid in battle if he could not trust his flank to his neighbor, the humble farmer? And what, even more pressingly, would be the fate of Sparta herself if the farmer could no longer afford his expensive shield? Ruin—as sure and violent as the hatreds of Messenia. The Spartan establishment, having grown fat on the lower classes, suddenly found itself, in the very hour of victory, staring catastrophe in the face. No longer, by the middle of the seventh century, could civic cohesion be regarded merely as an idle aspiration of down-at-heel farmers. It had become, even for the Heraclids, a matter of life and death.

Panic bred a truly extraordinary solution. Revolution came to Lacedaemon. The Spartan people, despairing of their future, were somehow persuaded to forget their time-honored class differences and submit to a majestic yet murderous experiment in social engineering. But how, precisely—and at whose instigation? The Spartans themselves, enthusiasts for dramatic tales of ancient heroes, were hardly the type of people to attribute their new order to anonymous social forces. Surely it could only have been the work of some visionary sage? Soon enough, a name, "Lycurgus," began to be floated. Barely a century after the establishment of *eunomia* in Sparta, and this mysterious figure had been definitively hailed as its architect. By and large, it was agreed that he had been a Heraclid grandee, uncle to a Spartan king, no less, and possessed of the sternest temperament, "high-principled and fair."[12] Such, however, were the limits of his biographers' consensus. Even oracles confessed that they were baffled as to whether Lycurgus was "human or a god"—although their inclination was, on balance, to believe the sage divine.[13] The Spartans shared this opinion: a temple was raised in the great man's honor, and his purported reform program increasingly located back in the mists of time, giving it, like the Heraclid bloodline, a pedigree as venerable as it was bogus. Control the past, and you control the future: as radical an act of surgery as had ever been attempted by a state upon itself was soon being represented as the essence of its traditions. Lycurgus, it would later be claimed, "moved and gratified by the beauty and loftiness of his legislation, now that it was completed and implemented, had longed to make it immortal and unbudging, for all time—or at least so far as could be achieved by human foresight."[14] The Spartans, by reverencing him, and possibly by fabricating him as well, had duly fulfilled his dream. Revolution, as they were the first people in history to discover, could best be buttressed if it was transfigured into myth.

The sense of strangeness that had long haunted the Spartans now came to animate the structures of their state. They had become, it appeared to the men of other cities, both more and less than human. Lycurgus was said to have been divine, and yet he had worn the aspect of a beast, of something feral, as well as that of a god. "He who brings into being the works of a wolf": this, portentous and menacing, was the literal meaning of his name. No longer, under the constitution established by Lycurgus, were the Spartans to be counted as predators upon their own kind, the rich upon the poor, the Heraclids upon the farmers, but rather as hunters in a single deadly pack. Every citizen, be he aristocrat or peasant, was to be subsumed within its ranks. Henceforward, even "the very wealthy were to adopt a lifestyle that was as much as possible like that of the ordinary run of people."[15]

Merciless and universal discipline was to teach every Spartan, from the moment of his birth, that conformity was all. The citizen would assume his place in society; the hoplite would assume his place in a line of battle. There he would be obliged to remain for the length of his life, "his feet set firmly apart, biting on his lip, taking a stand against his foe"[16]—with only death to redeem him from his duty. Indeed, Lycurgus, it was said, in a supreme illustration of what a citizen owed the state, had gone so far as to commit suicide, hoping by such a gesture that he might educate his people. "For it was his reasoning that even a statesman's end should be of some value to society, by setting it an example both virtuous and practical—and so it was that he starved himself to death."[17]

A grim philosophy, to be sure. Yet, self-denying though it might appear, it was valued by the Spartans precisely for the freedoms that it gave them. That their city had become a barracks and their whole society an immense phalanx braced for war reflected not coercion but rather a hard-wrought class consensus. The balance it struck between the rich and the poor was delicate. The Heraclids, although they had ceded sovereignty to the people, and also a seeming equality, nevertheless preserved their wealth, their estates, and much of their power. The poorer classes, initiated into the ranks of an elite and peerless army, gained a status they had hitherto been denied—and material security to boot. No more sordid scratching around for them, trying to make a living out of farming or trade. A warrior had no business with mending shoes, or sawing wood, or making pans. Such activities were best left to the citizens of other communities in Lacedaemon, the "*perioikoi*," or "about-dwellers," as they were dismissively labeled, second-rate men denied the rights of a full and tested Spartan.

Only one source of wealth, to the true soldier, could be counted worthy of his rank. Gratifyingly, for a people once haunted by land-hunger, the conquest of Messenia had provided ample scope for the aristocracy to be generous with their spoils. Hazy though the precise details are, it appears likely that one of the key policies of the Lycurgan reform program had been the partitioning of much of Messenia into allotments for the poor.[18] Not that any member of the master race ever farmed these grants in person: it was out of the question for a Spartan warrior to toil and sweat in a field. That was the function of the conquered Messenians. The Spartans, even prior to the crossing of Taygetos, had displayed a peculiar genius for the exploitation of vanquished foes. Their whole history bore witness to it. Learned scholars, curious about the name—"helots"—that the Spartans gave their wretched underclass, derived it from Helos, a town in Lacedaemon, conquered in the very earliest days of their expansion.[19] What had first been practiced on one side of the Taygetos range was refined and perfected on the other: a whole population was reduced to serfdom. The Messenians, laboring "like asses suffering under heavy loads,"[20] found themselves having to shoulder the full weight of Spartan greatness.

And no sooner had the conquerors found themselves growing rich off their helots than they began to cast around for more. By the early sixth century BC, with the west successfully pacified, the focus of their ambitions was inevitably turning north. There, however, blocking the path of empire, loomed a menacing rival. Argos, a city less than forty miles from the Lacedaemonian frontier, was a power just as restless and arrogant as Sparta, and had claims on southern Greece that were, if anything, more impressive. While the Spartans boasted of Menelaus as their forebear, the Argives could cite an even more celebrated figure, his elder brother Agamemnon, master of golden Mycenae, and commander in chief of the Greeks at Troy. Mycenae herself, although no longer the seat of kings, was still to be found, albeit a crumbled shell of her former greatness, huddled between ravines to the north of the plain of Argos. The Argives, despite taking regular pains to crush even the slightest hint of independence from her, had eagerly adopted her ancient pretensions. These, in the endless propaganda war waged by every Greek city, were certainly not to be sniffed at. Agamemnon, after all, had ruled as heir to his grandfather, the hero Pelops, an ivory-shouldered adventurer who had given his name to the entire peninsula which formed the south of Greece. Why, then, in any struggle for the mastery of "Pelops' island"—"*Peloponnesos*" in Greek—

should the Argives be content with second place? Surely Argos, not Sparta, should reign as the mistress of the Peloponnese?

As far back as 669 BC, during the earliest days of the Lycurgan revolution, the Argives had not merely countered the first assault upon their territory by the Spartans' new citizen army, but annihilated it. Half a century later, the Spartans were still struggling to impose themselves on states even immediately over their frontier. Taking the road north, after crossing a range of barren hills, the traveler from Lacedaemon would descend into a fertile expanse of fields and olive groves, the territory of Tegea, a city with the misfortune to lie midway between Argos and Sparta. To the Spartans, in particular, the richness of Tegea's farmland was an intolerable provocation, and in the early years of the sixth century, looking to seize it for themselves and turn the Tegeans into helots, they unleashed a full-scale war of annexation. The invaders, encouraged by an oracle's assurance that they would soon be "dancing upon the plain of Tegea,"[21] were sublimely confident of victory—so much so that they even brought surveying equipment with them and fetters for their new serfs. The oracle, however, had deluded them: their invasion was defeated, and the only dancing done by the Spartans was beneath the whip, as toiling prisoners of war, shackled by the chains they themselves had brought from Sparta.

This delivered such a blow to the Spartans' self-confidence that it forced an abrupt and decisive shift in their foreign policy. It had begun to dawn on them that the goal of reducing the whole of the Peloponnese to helotage was monstrously over-ambitious—and that hegemony could take a multitude of forms. There was no question that the Tegeans had to be brought to heel; perhaps, though, where naked oppression had failed, intimidation and force of prestige might yet succeed? The Spartans, employing their customary blend of low cunning and religiosity, duly dispatched a delegation to Tegea under cover of a truce. News had reached them of a strange find in a blacksmith's yard, the spine of what appeared to be a monstrous skeleton. The Spartans, sensing a possible propaganda coup, wished to stake this startling discovery for themselves. The prize was duly dug up, smuggled home, shown off, then reinterred. The skeleton, it was revealed, had belonged to none other than—a blast of trumpets!—Agamemnon's son. An identification more calculated to infuriate the Argives could not, of course, have been imagined; and yet the fanfare made over it by the Spartans had a far more calculated aim. The bones might have been stolen from Tegea, but Sparta, by enshrining them within her soil, was offering a public reassurance to others in the Peloponnese that she valued and respected their ancient traditions. No longer, as she had done in Messenia, was she aiming to trample them in the dirt. Cities which had demonstrated that they would rather fight to the death than be reduced to helotage could now submit to Sparta without fear of total ruin. Indeed, the Spartans hinted, it might even bring them some perks. To a Peloponnese long racked by rival hatreds, not to mention the menaces of Argos, Sparta offered the order of a protection racket, at least. Worse fates might be imagined. In 550 BC, just a few decades after her victory at the Battle of the Chains, Tegea entered into a league established and controlled by her fearsome neighbor.

Other cities soon followed. Like Tegea, they were wooed and reassured into submission. Spartan bone-hunters toured the remotest reaches of the Peloponnese, prospecting for the remains of further heroes, and having, in a landscape studded with the fossils of Pleistocene mammoths, considerable success. Not that the Spartans, in their ambition to forge a great league of subordinate cities, were content to rely on paleontology alone. Even as they promoted themselves as the guardians of their neighbors' mythic past, so they remained true to the ideals of the wolf pack, to the practice of terror and total war. The early defeats inflicted on their newly reformed army, far from denting their faith in the Lycurgan system, had only steeled them to perfect it. One century on, the transformation of their society into a killing machine had given the Spartans a rare and sanguinary mystique. To the hoplites of other cities, the wealthy elites whose armor, every season, would be brought out of haylofts and dusted down, and whose tendency, in best amateur spirit, was to regard warfare as a ritual, if often lethal, sport, the prospect of meeting the Spartans in battle was a dreadful one. That an entire city could mobilize itself was alarming enough; that the main object of its citizens was to meet and annihilate anyone who stood up to them was terrifying. Many non-Spartan hoplites, rather than test themselves against such an adversary, preferred simply to run away.

And the Spartans themselves, masters of psychological as well as every other form of warfare, knew precisely how to turn their enemies' blood to ice. From far off, the advance of their phalanx would be heralded by the shrilling of high-pitched pipes, and the earth would shake with the rhythm of their slow and metronomic approach. Then, as they emerged through the dust of battle, a dazzling "wall of bronze and scarlet"[22] would appear, for it was the practice of the Spartans to burnish their shields until they glittered, and to wear, supposedly on the personal prescription of Lycurgus himself, brilliant cloaks dyed the color of fresh blood.[23] Above the slow step of their marching, chilling battle hymns to ancient heroes would be raised, until officers, their distinctive horsehair crests running from ear to ear, would yell out a command and the phalanx would cease its paean. Immediately, upon the silence, a blast of trumpets would rend the air. The hoplites would quicken their pace, lower their spears—then start to run. Not necessarily, however, in a single mass: the wings might advance separately, like the horns of a bull, to turn the enemy flanks. The discipline required for such a maneuver, far beyond the ambitions, let alone the abilities, of amateur troops, served as grim testimony to the Spartans' addiction to drill. Such proficiency, to the hoplites of other cities, seemed almost like cheating. No dishonor, then, to acknowledge the greatness of a city that gave its men such training and such devastating skills. It was, everyone agreed, "a terrible thing to fight the Spartans."[24]

By the early 540s BC, when Croesus, the King of Lydia, was advised by an oracle to seek out "the most powerful of the Greek cities" as an ally in his looming war against the Persians, he had little hesitation in approaching Sparta. No greater tribute to her prestige could have been paid—nor a more direct snub to Argos. Indeed, with the friendship of a king as rich and powerful as Croesus, and with Tegea and much of the rest of the Peloponnese subordinated, it appeared to the Spartans that the time had finally come for a reckoning with the old enemy. Around 546 BC, even as the Lydian Empire was succumbing to Cyrus, the Spartans advanced, not to the aid of Croesus, as they were bound to do by the terms of their alliance, but directly against Argos. The Argives, harking back to an earlier age, immediately proposed a tournament, a clash between three hundred champions from their own city and three hundred of the invaders. The Spartans, ever enthusiasts for the example provided by tales of ancient heroism, agreed. At the end of the day, three men were left standing: two Argives and a solitary Spartan. The Argives, believing themselves the victors, duly returned to their city in triumph—leaving their adversary, blood-drenched but still very much alive, to accuse them of abandoning the battlefield, and to claim the triumph for himself. When the Argives disputed this in tones of high indignation, the Spartan's countrymen were there to back their champion up: meeting the enemy the next day with the full complement of their invasion force, they won a crushing victory. Strategically vital swaths of the Argive frontier were permanently annexed to Lacedaemon, and the Argives themselves, shaving their heads as a mark of their prostration, were left crippled for a generation. Even as the shears were getting to work in Argos, the Spartans were taking a precisely opposite vow: they would grow their hair long evermore, and wear oiled tresses, like red cloaks, as a mark of who they were.

It was in the midst of their celebrations, however, that news reached the Spartans of Croesus' fall. Their failure to live up to the terms of their alliance with the King of Lydia was an evident humiliation. Worse was to follow. Still unwilling to commit troops beyond the Aegean, Sparta dispatched instead only a small embassy, which duly met with Cyrus and was subjected to his celebrated put-down: "Who are the Spartans?" The Persians, certainly, had little cause to care. The lesson was sobering. Although Sparta appeared a colossus to the Greeks, in Asia she barely registered as a name, still less a power. Why should she?

77

Compared to the fantastical scale of Cyrus' dominion, all the Peloponnese was but an insignificant dot.

But the time would come when the Spartans would fling the Persians' mockery back in their teeth. "Who are the Spartans?" This question, asked in scorn, could just as well be asked in fear. Shielded behind their mountain frontiers, self-sufficient, xenophobic and suspicious, the Spartans took but never gave, spied but never revealed. Alone among the people of Greece, they made no attempt to distinguish between Greeks and non-Greeks, condemning all non-Spartans as "foreigners," and periodically expelling any found in their city. To their neighbors, at any rate, the wolf-lords of Lacedaemon were a source of obsessive fascination and fear. The riddle they posed their neighbors, like Cyrus' question, afforded no ready answers. The truth was veiled by fantasy, the reality by mirage. Ever conscious of the value of terror, the Spartans perfectly understood that it would diminish them to have the heart plucked out of their mystery. For in their mystery lay their dread.

Slaves of the Law

At the foot of the cliff on which the tomb of Helen stood flowed the swift and muddy currents of the Eurotas. Follow the gently winding course of the river northward, and a traveler would soon see, on the far bank, what looked like a huddle of straggling villages. There was little in the provincial appearance of Sparta to hint at the awe with which her citizens were regarded. "Suppose," as the Athenian Thucydides would one day put it, "that the city were abandoned, so that only her temples and the layout of her buildings remained—surely, as time passed, future generations would find it increasingly hard to believe that the people who once lived there had ever been powerful at all."[25]

This was of little concern to the Spartans themselves. A people steeled by the virtues of restraint and fortitude could have only contempt for grandiose architecture. Let the cowards of other states raise up walls around their cities. The Spartans had no need of masonry when they had their spears and burnished shields. Why build pompous monuments from wasteful marble when the truest mark of a man was that he lead his life as though in a military camp? Only temples—an intrusion of the unearthly and the eerie within the otherwise barracks-like spareness of the city—rose distinct above the common run of buildings. On these, at least, the Spartans could lavish their plundered riches. In the great shrine on the acropolis, a low-lying hillock which served as the citadel of the town, all the interior was faced with rectangular plaques of solid bronze. In another temple, just north of Sparta, a statue of Apollo, the archer-god of prophecy, stood sheathed in the purest gold.

Most haunting of all Lacedaemon's temples, however, was the shrine dedicated to Apollo's sister, the virgin huntress Artemis, "mistress of wild beasts."[26] Continuing north along the Eurotas past the center of the city, a traveler would soon pass beyond open exercise grounds into a marshy hollow, where stood a black and ancient idol of the goddess. The Spartans, in the first flush of their dominance over the rest of the Peloponnese, in around 560 BC, had built there a splendid temple all of stone; and yet, despite the gleam of its new masonry, the site retained an air of menace. It was not merely that frogs continued to croak from among the rushes that surrounded it, nor that a marsh haze might sometimes rise ghost-like from the river: the temple itself was a place to provoke goosebumps. Not all its fittings were recent. Hung upon the fresh stonework were adornments preserved from a much older shrine, faces of terracotta, some of them idealized portraits of beardless youths or grizzled soldiers, but others grotesque and twisted monstrosities, their stares cretinous, their mouths wide open in animal cries of savagery or pain.[27] These were the stuff of Spartan nightmares: rare was the citizen whose imaginings they would not have haunted, for the temple of Artemis, from his childhood through to his old age, was where he came to mark the staging posts of his life. Always present, blank-eyed yet watching him, were the masks. The faces of heroes to inspire him; and the grimaces of idiots, of gorgons, of deformed and toothless hags to remind him of the ugliness of failure. To fail was to be an outcast: lost beyond the bounds of the city, where only the shameful, the twisted and the bestial were to be found. All Spartans had to live with the implications of this truth. All had to live by the stern code that it forged.

For everywhere, as citizens, they were tracked and supervised. Each generation, like a jailer, kept its watch upon the next. The Spartans, who knew what it was to admire "choirs of boys and girls, and dance, and festivity,"[28] nevertheless mistrusted the exuberance of youth. Lycurgus, wolf-worker that he was, had dreaded where the energies of unchecked cubs might lead. Only with the whip, he had taught his countrymen, could young predators be adequately trained. As the Spartans well knew from the grim example of their own early history, the savagery of instincts and impulses slipped off the leash might all too easily tear a state apart. Having passed through one period of revolution, they had no wish to endure another. No leeway could be given to the natural restlessness and appetites of youth. Only discipline, unyielding discipline, could possibly serve to check them. If there had to be change in Sparta, whether of a failing custom or of a law that had had its day, then it was for the elderly to moot and pass the needed reform.[29] Why should any measure be accepted otherwise? After all, the elders of Sparta were living proof of what tradition could achieve: that it was capable of forging a master race of heroes.

So it was that Sparta, for all her fearsome reputation, was also widely lauded as the home of perfect manners. Only there, of all the cities in Greece, would a young man habitually step aside to make way for his senior; for he was, with such a gesture of respect, simultaneously paying honor to the laws and customs of his people. To such an extreme was this notion carried that the Spartans, appalled by the idea of a stripling unable to rise in the presence of his elders, frowned upon public lavatories. "The spears of young men" may have flourished in the city, but there was no doubting that "it is the old who have the power there."[30] Even the titular heads of state—for the Spartans, peculiar in all things, had not one but two kings—were obliged to respect their authority. Push too hard against the

limits of what was constitutional, and they would quickly find themselves arraigned by their city's supreme court, a legislative body that,
aside from the two kings themselves, consisted entirely of geronto-
crats aged over sixty. The Spartans duly called this intimidating body
the Gerousia—a name which, like the Romans' Senate, had the literal meaning of a council of elders. Since, aside from its role as the
guardian of the constitution, it also had the right to forestall all
motions put before it, and to present the fruits of its own delibera-
tions as effective faits accomplis, the Gerousia might easily exert a
stranglehold over politics in Sparta. Election to it was not only the
supreme honor that a citizen could attain, but was for life. "No
wonder that this, of all human prizes, should be the most zealously
contested." Even non-Spartans might concede as much: "Yes, athletic
competitions are honorable too, but they are merely tests of physical
prowess. Election to the Gerousia is the ultimate proof of a noble
spirit."[31]

This was not a nook in Sparta, not a cranny, but bony fingers would
intrude there. Even the newest-born baby was subjected to the prod-
dings of old men. Should an infant be judged too sickly or deformed
to make a future contribution to the city, then the elders would order
its immediate termination. Since the investment required from the
state to raise a citizen was considerable, this was regarded by most
Spartans as only proper. Indeed, a mother might well play the eugenicist herself, washing her baby in wine, which, as everyone knew, was
the surest test for epilepsy. What true Spartan parent, after all, would
wish to raise a son who might suddenly collapse in a fit? Better an early
bereavement than the risk of such disgrace. A cleft beside the road
which wound over the mountains to Messenia, the Apothetae, or
"Dumping Ground," provided the setting for the infanticide. There,
where they might no longer shame the city that had bred them, the
weak and deformed would be slung into the depths of the chasm,
condemned eternally to its tenebrous oblivion. This was no abandonment, as was conventionally practiced by other peoples, but a grim and
formal rite of execution. There was no hope of deliverance—such as

was said to have spared the infant Cyrus—for the unwanted Spartan child. He had to die, and be seen to die, *pour encourager les autres.*

And no doubt, for those permitted to live, the tracery of tiny bones which littered the depths of the Apothetae must have served to concentrate the mind wonderfully. Spartan children could not help but grow up proudly conscious of themselves as an elite, chosen as such at birth; and yet the state, in return for its patronage, imposed stern and fearsome obligations. Lycurgus, it was said, rather than commit his reform program to writing, had preferred to inscribe it upon the characters and bodies of those who were to live by it, so that they might serve one another as walking constitutions. Such a process of social engineering was only practicable, of course, if begun in the cradle. Babies, soft and helpless, had to be toughened and fashioned into Spartans. No swaddling for them. No cosseting of toddlers, either, no indulging of their whims. "When they were given food, they were to eat it, and not be picky; night-fears and clinginess were to be firmly stamped on; tantrums and whining too."[32] Unsurprisingly, Spartan nannies were widely admired for their brisk, no-nonsense approach. Yet, strict as they were, even they were put in the shade by the city's faculty of instructors. This had a role quite without precedent elsewhere in Greece, or indeed beyond. For the Spartans, in their concern to mold the perfect citizen, had developed a truly bizarre and radical notion: the world's first universal, state-run education system.

Why—it even provided for girls! If, as seems probable, baby boys were likelier to be condemned to the Apothetae than their sisters, then this implied no lack of concern among the Spartans for the vigor of their female stock. Healthy mothers made for a healthy warrior race. Just as boys were trained for warfare, so girls had to be reared for their future as breeders. The result—to foreign eyes, at any rate—was an inversion of just about every accepted norm. In Sparta, girls were fed at the expense of their brothers. To the bemusement of other Greeks, they were also taught to read, and to express themselves not modestly, as was becoming for women, but in an aggressively sententious manner, so that they might better instruct their own children in what it meant to be a Spartan. They exercised in public: running, throwing the javelin, even wrestling. When they danced, they would do so with such abandon that they might slap their heels against the bare skin of their buttocks. For, yes—and here the disbelief of foreigners would conventionally reach boiling point—it was the habit of Spartan girls, as they trained, to sport only the skimpiest of tunics, slit revealingly up the thighs. Sometimes—horror of horrors!—they might even disport themselves in the nude.

Visions of female flesh, oiled and tanned, glistened in the imaginings of many a Sparta-watcher. The Spartans themselves, sensitive to the mockery that labeled their daughters "thigh-flashers,"[33] would retort sternly "that there was nothing shameful about female nudity, nothing immoral in the slightest." In fact, "since it encouraged a sense of sobriety, and a passion for physical fitness,"[34] precisely the opposite. Yet, paramount though the requirements of Sparta's eugenic program undoubtedly were, an aura of the erotic still clung to the training grounds nevertheless. The fertility of a future mother was best gauged, a Spartan might argue, by the glowing of her skin and the perfection of her breasts. Physical beauty—the long blond hair and elegant ankles for which Spartan girls were celebrated—provided the readiest measure by which moral beauty too could be judged. An ugly daughter, inevitably, would cause her parents alarm and distress. Desperate measures might have to be taken. So shockingly plain had one baby been, it was said, that her nurse, clutching at straws, had finally taken her to Helen's tomb. There, outside the sanctuary, a mysterious woman had appeared and stroked the young girl's hair. The baby, this apparition had prophesied, "would grow up the loveliest woman in Lacedaemon."[35] And so it had come to pass: the girl had become a celebrated beauty and ended up the wife of a Spartan king. Evidently, the spirit of Helen still sometimes walked her native land.

Such a story revealed an important truth about the Spartan cast of mind. Egalitarian though the Lycurgan ideal was, it did not foster any notions of equality. The sense of frantic competition that made women wish to outshine their peers in beauty gnawed at everyone in the city. "What is the best kind of government?" a Spartan king was once asked. Back came his answer, unhesitatingly: "The one in which the largest number of citizens are able to strive with each other in virtue, without threatening the state with anarchy."[36] This was why the education system, in a seeming paradox, worked both to stamp a single mold on those who passed through it, and yet to identify and fast-track an elite. Evident in the upbringing of girls, it was even more so in the training of their brothers. The Spartan who best submitted to it was the Spartan who most excelled.

For it was the goal of instructors not merely to crush a boy's individuality, but to push him to startling extremes of endurance, discipline and impassivity, so that he might prove himself, supremely, as a being reforged of iron. When, at the age of seven, a young Spartan left his home to live communally with other boys, it was more than his sense of family that was being fractured and reset: the very notion that he possessed a private identity was, from that moment on, to be placed under continuous assault. Spartans termed his training the "*agoge*," a word more conventionally applied to the raising of cattle. His supervisor was a "*paidonomos*"—literally, a "herder of boys." Denied adequate rations, the young Spartan would be encouraged to forage from the farms of neighboring Lacedaemonians, stalking and stealing like a fox, refining his talent for stealth.* Whether in the heat of summer or in the cold of winter, he would wear one style of tunic, identical to that worn by his fellows, and nothing else, not even shoes. Strict limits on his conversation would be set, to foster the terse style of speech known all over Greece as "Laconic." Yet, even as a young Spartan submitted to these ferocious and uniform

---

*The famous story of the boy who hunted a fox for food, and then, rather than confess to having it under his cloak, let the creature gnaw away his stomach, surely derives from a genuine tradition in which young Spartans were encouraged to take on vulpine characteristics—to become, in a sense, like the cornered fox themselves. Certainly, as it stands, the story makes no sense, since surely not even the hungriest boy would choose to hunt a fox for supper.

disciplines, he was continuously being studied, compared and ranked: "As the boys exercised, they would always be spurred on to wrestle and contend with one another, so that the elders could then better judge their characters, their courage, and how well they were likely to perform when the time came for them, finally, to take their place in the line of battle."[38] Even girls might get in on the act: the boys would routinely be ordered to strip before them, to be subjected to either praise or mocking giggles. A true Spartan never had anything to hide.

A lesson most alarmingly brought home to a boy when, at the age of twelve, he became legal game for cruising. Pederasty was widely practiced elsewhere in Greece, but only in Sparta was it institutionalized— even, it is said, with fines for boys who refused to take a lover. Girls too, it was rumored, if not married, might expect to be sodomized repeatedly during their adolescence.[38] In both cases, the justification was surely the same: nowhere was so private, so intimate, but the state had the right to intrude there. Yet, traumatic though the experience of submitting must have been for most young Spartans, there were, for boys at least, some significant compensations. Not only was it acceptable for a lover to serve his young boyfriend as a patron; it was positively expected. The more honored a citizen, and the better connected, the more effectively he could further his beloved's career. Elite would advance elite: so it was that a boy, yielding to the nocturnal thrustings of a battle-scarred older man, might well find the secret wellsprings of Spartan power opened up to him.

Certainly, by the time he finished the *agoge*, a young man would know for sure whether he had been marked out for future greatness. To the most promising graduates was granted the honor of one final, bloody challenge. Enrolled into a crack squad known as the Crypteia, they would be sent into the mountains, armed only with a single dagger each, and ordered to live off the land. This period of exile from their city, however, was much more than a mere endurance test. Traveling alone, each member of the Crypteia would inevitably cross the Taygetos range and slip into Messenia. There, advancing soundlessly by night, as every graduate of the *agoge* had been trained to do, they would be expected to prove themselves as killers. Of all men, it was said, only the Spartans denied that homicide was necessarily a crime; for it was, in their opinion, perfectly legitimate to cull their slaves. Nervous lest the gods be provoked against them, however, the Spartans would proclaim each year a state of war against the helots, a maneuver of typically murderous circumspection, calculated to spare the Crypteia any risk of blood pollution.[39] How else, after all, save by careful pruning of the most able Messenians, could the Spartans hope to breed natural serfs? Just as they condemned to the Apothetae the dregs of their own city, so they aimed to extinguish any spark of talent or rebellion in their slaves. Only the truly servile could be permitted to reproduce. Individual masters who failed to stunt the growth and aptitudes of their helots would be fined. The matter would be brought to the attention of the elders. The Crypteia, tipped off, would then glide in and set about its business.

Hitman though he was, the young Spartan who brought his dagger to the throat of a condemned Messenian was performing something more than an execution: it was almost an initiation rite, a deed of magic. As he felt his blade slice deep, he was privileged to know himself an acolyte of the profoundest mysteries of his state. No Spartan could lead his people who had shrunk from killing in cold blood. The elders who gave the Crypteia its commissions were simultaneously putting its members to the test. Only once he had smelled for himself the hatred of a hunted Messenian, and seen it in his eyes, could a Spartan truly appreciate the full extent of his city's peril. Only once he had murdered could he truly appreciate what was required to keep it at bay.

Such, for the agent of the Crypteia, was the particular knowledge which he put on with his power. Not that ignorance could be permitted any Spartan, of course—whether male or female. Helen, it was said, while still a little girl, had been surprised as she danced before the sanctuary of Artemis, and raped. Messenian raiders, prior to the enslavement of their country, had similarly violated a whole chorus of dancers. And they might do so again, given half a chance. Every Spartan girl knew what her fate would be should her city's whip hand fail. It was left to her brothers, however, to test this certainty to the limits of their endurance. Every citizen, as part of his boyhood training, had learned what it was to suffer the lash. With their rough tunics slashed to ribbons, and their shoulders scarred and bleeding, the children of Lacedaemon's master race might sometimes, after rituals that demanded a whipping, look little better than the meanest, lowest-born slaves. And yet they had proved themselves the very opposite of servile. The whip which degraded the helot served to ennoble the Spartan boy. "Brief suffering leads to the joy of lasting fame,"[40] Lycurgus had instructed his people. It was those who endured the lash with the sternest fortitude who went on, no doubt, to be enrolled in the Crypteia. The master was most the master who could best endure the toils of a slave.

An insight which governed the Spartan throughout his adult life. Although a graduate of the *agoge* would never again have to endure the humiliation of a whipping, his life continued to be trammeled by restrictions that a citizen of any other Greek state would have found insufferable. A Spartan was not even permitted to control his own finances until he was thirty. Rather than live with his wife, he would be obliged instead to sneak from his barracks for hurried, animal couplings. He might bear the scars of battle, but a young man who came to blows with another could expect to be treated by his elders like a naughty child—or, indeed, a slave. Symbolic of his ambiguous status was the fact that a Spartan warrior in his twenties would wear his hair short, just like a helot. So too, even more shockingly, would a Spartan bride.[41]

In Greece, the only women generally seen with shaven heads were slave girls shorn of their tresses for wigs, but it was typical of the many peculiarities of the Spartans that they should have regarded what was elsewhere a mark of humiliation as an emblem of matronly pride. Having been raised to breed, the newly married Spartan woman—a fit, healthy and already anally proficient virgin—could at last embrace her destiny. Society encouraged her all the way. The more prolific she proved herself, the greater her prestige. If she produced three sons, her husband would be excused garrison duty; if she died in childbirth, she would at least have the consolation of having her name recorded for eternity upon a tombstone. In such a way did the state aim to make even motherhood a matter of the most intense competition.

Not, of course, that anything could compare with the status obsession of young men. The ruthlessness with which this was fostered became, in a Spartan's twenties, something truly carnivorous. The supreme honor, awarded to only three graduates at a time, was to be named by the elders a "*hippagretes*"—a "commander of horse." This title gave a young Spartan the right to nominate a further one hundred of his peers for membership in the Hippeis, an elite squad of three hundred, who operated distinct from the command structure which governed other military units, and served in the center of the battle line as the bodyguard of the commanding king. The jealousy of those overlooked by the *hippagretai* was naturally fearsome. Rejects were encouraged to keep an envious and watchful eye on the Hippeis, reporting any infractions, always looking to have its members dismissed in disgrace, angling to replace them. No wonder that brawls between young Spartans were so common. No wonder, either, that they had to be framed, even into their early manhood, by such ferocious rules of conduct.

Hence the unsettling paradoxes that governed Spartan society: humiliation was pride; restriction opportunity; discipline freedom; subordination the truest mastery. Even when, at the age of thirty, a Spartan finally became a full citizen, a "*homoios*," or the "peer" of his fellows, he continued to live in conditions that would have appeared to the elite of any other city akin to slavery. Every evening, he would be obliged to eat in a common mess; he would bring a set ration of raw ingredients which the cooks would mix into a black, bloody broth. So disgusting was this concoction that foreigners who were privileged to taste it would joke that at last they could understand why the Spartans had no fear of death. A shallow and uncomprehending jest. The Spartans themselves, who were not immune to a taste for witticisms, and indeed had raised a shrine to Laughter in their city, knew that some things were far too solemn to be joked about.

To a *homoios*, excess was always the enemy. In other states, the poor were skin and bones, and the rich might be nicknamed "the stout"—

but not in Sparta. In other states, it was the elite who would indulge themselves with wine and drunken dancing—but not in Sparta. In Sparta, it was the slaves. Sometimes, as the *homoioi* ate in their mess, a helot might be dragged in, a stoop-shouldered, bestial thing, dressed in mangy animal pelts, and with an ugly cap of flea-bitten dog skin on his head. For the entertainment and edification of his watching masters, the wretch would be forced to drink neat wine, to gulp it down until the liquor was spilling from his lips onto the skins. Laughing, the Spartans would then order the slave to dance. His cheeks bright red, his chin wet with spittle, the helot would weave and stagger and totter until he passed out in the dirt. His masters would then amuse themselves by pelting him with bones.

With some justice, then, it could be said of Lacedaemon that "the quintessence both of freedom and of slavery are to be found there."[42] One, after all, was the mirror image of the other. Upon the walls of the temple of Artemis, the masks of young warriors and wise old men were made to appear all the nobler for the ugliness of the masks that surrounded them, those of crones, imbeciles, savages and freaks. Similarly, to the sober *homoioi* at their mess table, all the rigors and cruelties of their training were given purpose by the spectacle of the drooling helot collapsed at their feet. The Spartans, who were the masters of their own bodies and appetites as well as of a vast population of slaves, were the freest men of all precisely because they were the subjects of the harshest and most unyielding code. "They have their liberty, yes—but their liberty is not an absolute. For even the Spartans have a master. And that master—the one who rules them—that master is their Law."[43]

Ancestral Voices

The evident perfection of their constitution, to say nothing of the xenophobia that it inevitably encouraged, led most Spartans to regard the world beyond their borders with a mixture of suspicion and disdain. A series of foreign-policy disasters had served only to encourage them in their insularity. The humiliation of the snub by Cyrus had been followed, in 525 BC, by an even worse debacle, when a sea-borne expedition against Samos, a powerful island just off Persian-occupied Ionia, had been comprehensively repulsed. From that moment on, rather than risk further entanglements in the Aegean, most Spartans were content to turn their backs on eastern adventures. Better by far to consolidate their supremacy closer to home. Dispatch too many of their peerless fighting men overseas and what was to stop the helots rising up in sudden revolt? Not to mention their supposed allies. Keep them all on a tight leash, and Lacedaemon would be secure. Let the frontiers of the Peloponnese, then, serve the Spartans as their walls.

And yet Pelops' island, despite its name, was not entirely "girt in by the sea."[44] Three days' march north from Sparta stood the great merchant city of Corinth, and beyond it, over a narrow strip of land no wider than six miles, lay the cities and mountains of mainland Greece. The Spartans, Peloponnesian though they were, could hardly afford to behave as though this isthmus did not exist. It was not merely that some of the cities which lay north of it, celebrated ones such as Athens and Thebes, were themselves major players in the power games of Greece. Instincts of sentiment as well as of self-preservation were at stake. The Spartans, despite their attempts to present themselves as the heirs of Menelaus, were Dorians, after all. The mountainous country north of the Isthmus was their ancestral homeland. Once the isthmus road had passed first Athens and then Thebes, it was obliged by the peaks which hemmed in the lowlands to thread along the coastline, until, at its narrowest point, there was barely room for two wagons to travel side by side. This pass was named Thermopylae—a site with considerable resonance for the Spartans, for it was from the peak that loomed high above it to the west, Mount Oeta, that Heracles, having immolated himself upon a pyre, had ascended from the flames to join the gods in their home upon Mount Olympus. Just south of Oeta lay a region equally rich in significance, the plain of Doris, from which the Dorians traced their name. South in turn of Doris stood a further peak, Parnassus, ravine-gashed and precipitous;

and then, on the far side of that mountain, the most sacred spot of all, a shrine holier to the Spartans than any in their own city, or indeed in all of Greece. At Delphi, the air was pure with prophecy. There, for nine months every year, the Lord Apollo was believed to have his dwelling. More than anywhere else in the world, it was where glimpses and revelations of the future might be uncovered. Deep within the oracle, the veil of time itself was rent.

That the Spartans should have had a particular admiration for Apollo was hardly surprising. Just as their ancestors had migrated to Lacedaemon, so the archer god had come to Delphi as an invader from the north. Leaving the halls of Olympus behind him, Apollo had traveled the world "with his far-shooting bow, searching for an oracle that might speak to mortal men."[45] He had found it where a monstrous python, bloated upon human prey, slumbered by a sweet-flowing, icy spring, its coils heaped against the sheer rock of Parnassus, while below it eagles soared over a lonely and dappled gorge. A single shot from his deadly bow had been sufficient to end the monster's reign, and from that moment on it was Apollo who had ruled as lord of Delphi. Sprigs of laurel planted by the god served to purify the sanctuary. In time, men raised a temple there, out of boughs cut from the laurel bushes, it was said, and Apollo had uttered prophecies through the rustling of the leaves. Since the youth of the god, foundation had succeeded foundation. The second had been built of fern stalks, the third of wax and feathers, the fourth of bronze—for the history of Apollo's oracle was a fabulous one, and marked by ceaseless change. In time, the laurel leaves themselves had fallen silent, and the god chose to speak instead through the ecstasies of a young priestess, the Pythia, in whose title could be heard an echo of Apollo's long-rotted foe. Around 750 BC, when Delphi's history first begins to emerge from myth, a temple of stone was raised. Shortly afterward, it appears, it was decided that only an old woman should be appointed to serve as the Pythia, although she was still, as a symbol of purity, obliged to wear a young girl's dress.[46] In 548 BC, the temple burned to the ground. Still, amid all this turmoil, the voice of Apollo spoke on.

There was no other oracle to compare with it. Indeed, such was the prestige of Delphi that it became, of all the many temples founded by the Greeks, the only one to be served by a body of full-time priests. While the notion of such a cadre would hardly have raised eyebrows amid the great temple bureaucracies of the East, it was, for the Greeks, a decided innovation. Travelers' tales of the bizarre doings of Egyptian or Babylonian priests never ceased to amaze them. The news that in Persia only a Magus could preside over a sacrifice was greeted with particular astonishment. In Greece, anyone, even women, even slaves, could sacrifice. Only the Delphians, far removed in their mountain valley from all other possible forms of income, made a living from the proceeds of their shrine. "Guard my temple," Apollo had instructed them, "receive the crowds of men."[47] The Delphians, obeying him, had lavishly cashed in. Other cities, far from begrudging the priests their professionalism, were happy to collude in it. The arrangement suited everyone. What better assurance could there be of the priests' even-handedness than that they charged everyone the same flat fee? When rival factions turned to the oracle for adjudication, they needed to be able to trust the words of the god absolutely. No one could afford to see Delphi's neutrality compromised. When, in 595 BC, the neighboring city of Crisa attempted to annex the oracle, the whole of Greece had been shocked into ruthless action.[48] A great league of cities had marched to the god's defense. The norms of civilized behavior, which banned chemical warfare as a crime against the gods, had been temporarily suspended: poison had been added to Crisa's water supply, so that "the defenders were afflicted by violent bouts of diarrhea, and had to keep rushing from their positions."[49] The walls were stormed, the impious city wiped out. Centuries later, the plain on which Crisa had once stood remained barren and bare of trees, "as though laboring under a curse."[50]

The terrifying lesson had been learned. Delphi was either an oracle for all the Greeks or it was nothing. Sacred flames rose eternally upon the public altar of the temple in illustration of precisely this truth: tended busily by priestesses, fed with pine and laurel wood, never permitted to go out, they blazed as the hearth fire of the whole of Greece.

Yet even those who were not Greek might approach Apollo and hope for an answer. Delphi's claims to holiness were on a truly global scale. In the beginning, it was said, when Zeus had first come into the kingdom of the universe, he had sought to measure the scale of his inheritance by releasing one eagle from the east and one from the west, and watching them fly, to locate the center of the world. The two birds had met at Delphi, and a great egg of rock, the "Navel Stone," or Omphalos, still marked the spot. It was only natural, then, that the priests should have welcomed foreign supplicants as merely their temple's due. When Croesus, for instance, faced with the growing threat of Persia, had sought divine guidance, he had sent messengers to all the world's leading oracles, with instructions, on a given day, to ask what their master was doing back in Lydia. Only Delphi had provided the right answer: that Croesus was boiling up a lamb and tortoise casserole. From that moment on, the King of Lydia had become the oracle's most generous patron. Unparalleled gifts of gold, mixing bowls, ingots and statues of lions had been sent to join the treasures that already cluttered the shadows of the temple. Apollo, in return, had offered Croesus foreign-policy advice. It had been upon the suggestion of the god, for example, that the King of Lydia had formed his alliance with the Spartans.

Not that this had saved him in the long run, of course. If Apollo's advice often appeared clear, then it was not always so. "The lord whose oracle is at Delphi neither speaks nor keeps silent, but offers hints."[51] Those who misinterpreted the god, who failed to recognize the ambiguities which might haunt his pronouncements, who blundered into actions on the basis of what they wanted to believe, would invariably come to ruin. Croesus, having grown reliant upon Apollo's counsel, had ultimately been deceived by his own vainglory and obtuseness into disaster. Pondering whether to attack Cyrus, he had consulted Delphi and received the answer that a mighty empire would fall if he did. Croesus had duly gone to war and seen his own empire fall.

When Apollo was accused of ingratitude toward his benefactor, his priests at Delphi retorted that the god, while he was unable to avert the course of destiny, had granted to Croesus three more years of prosperity than had been allotted him by Fate. This explanation was readily believed: kings had always been the favorites of the gods. Such was clear from the stories of ancient times, when the heroes had invariably possessed royal blood. But what was acceptable in legend had become, first to the aristocracies of the various Greek states and then to every class of citizen, increasingly offensive. The claim that one mortal might be privileged over his fellows did not, as in the East, serve to legitimize the concept of monarchy, but rather to tarnish it—for no Greek cared to imagine that he might naturally be a slave. "Only know the yoke of servitude," it was said, "and Zeus, the thunderer, will rob you of half your virtue."[52] It was all very well, perhaps, for the servile peoples of the East to live like women with a despot's foot upon their necks—but not for a freeborn Greek. Kings, unless safely confined to remote and effeminate lands, properly belonged in ancient poems. Only as a title awarded to certain priests did the rank, in some Greek cities, maintain a ghostly afterlife—for the intimacy which it had once been the privilege of royalty to share with the gods could not be lightly set aside, and venerable ceremonies might still depend upon it. Even as a priest, however, a "king" remained a figure of danger. The charisma natural to his title had to be scrupulously trammeled. No powers could be permitted him beyond the religious. Even his term of office, in a city such as Athens, was sternly limited to one year.

How extraordinary, then, it might be thought, that in Sparta, of all states, where the communal was everything, kingship should not merely have endured but been illuminated by a sacral, haunting glow. Other Spartans were *homoioi*—peers—but royalty was something more. As a boy a crown prince was exempted from the *agoge*. As commander in chief, a king led his countrymen into war. As head of state, he stood for no man in the city; nor was anyone permitted to touch him or even brush against him in public. Most eerie of all, and what truly set him apart from his countrymen, was his intimacy with the gods. Certainly, no mortal in the world could look for a closer relationship with the Delphic oracle than that enjoyed by a Spartan king. Each one, in an arrangement unparalleled in any other state, had two ambassadors, the "Pythians," on permanent standby, ready upon a royal gesture to gallop north and put questions to Apollo. Such were the privileges of breeding. The kings were, after all, the distant relatives of Zeus.

Their countrymen, naturally, looked to benefit from such a bloodline. Respectful of royalty though they were, the Spartans did not indulge it out of a craven servility. Just the opposite. While other Greeks flinched from the mystique of kingship, the Spartans, with that blend of common sense and superstition so typical of all their policy, looked to exploit it for their own ends. If the kings had the ears of Apollo, then the state had the ruling of the kings. Like magnificent but captive predators, they were kept, in the strictest Spartan manner, under close and ceaseless watch. By each other; by the Gerousia; by the mass of the people. Even when, as was increasingly the case by the late sixth century BC, the kings were absent from the city on campaigns, the surveillance never slackened.

In fact, if anything, the screws began to tighten. As Spartan greatness flourished, and the opportunities for foreign adventures with it, a once insignificant magistracy, the Ephorate, began to operate as both inquisitor and guardian of the kings. Five in number, the ephors were elected annually from the whole assembly of citizens, and so could legitimately claim to represent the people. A king, although he might ignore their first and second summons, was obliged to rise and answer their third. This calling of royalty to account by the Ephorate, a ritual which would occur at least once a month, represented a piquant reversal of roles. In the beginning, it was said, the ephors had served the kings as their servants, but over the years, by a secretive and cunning process, they had advanced to become their masters' shadows. Faceless in comparison to the kingship they may have been, and yet they too had unearthly powers. They would meet in darkness and trace the future in the sky. Should it be discovered there that a king was "an offender against the gods,"[53] the ephors had the right to dismiss him from his throne. They could then take it upon themselves to do as the king himself traditionally did, and dispatch messengers to Delphi. The oracle, it was assumed, would confirm the judgment of the heavens.

But would it? In a death struggle between a king and the Ephorate, which side would Apollo and his priesthood back? This was not a question that the Spartans, with their deep-seated fear of constitutional upheaval, much cared to ponder. Nor did they expect to have to: Sparta was a city governed, in the final reckoning, not by kings or ephors, but by custom, and by the inimitable character of her people. To the quality they most universally prized the Spartans gave the name "*sophrosyne*": soundness of mind, moderation, prudence, self-restraint. Great though the powers of a king or an ephor might be, both were steeled, as Spartan citizens, not to push them to the limits. "For it is always your nature," as a Corinthian would one day complain, "to do less than you could have done, and to hold back from heading where your judgement might otherwise lead you."[56] But such criticism could be taken by the Spartans as commendation. *Sophrosyne* in everything: the spirit of revolution in Lacedaemon had been well tamed. Just as a warrior was subsumed within the discipline of the phalanx, so were the ephor and the king within the state: no selfishness, no running amok, no sudden lurching from the ranks.

Then, in 520 BC[55] a new king came to the throne. He laid claim to power as he would wield it, ruthlessly, and touched by scandal. Even before his birth, Cleomenes had been entangled in a snarl of shocking rumors. His father, the king, unable to impregnate his much-beloved first wife, had been ordered by the ephors to divorce her and take a second; but the king, although reluctant to defy the Ephorate openly, opted instead to practice bigamy. No sooner had his new bed-partner borne him Cleomenes than his original wife, to everyone's astonishment, outdid her rival and delivered three sons in quick succession. Since she was the king's niece as well as his beloved, this, unsurprisingly, had left Cleomenes much resented by his father. The king, flaunting his favoritism, had pointedly named the eldest of Cleomenes' half-brothers Dorieus—"the Dorian"—and then entered him for the *agoge*, which the prince had duly passed with flying colors. Posing simultaneously as legitimate heir and man of the people,

Dorieus had put the hapless Cleomenes, his unwanted elder brother, thoroughly in the shade. "Everyone ranked him first of all the youths of his generation. And Dorieus himself had little doubt that his many qualities would serve to win his father's throne."[56]

But the Spartans were nothing if not a legalistic people, and Cleomenes retained first claim on the kingship. No sooner was his father dead than he moved to seize the throne. Dorieus, for all his flash and popularity, found himself outmaneuvered. Cleomenes, tightening his grip upon power, next looked to drive his half-brother out of Sparta altogether. Dorieus' exile, when it came, might have been dressed up as an exotic foreign mission, but there could be no disguising the scale of his defeat. Sparta had proved too small for both brothers. Nor would there be any comeback for the increasingly shiftless Dorieus. After an abortive attempt to found a colony in Africa, he ended up a mercenary in Sicily, where he fell in an obscure and inglorious scuffle. Cleomenes, back in Sparta, could henceforward reign secure.

All the same, the circumstances of his accession would continue to cast their shadows. Perfectly aware that many of his countrymen regarded him as at best semi-legitimate, Cleomenes chose to respond with bravura and defiance. Not for him the sober traditionalism expected of a Spartan king. Nor, just as pertinently, the caution. Whether out of a desire to prove himself to his detractors, out of scorn for their limited horizons, or because, shrewd and quick-witted, he believed that he was serving his city's best interests, Cleomenes had resolved from the very beginning to throw his weight around. The ease with which he had dispatched Dorieus suggested that this might prove considerable. For the first time since the Lycurgan revolution, a king sat on the throne of Sparta who was determined to test his prerogatives to the full.

All of which promised turbulent times ahead for the Spartans. It also threatened cities far distant from the confines of Lacedaemon. A strongman in charge of Greece's deadliest war machine was an alarming prospect for the whole of the Peloponnese—and beyond. In 519 BC, barely a year after his accession, Cleomenes led an army across the

Isthmus. It was a menacing—and, as time would prove, portentous—statement of intent. The new king was not to be bounded by the limits of his backyard, and already, so early in his reign, his attentions were fixed firmly on central Greece: on Delphi, where the priests were soon embroiled in bribery and scandal; on Boeotia, the great cattle-rearing plain dominated by Thebes but also dotted with smaller cities, resentful of Theban bullying and offering any interloper plenty of scope for making mischief; and on Attica, the strategically vital region of hills and farmland through which the main isthmus road passed as it wound north. On Attica, and the city of Athens, more than anywhere, indeed. For Athens was a growing power—and so a potential threat. She had to be neutered. Cleomenes, though sometimes impulsive, could hardly be counted a maverick just because he had developed a taste for preemptive force.

Yet tremors were starting to build deeper than he, or indeed anyone, could sense. Cleomenes' meddling in Athenian politics would help precipitate a political earthquake. It would be the most far-reaching upheaval in a Greek city since the time of Lycurgus himself. Its aftershocks would be felt, not only throughout Greece but also, rippling across the Aegean, eastward into the empire of the Persians. Even, though far distant, within the chanceries of Darius himself.

Revolution was coming to Athens—and war to the whole world.

4

ATHENS

Earth-Born

In Greece, a city was hardly a city without a bizarre foundation myth. The Spartans were far from alone in obsessing about their roots. With the anxiety of people who were always looking over their shoulders at rivals, concerned to pull rank, to put down others, to claim pre-eminence, Greeks in cities everywhere told tall stories about their past. Some were taller than others. The Argives, for instance, although Dorian, like the Spartans, and therefore similarly able to claim the bloodline of Heracles, were hardly the people to rest content with the same pedigree as their hated neighbors. Even as they were being repeatedly bested by the Spartans on the battlefield, their genealogical fantasies grew increasingly bombastic. It was an Argive woman, they boasted, who had been the ancestress of the Egyptians, the Arabs and a host of other peoples. In fact, there was barely a nation in the world that did not possess some blood link to Argos—or so the Argives liked to claim.

Extravagant pretensions of this order were not the only way to put the Spartans in their place. The citizens of Tegea, for instance, whose history boasted few famous names, could still afford to sneer at their fearsome neighbors as parvenus—for they, unlike the Dorians, had always lived in the Peloponnese. Deep roots, among the Greeks, were a sure source of prestige. The Argives, not content with swanking about their glitzy overseas connections, boasted that they, too, were natives of their homeland, and always had been. Their Dorian ancestry, which might have been thought to render this assertion problematic, was cheerfully ignored. Logic was rarely a feature of the Greeks' foundation myths. In the Peloponnese, particularly, where there were any number of competing traditions, claims swirled amid counterclaims, and the past might easily be adapted on the hoof.

The ultimate, of course, was for an entire region to claim never to have been conquered, but always to have preserved its customs, and its liberty, from invaders. "The same ethnic stock, generation after generation, the same people, they have always lived in this, our native land—and it is they, by virtue of their merits, who have bequeathed it to us, a country eternally free."[1] The Athenians, throughout their history, never tired of this kind of talk. No folktales of migration, of the melting pot, for them. Instead, with a smugness that other Greeks found wearisome in the extreme, they pointed to the sacrosanct quality of their borders, of how no Heraclid or Dorian had ever succeeded in forcing them, and of how, like "the wheat and the barley" that grew in the Attic fields, "the vines, the olives and the figs,"[2] they were earth-born, soil-sprung—"autochthonous."

This was no metaphor, no labored conceit. To the Athenians, it was the simple, literal truth. When they trod their native land, the dusty paths that wound over the hills of Attica, her plains and rocky valleys, they knew they were as much a part of the landscape as the clumps of marjoram and heady-smelling thyme, or the meadows of spectral asphodels, beloved of the gods, or the marble that might sometimes be glimpsed through the scrub of a mountain slope. Here was a mystery profounder by far than those claimed by other Greeks when they traced fabulous bloodlines for themselves and boasted of divine descent. Indeed, it would have been blasphemy for an Athenian to pretend to any such thing. After all, the goddess whom they worshipped as their protector and from whom they took their name was Athena: the gray-eyed warrior, mistress of the arts, daughter of Wisdom—and a virgin. Not for her, sublime and enigmatic, the indignities of childbirth. No man would ever possess her. The nearest anyone had come to achieving that was when her brother Hephaestus, the crippled blacksmith of the gods, whose talents of craftsmanship were as limitless as his bandy legs were weak, had been so overcome with desire for his sister that he had hobbled after her, sweaty and soot-stained, and sought to take her in his arms. Athena, with icy contempt, had brushed him aside—but not before Hephaestus, shuddering with excitement, had ejaculated all over her thigh. Wiping the mess off with a tangle of wool, the goddess had then dropped it, still sodden, down onto Attica—where the semen, like heavy dew, had moistened the womb of Mother Earth. From this fertilizing of "the grain-giving fields" had been born a child with the coiled tail of a snake. Athena, adopting him, had named him Erechtheus.[3] She had settled him on the Acropolis, "in her own wealthy temple," and there, "to this day, with each revolving of the year, the sons of Athens offer him bulls and rams."[4]

Hardly the kind of story that a Heraclid would promote. That the Athenians were content to ascribe the origins of their city to a discarded toss rag speaks eloquently of the significance that the myth possessed for them. Over the centuries it would be increasingly elaborated, but its roots were ancient, and reflected an equally ancient truth. The Athenians were indeed, just as they insisted, a people distinct. Whether their borders had really remained as sacrosanct as they would later claim seems improbable, but Attica, of all the regions of Greece, had certainly best weathered the storm that brought the palace of Menelaus and many other proud capitals blazing into ruin. Throughout the turmoil and obscurity of the centuries that followed, the various communities of Attica had preserved a sense of themselves as a discrete nation, united by shared customs, dialect and race. Emerging from their dark age, they were still able to recollect that they, at any rate, had never been homeless migrants, but were "the oldest people of Greece."[5]

True, Athens, right until the seventh century BC, was, like Sparta, little more than a shabby village, huddled ingloriously around the rock of its acropolis. Nor did the people of other settlements yet think of themselves as Athenians, or even, it may be, as citizens of a single state.[6] Yet the Acropolis itself, sheer and immense, served all the communities of Attica as a natural focus of veneration, since every valley led to it; nor was there any other Attic sanctuary that could rival its aura of mystery. Rectangles of masonry so heavy that it was evident only giants could have raised them ringed its summit in an immense wall. Ruins incalculably ancient testified to its use in former times by heroes and kings.* Sanctified by the presence of Athena, whose dwelling place it was, its rock served also as the tomb of Erechtheus, the earth-born one. So it was that all the people of Attica, not just the Athenians, could look upon the Acropolis and be reminded of the soil from which they had sprung, of the inheritance which they shared, and of the loyalty to their homeland which they owed.

The result was a regional identity unlike any other in Greece. That Athens stood dominant as the only city in the whole of Attica was, in the eyes of other Greeks, both startling and aberrant. Boeotia, an area of similar size to its neighbor, was carved up between no fewer than ten squabbling states. Argos, the most populous city in the Peloponnese, ruled a plain that was barely half the size of Attica. Only Sparta, of the Greek powers, controlled a broader swath of territory than Athens did—but hers had been won, and was held, at the point of a sword. The Athenians themselves had never attempted anything remotely as energetic. In the seventh century BC, while the Spartans were completing their pacification of Messenia and cities throughout Greece were swirling with violent currents, a visitor to Attica from Argos or Corinth would have found it a somnolent backwater. The Athenians positively shrank from dipping their toes into the flood tides

---

*Fragments of a Bronze Age palace would still have been visible on the summit of the Acropolis in the seventh century BC.

of the modern. Not for them the military and political revolutions that were affecting the rest of Greece, and were transforming Sparta, in particular, into something perilous and new. Rather than submit to a similar experiment, the Athenians preferred the security of parochialism and nostalgia. In comparison to those on even the smallest Aegean islands, their temples were poky and unimpressive; their funeral practices self-consciously archaic; even their pottery, which provided employment for a full quarter of the city, and had once been the most innovative in Greece, increasingly harked back to the past. Just as the rest of the Greek world was fixing its gaze on dazzling new horizons, the Athenians seemed to be set on returning to the age of the Trojan War.[7]

And indeed, in the structure of their society, it was as though they had never really left it. Out in the fields and groves of Attica, a whole day's journey from Athens, perhaps, or maybe more, a man might easily live less as a citizen than as a serf, as a sharecropper, paying a sixth of all he earned to a distant landlord. The landlords themselves, in the traditional manner of heroes, lived well apart from the common run, marrying into one another's houses, parceling out magistracies to one another, and sneering at everyone else with a roistering contempt. Such was the desire for exclusivity of some aristocratic clans that they even turned their noses up at what was commonly an Athenian's proudest boast, and would trace exotic foreign lineages for themselves from the assorted stars of the Trojan War. One family, the Pisistratids, claimed descent from a Messenian king; another, the Philaids, from Ajax, the tallest warrior to have fought on either side at Troy, and a king of Salamis, an island just off the Attic coast. Well might the Athenian nobility have awarded themselves the title "Eupatrids," or "Well-bred." There was no other aristocracy in Greece quite so snobbishly stuck in the past.

But the forces for change in the world beyond Athens were not easily kept at bay, and by 600 BC even the Eupatrids were starting to embrace them. Cosmopolitanism, for those with sufficient fashion sense, had long promised ready entry to an international fast set. Its members felt their truest sense of identity not with compatriots from the grubbing lower classes but with fellow sophisticates from across the entire Greek world. "I simply adore the good things of life":[8] a statement unimaginable upon the lips of a stern and shaggy hero, but raising no eyebrows whatsoever among those who believed that luxury held up a mirror to the gods. Even a woman, if her tastes were sufficiently elegant, her jewelry golden, her robes soft and richly dyed, might hope to glimpse and converse with the divine: "Come, rainbow-throned and immortal goddess of love, if ever in the past you heard my far-off cries and heeded them, leaving your father's halls, travelling in your chariot of gold, your pretty sparrows bearing you swiftly upon the fluttering of their wings, down from heaven through the sky to the dark earth."[9] A prayer well worth raising—for pleasures, properly enjoyed, might indeed lift scales from mortal eyes, and a dinner party provide a better-ordered realm than any state. The seductions of high society, delicate and perfumed as they were, exerted on those who could afford them an almost spiritual allure. Taste as well as breeding had become the mark of the elite.

Yet what defined it also served to threaten it. The passion for luxuries, most of which had to be shipped from glamorous locations overseas, inevitably boosted the fortunes of those with their fingers in the import-export trade. Capital, which had previously been tied up almost exclusively in the estates of the nobility, grew increasingly liquid. By 600 BC, a momentous innovation was being introduced to the cities of Ionia: coinage. Over the following decades, it would cross the Aegean and begin to circulate in Greece. The aristocracy, unsurprisingly, reacted with disgust and mounting alarm. They bristled at the prospect of a businessman having the same spending power as a Eupatrid, and responded with increasingly frantic insults. "*Kakoi*," they called the *nouveaux riches*: the "low-born," the "unpleasant," the "cheats." The *Kakoi* themselves, however, as they could afford to do, merely shrugged their shoulders and continued to rake in the cash. After all, as a Spartan had once pointed out, back in the days of his own city's social upheavals, "A man is nothing but the sum of what he owns." Fitting slogan for a new and perplexing age.

"Gold is the only thing that makes for breeding now." So, with a curling of the lip, might the *déclassé* nobleman complain. "There is no other basis of esteem."[10]

The Spartans themselves, of course, once so convulsed by precisely such complaints, had long since evolved their own remedy. To many, in the Attica of the 590s BC, it must have seemed as though history were repeating itself. Once again, just as in Lacedaemon a century previously, a whole region of Greece was crippled by an agrarian crisis. Never before had the property market been so fluid. As impoverished noblemen, threatened with the loss of their patrimony, tightened the screws on their tenants, so misery was passed down the food chain to the very poorest, from the mansions of great families to the barest, rockiest plots. Creditors, mapping the limits of mortgaged olive groves and fields, filled the countryside with ominous lines of stones. They might just as well have been marking out the graves of ruined peasants.

As it worsened, the land famine drew an inevitable recourse. Just over the straits from southern Attica, temptingly, indeed irresistibly, close, lay the island of Salamis. Athenian scholars, adducing complex arguments from ancient epics, were able to demonstrate, at least to their own satisfaction, that Ajax's old kingdom belonged to them. News, certainly, to the citizens of Megara, a small city midway between Athens and Corinth, which also laid claim to Salamis, and indeed had planted it with settlers. The two cities duly went to war. Athens was defeated and forced to sue for peace. All the more galling for the vanquished was the fact that Megara, tiny as she was, ranked only as a third-rate power. The Athenians plunged into a gloomy introspection. Racked by crisis at home, humiliated abroad, they could no longer deny that they were punching woefully below their weight. Something was rotten in the state of Athens.

Spectral figures began to be glimpsed on the streets of the city, seeming portents of imminent ruin. So desperate did the situation appear that the Athenians, with that Greek enthusiasm for one-man think tanks best exemplified by the tales told of Lycurgus, began to cast around for a sage. Fortunately for them, a ready candidate was at hand. In 594 BC,[11]

Solon, universally held to be the wisest man in Athens (not to mention one of the seven wisest Greeks who had ever lived), was given the archonship, the city's supreme magistracy, and entrusted with the task of saving the state. His appointment, remarkably in a society as class-riven as Athens', met with universal applause. The blue-blooded descendant of an ancient Attic king, Solon had also dabbled in trade, while simultaneously letting slip to the poor his sense of outrage at their plight. Here was a man who could appeal to all his constituencies.

Skilled though he was at tailoring his pitch to his audience, however, Solon was no mere idle trimmer. His brand of wisdom was of a peculiarly muscular variety. It was he, only a year before becoming archon, who had rallied Greek opinion to the defense of Delphi when the impious city of Crisa had sought to annex the oracle. His own city's defeat by Megara had inspired him to even greater heights of outrage. "Let's head for Salamis," he had urged in impassioned verse, "fight for that beautiful island, wipe ourselves clean of the disgrace."[12] Now, as head of state, he was in a position to do more than sloganeer. It was evident to Solon that the two great crises facing Athens, agrarian and military, both sprang from the same root: rural impoverishment was enfeebling the reserves of Attic manpower; farmers were sinking ever deeper into serfdom. The poor, if truly desperate, might even stake their freedom against their debts, perhaps ending up chained and shackled as slaves in their own fields. Solon, had he displayed the calculating mercilessness of a Lycurgus, could easily have sponsored this trend, and condemned his city's poor to a permanent helotage. Instead, he chose to redeem them. Even those who had been sold abroad, even those "who had forgotten how to speak the Attic dialect," were liberated, while in Attica itself, wherever property had been mortgaged, Solon ordered a general pardoning of debts. Out in the fields, men were set to work "digging up the boundary-stones where they had been set in the dark earth."[13]

Most landlords, naturally enough, were outraged; but Solon, playing the selfless sage to the hilt, argued sternly that his reforms were in their interests, too. After all, without the bedrock provided by a free peasantry, what hope was there of capturing Salamis, or of preserving Athens from social meltdown, or of winning for the city a rank commensurate with her size? Yes, Solon had sought to ease the sufferings of the poor—but he had also labored hard to keep the rich in power. The Eupatrids, holding their noses, had duly been persuaded into an alliance with the *Kakoi*; wealth rather than birth made the prerequisite for office; the poor, although granted membership of a citizens' assembly, denied the privilege of speaking in it. It was a triumph not for revolution but for a hard-fought middle way. "Envied for their wealth though they were," Solon pointed out, "I sought to preserve the powerful from the hatred of the oppressed. Taking my stand, I used my strong shield to protect both sides of the class divide, allowing neither to gain an advantage over the other that would be unjust."[14]

The boast, in short, of an instinctive centrist. Solon's watchword was the traditional one of *eunomia*: that familiar Greek dream of a just and natural order, one in which all would know their place, and "rough edges would be smoothed out, appetites tamed, and presumption curbed."[15] What was such an ideal, after all, if not the birthright of the earth-sprung Athenian people? Far from launching a novel political experiment, Solon saw himself as engaged in an act of restoration and repair. With a talent for reinventing history that would have done credit to a Spartan, he persuaded his city that the constitution he had drafted was in fact the very one she had possessed in her distant past. Copies of his laws, inscribed in public on revolving wooden tablets, served to spell this out to every class of citizen. To the poor, they guaranteed freedom and legal recourse against the abuses of the powerful; to the rich, they gave exclusive right to magistracies and the running of the city. What could be fairer, more natural, more traditional, than that?

Before relinquishing power and departing Athens for a ten-year Mediterranean cruise,* Solon decreed that his laws should remain in

---

*It was during the Egyptian leg of this trip that Solon, according to Plato, was told the story of Atlantis.

force for a minimum of a century. No sooner had he set sail, however, than familiar problems began to raise their ugly heads. *Eunomia* was not as easily maintained in Athens as the departed Solon had cared to hope. Their powers left untrammeled, the nobility swaggered and feuded just as they had always done. Beyond Athens herself, Attica remained a patchwork of rival loyalties and clans. The war for Salamis, although it scored some successes, continued to drag on. Despite all Solon's efforts, Athens remained very much the sick man of Greece.

Even so, his reforms had set in motion something momentous. Moved by the legends of his city, and by her claims to antiquity and to the favor of the gods, Solon had taken for granted that here was a heritage upon which every Athenian had a claim. Scandalized at the sight of his countrymen laboring in bondage amid the dust from which their ancestors had sprung, he had ordered their chains struck off. There could be no doubting, from that moment on, who was an Athenian and who was not. Nothing, of course, like the spectacle of another's servitude to boost one's self-esteem: thanks to Solon, even the poorest peasant could now look down upon a slave, and know himself to be as free as the haughtiest Eupatrid. Admittedly, he was not as much of a citizen; how could he be when he was barred from standing for office or making his voice heard in debate? Yet the rich, even though they still hugged political power to themselves, could not entirely afford to ignore him and his fellows. The poor may have been silent in the Assembly—but not without a vote. "For in their hands lay the power to elect officials, and to review their performances—and indeed, had the people been denied even this privilege, then they would still have ranked as little more than slaves."[16]

Clearly, a new and intriguing cross-current had been added to the endless swirl of aristocratic rivalries. How best to negotiate it was a challenge that every ambitious nobleman would henceforward have to meet. There was certainly no call for him to kowtow to the poor— the very idea would have been ludicrous!—but success or failure, even for a Eupatrid, might now depend on a show of hands. Tanners, carpenters, farmhands, potters, blacksmiths: any or all of these might come to the Assembly to use their votes. Even as they continued to make policy in the closed rooms of their mansions, the elite could not afford entirely to forget where sovereignty now resided. As befitted a city with earth-sprung origins, it lay not only with the Eupatrids, nor even with the rich alone, but with the Assembly of all the Athenians, with the people—with the "*demos.*"

I Capture the Acropolis

It was no surprise that Athena should have chosen the Acropolis as her residence. For a start, there was the view. Five hundred feet above the rest of Athens, even a mortal could see for miles around. To the south, an hour's walk away, lay Phalerum, the open bay which served the Athenians as their port; to the west, blocking off the view of Salamis, the peak of Mount Aigaleos; to the northeast another mountain, Pentelikon, where workmen from Athens would travel to quarry marble, gashing its slopes with scars. To a goddess, of course, shimmering through the brightness of the sky, this would have presented no obstruction; but to mortals, road-bound, it was altogether more of a challenge. Two trails circumvented the mountain, one winding northward, the other circling south. Noblemen, in particular, heading out from Athens, were frequent travelers on the loop around Pentelikon—for beyond it, level and beach-fringed, lay the perfect location for one of the aristocracy's favorite sports. Horses and their trainers flourished at Marathon.

But the steepling heights of the Acropolis afforded more than a view alone. Down beyond its cliffs, in the cramped and booming city, the narrow alleyways were no fitting home for a goddess. Unpaved, often rocky, and invariably encrusted with filth, the streets of Athens wound and twisted without plan. Dogs and chickens, goats and pigs and cows, all of them added to the stench—and to the fleas. Carts, rumbling and creaking along specially scored grooves, added to the noise. Athens, by the 560s BC, had long since stopped stewing in her

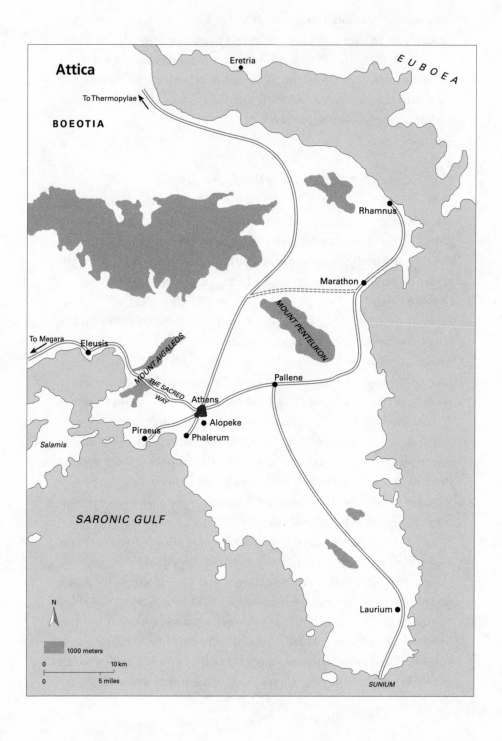

Attica

EUBOEA

Eretria

BOEOTIA

To Thermopylae

To Megara

Eleusis

MOUNT AIGALEOS

THE SACRED WAY

Rhamnus

Marathon

MOUNT PENTELIKON

Pallene

Athens

Piraeus

Alopeke

Phalerum

Salamis

SARONIC GULF

Laurium

SUNIUM

N

1000 meters

0   10 km

0   5 miles

own backwardness. There were always wagons in the city, piled high with wares, and especially pottery, for in ceramics Athenian craftsmen now led the world. One area of the city was even named after it—although, in truth, the Ceramicus was just as famous for its cemetery and cheap whores.

How very much more elevated, then, in every sense, were the heights of the Acropolis. The bare rock left no doubt as to their sanctity. There, growing from the stone, rose the primal olive tree, gift of Athena and as old as Athens herself. Indeed, it was said to be immortal; but the Athenians, playing safe, and naturally not wishing to see it stripped bare of its foliage, had elected to ban goats from the hill; all save one, once a year, which would be led up to the summit and offered in sacrifice to the gods. Indeed, only a single creature was permitted on the sacred rock: a serpent. This lived in an enclosure near the tomb of Erechtheus, the snake-tailed, earth-born first citizen of Athens, where priestesses would lovingly feed it honey cakes. Men whispered that if it vanished, then the city was doomed to fall.

Yet that the snake was content to reside on the Acropolis at all could be reckoned a miracle. Sanctified it might be, yet it was hardly a place of calm. For years, it had been a permanent building site. Around 575 BC, a great stone ramp, some 250 feet in length, had been pile-driven up to the gateway of the ancient citadel, permanently improving access to the summit—and the workmen had promptly moved in. Over the following years, the hammering had never stopped. What had previously been a jumble of primitive ruins was transformed into a shrine as spectacular as any in Greece. Not only masonry, but statues of every conceivable size crowded the summit: those of young men with snail-shell curls and mocking smiles; of dimpled maidens with falling tresses, pleated cloaks and skin-tight gowns; of gorgons, luridly painted; of prancing horses and snarling lions. In images such as these, faint, perhaps, but unmistakable, could be caught a glimpse of the influence of the East, fabulous and rarefied, the home of unimaginably rich and mighty kings. The days of provincialism, in short, were well and truly over. There was nothing remotely inward-looking about the Athenians' sanctuary now.

Except that none of the work was actually done in the name of the Athenians. Far from signaling an outbreak of civic harmony, the dust-clouds on the Acropolis conveyed precisely the opposite message. Every building project was the gift of a different clan. What better way, after all, for a Eupatrid to show off than to adorn the city's skyline? To excel was, for a nobleman, not merely to cut a political dash but to emulate the age of heroes, to mimic the deathless gods. "Always be the bravest," warriors in the Trojan War had been admonished. "Always be the best."[17] Centuries later, this was a message that an aristocrat still drank in with his milk. For the upper classes across the whole Greek world, it served as a virtual manifesto. This was why, if a partiality for dinner parties was one mark of the cosmopolitan elite, then another distinguishing feature had become, during the seventh century BC, a relish for sport: spectacular contests of stamina and skill, in which the *jeunesse dorée*, glistening and gym-perfected, would compete with their fellow noblemen for public glory. True, the first victor at the Olympic Games was said to have been a cook, and an occasional goatherd might still sneak a fairy-tale victory, but in general only those with time and money could afford to put in the ten months' training officially required by the rules. By the first half of the sixth century, the games at Olympia had been supplemented by a whole circuit of other festivals, so competitors might, and often did, spend year after year on the road, sculpting and toning their bodies, schmoozing with other members of the Greek world's *crème de la crème*. In 566 BC, even the Athenians, who in the previous century had been defiantly sniffy about the Olympics, got in on the act. A magnificent festival in honor of Athena, the Great Panathenaea, was inaugurated in their city, at which the prizes included, as well as glory, a huge amphora of olive oil. *Grands projets* on the Acropolis, an athlete's trophies: both spoke of "the sweetness" that was "triumph and wondrous fame."[18]

Yet the applause was not universal. Glamour and self-glorification might be all very well at Olympia, but not, say, for hoplites advancing into battle. It was notable that the Spartans, raised as they were to subordinate their individuality to a collective, were the only people in Greece to play team games; notable also that they displayed a marked ambivalence toward their Olympic athletes. A competitor from elsewhere in Greece who won first prize at the Games might expect to have statues raised in his honor, or receive a bounty, or even breach a section of his native city's walls, "to convey," so it was said, "that a state with such a citizen hardly had need of fortifications."[19] No such nonsense for the Spartans—not least because they had no city walls to pull down in the first place. Naturally, since their prestige was at stake, their athletes were expected to compete and win at Olympia, but memorials to their victories, back at Sparta, were conspicuous by their absence. The returning champions themselves were granted no reward save the distinctly hazardous one of a posting to the front line of battle, directly before the king.

For always, with the exceptional, with the godlike, there was menace. There rose, in the universe of things, a scale of perfection, towering like Mount Olympus, with the immortals on the summit, and mortals down in the foothills, eternally looking to climb higher. But it was perilous for a man to reach too far. The dangers that resulted might plunge not only the hero but all who knew him— indeed, all his city—into ruin. That the Athenians, for instance, back in the days of their insularity, were not being merely provincial in their suspicion of international athletics had been amply demonstrated by the fate of Cylon, a Eupatrid, and one of their few Olympic stars. The champion, returning home with his victor's olive crown, had eventually grown so puffed up with conceit that he had dared, in 632 BC, to occupy the Acropolis and proclaim himself master of Athens. The scandalized city had been plunged into street fighting. Cylon and his followers had found themselves barricaded on the hill; they had sought sanctuary in a temple; granted a promise of free passage by the archon, they had duly emerged, only to be stoned and put to death.[20] A salutary lesson on the bitter fruits of setting one's sights too high.

Except that in states more in tune with the modern than Athens, men such as Cylon had already proved themselves vanguards of the future. There were few leading cities anywhere in the Greek world that did not at some point during the seventh and sixth centuries BC fall into the hands of a high-aiming strongman—with Sparta, as ever, the exception that proved the rule. "*Tyrannides*," the Greeks called such regimes—"tyrannies." For them, the term did not have remotely the bloodstained connotations that the English word "tyrant" has for us. Indeed, a Greek tyrant, almost by definition, had to have the popular touch, since otherwise he could not hope to cling to power for long. Trumpets, slogans and public works: such were the enthusiasms he would invariably parade. He would also be expected to provide, to a people that might have been racked by faction-fighting for decades, the stamp of firm government—at the very least. Most provided a good deal more: Periander, a celebrated tyrant of Corinth, for instance, proved so consummate a statesman that he was remembered, along with Solon, as one of the seven sages of Greece.* Naturally, in exchange for granting his fellow citizens the blessings of order and prosperity, a tyrant could be expected to make a few demands of his own. He might require that certain illegal measures, certain regret-table precautions, be overlooked: bodyguards, for instance; controls on free speech; the occasional midnight knocking on doors.

It was the tyrant's own peers, of course, who would wince most painfully at these humiliations. Few greater torments could be imag-ined for an aristocrat than to endure a tyranny: the equivalent of watching a single champion win every race, year after year. No wonder

---

*Other traditions, it is fair to say, remembered Periander in a far less favorable light. He is said to have been so crazed that he killed his wife, then made love to her corpse; to have castrated three hundred boys from an enemy city; and to have given silent advice on statecraft to a fellow tyrant by walking through a field and lopping off the tallest ears of corn with a stick. The contradictions in the historical record well reflect the ambivalence with which the Greeks tended to regard the institution of tyranny.

that Megacles, the archon who had tricked Cylon's followers from their temple sanctuary to their deaths, had been willing to risk the taint of sacrilege—for he had been head of the Alcmaeonids, one of the grandest of all Athenian clans, descended from a king, proud and high-aspiring, and certainly no man's slave. And, to be sure, the penalty he and all his family paid had been a terrible one. Even in defense of freedom, a crime such as Megacles had committed against the gods could not be readily forgiven. It had taken a full thirty years of furious foot-dragging by the Alcmaeonids before they were finally brought to court; but Megacles' clan, in the end, around 600 BC, had all been sentenced to exile in perpetuity.[21] The moldering bones of their ancestors had been dug up and dumped beyond the borders of the city. The Alcmaeonids had become a family accursed.

But even absent from Athens, they continued to cast a long and glamorous shadow. Indeed, if anything, the curse only contributed to their menacing allure. It was typical of the Alcmaeonids' cool effrontery that the moment they were exiled they entered into a hugely profitable relationship of mutual back-scratching with—of all people—the priests at Delphi. Megacles' son Alcmaeon, displaying a particularly shameless aptitude for hypocrisy, led the campaign against the sacrilegious city of Crisa. He then successfully wangled himself into serving as the middleman between the grateful oracle and King Croesus, and reaped fabulous rewards—for Croesus was so pleased with his agent's diplomacy that he invited him to visit the royal treasury in Sardis and take away all the gold that he could carry.[22] Alcmaeon capitalized on this offer, it was said, by wearing a baggy woman's tunic and the loosest boots that he could find, and then filling them with gold dust; so that "when he came staggering out, he could scarcely drag one foot after the other, his tunic bulged obscenely, and even his cheeks were stuffed full to bursting."[23]

Still the Alcmaeonids' gaze remained fixed longingly on their native city, even though the view by the 560s BC had become an increasingly discouraging one. Athens in that decade seemed firmly under the thumb of a Eupatrid of immense hauteur, Lycurgus, head of the Boutads, a clan of such impeccable breeding that it could claim descent from the brother of Erechtheus himself. This bloodline provided Lycurgus with an almost proprietary claim on the Acropolis—a perk which, with the eye of a natural impresario, he had exploited to the full. Lycurgus, almost certainly, had been responsible for the construction of the massive ramp leading to the summit, and for the inauguration of the city's premier new festival, the Great Panathenaea. Indisputably, he officiated in the most venerable temple on the entire Acropolis, that of Athena Polias, the "Guardian of the City."[24] Modest and old fashioned this shrine may have been, but it contained within its murk an object of incalculable holiness: a statue that had fallen from the sky in far-off times, a self-portrait fashioned out of olive wood by Athena herself.[25] Ramp, festival, idol: Lycurgus' fingerprints were over them all. Staged for the first time in 566 BC, and then every four years after that, whenever the Great Panathenaea was held, a great procession would climb the ramp to the temple of Athena and present to the statue, which was already wearing around its neck a golden gorgon's head, a beautifully embroidered robe, woven by the noblest maidens of the city. Hoplites and cavalrymen, venerable elders and young girls, even foreigners resident in the city, all would take their places in the spectacular cavalcade. A show, in short, that provided the Boutads with publicity to die for.

Not that Lycurgus was the only headline act in the 560s BC. Amid all the excitement of the festivities back in Athens, a general by the name of Pisistratus was at last bringing to an end the running embarrassment of the war for Salamis. Although he certainly did not lack for connections—he was even said to have been Solon's beloved as a boy—Pisistratus had no illusions that he could challenge the Boutads when it came to snob appeal. By the end of the decade, however, with Megara defeated and Salamis at last securely in Athenian hands, he had fostered a formidable prestige. Not merely a war hero, Pisistratus was also a charmer and a schemer, blessed with the popular touch, and possessed of a rare eye for the opportunities created by Solon's reforms. Having first cast himself as the spokesman for the poorest of the rural poor, he then faked a dramatic assault upon himself, and appealed to the Assembly for bodyguards. Despite the lucubrations of Solon, his by now ancient former lover, who emerged from retirement to warn banefully of a looming tyranny, Pisistratus was given what he had requested—and promptly occupied the Acropolis.

The Alcmaeonids, still in exile, but sniffing the air, now suddenly smelled their chance. Feelers were put out to the Boutads; Lycurgus, stunned by the coup into a dramatic reappraisal of his objections to an Alcmaeonid return, found himself hurriedly swallowing them. A rapprochement between the two great clans was duly concocted. Against such a heavyweight pairing, there was little that Pisistratus could do. His position began to crumble by the day. Rather than make a doomed stand, as Cylon had done, he opted to cut his losses and flee into exile.

Perhaps, however, amid the seeming ruin of all his hopes, Pisistratus was able to reassure himself that his time would come again. He must have calculated that the Alcmaeonids—devious, arrogant and obscenely wealthy—would hardly make easy partners for anyone. Whatever the precise terms of their agreement with Lycurgus, it appeared unlikely that they would rest content with playing second fiddle to him for long. And, sure enough, no sooner had they returned to Athens than the Alcmaeonids were fixing their calculating gaze upon that natural stage for self-advertisement, the Acropolis, and tapping their reserves of Lydian gold. It appears probable, at the very least, that an immense stone temple raised around this time, and the first of such a scale built on the Acropolis, was the work of the Alcmaeonids.[26] Who else would have had the resources—or the motive—to sponsor such a project? Lavishly decorated, with brightly painted snakes, and bulls, and lions, with fish-tailed Tritons, and triple-bodied men with trim blue beards, the temple could hardly have been a more flamboyant statement of intent. Certainly, it put the shabby old shrine of Athena Polias, and the Boutads with it, thoroughly in the shade.

But new, in the opinion of the Athenians, was not necessarily best. The Alcmaeonids' temple may have been spectacular, but it lacked what gave the older shrine its peculiar sanctity: the presence of Athena herself. By the mid-550s, as the relationship between Alcmaeonids and Boutads turned increasingly bitter, the former were beginning to cast around for a fresh way to trump Lycurgus, and claim the favor of Athena for themselves. They found it, with a fine display of opportunism, in alliance with the very man they had driven into exile barely five years previously—and the concoction of a wonderfully far-fetched plot. First, to cement the dynastic alliance, Pisistratus was obliged to separate from his wife, a blue-blooded Argive by the name of Timonassa, and marry into the Alcmaeonid clan. Next, returning to Attica, he headed to a village just south of Mount Pentelikon. A flower-seller lived there, a towering woman of exceptional beauty, with the apt name of Phye—"Stature." Pisistratus, adorning this peasant woman with the helmet and armor of Athena and placing her in a chariot, had her driven on the road that led to Athens, with messengers going before them both, proclaiming that the goddess was leading her favorite in person to the Acropolis. An outrageous stunt—but Pisistratus somehow pulled it off. No one thought to laugh at the procession; rather, all flocked to gawk at it. To many Athenians, awestruck by the spectacle of a goddess riding through the streets of their city, it seemed a magical and wondrous epiphany; to others, watching as the chariot wound its way to the Acropolis, a dazzling piece of theater. After all, not even that consummate showman Lycurgus had thought to have Athena appear in person to grace his temple. The Alcmaeonids had, in every sense, pulled off a coup.

And Pisistratus, having captured the Acropolis a second time, had already outlived his usefulness to them. Smoothly stabbing their in-law in the back, the Alcmaeonids began to circulate a shocking rumor.[27] Not only, it was whispered, had Pisistratus been denying his wife the pleasures that were the due of any bride; he had also, like the monster he self-evidently was, been sating his own desires upon her purebred body in loathsome and unnatural ways. Family honor, once Athens was buzzing with the scandal, positively obliged the Alcmaeonids to turn on their erstwhile partner; even if it meant building bridges with Lycurgus, their erstwhile foe. Pisistratus, once again confronted by an alliance of the city's two most powerful families, retreated hurriedly into a second ignominious exile. Athens was left, as before, in the hands of the Alcmaeonids and the Boutads. This time, however, there could be no doubt as to which was the preeminent clan.

But in double-crossing Pisistratus, the Alcmaeonids had sorely underestimated their man. Indeed, by using him and then dropping him in so perfidious a manner, they had provided him with an invaluable master class in the darker political arts. Pisistratus, over the next decade, would show that he had learned the lesson well. Somehow persuading the jilted Timonassa to return to him, he also succeeded in patching up his friendship with her relatives back in Argos. Wealthy backers in Thebes were similarly charmed into giving him sponsorship. A fortune was raised, and an invasion force recruited. By 546 BC, Pisistratus was ready. He and his men landed on the shallow beaches at Marathon. Here he was assured of a warm welcome—for the Pisistratids had always had close family links with the villages on the plain. The Alcmaeonids appear not to have been unduly alarmed. Taking the southern road around Mount Pentelikon, they led an army in a desultory manner as far as the village of Pallene. There, in a manner that spoke loudly of their contempt for their former stooge, they halted to have their lunch, even though Pisistratus was closing in. The engagement, when it came, was a rout: the Athenians, surprised mid-snack by an army that included both Theban cavalry and a thousand crack Argive hoplites, turned and fled in a rabble back to Athens. Left behind in the dust of Pallene lay at least one Alcmaeonid, killed "in the front line of battle."[28] The surviving members of the family, rather than returning with their defeated army to Athens, there to await the vengeance of Pisistratus, fled across the Attic border—exiles once again.

Pisistratus himself, meanwhile, relishing his triumph, continued his advance on Athens. It hardly needed a goddess now to proclaim him her favorite. Once again he climbed the great ramp that led to the

Acropolis and took possession of the summit. Surpassingly gracious, Pisistratus then informed his fellow citizens "that they should not be alarmed or downcast, but should go and attend to their private business, leaving all the burdens of state for him to shoulder."[29] The Athenians, in acknowledgment of their submission, turned and did as their new master had instructed, reckoning—and relieved, perhaps—that this time the tyrant was surely there to stay.

Drama out of a Crisis

And so it proved. No more foreign travels for Pisistratus. With a silky ruthlessness that showed he had nothing left to learn now from the exiled Alcmaeonids, he alternately menaced and lulled his fellow Eupatrids into an unprecedented docility. The children of prominent rivals were packed off as hostages to the Aegean island of Naxos. Slaves from the steppes of Scythia, a savage wilderness far to the north of Greece, appeared suddenly on patrol in the streets, an alarming sight for any citizen, armed as the police squads were with bows and arrows, and wearing outlandish pointed caps. Competitive building on the Acropolis, now that there was only the one show in town, slowly ground to a halt. Yet Pisistratus, even as he kept the city's richest pickings for himself, was careful also to throw his rivals the occasional juicy scrap: a magistracy, perhaps, or an overseas command.

Even the grandest were content to accept his patronage. Miltiades, for instance, head of the Philaids, was given permission to lead an expedition across the Aegean to the Hellespont, the narrow strait which divides Asia from Europe, and is known today as the Dardanelles. Miltiades, relieved to be able to spread his wings, enthusiastically seized his chance. Arriving in the Hellespont, he landed on the Chersonese, the thin peninsula which forms the European bank of the strait, and from which access to the Black Sea, and its corn-gold shores, could easily be controlled. There he threw himself into a brisk war of pacification, not only against the natives, but against any Greek colonists already established there who might presume to stand in his way. Then, with his authority firmly established over the whole peninsula, he settled down, with Pisistratus' blessing, to establish a tyranny of his own. This left everyone—the hapless victims of his campaigns aside, of course—a winner. Certainly, no news could have been better designed to gladden Athenian hearts. Attica, with its thin soil and booming population, had long since outgrown self-sufficiency, and the dread of starvation, even as Athens prospered, was never far away. To Pisistratus, the man who could boast of having sent Miltiades to the Chersonese, and thereby securing it for the Athenian people, immense gratitude was naturally due. The tyrant himself—who had succeeded in keeping his fellow citizens in bread, secured a vital trade route for Athenian business and disposed of a potentially dangerous rival, all with one deft move— could reflect with satisfaction on a job well done.

This killing of multiple birds with a single, well-directed stone was a classic Pisistratid throw. Why, after all, rest content with neutralizing the Eupatrids when there were businessmen, potters and farmers to woo as well? Solon, years previously, had dared to ask an identical question—but he had shrunk in horror from the answer. "Only hand another man the goad I was given," he had warned with grim self-satisfaction, "someone unscrupulous and on the make, and you will see how he lets the mob run wild."[30] Solon had spoken with the moral authority of a man who had spurned the temptations of tyranny; but Pisistratus, despite having wholeheartedly surrendered to them, could claim with some justification that he was only following his old lover's middle way. If his manipulation of aristocratic rivals owed much to a path already blazed by the Alcmaeonids, then he was, in his concern for the *demos,* just as obviously drawing on the example of Solon himself. This was why, autocrat though Pisistratus undoubtedly was, his scrupulous show of respect for the Assembly—"like a citizen rather than a tyrant,"[31] observers said—was more than mere spin. Not for him the nose-wrinkling of his fellow Eupatrids as they deigned to curry favor with stinking laborers or tradesmen. Pisistratus actively courted popular enthusiasm for his regime. He would tirelessly tour the countryside, pressing the flesh of the humblest fieldhands, bringing justice to the remotest croft, "so that those with complaints would not have to travel all the way to Athens, and get behind with their business."[32] Meanwhile, back in the city itself, builders were set to work on the construction of a spectacular new square at the foot of the Acropolis, one that would soon sound to fresh water, bubbling from nine fountains, and gleam with the brilliance of freshly chiseled marble. How could any Athenian, gawking at such unexampled scenes, have any doubts about the tyrant's greatness or his beneficence? Athens truly seemed to have entered "a golden age."[33]

There was certainly little enthusiasm for any talk of liberty. In the spring of 527 BC, when Pisistratus finally passed away peacefully in his own bed, his two sons, Hippias and Hipparchus, succeeded without challenge to his nineteen-year reign of peace. An ambassador of the Persian king, should one have been sent to attend to the business of so remote and obscure a city, would have had no difficulty in identifying the form of government that appeared to prevail in Athens—and to be sure, in the character of the two brothers' reign there was indeed a whiff of monarchy. Their tastes, to a degree exceptional even by the standards of their father, ran to the monumental. Any citizen who doubted that had only to look to the southeast of Athens, yet another scene of hammering and chiseling, where the Pisistratids, not content with the ongoing beautification of their father's magnificent square, had embarked upon an even more ambitious showcase: a temple to Zeus so breathtakingly vast that philosophers, goggling at the site centuries later, would compare it to the pyramids.

But Hippias and Hipparchus were no pharaohs. Showy though their building projects were, they actually held no formal rank within the city at all. Just as the site on which the great columns of their temple were being erected was an ancient one, long sacred to Zeus, so the Pisistratids themselves, confronted by the natural conservatism of their fellow citizens, had felt it best to root their authority in the subsoil of tradition. It was one thing for them to indulge in the enthu-

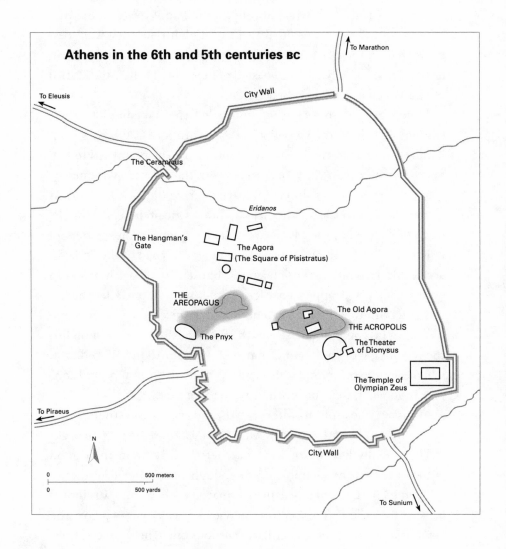

Athens in the 6th and 5th centuries BC

To Marathon

To Eleusis

City Wall

The Ceramicus

Eridanos

The Hangman's
Gate

The Agora
(The Square of Pisistratus)

THE
AREOPAGUS

The Old Agora

THE ACROPOLIS

The Pnyx

The Theater
of Dionysus

The Temple of
Olympian Zeus

To Piraeus

N

City Wall

0   500 meters
0   500 yards

To Sunium

siasm for architecture that had always been expected of the upwardly mobile Eupatrid, but it was quite another to flaunt the basis and true character of their power. If rivals proved obdurate, they were best murdered on the quiet. What went on behind closed doors, in darkened cellars, could hardly be boasted of in public. The Pisistratids had to veil as well as publicize their tyranny.

Decorously, therefore, they concealed the nakedness of their supremacy behind the veil of Solon's constitution. Candidates from families other than the Pisistratids continued to be permitted to run for the archonship. Most, of course, were the tyrants' placemen—most, but by no means all. Two, in particular, would have leapt out at anybody scanning a list of the city's archons. One of these, startlingly, was a Miltiades: not the adventurer who had been a contemporary of Pisistratus, but his nephew, recently emerged as head of the Philaids, and would-be tyrant of the Chersonese himself. Just above him was an even bigger jaw-dropper: an Alcmaeonid, no less, one Cleisthenes, restored both to Athens and to her highest office by the favor of the tyrants. Who could doubt, seeing the former exile on the archon list, the legitimacy of the regime that had put him there? Who doubt, when even the most implacable enemy of the tyranny appeared content to adorn it, that the brothers were there to stay?

Yet it was possible to interpret the return of Cleisthenes in a very different light. Could the Alcmaeonids, those inveterate back-stabbers, really have buried the hatchet? To rely upon their good faith was certainly a gamble. Sure enough, soon after Cleisthenes had served his term of office, he overplayed his hand and was forced back into exile.[34] This could be viewed as a victory for the Pisistratids—but it was a peculiarly perilous one. The source of their legitimacy, after all, was their ability to keep peace and public order. Descend to faction-fighting and their grip on power would start to slip. While they could hardly permit popular unrest, neither, awkwardly, could they risk indulging in too much of the repression that might stem it. Seen in such a light, even the temple of Zeus might appear less a monument to their self-confidence than a colossal bluff.

And in truth, such illusions were the hallmark of the regime. Look one way, and Athens might indeed appear a monarchy. Look another and something very different. The citizen inspecting the archon list, if he turned eastward, would see, along the margin of the open space, the glint of money changing hands, and hear the clamor of business—for the square, that imperious exercise in Pisistratid self-promotion, was already being colonized by commerce. Merchants had grown fat on the tyranny. Silver weighed heavy on counting tables all over the city, coins standardized, it seems likely, by the Pisistratids themselves, stamped on one side with Athena and on the other with her sacred owl—a currency so pure that already it had come to rank among the strongest of any city's. But if it had served to make the rich more of a force to be reckoned with than ever, it had also raised the profile of those on whom big business depended, whether the potters of the Ceramicus or the farmers who supplied the olive presses. Hippias and Hipparchus, like their father, courted them all. Every class in Athens was wooed and flattered somehow. Just as the archons were encouraged to pretend that the constitution was something more than a glorified sham, so the people were still cast as citizens who were sovereign, earth-born, free. Potters and farmers, told that often enough, might even end up believing it. Such a delusion naturally served the tyrants' own purposes well. Actors rarely appear more authentic than when convinced of the reality of their parts.

Of the many memorials raised by the tyranny to itself, then, perhaps the most fitting was not the temple of Zeus, nor any other *grand projet*, but rather an addiction among the Athenians to the wearing of masks, the mouthing of scripts and the playing of roles. Later generations, looking back to the mysterious birth of tragedy, would have no hesitation in attributing to the tyrants' original patronage a prestigious new festival, the City Dionysia, which had as its centerpiece a contest between rival tragedians—nor in imagining what the motive for such sponsorship might have been. After all, "only allow ourselves to praise and honour make-believe," as Solon was said to have warned, "and the next thing will be to find it creeping into the very business of state."[35] Which was, of course, for the Pisistratids, precisely the appeal.

Yet they too, lost in a hall of mirrors of their own making, appear sometimes to have longed for a guiding hand. How best to find one in a city in which the boundaries between fantasy and fact, propaganda and truth, had grown so blurred was naturally a challenge. Fearful of overreliance on any human agency, the two brothers opted instead to put their faith in the supernatural. Hippias, it was said, "had a deeper understanding of oracles than any other man living,"[36] and together with his brother sponsored a vast archive of prophecies, which they hoarded lovingly on the Acropolis. When Hipparchus discovered that the archivist, an intimate of his by the name of Onomacritus, had been doctoring them, the tyrant was so upset that he banished his friend on the spot. Intelligence, after all, was only ever as good as its source. Bearing this in mind, the two brothers placed a particular reliance upon their own dreams—and to such effect that they ruled their city without challenge for thirteen years.

Then, one blazing night in the summer of 514 BC, on the eve of the Great Panathenaea, Hipparchus had a vision that he failed to understand. A young and very beautiful man spoke to him from beside his bed, warning him in the urgent and cryptic manner of dreams that crimes must always be paid for. Hipparchus, waking with a jolt, would surely have devoted himself to identifying the offense he might have committed and making amends—but it was the morning of the Great Panathenaea and he did not have the time. Instead, leaving his home, he hurried across his father's square, heading for the Ceramicus, where his brother was organizing the great procession that would soon be departing for the Acropolis. As he passed a temple on the edge of the square, Hipparchus saw two men he recognized pushing their way toward him. Perhaps then, too late, he made sudden sense of his dream. For the two men were coming to murder him. One, Harmodius, was the handsomest man in Athens, "in the full splendour of his youth,"[37] while the other, Aristogiton, was his lover—and Hipparchus, who had an aesthete's eye for beauty, had attempted to split the couple for his own predatory ends, and thereby mortally offended them both. Dreading the power of the tyrant, and knowing that they had no other recourse, the two lovers had been biding their time, waiting until a festival such as the Panathenaea, at which everyone wore swords, when they would have their chance. Now, with Hipparchus before them, and with his bodyguards distracted by the crowds, they cut him down.

That was the limit of their conspiracy. Harmodius himself was killed on the spot; Aristogiton, although tortured for a few days, revealed nothing of any broader plot. Yet could Hippias afford to believe that the two assassins had acted on their own? Hipparchus, after all, had been murdered because he had abused his power; and the whisper on the streets was that he had been the victim, not of a crime of passion, but of a heroic blow struck in the cause of freedom. Hippias began to grow paranoid. With the ebbing of his confidence, the shadow play which he and his family had long orchestrated appeared increasingly a sham. The balance that they had always struck with such delicacy—between the true nature of their regime and the sets which had served to adorn it, between menace and a gracious magnanimity—was fatally upset. Despairing, the bereaved and panicky Hippias began to rely increasingly upon naked terror. Executions, previously carried out in back rooms, were soon washing the city in blood. Repression bred conspiracy; conspiracy led to further repression. The pretense that Athens was anything other than a police state began to seem a savage joke. Hippias, formerly "a man who was always easily approachable,"[38] now hunkered himself away among his Scythians and his other foreign mercenaries, as though he were some alien despot, as though barely Athenian at all.

Yet who was there to dispose of him? Heated talk of revolution in the salons of the aristocracy or in the bars of the Ceramicus was all very well—but someone had to take a lead. All eyes turned to Cleisthenes, who duly materialized, jackal-like as ever, on the northern frontier of Attica, barely a year after Hipparchus' death. Presented with the opportunity to throw out Hippias, however, the Athenians signally failed to take it. Resentful of the tyranny though they had become, they were hardly more enthusiastic about restoring the Alcmaeonids to power. Cleisthenes, once his invasion force had been annihilated by Hippias' mercenaries, had no choice but to slink back across the border. Behind him, on the battlefield, he left the corpses of those few Athenians who had dared to support him. "Good warriors, and nobly born—they showed the blood that flowed in their veins."[39]

For the Athenians, it appeared, a grim truth had been revealed: the only alternative to slavery was banishment or death.

Power to the People

Not that the irrepressible Cleisthenes himself had given up. Wallowing in self-doubt was hardly the Alcmaeonid way. Even as he licked his wounds, the man who remained the tyranny's most dangerous adversary was scouting around for fresh allies. Cleisthenes knew that he was far from the only man who wished to see Hippias fall. A second quality schemer, positively Alcmaeonid in his eye for the main chance, and far exceeding the Alcmaeonids in the resources available to him, also had an interest in destabilizing Athens. Indeed, King Cleomenes of Sparta, back in 519 BC, during his first expedition north of the Isthmus, had already had a stab at it. On that occasion the Plataeans, citizens of a small city ten miles south of Thebes, had approached him for support against their overweening neighbor; and Cleomenes, with malevolent cunning, had advised them to turn for help instead to Athens. Unable to resist this flattering appeal, the brother tyrants had duly marched to the Plataeans' defense and won an overwhelming victory: a result which, although gaining for the Athenians the undying loyalty of little Plataea, had, of course, dealt a death blow to their friendship with the powerful Thebans. Since this had been a mainstay of Pisistratid foreign policy since at least the time of their father's second exile, the whole episode could be reckoned a major blunder. Cleomenes had been left rubbing his hands in glee.

But could Cleisthenes, putting out feelers six years later, persuade the Spartan king to intervene openly against Hippias? It might have appeared a quixotic hope. The Pisistratids, despite their marriage alliance to Argos, had been careful to hedge their bets and stay on the good side of Sparta, too—so much so that Hippias was officially ranked as "a friend of the Spartan people." Before approaching their king, however, Cleisthenes would surely have done some homework on his man. He would have known that Cleomenes, with his proven enthusiasm for meddling in the business of cities beyond the Peloponnese, was hardly the model of a hidebound Spartan king. A politician with Cleisthenes' silver tongue would have been confident of convincing Cleomenes of what the latter was no doubt inclined to believe anyway: that Hippias, with his megalomaniacal building projects and his alliance with Argos, was a menace to Spartan interests. Yet Cleomenes, no matter how unorthodox in his approach to international relations, could hardly be expected to launch an unprovoked attack against a man who was, after all, "a friend of the Spartan people"—not without some trumped-up justification, at the very least. Here too, however, the ever-resourceful Cleisthenes was able to oblige. Not for nothing had the Alcmaeonids made themselves the favorites of Delphi—even to the extent of paying for lavish refurbishments after the great fire of 548 BC. Now, after decades of devoted patronage, it was payback time. Spartans who consulted the oracle received a single, invariable reply. No matter what questions they put to Apollo, the same answer always came back—"it was their duty to set Athens free."[40] When this startling news was reported back to Sparta, it was greeted with consternation. Perhaps only Cleomenes, tipped off by Cleisthenes as he must have been, failed to share in the general perplexity and alarm.

Not that there could be any question, for a people as devout as the Spartans, of ignoring Apollo's command, no matter how bemused by it they might be. "After all, while it was perfectly true that the Pisistratids were good friends of theirs, what were human ties when set against the orders of a god?"[41] The first expedition sent against

Athens—perhaps reflecting the Spartans' continued unease at the illegality of what they were doing—was low key and undermanned, and Hippias was able to repel it easily. The second, with their prestige now directly at stake, was overwhelming. In the summer of 510 BC, a Spartan army led by Cleomenes himself advanced from the Isthmus and crossed into Attica. This time, almost disdainfully, it swatted aside Hippias' mercenaries. Scuttling back into Athens, the tyrant holed himself up with his family on the Acropolis, where Cleomenes promptly barricaded him, blocking off every place of refuge with such an attention to detail that when Hippias sought to smuggle out his children to safety, they dropped straight into the Spartans' hands. Their father, bargaining desperately for their lives, was issued a stern ultimatum: he must leave Attica at once. Stunned by the abruptness of his fall, Hippias found himself with little choice but to accept these bitter terms. His only consolation as he left the city he had ruled for so long would have been to reflect that exile, for any tyrant, could be considered something of an occupational hazard—and that, as his father had amply demonstrated, there was nothing to stop him from plotting his return. In the short term, however, the tyranny was finished. Athens, dramatically, unexpectedly, was free.

But what did her freedom mean? On that score, the two men whose maneuverings had done most to restore it to her held ominously contrasting views. Cleisthenes, no matter what he might have promised Cleomenes while in exile, had not the slightest intention of seeing his city become a client state of Sparta. Cleomenes himself, meanwhile, having risked Spartan lives in the cause of a thoroughly illegal war, was looking for precisely such a return on his investment. Even if he could not have a regime that was actively subservient, he wanted, at the very least, an Athens so racked by factionalism that she would cease to function as a threat to Sparta. Soon enough, the compact between the two conspirators began to break down. In the shadowboxing that followed, the advantage appeared to be all Cleomenes'. Certainly, Eupatrid suspicions of Cleisthenes remained as dark as ever, and there were any number of aristocrats, now that the dead hand of the tyranny had been removed, keen to get back to the good old days of ganging up against the Alcmaeonids. Opposition to Cleisthenes began to gravitate around a rival nobleman by the name of Isagoras, "a former friend of the tyrants"[42]—and to such effect that he was elected in 508 BC to the archonship. Cleomenes, by now openly aligned against his former partner, let it be known from Sparta that he thoroughly approved. So vital had Isagoras regarded the backing of the Spartan king, and so desperately had he craved it, that it was rumored he had gone so far as to pimp Cleomenes his wife.

Cleisthenes, though he had stooped to many low tricks in his time, had never sunk quite as low as that. For all his mastery of scam and spin, he was much more than the grasping opportunist of his enemies' propaganda. Resolute in his determination not to see Athens sunk to the status of a Spartan client state, he could also recognize that Isagoras and his allies were fighting a war that had already had its day. Few Athenians might have recognized it, but the character of their city had changed forever. Authority, under the tyrants, had become a thing of shadow, melted from the grip of the elite who had once hugged it so tightly to themselves. Now that the tyranny itself was gone, it was difficult to say where precisely power resided. With those few families, the Alcmaeonids themselves, perhaps, or the Philaids, who still had a personal base? Perhaps, but Cleisthenes' own experiences since his return to Athens had demonstrated that even the very grandest Eupatrids, weakened by exile or by the humiliations of collaboration, had been perilously leeched of their prestige. Menaced by Isagoras, he chose to turn for support not, as was traditional for one of his background, to other factions among the elite, to those of wealth and breeding, but to a wholly original source. Addressing an assembly of the citizens, Cleisthenes proposed what was in effect a revolution.[43] If the people, as Hippias, as Pisistratus, as even Solon had always claimed, were truly sovereign, very well then—let them have authority over the city to match. Let them debate policy, and vote on it, and implement it, without regard to qualifications of class or wealth. Let power—*kratos*—be invested in the *demos*. Let Athens, in short, become a *demokratia*.[44]

A program so startling, so baldly radical, that it was wholly without precedent. His opponents, caught off balance, responded with howls of rage and disbelief. While Cleisthenes' proposals, unsurprisingly, "won him the wholehearted backing of the people,"[45] they appeared to Isagoras and his followers a scam of quite terrifying irresponsibility, reckless and cynical even by the standards of past Alcmaeonid maneuvering. Yet, if anything, the truth was even more unsettling for the aristocracy. The measures Cleisthenes was putting forward, in the sweep of their ambition, and in the brilliance of their design, did not have the character of a cornered gambler's makeshift throw. Far from it: they showed every sign of having been most carefully worked out. Cleisthenes would have had no lack of opportunity, in the bitterness of his exile, to reflect upon how all the ambitions of the nobility, all the pretensions of his own and of the other Eupatrid clans had led only to decades of internal feuding and to the indignities of a tyranny. Athens was sick—so much everyone agreed. What possible hope, then, for a cure? Only one, Cleisthenes and his associates appear to have decided. To break the mold; to harness the ambitions not only of the elite but of all the Athenian people; to create, from their energy, a future for Athens that would at last match the full measure of her potential. A great, a momentous, a breathtaking gamble—and on it Cleisthenes appeared willing to stake everything.

Except that, suddenly, his nerve failed him. In the early summer of 507 BC, a herald arrived from Sparta, and demanded, citing the ancient curse, the expulsion of the Alcmaeonids. Clearly, in the game of cat and mouse between the two former allies, Cleomenes still had plenty of moves to make. Cleisthenes, as though dreading what might come next, promptly turned tail and fled. Soon afterward, Cleomenes himself, accompanied by a small bodyguard of soldiers, came breezing into town. Briskly, he ordered a further purging of anti-Spartan elements, seven hundred families in all. Then, swaggering up to the Acropolis, he settled down with Isagoras to dictate a new constitutional order. Naturally, there was to be no place in it for any nonsense about democracy. Just as naturally, Isagoras, who had already loaned his wife to Cleomenes, was now obliged to pimp Athens herself to Sparta.

As the two men, king and traitor, deliberated, however, there came from the streets far below them an ominous and violent sound: that of rioting. Peering down from the battlements, Cleomenes saw angry crowds massing before the gates of the Acropolis, blockading him and his soldiers on the summit. To put it mildly, this was unexpected. Who could possibly be directing the riot? Cleisthenes was in exile. His associates had also been expelled. Slowly, as the hours passed, the unpalatable truth dawned. The Athenian people themselves, infuriated by Cleomenes' presumptions and Isagoras' treachery, had risen spontaneously in defense of their promised freedoms—nor did they appear in any mood to be placated. For two days the blockade was maintained. By the third, Cleomenes, "hungry, filthy, and stubble-chinned,"[46] had had enough. A truce was arranged; the Spartans, humiliatingly, were obliged to accept safe conduct to the border; Isagoras, somehow escaping the city too, managed to slip away into exile. His fellow collaborators, meanwhile, were rounded up and put to death. Democracy, having staked its future amid the smoke and bloodshed of revolution, had endured the first attempt to snuff it out.

Brought the news, Cleisthenes promptly hurried back in triumph. The victory, however, as everyone knew, was hardly his alone. Even his most diehard opponents now had to accept that there could be no retreating from the reform program he had promised the Athenian people: for it was, after they had stormed the Acropolis and defeated Cleomenes, their simple due. Indeed, with the lynching of Isagoras' followers still fresh in everybody's mind, it had become possible even for the upper classes to feel a certain sense of relief that Cleisthenes was back on the scene. Better him and his carefully planned package of reforms than blood flowing in the streets, and Eupatrid corpses strung up on the Acropolis, rotting in the heat.

So it was that midway through that momentous year of 507 BC, an Alcmaeonid relative of Cleisthenes was able to take over smoothly from Isagoras as archon and resume the transformation of Athens into a state like no other in history. While "*eunomia*"—good governance—had been the watchword of previous Greek reformers, from Lycurgus to Solon, that of Cleisthenes and his associates was subtly, and yet radically, different: "*isonomia*"—equality. Equality before the law, equality of participation in the running of the state: this, henceforward, was to be the Athenian ideal. True, some citizens remained much more equal than others: it remained the case, for instance, that only the upper classes could run for high office. Nevertheless, although certain relics of the old order had been preserved from the democratic tide, many more were soon to lie submerged beneath it for ever: Solon, for one, would barely have recognized the flood scene. Athens had become a city in which any citizen, no matter how poor or uneducated, was guaranteed freedom of public speech;[47] in which policy was no longer debated in the closed and gilded salons of the aristocracy, but openly, in the Assembly, before "carpenter, blacksmith or cobbler, merchant or ship-owner, rich or poor, aristocrat or low-born alike";[48] in which no measure could be adopted, no law passed, save by the votes of all the Athenian people. It was a great and noble experiment, a state in which, for the first time, a citizen could feel himself both engaged and in control. Nothing in Athens, or indeed Greece, would ever quite be the same again.

And that, for Cleisthenes and all who supported him, was absolutely the point. The sponsors of the Athenian revolution were no giddy visionaries moved by shimmering notions of brotherhood with the poor, but rather hard-nosed pragmatists whose goal, quite simply, was to profit as Athenian noblemen by making their city strong. To this ambition, and to the whole immense project that followed from it, they brought a desperate energy. Time, as they well knew, was hardly on their side. It was not only that Cleomenes, "who felt that the Athenians had shown him disrespect in word and deed,"[49] was set on revenge; Cleisthenes also feared, with both Hippias and Isagoras plotting their returns, that the city might implode at any moment into rival factions. Dynastic feuding, having brought Athens to the point of ruin, was simply too lethal to be tolerated any further—an analysis which even the dynasties themselves appeared reluctantly now to have accepted.

Yet how to neutralize them? Cleisthenes' solution was both brilliantly simple and quite ferociously ambitious: to suppress a citizen's identification with family, neighborhood and local clan chief altogether. Since these were instincts that had long come naturally to almost everyone in Attica, the plan to scotch them required peculiarly ingenious and detailed measures. Punctiliously, Cleisthenes sliced up the countryside, with its ancient tapestry of towns, estates and villages, into almost 150 separate districts. It was from these, the "demes," and no longer from their families, that the citizens of the new democracy would henceforward be obliged to take their second names. Their civic identity too—for a young man, when he came of age, might become a citizen of Athens under Cleisthenes' reforms only by being enrolled within a deme. This was to apply to the haughtiest Eupatrid and the humblest plowman in the field alike: both, as fellow demesmen, would share the same second name. Not all Eupatrids were necessarily thrilled by this innovation, of course. Some of them, particularly those so grand that they had an estate or village, and thereby a deme, named after them, made their disgruntlement with the new order all too clear. The Boutads, for instance, fed up with having to share their distinguished nomenclature with riffraff, pointedly gave themselves a new name: the Authentic Boutads.[50]

Still, they had to be careful. Sniff too pointedly at one's fellow demesmen, and even an Authentic Boutad might find himself excluded from public life. Cleisthenes, with his customary preemptive cunning, had ordained that demesmen should select delegates from among themselves to travel to Athens, and there prepare the agenda for the Assembly. What aristocrat worth his salt was going to put snobbery above such a plum opportunity? Just as Cleisthenes had to encourage the Eupatrids not to sulk in their tents, so he had to beware a counter-danger: that an ambitious nobleman might use his deme as a springboard to tyranny. Against that peril, deploying both their habitual foresight and their fiendish taste for complicating anything they touched, the founders of the democracy massed a whole array of checks and balances. Attica, already partitioned into demes, was scored with further patterning and fretwork. Demes were bunched into "thirds," a "third," as the name implied, was then grouped with two others to form a tribe. Since the thirds would all be drawn from separate corners of Attica—one from a mountainside, perhaps another from the coast, and another from nearby Athens herself—every tribe, of which there were ten in all, inevitably served to snarl up ancient roots. In place of the primal simplicities of the clan, the Athenian people could now enjoy infinitely more artificial and finely calibrated loyalties. Tribes, thirds and demes: here were complexities not easily manipulable by even the best-connected aristocrats.

But could they be made to work? Since no one had ever attempted to found a democracy before, no one actually knew. Watching the progress of the revolution in mounting alarm, Athens' neighbors could hardly afford to take its failure for granted—and Cleomenes, in particular, had good reason to fear the worst. If Cleisthenes and his associates, laboring furiously to entrench their reforms, always kept one nervous eye on the Spartans, then so too did the Spartan king, as he plotted counterrevolution, dread that he might be in a race against time himself. Fabulously intricate though the democratic reforms were, their potential appeared to Cleomenes ominously clear. No longer divided among themselves, the citizens of a democratic Athens would at last be able to present a united front to their neighbors. The sheer size of Attica would give them a truly fearsome capability. For centuries a military pygmy, Athens appeared on the verge of becoming, almost overnight, a heavyweight.

And most wounding of all for Cleomenes was the fact that he, by deposing the Pisistratids, had effectively served as the midwife of the Athenians' rogue regime. He was well aware that many of his countrymen, resentful of his proactive foreign policy, were starting to whisper against him, muttering about overstretch and complaining that all his meddlings in Athens had led only to disaster. For the moment, no one was strong enough to challenge him openly. The ephors were still reluctant to tread on his toes, and his fellow king, Demaratus, son of the once-plain girl who had been granted beauty by the apparition of Helen, remained firmly in his shadow. Yet the longer the Athenians thumbed their noses, the greater was the damage to his prestige, and the more closely he would need to guard his back. Preparing for his final bout against Cleisthenes, Cleomenes could not afford to take any chances. No wandering into Attica with a few bodyguards this time. When, in the summer of 506 BC, he and Demaratus finally advanced across the Isthmus, Isagoras in their train, the two kings led a strike force formed not only of their own steel-limbed countrymen but of contingents summoned from across the Peloponnese. They had other allies, too. The Thebans, still smarting from the Athenians' alliance with Plataea, readily joined the party by invading from the west. Meanwhile, crossing the straits that separated Attica from the long, narrow island of Euboea to the north, an army from the city of Chalcis formed the third prong of what now stood revealed as a brilliantly coordinated assault. Cleomenes had done his work well. Athens was effectively sur-rounded. The infant democracy seemed certain to be strangled in its cradle.

Yet as the Athenians, opting to confront their deadliest opponents first, prepared to march southward to meet the two Spartan kings, they might have found a plausible omen of hope in the route ahead of them. The road was no ordinary one. Every September a great procession of the Athenian people would take it, garlanded with myrtle, dressed in white, raising, as they walked, the "*iacche*," an ulu-lation of joy and triumph. Not for nothing was the road known as the "Sacred Way"—for it led, seventeen miles from Athens, to the holy shrine of Eleusis, where a great mystery would be taught: that from death life might arise and from the darkest despair the light of hope. No more propitious place for a defense of the city's liberty could pos-sibly have been imagined—and sure enough, when the Athenians arrived at Eleusis, they discovered that a miracle had indeed occurred.

The Spartans, and all the vast host that had marched with them, had gone. Demaratus, it was said, jealous of his fellow king and mistrustful of his foreign adventures, had been fomenting dissent. Many of the Peloponnesian allies, led by Corinth, had duly deserted; Cleomenes, finding himself suddenly without an army, had been forced, in impotent fury, to abort the invasion. The Athenians, stunned by the sheer scale of their deliverance, could presume only that the gods had come to their rescue—although some of them, remembering Cleisthenes' previous facility with backhanders, may have wondered whether they actually owed as much to Alcmaeonid gold.

Not that the Thebans, in their hatred of Athens, could be bribed. Swinging swiftly northward to meet them, the new model army of the democracy now faced its first authentic test. Cleisthenes, and everyone who had labored so hard with him on his reforms, braced themselves for the result. One question, in particular, was about to be answered. Accustomed as the average Athenian was to fighting in the train of a great aristocrat, would he now feel sufficient loyalty to a novel and wholly artificial innovation, his tribe, to stand in the line of battle, to cover the flank of his fellow demesman, to fight not for a clan lord but for an ideal, for liberty, for Athens herself? The answer, resoundingly, triumphantly, was yes. The Theban invasion force was annihilated. On the same day, crossing into Euboea, the Athenians forced Chalcis to sue for a humiliating peace, and accept, on what had previously been her own territory, a huge colony of four thousand Athenian settlers.

And so it was that the Athenians found themselves suddenly a great power. Not just in one field, but in everything they set their minds to, they gave vivid proof of what equality and freedom of speech might achieve. As the subjects of a tyrant, what had they accomplished? Nothing exceptional, to be sure. With the tyrant gone, however, they had suddenly become the best fighters in the world. Held down like slaves, they had shirked and slacked; once they had won their freedom, not a citizen but he could feel that he was labouring for himself.[51]

It appeared that democracy might indeed be made to work.

A boast that the Athenians now joyously proclaimed to all the world. Returning to their city, they commissioned, in the ecstasy of their deliverance, an immense victory memorial—a chariot led by four horses fashioned completely out of bronze—and placed it directly beyond the gates to the Acropolis. There, raised on what had previously been the supreme showcase for aristocratic megalomania, the intimidating sculpture gleamed, the first thing that anyone entering the citadel would see, a monument raised not to any individual but to "the sons of the Athenians"[52]—to the people as a whole. Elsewhere, too, all across Athens, the renewed din of chiseling bore ample witness to the democracy's enthusiasm for a facelift. Masons who had previously been laboring on the Pisistratids' gargantuan temple could now be found at work on the sloping hill west of the Acropolis, the Pnyx, hewing from its rock an immense new meeting place for the Assembly, capable of seating up to five thousand at a time: a first and fitting monument to government by the people. Meanwhile, stretching away northward beyond the Pnyx and the Acropolis, in the great square raised to himself by Pisistratus, other workmen were systematically excising all traces of the tyranny. The half-completed temple of Zeus was left to stand as a monument to the tyrants' folly, but the massive public space that Pisistratus had cleared in the heart of the city could not so easily be abandoned—not least because the citizens of the new democracy needed such a meeting place. "Agora," they began to call it—the word for an area that all Greek cities had, a space where people might freely gather. The previous Athenian *agora*, to the northeast of the Acropolis, found its venerable public buildings supplanted, while the new one, of a scale and beauty altogether more worthy of the dignity of the people, was duly enshrined as the symbolic heart of the democracy.[53]

A point rammed home by the installation, right in its center, of a hefty bronze of the two tyrannicides. Their swords drawn, their faces

139

stern, their bodies heroically if improbably nude, Harmodius and Aristogiton were portrayed as the joint saviors of Athens and the founders of her freedom. Considering that there were no other public portraits to be seen in the whole of Athens, the dominant position of these statues in the Agora was startling enough. What made it even more jaw-dropping, of course, was the fact that Harmodius and Aristogiton, far from having sacrificed themselves for liberty, had in reality cut down Hipparchus in a squalid lovers' tiff. Indeed, if anyone deserved to be hailed as the city's liberator, it was probably the King of Sparta—but the Athenians did not care to dwell on that. Hence the value to them of the tyrannicides. Like every other revolutionary state in history, Cleisthenes' regime had an urgent need of heroes. Harmodius and Aristogiton, gratifyingly sanguinary, even more gratifyingly dead, were duly spun as democracy's first martyrs.

The hype also served a more profound purpose. Cleisthenes understood his countrymen well; he knew that the Athenian people, revolutionaries though they had rather startlingly proved themselves to be, remained, in their souls, traditionalists still. Far from glorying in the novel character of the democracy, they craved reassurance that it was rooted in their past. Cleisthenes, ever subtle, had therefore been sure to adorn even his most daring experiments in the fustian of tradition. The tribes, for instance, had all been given the names of antique heroes, as though, like the Athenians themselves, they had sprung not from Cleisthenes' fertile brain but directly from the soil. Even the democracy itself, so its founders implied, far from being something new, was in fact the primordial birthright of all the people of Attica, having originally been bequeathed to them back in the days of legend by the celebrated hero Theseus, slayer of the minotaur. Seen in such a light, what were the two tyrannicides themselves but monster killers, selfless patriots who had died in order that Athenian democracy might be restored? Smoke and mirrors all, of course—and hardly paying to Cleisthenes and his associates anything remotely like their due. Yet it is perhaps the clinching proof of their greatness that even Cleisthenes himself, scion of a family rarely noted for its modesty, should have recognized how essential it was to veil the full scale of his achievement behind such fantastical shadows. In founding democracy, he had invented his city's future; but he had also, just as crucially, fabricated its past.

No statue of Cleisthenes in the Agora, then. Nor any place for him in his countrymen's affections as their democracy's founding father. Indeed, no sooner was he dead than the Athenians, indulging themselves in an extraordinary bout of amnesia, started to forget that they had passed through a revolution at all.* So natural did their new form of government already appear to them, so deeply rooted in the Attic soil, that a true understanding of its origins, just as Cleisthenes had calculated it would, began to fade. It was a bittersweet paradox: in the false-memory syndrome that buried Cleisthenes in obscurity was the ultimate proof of his stunning success. Not merely to have redeemed his country from civil war, but to have set it upon enduring foundations—only Darius, of Cleisthenes' contemporaries, could compare. To be sure, between the Persian, monarch of all the world, and the Athenian, friend of the people, there might have appeared few correspondences; and yet in truth, in the scale of their achievements, and in what they betokened for the future, the two men were indeed well matched. Both had come to power amid bloodshed and given their countries peace; both had tamed the ambitions of a turbulent aristocracy; both, in doing so, had crafted a radical new future for their people and yet opted to disguise their originality behind the lumber of the past. Both, most portentously of all, had created something restless, and dangerous, and new.

Nor, for all that Athens, set upon the remote margins of the world as she was, stood shrouded in a natural obscurity, was Darius quite as oblivious to her now as he had previously been. Reports of her revolution had arrived in Persepolis. In 507 BC, while the Athenians were

---

*It is a mark, perhaps, of the oblivion that descended upon Cleisthenes' memory that we are not even sure of the precise date of his death. Some time around 500 BC seems likeliest.

nervously awaiting the Spartan onslaught, and noting, with alarm, that Hippias had taken refuge on the southern side of the Hellespont, in territory held by Persia, they had sent an embassy to Sardis. There sat Artaphernes, brother of the King of Kings, ruthless and shrewd. When the Athenian ambassadors had arrived at his court and begged him for an alliance against the Spartans, Artaphernes had graciously granted their request. Naturally, however, he had set a condition of his own: the usual gift of earth and water. The Athenian ambassadors, shrugging their shoulders, had accepted his terms. On their return to Athens, when they reported the news of the submission they had made to Artaphernes, "they were severely censured"[54]—which no doubt enabled the democracy to feel good about itself. The Athenians, however, did not repudiate the alliance with Persia—or their own submission. Better safe than sorry. Even after the great victories of 506 BC, who knew when Cleomenes might be back? An insurance policy against the Spartans was no bad thing—even if it had cost a symbolic humiliation. And what was a gift of earth and water? A gesture—nothing more.

Or so, at any rate, it pleased the Athenians to assume.

5

SINGEING THE KING OF PERSIA'S BEARD

The Great Game

Artaphernes had been well rewarded by his royal brother for the blow that struck down Bardiya. Sardis was by any reckoning a great and fitting prize. The capital of the west, it ranked, in the opinion of the Persians, as one of the four corners of their dominion, a city so fabulously wealthy that even its rivers ran with gold. Croesus, when not bribing the Delphic oracle or being stung by the Alcmaeonids, had used the proceeds to mint the world's first golden coinage, an innovation that had helped him become, if anything, even more obscenely rich than he had been before. Forty years on, and with Croesus long since dead, his Persian conquerors could still enjoy the fruits of his lavish spending.

Even those familiar with Babylon would have found it hard to sniff at Sardis. Showcase of the city was a magnificent temple to Cybele, a mother goddess as ancient as the hills, and capable of inspiring such extremes of devotion in her worshippers that they might end up dancing on a mountainside, writhing in orgies, or even, should the rituals be going with a particular swing, hacking off their testicles. Beyond the temple, rising in rings like those of Ecbatana, loomed the celebrated walls of Sardis. The innermost one, circling the acropolis, was so immense that Croesus had been led into the fatal error of assuming it impregnable. The acropolis itself, a red shard of mountain jagging up from the river plain, was even more intimidating, topped as it was along one of its spurs by what had once been the royal palace, and was now the brooding stronghold of Persian power. From there, gazing down at the sprawl of the lower town, or far westward over vast expanses of wheat and barley, and the road that led onward for three days to "the bitter sea," Artaphernes might well have felt himself the equal of any king.

With one exception, of course. Master of the west he might be, but Artaphernes—"faithful Artaphernes"—knew better than to forget for even a moment that he was merely his brother's vassal, his servant, his "*bandaka*." Although, to instill in the locals a due sense of Persian majesty, he had modeled his court on Darius' own, he ruled it not as a king himself but rather as the "Guardian of the King's Power"—as a satrap.* Darius, having won his throne amid an inferno of rebellions, had no intention of permitting overmighty subjects ever again to endanger either his or Persia's greatness. The merest command from his secretariat, then, and a satrap would be obliged to jump. For a provincial capital, the arrival of a royal letter was a major and often alarming event. Certain satraps, presented with a missive from the Great King, might go so far as to prostrate themselves before it and humbly kiss the floor.

Excess of zeal—or simple common sense? No one could ever tell who might be in the shadows, keeping watch, taking notes. Some claimed that the king appointed spies specifically to tour his empire, all-seeing officials known simply as his "eyes." Others suspected an even more unsettling truth:

---

*The Greek word *"satrapes"* was a transliteration of the original Persian *"xsachapava."*

The king's subjects, after all, would be put on their guard by any inspector whom they knew to be his "eye." What really happens is quite the opposite—for the King will listen to anyone who claims to have seen or heard anything untoward. Hence the saying that he has a thousand eyes and a thousand ears.[1]

Here was paranoia on an almost global scale. No matter where within the inconceivable vastness of the empire his subjects might be, Darius could be imagined as always watching them, as overhearing all they said.

It was not enough for a servant, however, even one as favored as Artaphernes, to owe his duty simply to the king. Master accountant and insatiable for tribute though Darius was, yet he demanded from his satraps something more than revenue alone. "By the favour of Ahura Mazda," he reminded those who served him, "I am the kind of man who is a friend to the right, who frowns upon the wrong, who has no wish to see the weak oppressed by the strong."[2] Darius spoke, as was his privilege, as the fount of law for all the world, but he was also closely reflecting how the Persians saw themselves. No people had a greater faith in their own virtue. So stern were the demands of justice, the Persians liked to believe, that they might outface even those of class and breeding. A peasant, his upright nature spotted by the unblinking eye of the Great King, might be promoted to the judicial bench; once installed there, he might find himself seated upon strips of drying skin, the hide of his corrupt predecessor, justly flayed alive. This was the kind of anecdote, both edifying and gruesome, that never failed to delight the Persians. Naturally—for it helped to confirm all their dearest preconceptions. There was no other people, they could reflect contentedly, with a sense of justice, an aptitude for rule that could remotely match their own. What good fortune for lesser nations, then, that they should all have ended up the slaves of the Persian king!

A justification for world conquest, of course, that the Persian King himself had already made his own. Upon Darius' satraps, however, out on the empire's fringes, far from the royal presence, it imposed particular demands. The obligation to provide justice for the same provincials whom they were simultaneously fleecing was not straightforward. Where it might easily lead could be discovered by a visit to the royal mint at Sardis, where coinage, just as it had been in Croesus' day, continued to be struck, stamped now with the image of Darius as an archer, bending back the royal bow of power, the warrior champion of truth, of justice, of Arta. Then, chinking, glinting brightly, the gold would be crated and carted off to Susa.

Perhaps a certain brutal hypocrisy was merely the mark of any successful satrap. Nor did it necessarily make the trumpeting of the "*pax Persica*" a total sham. Even though he was sure to keep a regular supply of tribute wagons rumbling out of Sardis, Artaphernes did not look to bleed his province dry. That would have been to risk the goose that was laying the Great King his splendid golden eggs. As under Croesus, so under Artaphernes, Lydia continued to boast a class of native super-rich. One of these, a mine owner by the name of Pythius, was so successful in husbanding his assets that it was said only Darius lay ahead of him on the empire's rich list. Lydians like Pythius, to whom Persian rule had opened up global horizons, had not the remotest interest in agitating for independence. Artaphernes, quite as subtle as his brother, encouraged such collaboration wherever and however he could—and not merely among the rich. Lydian functionaries still dutifully ran the province for their masters, just as they had done under Croesus. Their language, their customs, their gods, all were scrupulously tolerated. Only in temples particularly associated with Croesus and his dynasty might symbols of the old regime be pulled down or adapted into fire altars—and even then no attempt was made to force the worship of Ahura Mazda down unwilling Lydian throats. Indeed, if anything, it was the conquerors who adopted the natives' customs. Perhaps the most startling evidence of this could be seen eight miles to the north of Sardis, a wonder visible from Artaphernes' palace: eerie mounds of stone and turf looming over the cornfields like waves whipped up from a golden swell. Three of these were the graves of famous Lydian kings; but around them, filling the necropolis, rose newer, smaller tombs, the resting places of both wealthy natives and their Persian masters.³ Even in the dust and silence of a cemetery, then, Artaphernes' Sardis was an unabashedly multicultural place.

Not that the Persians' tolerance of foreigners and their peculiar habits in any way implied respect. Just as Cyrus, conquering Babylon, had felt free to claim the favor of a whole multitude of gods precisely because he believed in none of them, so too did Artaphernes, by appropriating the Lydians' traditions and twisting them to his own ends, display his appreciation of a bleak and baneful truth: the traditions that define a people, that they cling to, that they love, can also, if cunningly exploited by a conqueror, serve to enslave them. This maxim, applied by the Persians across the vast range of all their many satrapies, was one that underpinned their whole philosophy of empire. No elite anywhere, they liked to think, but it might somehow be seduced into submission.

And when no elite existed, one could always be imported from elsewhere. Cyrus, even as he flattered the Babylonians with the attentions he paid to Marduk, had not ignored the yearnings of the city's deportees, exiles such as the Judaeans, brought to Babylon decades previously—for the Persians had recognized in these wretched captives, and in their homesickness, a resource of great potential. Judaea was the pivot between Mesopotamia and Egypt; a land of such strategic significance might certainly be considered worth a small investment. Not only had Cyrus permitted the Judaeans to return to the weed-covered rubble of their homeland, but he had even paid for the rebuilding in Jerusalem of their obliterated Temple. Yahweh, the Judaeans' god, was said to have hailed the Persian king in gratitude as His "anointed," His "Christ,"⁴ and asserted that for the messiah of his chosen people the earth itself would prove the limit. "I will break in pieces the doors of bronze and cut asunder the bars of iron, I will give you the treasures of darkness and the hoards in secret places, that you may know that it is I, the Lord, the God of Israel, who call you by your name."⁵

This comical notion, that Cyrus might somehow have owed all his greatness to the Judaeans' boastful god, was one that the Persians were nevertheless perfectly content to indulge; for they well understood the longing of a slave to believe himself his master's favorite. There was no greater source of self-contentment for a subject nation, after all, and no surer badge of its continued servitude, than to imagine that it might have been graced by a special relationship with the king. So it had always been: the Persians themselves, back in the days of their nomadic insignificance, had hardly been oblivious to the magnificence of Mesopotamia. Now the masters of the world, they could still remember what it was like to experience the gravitational pull of wealth and power and glamour.

The Greek upper classes too, long before the coming of the Persians, had been intrigued by the golden splendors of the kingdoms of the East. Athletics and dinner parties were not the only passions of their smart sets; as the decor on the Acropolis bore flamboyant witness, so too was anything that smacked of the Orient. If this was evident even in a backwater such as Athens, then how much more so back across the Aegean, on the shores of Asia itself, where the Ionians had for centuries been cultivating a taste for the exotic. "In the *agora* you can see them, sporting their purple cloaks, soused in heady perfumes, tossing their exquisite locks."[6] Yet still the Ionians, to their masters, were an enigma—and a challenge. All they ever did, it seemed to the Persians, was quarrel. This interminable feuding, which had helped immensely when it came to conquering them, also made them a uniquely wearisome people to rule. Where the Lydians had their bureaucrats and the Judaeans their priests, the Greeks seemed to have only treacherous and floating factions.

As a result, even with their aptitude for psychological profiling, the Persians struggled to get a handle on their Ionian subjects. True, some advisers in Sardis held out high hopes for the priests of Apollo, identifying them as the nearest thing the Greeks had to an order like the Magi, and recommending lavish patronage of their shrines as a possible means to winning Ionian hearts. Enthusiasm for such a policy went all the way to the top, for even Darius himself might fire off a stinging rebuke if it were reported to him that his officials had been infringing Apollo's prerogatives. Yet the king was to be sorely disappointed if he hoped thereby to recruit the Greeks' god of light to the sacred cause of "Arta." It was simply not in Apollo's character to offer his worshippers lectures on the truth. As at Delphi, so at his great oracle of Didyma on the south Aegean coast, he much preferred to speak in teasing riddles—which was at least an improvement on the behavior of his fellow Olympian, Athena, who positively delighted in sponsoring men with a talent for telling lies.

Whatever were the Persians to make of such gods? Nothing, really, could have been more shocking to their sensibilities—unless it was the trend, among the more adventurous of the Ionian elite, to deny a divine plan for the universe at all. The first philosophers may have been raised within the Persian Empire, but they could hardly be considered supportive of the Great King's claims or ideals. Where Darius saw in the rise to power of his people certain evidence of the animating favor of Ahura Mazda, a daring Ionian might see only the operation of the principles of nature. As to the character of these principles, that was also the subject of heated debate. One sage might argue that the world was formed entirely out of air, thereby reducing the Persian Empire and all its works merely to the interplay between condensation and rarefaction. Another might press the counterclaim of Zoroaster's sacred element of fire, seeing in it, however, not the immanence of truth, or justice, or righteousness, but only a ceaseless flux. To such a philosopher, the belief that any profounder order might lie behind it was merely the stupidest pretension. "All things are constituted from fire and all things will melt back into fire."[7] Not much for a propagandist at the satrapal court to work with there.

Yet Artaphernes' dependence on tyrants to administer Ionia, forced on him by the lack of any obvious alternative, hardly served to set Persian power on a rock-solid footing, either. Indeed, it might have been designed to illustrate a theory much favored by certain philosophers, and one that to them appeared simply an observable fact of life: that everything in the world was conflict and tension. Ionian noblemen, after all, were no more keen on being subjected to a tyranny than were their counterparts across the Aegean. The Persians, by favoring one faction over another, were inevitably sucked into the Ionian aristocracy's endless feuding. Whereas in Sardis they could base their administration upon an efficient and respectful bureaucracy, in Ionia they had to found it upon intrigue, factionalism and espionage. A Persian agent there had to prove himself quite as adept at back-stabbing as any Greek. For Artaphernes himself, the challenge was to pick winners, keep them in power until they had outgrown their usefulness, and then dispose of them with a minimum of fuss.

No wonder that his protégés, perfectly aware of the role they had been allotted within the satrap's scheme of things, felt themselves under an infinitely greater pressure than that which weighed upon their counterparts in Greece. Although clearly indispensable, Persian backing came at a perilous cost—for an Ionian tyrant had to deflect not only the jealousy of his peers but the suspicions of a turbulent and xenophobic lower class. While the aristocracy, suckers for Oriental chic, had proved themselves natural collaborators with their counterparts from the East, their countrymen retained an invincible contempt for foreigners of any kind. Thales, for instance, a man ranked by the Ionians as the most brilliant of their sages—as the first philosopher, indeed—was reckoned to have given a fine example of his wisdom by observing how grateful to Fate he was for three things: "first, that I am not a beast but a man; second, not a female but a male; and third, not a foreigner but a Greek."[8] The Ionians liked to call their neighbors "barbarians": people whose languages were gibberish; who went, "bah, bah, bah." This failure to speak Greek, self-evidently contemptible, was also widely believed to veil more sinister failings. Ionian suspicion of foreign habits long predated the humiliation of conquest by the Persian king. The same Lydians so admired by upwardly mobile aristocrats back in the days of Croesus, for instance, had been widely despised by the vast majority of Ionians who were unable to afford purple cloaks, perfumes or golden supperware. Scandalous stories had been enthusiastically told of Croesus' predecessors, in particular. One, it was said, had patented female circumcision in an effort to economize on eunuchs; another had been in the habit of showing off his naked queen to voyeurs; yet another was claimed, revoltingly, to have developed a taste for cannibalism, and to have woken up one morning after a night of heavy drinking to find his wife's hand protruding from his mouth.

What kind of Greeks could choose to ape monsters such as these? Clearly, critics of the nobility liked to imply, only those who were perverts and degenerates themselves. Lydia, like her notoriously expert whores, was both diseased and predatory; those who surrendered to her embraces deserved all the scorn they got. Strip away the veil of barbarian delicacies so prized by the aristocracy—the silken eroticism, the refinements, the displays of wealth—and the reality would be an infinitely sordid one: the court at Sardis could fittingly be portrayed as a prostitute "speaking Lydian," kneeling in a back alley, thrashing her client's testicles while shafting his dripping arse. "The passageway reeked. Clouds of dung-beetles came whirring after the stench."[9] A vile and shocking scene: fitting metaphor for a vile and shocking truth. The aristocracy were wallowing in shit—and tyrants, the worst offenders, were in it up to their necks.

Which left the tyrants themselves with an invidious choice: either to rule as traitors or to be lynched by angry mobs. If they were to be given the opportunity to strike a devastating blow against their overlords— even, perhaps, to finish off the King of Kings himself—what then? A fantastical hypothetical—except that, back in 513 BC, the question had suddenly become pressingly real.[10] Darius, fresh from his triumphs in India, had rolled into Sardis with a vast army, crossed from Asia into Europe, and then vanished north into what is now the Ukraine on a great raid against the Scythians. The various Greek tyrants, ordered to play their part in the Persian war effort, had been sent with their squadrons into the Black Sea to build a pontoon bridge across the mouth of the Danube and await their royal master's return. Among them, recently brought under the Persian yoke and not very happy about it,

151

had been the Athenian aristocrat Miltiades the Philaid, tyrant of the Chersonese. Counting the weeks and watching the skies turn steadily more leaden and icy, he had conceived an audacious plan. What if the Greeks, by cutting the bridge, were to strand Darius and his army on the Danube's freezing northern bank? Scythia was certainly no place to pass a winter. The snowstorms were appalling, and the natives partial to drinking human blood. Conceivably, just conceivably, it lay within the power of the Ionians to doom the Great King's whole expedition. A dangerous, teasing thought—and by late autumn, with Persian out-riders only days away, an increasingly urgent one, too. A conference of the tyrants had duly been convened. Miltiades had pressed his case. For a brief, intoxicating moment, the other Greeks had allowed themselves to be swayed; until reason, inglorious but pragmatic, had prevailed. After all, as every Ionian tyrant was perfectly aware, "there was not one of them but he owed Darius his position as head of state."[11] So they had voted to stay loyal and to keep the bridge afloat. Discreetly suppressing any mention of the treachery they had been contemplating, the assem-bled tyrants—Miltiades included—had duly welcomed back their master. The prospect of liberty might have been sweet, but not so sweet, it appeared, when weighed in the balance, as the reality of power.

And for one Greek in particular, a man as sensitive to the opportu-nities opened up to him by Persian rule as any Lydian or Mede, that power was especially precious. Histiaeus, the chief opponent of Miltiades' braggadocio on the Danube, had spoken out as tyrant of the Aegean's sole world city, the acknowledged "glory of Ionia,"[12] Miletus. The birthplace of Thales, and of philosophy itself, the city was an eco-nomic as well as a cultural powerhouse. The port's four magnificent harbors, thronged with a great bobbing forest of masts—those of grain ships from the Crimea, merchant ships from Syria, from Egypt, from Italy, warships, sleek and menacing, from the Great King's own battle fleet—were unparalleled anywhere else in the Greek world as scenes of opulence and bustle. So prized was Miletus by the Persians, both as trading entrepôt and naval base, that she enjoyed, in comparison to the other Ionian cities, a uniquely privileged form of vassalage, one that enabled her to pretend almost to the rank of ally. While being sure never to let this status go to his head, Histiaeus had nevertheless relished the advantages it had given him over his fellow tyrants—and the opportunity, above all else, to establish a personal relationship with the world's most powerful man.

On his return from Scythia, the Great King had duly rewarded Histiaeus for his stalwart support of the Persian expedition by summoning him to Sardis, and inquiring graciously of his Milesian *bandaka* if there were any gift that he had his eye on. Since the army that Darius had left behind in Europe was at that very moment advancing westward from the Chersonese into Thrace, painstakingly conquering the north coast of the Aegean and its interior, Histiaeus, greatly daring, had wondered if he might perhaps be gifted a portion of this splendid new satrapy? The Great King had inclined his head; the request had been granted; Histiaeus had found himself the owner of an area of Thrace named Myrcinus. It was no mean reward: situated on a broad river not far from the empire's new border with the kingdom of Macedon, Darius' gift came complete with silver mines and forests, excellent raw material for a fleet. Histiaeus, unsurprisingly, was delighted. No longer confined to Ionia, he dared to dream of greater things.

But already, even as he hurried to Thrace to found a city on his new property, eyebrows had begun to be raised among the Persian military. After much nervous clearing of throats, words had very respectfully been put to the royal ear. It had been suggested to Darius that Greeks, especially subtle and ambitious Greeks such as Histiaeus, were simply not to be trusted with too much power. It was out of the question, of course, for the Great King, having presented Histiaeus with a reward, to snatch it back; still less for him to admit that he might possibly have made an error. Instead, summoning the Milesian to Sardis, Darius had announced that Histiaeus was to be graced with yet further marks of high esteem: the magnificent title of "Royal Table-Companion," and an official post as the king's adviser on Greek affairs. Naturally, since Darius would shortly be leaving Sardis, Histiaeus would now have the supreme honor of accompanying his master on his travels. A fixed grin no doubt plastered on his face, Histiaeus had duly been obliged, in 511 BC, to pack his bags, turn his back on his homeland, and leave for Susa.

Even languishing in the gilded cage of the royal court, however, he did not abandon all his hopes of exploiting Persian dominance to establish an Aegean power base for his dynasty. Back in Miletus, Histiaeus' stand-in as tyrant, his nephew Aristagoras, was soon proving himself a chip off the old block, and a keen student of his uncle's methods. In 500 BC, he approached Artaphernes with a scheme that he trusted might prove to their mutual benefit. Why not, Aristagoras suggested smoothly to the satrap, send an expedition against the island of Naxos? It was a rare prize, lying midway on any likely invasion route across the Aegean to Greece, and ripe for the plucking. The island was riven by factions; class war was threatening; the aristocracy were positively begging for Persian intervention. Sardis could provide the ships; Aristagoras himself would provide contacts within the disgruntled Naxian aristocracy. Everyone would be a winner.

Artaphernes, after consultations with his royal brother, duly gave the plan the nod—to Aristagoras' immense, but unspoken, relief. Although he could hardly let slip as much to the satrap, he was finding the delicate balance between the rival demands of his Persian masters and his own people an increasingly precarious one to maintain. Miletus had always been notorious, even by the standards of other Ionian cities, for the savagery of her class hatreds; but recently they had threatened to turn peculiarly internecine. The revolution in Athens, a city which claimed, in the mists of the fabulous past, to have sent the first colonists to Ionia, had been followed as enthusiastically in Miletus as in the islands of the Aegean. Calls for the establishment of a similar democracy, for the overthrow of the tyranny and an end to barbarian rule, were growing increasingly violent in the city's streets. Aristagoras, embarking with the Persian task force for Naxos, knew that he was playing for very high stakes indeed; the consequences of failure simply did not bear contemplation.

154

Soon enough, however, he would find himself facing them. Everything that could go wrong with the expedition did go wrong. The attempted conquest of Naxos proved a debacle, and Aristagoras, setting the seal on the disaster, then had a monstrous falling-out with the expedition's Persian commander—who just happened to be Artaphernes' cousin. When news of this reached Sardis, the satrap, with the decisiveness he habitually brought to his administration of Ionian affairs, resolved that Aristagoras would have to be replaced, and signed an order to that effect. But Aristagoras himself, with nothing now left to lose, and strongly backed by his uncle in far-off Susa, responded to his dismissal with a startling, not to say acrobatic, volte-face. Abdicating his tyranny before it could be taken from him, he suddenly pronounced himself a keen enthusiast for democracy—so keen, he added loudly, that he would like to see it established in all the Ionian states. This, of course, was to toss a flame into a kindling box: revolution duly flared throughout Ionia, tyrannies were toppled everywhere and democracies proclaimed in their place. Those tyrants who managed to avoid being stoned to death all fled to Artaphernes.

Whose fury was naturally terrible. The Ionians, by raising the banner of democracy, had taken a fateful and perilous step. Having defied the orders of Darius' appointed satrap, and ousted the regimes he had imposed, they had effectively chosen to declare war on the King of Kings. In the first giddy flush of their liberty, this seemed barely to concern most of them. Aristagoras, however, knew better. He, at any rate, had no illusions as to the scale of the challenge his countrymen now faced. A superpower such as Persia was not lightly challenged; Artaphernes' desire for revenge was sure to prove swift and devastating. If the rebellious cities—and their dreams—were not to be crushed utterly, they would need, at the barest minimum, not merely a united front but an effective fleet and allies too.

But how to secure them? Aristagoras' fertile mind was already cooking up any number of hopeful plots. The first was particularly audacious. One of his agents, pretending to be an officer loyal to Artaphernes, coolly sailed into the port some miles north of Miletus

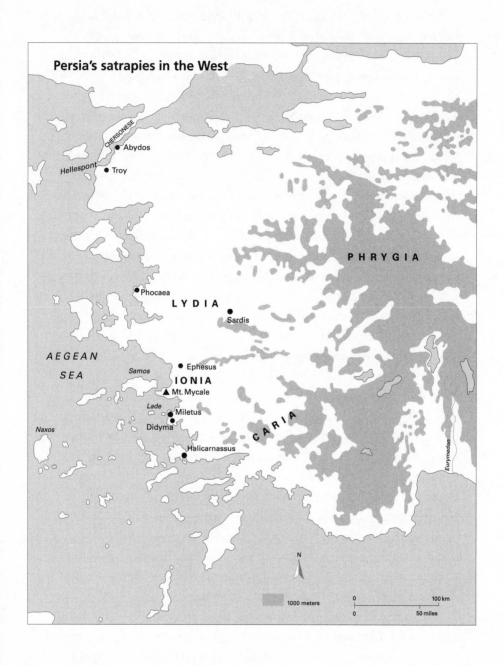

Persia's satrapies in the West

CHERSONESE
● Abydos
Hellespont
● Troy

PHRYGIA

● Phocaea
LYDIA
● Sardis

AEGEAN
SEA

Samos
● Ephesus
IONIA
▲ Mt. Mycale

Lade
● Miletus
Didyma
CARIA

Naxos

● Halicarnassus

Eurymedon

N

1000 meters

0   100 km
0   50 miles

where the Persian navy was docked, rounded up all the Ionians serving there as admirals, and proceeded to sail off to Miletus with the fleet.[13] It was a daring and spectacular triumph—and encouraged Aristagoras to embark on a secret mission of his own. In the winter of 499 BC, he boarded a warship and glided out from the great harbors of his city. Across the bay to the north of Miletus he could see a great spine of rock, the ridge of Mount Mycale, rising above the sea. This was where the Greeks of Asia, in happier times, had been accustomed to meet to celebrate their common bonds, at the sanctuary of the "Panionium"—"the shrine of all the Ionians." There would be opportunity enough, perhaps, for councils of war there, for assemblies of generals, and the plotting of strategy—but not now. Aristagoras had other, more pressing business. Onward he sailed. Mount Mycale and then, just beyond its westernmost tip, the island of Samos both began to fade over the horizon. Ahead lay the open sea—and the currents that led to Greece.

A Low, Dishonest Decade

499 BC. Winter in Lacedaemon. Just offshore from Gythion, the small port which served the Spartans as their naval base, the islet of Cranae was windswept and deserted; and yet it bore, for all who gazed at it, indelible associations of summer heat and blazing stars. There it was, beneath the open sky, that Helen and Paris had spent their first night together, an entwined delirium of passion that had led, in short time, to a conflagration engulfing both East and West, and Spartan warships plowing the waters off Troy. A promising omen? Aristagoras, gazing at the notorious island as his ship pulled into Gythion, would certainly have hoped so. His mission was nothing less than to recruit the Spartans to a second great Asian war.

Taking the thirty-mile road that led to their city, Aristagoras rehearsed the incentives that he would dangle before his hosts. The Persians were rich beyond the dreams of avarice; they were perfumed and effeminate; why, "they even fought in trousers."[14] Could any foe be more tempting? Particularly since the Spartans had, in one of their kings, a leader with a proven relish for launching preemptive strikes. Cleomenes, even after the debacle at Eleusis, still stood unchallenged as the strongman of Sparta. Demaratus, the colleague whose agitation had done so much to abort the Athenian campaign, had been decisively shoved back in his place. Returning from Attica, Cleomenes had openly accused his fellow monarch of sabotaging the war effort, and pressured the Spartan assembly to pass a law forbidding both kings ever again to go on the same campaign. His rival was effectively confined to barracks. Indeed, the wretched Demaratus was left so thoroughly in the shade that he had been reduced to the desperate straits of entering a chariot at the Olympic Games; worse, when he won he had actually boasted about his victory. If this was vulgar behavior for any Spartan, it was unheard of for a king.

But Cleomenes, too, still bore scars from the Athenian misadventure. When he met Aristagoras to discuss the crisis in Ionia, the Spartan commander-in-chief astonished his guest by flatly turning down his appeal for aid. Assuming that he was being stung for a bribe, Aristagoras followed Cleomenes home, proffering ever higher figures as he did so. Not even the presence of the king's eight-year-old daughter, Gorgo, served to inhibit him—a major oversight, in view of the priggishness conditioned from a tender age into Spartan girls. "Daddy," the bright-eyed Gorgo piped up suddenly, "this foreigner is out to corrupt you. Leave him well alone!"[15] A display of precocious rectitude to thrill her father's heart; but Cleomenes, even had his daughter not been there to hold him to the straight and narrow, would surely still have sent Aristagoras packing. The taste of the Athenian debacle was still too bitter in his mouth. Worse, there were reports from the north that the Argives, the old enemy, were regrouping, plotting yet another showdown. The Spartans would need all their reserves of manpower to deal with the looming crisis. Cleomenes had not the slightest intention of diverting a single hoplite overseas.

Which is not to say that he was contemptuous of the Persian threat. By now a seasoned strategist, Cleomenes could certainly recognize a threat to Sparta in the growing scale of the Great King's ambitions. But not to Sparta alone—nor even preeminently. Watching the disconsolate Aristagoras leave Lacedaemon, Cleomenes would have had a shrewd idea as to his next port of call. The Ionians, that winter, were not the only rebels against the Great King. A city of them was to be found in Greece, too. The Athenians, having sought Persian assistance against Cleomenes back in 507 BC, had come bitterly to regret their gift of earth and water. In what Cleomenes himself could only regard as the most exquisite poetic justice, Artaphernes, that instinctive tyrant-sponsor, had ordered the Athenians to take back Hippias, the exiled Pisistratid. The Athenians, naturally, had refused. As a result, from that moment on, to all intents and purposes they had been at war with Persia. Who was Cleomenes, of all people, to bail out the Athenians? Their mess: their problem. And when, as he was sure they would, they answered Aristagoras' appeal by sending a task force to Ionia, they would be running risks, and suffering casualties, and probing the Persians' strength as proxies of Spartan intelligence.

A fact of which the more calculating of the Athenians were uncomfortably aware. Wise heads among the aristocracy, alert to the vastness of Persian power and practiced in realpolitik, listened to Aristagoras and his war-mongering with horror; but it was not the aristocracy who ruled the Assembly now. The Athenian people, eager to pay back Artaphernes for ever having received their submission, buoyed by the idea of making cause with their kinsmen across the sea, and intoxicated by the prospect of easy loot, voted enthusiastically to send a fleet of twenty ships to join the assault on Persia. War fever, as Aristagoras jovially pointed out, was an intoxication to which democracies appeared peculiarly prone. After all, "where he had failed with Cleomenes, a single individual, he had now succeeded with the Athenians, an assembly of thirty thousand."[16]

Unfortunate for him, then, and for the Ionians, that there were no other democracies on hand. Indeed, aside from Eretria, a merchant port on the island of Euboea which had long felt its interests threatened by Persia, Athens was the only city in the whole of Greece to swallow

Aristagoras' patter. But this sobering statistic, far from giving her citizens pause for thought, served only to fuel their already shining sense of exceptionalism and mission. In the spring of 498 BC, democracy's first ever task force duly slid out of the harbor of Phalerum. Heading eastward along the Attic coastline, it was soon joined from the north by five ships from Eretria, and then, prows pointed boldly toward Ionia, sailed onward and out of the Athenians' sight. Not out of mind, however. Wherever the Athenian people gathered together that early summer, whether in the bars of the Ceramicus, in the Agora or down in Phalerum, news was feverishly awaited. Weeks passed. Then, at last, news began to filter through. The soldiers of the democracy were reported to have scored a glorious success. Disdaining to cower and skulk on the Ionian coast, they had dared instead to strike directly at the heart of Artaphernes' power. Marching with their Ionian and Eretrian allies over the mountains that guarded Sardis, they had followed secret, winding paths, and then, taking the Persians wholly by surprise, had descended suddenly into the plain. Artaphernes had been sent scampering into his palace. The lower city had been burned. A Persian expedition against Miletus had been forced to turn round. Athens had done her duty; and the Ionians, thanks to her heroic efforts, had surely now been freed for good.

Mission accomplished? So it might have seemed. It did not take long, however, for the sunny news from Ionia to darken. Yes, Artaphernes had holed up in his palace; but the Greeks, few in number and lacking siege engines, had failed miserably to breach its formidable walls. Nor, with fire blazing through the lower town, had they been able to preserve the temple of Cybele from the inferno. This sacrilege was so fearful that the Greeks, already dispirited by their failure to capture Artaphernes, had promptly retreated to the mountains. Stumbling wearily back to the sea, they had then found themselves shadowed by squads of Persian horsemen. Barely a mile from their ships, they had been forced to turn and make a stand. "Easily beatable":[17] this was how Aristagoras had repeatedly described the Persians during the course of his shuttle diplomacy. Now, wilting beneath a hail of their arrows, choking on dust clouds raised by their tireless cavalry, the Athenians had discovered the baneful truth. The Greek line, bronze-clad though it was, had begun to break. The Eretrian commander, struggling to hold it together, had been killed. The Athenian survivors, separated from the main body of the Greek army, had straggled back to their ships, hoisted their sails and fled.

Greeting the return of the broken fleet with alarmed perplexity, their fellow citizens could at last appreciate that Aristagoras had fed them a con. The Ionian's claim that the Persians were womanish and feeble stood exposed as the product of wishful thinking. The Athenian Assembly, veering wildly from jingoism to funk, dismissed all further appeals from the war zone, frantic though these were, and bitter with reproach. Indeed, having originally sold Athens a false prospectus, Aristagoras could now point to some genuine successes; for the burning of Sardis, although it had struck the Athenians as a disaster, had blazed the news of Persian humiliation far and wide. From Cyprus to the Chersonese, the sparks of rebellion were bursting into flames, and Artaphernes, his prestige badly damaged, was finding the task of stamping them out a desperate one.

The Athenians, however, with the obduracy of born-again isolationists, remained resolutely unimpressed. It appeared clear to them now, from the brief glimpse of Persian power that their expedition had afforded, that all Aristagoras' schemes and ambitions were merely so many castles built of air. Most ominously, as they had found out for themselves, the Ionian hoplites simply had no answer to the range and speed of the Persian cavalry—so much so that by the summer of 497 BC, barely two years into the revolt, the rebels had all but been swept into the sea. Only Miletus, birthplace of the insurgency, still held out; and although the Ionian fleet remained unconquered, there were no supplies or fresh recruits to be had from the waves. So grim did the situation appear that Aristagoras, despairing of the Athenians, decided to take a leaf out of his uncle's book and travel to Myrcinus, Histiaeus' private fiefdom in Thrace, to secure fresh timber for the fleet and silver for mercenaries. The natives, however, proved even less supportive of the war effort than the Athenians had been: far from welcoming their landlord, they opted instead to make their own bid for freedom, and knifed him dead. So, squalidly and obscurely, perished Aristagoras, instigator of the great revolt against the King of Kings—and the one man to have provided it with genuine leadership and purpose.

The Ionians' hope of victory, already flickering, now began to dim to the point of near-extinction. It would take the Persians, laboring hard to rebuild the fleet stolen from them at the beginning of the revolt, another three years before they felt ready to challenge the rebels for control of the sea. Yet, during that time, with Aristagoras dead, and no one stepping forward to replace him, the Ionians' war effort appeared struck by paralysis, as though with horror at the catastrophe they knew was surely nearing. Faction leader turned against faction leader; class against class; city against city. More lethal in its effects than any number of cavalry squadrons, Persian gold began to do its work. Defeatists and appeasers flaked away. Still the Ionian fleet, moored along the islands off embattled Miletus, held to its position, more than 350 battleships, a fearsome number, save that as they rotted in the storms of winter and steamed in the summer heat they began to reek of dread and desperation, a stench that hung menacingly in the air, and reached as far as a fretful Athens.

For there, with the dual realizations that any bulwark the Ionians might have given them was surely doomed, and that the far-seeing and pitiless eye of the King of Kings would soon be fixed unblinkingly on their city, the Athenians were panicking, too. The ebullient self-confidence that had swept the democracy to its first intoxicating victories was already fading fast. Defeat in Ionia was not the only bloody nose that the Athenians had recently been given. For a whole decade now, they had found themselves embroiled in a bothersome war with the small but tormentingly energetic island of Aegina, a nest, as the Athenians saw it, of pirates and scavengers, and one that stood infuriatingly only fifteen miles south of Salamis, in the heart of the Saronic Gulf—directly astride their shipping lanes. Guided in her policy as she was by landowners, instinctive lubbers with their roots in the soil, Athens had never thought to build herself a navy. Nor, despite the relentless buzzing of Aeginetan privateers, did she think to do so now. Who, after all, was going to stump up the cash? Not the poor, self-evidently; and certainly not the rich, who took it for granted that they should stand and fight with shield and spear on dry land, as men of their background, men who could afford decent armor, had always done. Yet this disdain for seapower, although it certainly helped to preserve the hoplite class from the indignity of having to grunt and sweat at an oar, did not contribute greatly to the war effort against Aegina. Indeed, such was the Athenians' impotence against enemy raids that they were forced, on one occasion, to watch helplessly as their whole harbor went up in flames. True, the wide bay of Phalerum was not easily defended; nor were the Aeginetan pirates in any position to challenge Athens by land; but the fact that the war was a nuisance rather than a terminal menace in no way diminished the democracy's sudden sense of drift. One question, in particular, could hardly fail to trouble the voters. If they found it impossible to defeat a tiny pinprick of an island just off their coast, what hope would they have against the righteous fury of a superpower?

As the storm clouds of seeming Persian invincibility loomed ever darker over Ionia, so strange shadows from the past returned to haunt Athens, too. In the summer of 496 BC, the Athenian people elected as their head of state a man whose very name appeared to hint at an imminent climbdown from liberty. Hipparchus was not merely the son of a prominent Pisistratid minister, but had even married his sister to Hippias, the exiled tyrant. The ideal candidate, perhaps, to open channels to his brother-in-law, negotiate favorable terms with Artaphernes, and secure a pardon for the burning of Sardis from the Great King. In the event, the democracy stood firm: despite all the continuing bad news from the Ionian front, Hipparchus served out his year of office without engaging in active collaboration. Yet the temptations of surrender, which the peace party naturally preferred to term realism, continued to gnaw away. Rumors of treachery—of "medizing"—swirled through the city; and inevitably, as they had done for a century, the darkest suspicions of all attached themselves to those champion opportunists, the Alcmaeonids. Cleisthenes may have been the patron of democracy, but few doubted that his clan, given sufficient incentive, would opt to sell it out. That nothing was ever proved against them served only to fuel the democracy's paranoia. The Great King's gold was surely flowing somewhere, somehow, into Athens. If not to an Alcmaeonid, then to somebody else. Politician kept suspicious eye on politician, tracked the news from Ionia with growing foreboding, and maneuvered for advantage.

To the Eupatrids, of course, this was an old game. Appeasement came naturally to them. As in Ionia, so in Athens, the aristocracy had long affected a faddish Orientalism. The notion that they should risk the obliteration of their city rather than arrive at an accommodation with the all-powerful King of Kings was hardly one that they could be expected to embrace. Enthusiasts for the new political order, realizing this and marking the pall of black smoke that hung over Ionia, came increasingly to mistrust the old elite and to doubt their loyalties. Admittedly, not all Eupatrids could necessarily be regarded as collaborators in waiting: Miltiades, for instance, grandest of the grand though he was, had been an active freedom-fighter in the Chersonese since the very start of the Ionians' great revolt. But even he ruled his fiefdom as a tyrant: not much of a recommendation to those in Athens growing nervous for their democracy.

Where, then, could they look for leadership? Perhaps to a new generation of politician, and a new breed. One not unsettled by the talk of people power, as the scions of the great families were, but inspired by it instead. Revolution, so alarming to the Eupatrid elite, appeared to promise rare opportunities to talented citizens on the make. Barely a decade into the life of the democracy, for instance, a young man by the name of Themistocles could credibly set his eyes on the supreme office in Athens, the archonship, despite coming from a family with no obvious political pedigree at all. Though of aristocratic birth, his father had never shown the slightest interest in holding public office; his

mother—horror of horrors—was not even Athenian-born. In an earlier and more chauvinistic age, a misfortune of this order would have
been sufficient to deny Themistocles his citizenship altogether; only
Cleisthenes' reforms and the need to pad out the ten tribes with a full
complement of able bodies had ensured a change to the law. As a result,
Themistocles' sense of loyalty toward the new order was of a peculiarly
personal nature—and left him hankering after public office rather as a
man in a delirium might crave a cure. Themistocles had recognized,
with the instinctive cynicism that would always mark his love affair
with celebrity, that in a state run by the people there could be only one
certain gauge of fame. "How can you rate me," he would ask his friends,
"when I have not yet made anyone jealous?"[18] The horizons opened up
by the new order glimmered before him as a kind of agony.

In 494 BC, this brilliant and ambitious young man celebrated his
thirtieth birthday—and became old enough, after years of waiting, to
stand for election to the archonship. The following year, he resolved,
he would have a go at it—and do so, furthermore, with a good chance
of success. He might have been inexperienced in public life and of
obscure background, but he nevertheless had all the makings of a
star. Bull-necked, crop-haired, solid of body and face, Themistocles
had the appearance, so posterity would judge, "of a true hero":[19] one
indomitable, indestructible, packed with strength. Yet he was simultaneously, in his intelligence, the very opposite of muscle-bound: the
workings of his mind, infinitely mobile and serpentine, would ultimately become a thing of wonder to his fellow citizens—and of alarm.
Not a dark art required of the politician under the Athenians' new
form of government but Themistocles showed himself its master: he
could infight, he could network, he could spin. Above all, and most
crucially, he knew how to make himself visible. Rather than live out
on the family estates, for instance, he chose to settle instead downwind
of the Ceramicus, near the "Hangman's Gate," where the bodies of
executed criminals and suicides were dumped: an insalubrious address,
to be sure, but also—and here was the attraction for Themistocles—
within walking distance of the Agora. Concerned not to have the

great and the good put off visiting this ill-omened spot, he began inviting celebrated musicians to rehearse inside his home; keen to make friends and influence people, he set up as an attorney, the first candidate ever in a democracy to rehearse for public life by practicing the law. Above all, naturally affable and gregarious as he was, he wooed the poor; and they, not used to being courted, duly loved him back. Touring the taverns, the markets, the docks, canvassing where no politician had ever thought to canvass before, making sure never to forget a single voter's name, Themistocles had set his eyes on a radically new constituency.

Not that ambition was his only motivation. While nothing that Themistocles did was ever entirely divorced from self-interest, he had seen in the poor not merely voters but the future saving of his city. A startling notion to his peers; "yet it was the genius of Themistocles that he could gaze far into the future, and penetrate there every possibility, both for evil and for good."[20] More clearly than any of his elders, the tyro politician recognized that the best chance for his city's survival lay not on dry land but on the sea—and that any warship would depend for power upon the massed muscle of its rowers. This was hardly a convincing prognosis, it might have been thought, when Athens possessed barely a harbor, let alone a battle fleet. Themistocles, however, his gaze fixed in visionary fashion upon the long term, was undaunted. Drawing up his manifesto, he began to argue for the urgent downgrading of the existing docks and their replacement by a new port at Piraeus, the rocky headland that lay just beyond Phalerum beach. The shoreline there afforded not one but three natural harbors, enough for any fleet, and readily fortifiable. True, it lay two miles further from the city than Phalerum, but Themistocles argued passionately that this was a small price to pay for the immense advantages that a new harbor at Piraeus would afford: a safe port for the Athenians' ever-expanding merchant fleet; a trading hub to rival Corinth and Aegina; immunity from Aeginetan privateers. And perhaps, in due course, if the money could be found and the circumstances appeared to demand it, then perhaps, just perhaps, a naval base as well . . .

Themistocles, who had no wish to alarm the landed gentry with wild talk of sea power, chose not to belabor this final point. Yet its shadow, in that spring of 494 BC, was palpable across Athens. The news from the East was darkening daily. The Persian war fleet was finally on the move. The Ionian leaders, it was reported, smuggling themselves ashore onto the spur of Mount Mycale, then skulking up its side like refugees in their own land, had assembled at the Panionium, their long-abandoned communal shrine. There, clearing away the weeds, they had resolved to make their stand against the Persians, and stake their future on a single, desperate throw. The revolt, as its leaders were agonizedly aware, was now on a razor's edge: "On one side, freedom— on the other slavery, and the slavery of runaways, at that."[21] No choice had been left the Ionians but to man every warship that they could, to throw in their every last reserve. Round the cape of Mycale they had sailed, south toward Miletus and the small island of Lade. There, two miles outside the great city's harbors, they had made their base. Beyond them were six hundred enemy warships—and the prospect of a decisive battle. Yet, for days, as though overwhelmed by the monstrous scale of the looming engagement, neither side had ventured to stir; and nerves, across Ionia, across Athens, across the whole Greek world, began to jangle. Still the stalemate continued; and still, on harbor fronts everywhere, men waited anxiously for the news.

Then, toward summer, tidings at last, as bleak and flame-lit as had always been dreaded. The Ionians, starving on their tiny island base, had proved easy prey for enemy agents. When their fleet, advancing to meet a sudden Persian attack, had sailed out into the bay of Miletus, its line of battle had promptly crumbled. Some captains from Samos, the island facing Cape Mycale, had cut a private deal with the Persians, not merely to save their own skins but to doom the city in whose commercial shadow they had lived for so long. As whole squadrons copied the renegades' example and began turning tail, defeat for the rest of the Ionian fleet had become inevitable—and the position of Miletus untenable. With corpses washing up in their harbors, disease rife in their streets, and all hopes of victory now lost in the waters off

Lade, the Milesians had soon succumbed to the assault of the Persian siege engines; and Artaphernes, taking possession of the city, had wreaked upon it a terrible, almost Assyrian, revenge. The jewel of the Aegean, once the favored ally of the Persian king, had been given over completely to fire. Her men had been slaughtered, her women raped, her sons castrated, her daughters enslaved. As the wretched survivors, tethered in the train of wagons piled high with the treasures of their holiest shrines, began shuffling off on their long journey to the work camps and harems of Persia, they had passed settlers heading the other way, loyalists granted possession of their land by Artaphernes. Such was the fate that the Great King had sworn would befall all rebels against his power; and as the Great King had sworn, so, sure enough, it had come to pass.

Where next would he fix his gaze? Did the shadow of his anger have any limits? If news of the obliteration of Miletus was greeted in Athens and Eretria by naked terror, there ran through their neighbors, too, a palpable shudder of apprehension. Preoccupied with their own squabbles as they always had been, even the most parochial Greek cities were now obliged to lift their gaze and recognize in Persian power a new and prodigious factor in their calculations. But to what effect? There were many options open—and not all of them glorious. The Argives, for instance, whose enthusiasm for liberty ran a very distant second to their loathing of the Spartans, had made up their minds even before the fall of Miletus.[22] Flourishing one of the bogus genealogies that had long been a feature of their foreign policy, Argive ambassadors had crossed to Sardis and informed the startled Persians that they were in fact descended—roll of drums—from an ancient king of Argos. A somewhat far-fetched theory, it might have been thought; except that the putative ancestor dredged up by the Argives, a gorgon-slaying, princess-rescuing hero by the name of Perseus, certainly sounded as though he might have been an ancestor of the Persians. A murky compact had duly followed, for Persians and Argives alike had excellent reasons for indulging the fantasy that they were relations: the former could anticipate a welcome base in the

Peloponnese; the latter could rub their hands and dream of a Sparta reduced to rubble by their distant cousin, the King of Kings.

The Spartans themselves, despite a hostility to Persia that dated back to their rebuff at the hands of Cyrus, had long been content to regard Argive pretensions of kinship with the barbarians as pathetic rather than menacing. That quickly changed, however, as the grim news from Ionia began to arrive. A victorious Persia, a revanchist Argos: here was a prospect risen from the Spartans' darkest nightmares. Cleomenes, having originally spurned the chance to fight the barbarians in Ionia, now looked to strike at them in a manner far more calculated to bring a glow to his countrymen's hearts: by assaulting Argos. In the summer of 494 BC, even as the Persians were pulverizing the rebel forces in Ionia, Cleomenes duly led his countrymen northward on their own mission of annihilation. Nothing was permitted to stand in their way. Informed by his seers that an Argive river god would doom the Spartans if they crossed his waters, Cleomenes snorted, "How very patriotic of him,"[23] and disdainfully took another route. Next, having shattered the Argive army in a great battle beside the village of Sepeia and pursued the survivors to a sacred grove, he called out to individual Argives that their ransom money had been paid. As they emerged from the sanctuary, Cleomenes had them executed one by one. When the remaining fugitives finally understood this murderous trick, Cleomenes coolly ordered the incineration of the holy grove.

A shocking crime, of course—as shocking, in its way, because ordered by a Greek, as the harrowing of Miletus. Even though Cleomenes, to spare himself the taint of sacrilege, had ordered helots to fire the grove, the black smoke that billowed up from the holocaust, greasy and polluted with human flesh, provided a gruesome statement to other cities of Spartan intent. No threat to Lacedaemon would be tolerated. Argos, culled of an entire generation, dismembered of her territory, left so enfeebled that even tiny Mycenae was able to wriggle free of her grip, stood as a mutilated example of what might result from any challenge to Spartan power. The Persians too

169

could count themselves included in the warning. Any invasion would be met with implacable resistance. Sparta was pledged to hold her ground and fight, no matter what.

It seemed, then, as though Athens might not have to stand alone against the vengeful King of Kings after all. Yet the Athenians themselves, by the winter of 494 BC, appeared paralyzed by that same indecision which had so fatally afflicted their Ionian cousins. Perhaps they were numbed by the continuing bleakness of the news from across the Aegean. Ionia, once so prosperous, so brilliant, so fair, was reported to have become a wasteland. Weeds rose in the footsteps of the Persian reprisal squads; fugitives who had taken to the hills were being harried by dogs and human dragnets; those few Milesians not to have been deported sat shivering amid the blackened ruins of the birthplace of philosophy. The prospect that they might share a similar fate was almost too much for the Athenians to bear. In the spring of 493 BC, when a tragedy was staged at the City Dionysia that drew not on a scene from mythology, as the audience had been expecting, but directly on the fall of Miletus, "everyone in the theatre was moved to tears."[24] The tragedy was promptly banned and the playwright, as a punishment for having invented agitprop and upset the citizenry so, was heavily fined. The Athenians' response to the Persian threat seemed to be to bury their heads deep in the sand.

And yet, just as they knew in their hearts that the Great King's task force was coming, so they knew that its arrival would leave them with only two effective options: to appease, collaborate, surrender— or to fight. The choice could not be put off for much longer. Evidence for that was everywhere. No sooner had the theatergoers wiped away their tears than another vivid reminder of the storm clouds gathering to the east had arrived in Phalerum harbor. Miltiades came trailing clouds of glory: having fought the barbarians far more heroically than any other Athenian had done, he had escaped the vengeance of the Persian fleet by the skin of his teeth, dodging a squadron sent specially to intercept him and being pursued all the way to Athens. But he also had many enemies closer to home: hated by his peers and feared by the people, his glamour appeared ill suited to an embattled democracy. No sooner had he disembarked than he found himself being prosecuted "for his tyranny in the Chersonese."[25] The trial was set for later in the year.

Much more would hang on the verdict than the fate of Miltiades alone. Would the Athenians have the courage to acquit a man they had long feared as a potential tyrant, yet whose track record as a Mede-fighter was second to none; or would they surrender instead to the more immediate—and traditional—pleasures of factionalism? Every citizen was bound to have a view; but the one with the greatest influence promised to be the chief archon, the annual head of state. This was sufficient to give a particular edge to the elections of 493 BC; and when victory was won by a candidate firmly identified with the anti-appeasement cause, Miltiades must surely have breathed a deep sigh of relief. True, Themistocles was much given to envy, and the temptation to work for the ruin of a charismatic rival must have been considerable; but he resisted it. Miltiades, brought to trial, was acquitted. Shortly afterward, he was elected military head of his tribe—one of ten generals charged with providing advice and support to the Athenians' supreme commander, the war archon. This, as surely as the burning of the grove at Sepeia had been, must have appeared to Persian spies a defiant statement of intent. It certainly served to give Miltiades a critical influence over the formulation of his city's defense policy. The democracy, it appeared, had finally made up its mind. The Athenians, like the Spartans, had committed themselves to fight.

The Road to Marathon

No one in Athens had the slightest doubt that the Great King was personally resolved upon the destruction of the democracy. When Darius had been brought the news that Sardis was burning, it was said that he had called for his bow, that awful totem of royal power, and fired an arrow high into the air, praying to Ahura Mazda as he did so that he might punish the Athenians as they merited. Such was his fury that the royal appetite was supposed never entirely to have recovered from the shock. Day after day, it was rumored, year after year, every time that Darius sat down at his table to eat, a servant would whisper softly into his ear, "Master, remember the Athenians."[26]

No mean feat, of course, for a previously obscure people on the very edge of the world to be mentioned daily within the inner sanctum of Persepolis. The Athenians, even as they made their flesh creep by imagining themselves singled out for the Great King's vengeance, could also feel a certain shiver of desperate pride at the idea. Indeed, the fact that Darius had signally failed to come sweeping across Asia against them suggested that they might just possibly be flattering themselves. Certainly, the true scale of the Great King's empire and the demands upon his attention were utterly beyond the comprehension of most Greeks. Cleomenes, informed during the course of his abortive interview with Aristagoras that Susa lay more than three months' march beyond the sea, had leapt up in startled disbelief; and yet, east of Susa, the Great King's dominions took a further three months to cross in turn. It would have been small comfort for the Athenians, as they awaited their hour of doom, but teaching them a lesson was not the only, nor even the most pressing, of Darius' concerns.

But that is not to say it was no concern at all. The Great King's memory was capacious and his reach global. Not a crisis on a far-distant border but he would be kept closely informed of it. Staggering as the distances within his dominion were, so was the ingenuity with which his servants worked to shrink them. No one could fail to be dazzled by the speed of the Persians' communications. Fire beacons, flaring from lookout to lookout, might keep the Great King abreast of an incident almost as it brewed. In the more mountainous regions of the empire, and particularly in Persia itself, where the valleys offered excellent acoustics, more detailed information might be brought by aural relay. The Persians, schooled "in the arts of breath control, and the effective use of their lungs,"[27] were well known to have the loudest voices in the world; many a message, echoing from cliffs and ravines, had been brought within the day over terrain that a man on foot would have struggled to cover within a month. As the Persians understood to a degree never before rivaled, information was dominance. Master information, and master all the world.

The ultimate basis of Persian greatness, then, was not its bureaucracy, nor even its armies, but its roads. Precious filaments of dust and packed dirt, these provided the immensity of the empire's body with its nervous system, along which news was perpetually flowing, from synapse to synapse, to and from the brain. The distances which had so appalled Cleomenes were routinely annihilated by royal couriers. Every evening, after a hard day's ride, the messenger would find a posting station waiting for him, equipped with a bed, provisions and a fresh horse for the morning. A truly urgent message, one brought at a gallop through storms and the dead of night, might arrive in Persepolis from the Aegean in under two weeks. This was an incredible, almost magical, degree of speed. Nothing to equal it had ever been known before. No wonder that the Great King's control of such a service—the original information superhighway—should so have overawed his subjects, and struck them as the surest gauge and manifestation of Persian power.

Access to it was ferociously restricted. No one could set foot upon the king's roads without a pass, a "*viyataka.*" Since every travel document was issued either directly from Persepolis or by a satrap's office, mere possession of one spelt prestige. Indeed, it was in the "*viyataka*" that those twin manias of Persian imperialism, for shuffling forms and for rigid social stratification, most perfectly met and fused. There was no better way for an official to discover his precise place in the imperial pecking order than to arrive at a posting station for the night, hand over his *viyataka* to the manager, and count out the rations that it brought him in return. If he were one of the greatest men of the kingdom—one of Darius' six coconspirators, say—then he and his retinue might receive up to a hundred quarts of wine. If he ranked at the bottom of the food chain, then he might find himself, humiliatingly, on a lower wine ration than a particularly favored horse. So satisfying did the Persians find the *viyataka* as a basis for ordering the world that not only officials and soldiers but women and children, and even birds, found themselves definitively fixed within the imperial scheme of things by ration chits. A duck, for instance, if it were being fattened for the royal table, could look forward to downing a quart of wine every day. A young girl, by comparison, might have to get by on one a week.

Men, women, children, horses, waterfowl: none could elude the meticulous prescriptions of Darius' bureaucrats. It was not only within the satrapal courts that the Great King had his "eyes," forever watching, scanning, tracking. Every transaction carried out within a posting station required a form to be stamped by both manager and recipient, and then forwarded to a central archive in Persepolis. So tightly controlled were the itineraries of travelers on the royal roads that those who dawdled on the way and failed to arrive at a given destination on an allotted date could expect to forfeit their rations for the night. Those who traveled on the roads without a *viyataka* at all would not merely go hungry but very quickly be hunted down and killed. Even mail, if it were sent without royal or satrapal approval, would be destroyed. Only the most cunning could hope to evade the vigilance of the highway patrols. Histiaeus, for instance, back in 499 BC, desperate to communicate with his nephew in far-off Miletus about his plans for revolt, had shaved the head of his most trustworthy slave, tattooed a message on the gleaming scalp, and patiently waited for the hair to grow back. "Then, once the slave had a full head again, Histiaeus sent him to Miletus with orders to do nothing except tell Aristagoras to shave him, and inspect what stood revealed."[28] Such was the inventiveness required of those without a *viyataka*.

How, then, were enemies of the Great King ever to compete with all Darius' prodigious resources of intelligence? Not very well, was the answer. The Ionian rebels, for instance, pinned on the outermost rim of Asia, had only ever had the haziest notions of Persian troop movements and intentions—a failure set into stark relief by the startling ability of Darius, 1500 miles from the theater of war, to track events almost as though he were on the spot. It was he, for instance, in the early weeks of 494 BC, who had personally drawn up plans for the final offensive that a few months later would result in the great Persian victory at Lade and the sacking of Miletus. Darius' information on that occasion had been particularly precise and detailed, for his leading military specialist on Greek affairs, a general by the name of Datis, had traveled directly by express service from Ionia to keep him abreast of the latest news from the front. Nothing could better have indicated the supreme importance attached to intelligence by the Great King than that a man of Datis' stature should have made the long journey to Persepolis in person. Datis—like Harpagus, the original conqueror of Ionia—was a Mede; but he was also, in the competitive world of ration chits and security passes, quite as weighty a player as any Persian grandee. His daily wine ration was seventy quarts: a drinking allowance at which a sister of the King would not have turned up her nose. Due reward for an exceptional military ability and record.

True, the Persian intelligence services did not always have things their own way; nor was Darius' eye for talent necessarily infallible. One of the worst debacles had occurred a couple of years before Datis' arrival in Persepolis, when the Great King, in a startling display of misjudgment, had sent Histiaeus back to Sardis as his personal agent. Appalled at having to welcome the slippery Milesian to his headquarters but reluctant to offend his brother, Artaphernes had pointedly revealed to Histiaeus the full scale of his suspicions, hoping thereby to intimidate his unwelcome guest into openly going over to the enemy. " 'Let's not beat about the bush,' " the satrap had menaced. " 'Aristagoras may have worn the shoe, but you were the one who made it.' "[29] Histiaeus, turning pale, had got the message, but flight from Sardis that very night had hardly ended his capacity for mischief. Fishing in the murky waters of espionage circles with consummate skill, revealing himself first to one side then to the other as a double agent, he had sought to turn Artaphernes' more underhand methods back against their perpetrator, daring even to foment rebellion within the satrapal court itself. Greeks, it appeared, were not the only people who could be set against one another: the crisis briefly appeared so threatening that Artaphernes, struggling frantically to maintain his authority, had been forced into a wholesale purge of his countrymen. Such ruthlessness, fortunately for the satrap, had been just sufficient to prevent a disintegration of the Persian provincial command—and, of course, from that moment on, Histiaeus had been a marked man. No episode in the entire quashing of the Ionians' revolt can have given Artaphernes greater pleasure than the capture, a year after the victory at Lade, of his brother's treacherous former favorite. Hauled to Sardis in chains, the irrepressible Histiaeus had coolly insisted that he be returned to the Great King—a demand which Artaphernes had duly met by impaling him, and then sending his severed head, pickled and packed in salt, by express post to Susa.

The execution of Histiaeus, and the parallel escape of Miltiades to Athens, had marked the effective end of Ionian resistance. Not of Artaphernes' labors, however. Having won the war, it was now his equally arduous task to win the peace. Ionia had been trampled underfoot by six summers of savage warfare. Fields lay uncultivated, ships rotted idly in stagnant harbors, roads had vanished beneath grass, villages and whole cities stood abandoned in blackened ruin. As the Ionians starved, so, inevitably, they began to scrap desperately over the few fields not lost to nettles and brambles; and, bled of nearly all their energy and manpower though they were, they reached for their weapons again. Artaphernes, having none of it, stepped in at once. Representatives of the various Ionian states were summoned to Sardis and briskly ordered to swear an oath of perpetual amity. Henceforward, all border disputes were to be settled not by the armed squabbling that was traditional among the Greeks but by arbitration, backed up directly by the sanction of Persian force. As even the Ionians themselves acknowledged, this was a development "not entirely to their disadvantage."[30] To protect his subjects from their own worst instincts, to promote stability, to facilitate a regular flow of tribute: this, as it had always been, remained the satrap's default policy. Terror having served its purpose, Artaphernes could now return with a sigh of relief to the winning of his subjects' hearts and minds. Having been made all too aware of the Ionians' distaste for tyranny, he was even prepared to indulge in certain circumstances their preference for democracies. After all, just as long as the king's peace was kept, it scarcely mattered how the Greeks chose to rule themselves.

This indulgence was not extended, of course, to those who remained in arms. Even as Artaphernes applied to bleeding Ionia the balm of a settlement long remembered afterward as a model of fairness and justice, so the continued defiance of the Athenians remained an open wound. A standing menace too. The longer that the punishment of Athens was delayed, the greater was the risk that terrorist states might proliferate throughout the mountainous and inaccessible wilds of Greece: a nightmare prospect for any Persian strategist. Geopolitics, however, was far from the only prompting at the back of the Great King's mind. Not for nothing had Ahura Mazda delivered the world into his hands. No more sacred duty had been laid upon him than the obligation to storm, wherever they might fester, the strongholds of the Lie. Athens was a nest of rebels, to be sure—but the city also stood revealed, far more sinisterly, as the home of demons, "*daiva*," false gods who had chosen the path of rebellion against the Lord Mazda, "following the course of Wrath, sickening the lives of men."[31] Only fire, of the kind that had already cleansed and purged the shrines of the Ionians, could possibly redeem Athens and her temples from the Lie. For the spiritual good of the universe, as well as the future stability of Ionia, the entire Aegean would have to be transformed into a Persian lake—and without delay. Staging post in a thrilling new phase of imperial expansion and holy war: the burning of Athens promised to be both.

But how best to achieve it? Two policies suggested themselves: to complete the conquest of the land approaches along the coast of the north Aegean; and simultaneously to menace the cities of Greece into surrender. In pursuance of the first goal, a fleet and a fresh army were dispatched to Thrace in the spring of 492 BC, with orders to extend Persian dominance ever further westward, into Macedonia and perhaps beyond. Their commander, a dashing young nobleman by the name of Mardonius, arrived on the western front already bathed in the golden glow of natural charisma. The son of Gobryas, Darius' closest friend among the Seven, his intimacy with the royal household had been confirmed by his marriage to the Great King's daughter. But Mardonius was not merely prodigiously well connected; he was also a general of authentic élan and flair. Alexander, the King of Macedon, quickly bowed to the inevitable: Macedonia was formally absorbed into the dominions of the Great King, whose remit now extended to the foothills of Mount Olympus. True, the victory was slightly tarnished when Mardonius' entire fleet was shipwrecked in a storm off Mount Athos, and Mardonius himself, launching an overexuberant assault on a troublesome mountain tribe, was badly wounded—but these setbacks were hardly severe enough to undermine Persian prestige. Macedonia, certainly, remained solid for the Great King; Alexander, practiced weathervane that he was, could still tell precisely which way the wind was blowing.

But the key question for Persian strategists was whether the Greeks to the south would show themselves similarly sensitive to the political weather. In 491 BC, a year after the conquest of Macedonia, ambassadors were sent on a exploratory tour of Greece, with demands for earth and water. Most cities, gratifyingly, scurried to oblige. Some, however, did not. Two, in particular, could not have made their adherence to the darkness of the Lie, and to the *daiva*, those "spawn of evil purpose,"[32] any clearer. In Athens, not only were the Great King's demands dismissed out of hand, but his ambassadors, in blatant defiance of international law, were put on trial by the Assembly, convicted and put to death. Perhaps—given that Athens was a proven terrorist state, and that the man who had initiated the diplomats' execution was Miltiades, a notorious fugitive from the Great King's justice—this outrage was no surprise. More shocking, and more disturbing in its implications, was that the Spartans chose to blacken themselves with an even worse act of sacrilege. There was no trial for the Great King's ambassadors in Sparta: instead, flung down a well, they were told before they drowned that "if they wanted earth and water, they could find it there."[33]

This, in its naked defiance, its savage wit and its cavalier disregard for religious convention, was a spectacular that had Cleomenes' fingerprints all over it. The Athenian democracy, it appeared, had indeed arrived at an accommodation with the Spartan king who had twice tried to destroy it. When the Athenians, discovering that Aegina had handed over earth and water to the Great King, reported the news to Sparta, Cleomenes traveled in person to berate the medizers. The merchant princes of Aegina, however, with their dependence on international trade, were reluctant to offend the great superpower to the east—even on the say-so of a Spartan king. Searching for a way to outflank Cleomenes, they appealed to Demaratus, his fellow king. Demaratus, grateful for any opportunity to stab his hated rival in the back again, eagerly pledged his support. The Aeginetans were encouraged to stand firm. Cleomenes was rebuffed.

Covert though Demaratus' role in this business had been, however, it was not so covert that his colleague failed to sniff it out. Cleomenes' counterthrust, delivered immediately on his return to Sparta, was brutal and cunningly aimed. Resolved now to finish off his insufferable colleague once and for all, Cleomenes approached Demaratus' cousin, a spiteful nonentity by the name of Leotychides, and promised him the throne if he would help bring down his kinsman. Leotychides, unsurprisingly, jumped at the chance. As his enemies were well aware, Demaratus had an old skeleton just waiting to be dragged out of the closet. Tangled though the circumstances of Cleomenes' own birth were, those of his fellow king were hardly less so. Demaratus' mother, the once plain girl granted the gift of loveliness by the apparition of Helen, had become such a beauty that the King of Sparta, overwhelmed by her charms, had used his royal muscle to abduct her from her husband. Seven months later, the new queen had given birth to a son. But was the father the king or the commoner? A question long settled, it might have been thought, by the fact that the queen's son—Demaratus himself—had by 491 BC been on the throne for twenty-four years. A mere detail to Cleomenes, though; and when Leotychides, raking up the issue of Demaratus' legitimacy, proposed taking the case to Delphi for arbitration, judicious bribes to the priesthood had already guaranteed Apollo's complicity.

The oracle duly pronounced against Demaratus. Back in Sparta he was formally deposed by the ephors, and Leotychides, pliable and venal, took his place. Accompanied by his new colleague, Cleomenes promptly returned to confront the Aeginetans, who this time, rather than dare defy two Spartan kings, capitulated on the spot. They even agreed, when Cleomenes demanded it, to hand over hostages as a token of their good behavior to their bitterest foes, the Athenians. No longer would a Persian task force arriving off Attica be able to use Aegina as a base. Cleomenes, long reviled by his neighbors, suddenly found himself widely lauded for his selfless labors "in the common cause of Greece."[34] Persian agents were confirmed in their judgment of the Spartan king as their most dangerous and able foe, and the major obstruction to the Great King's plans for the West.

Yet all was far from lost. As the Persians had often had good cause to appreciate, there was no Greek front so united that it might not at any moment disintegrate. Just when Cleomenes appeared to have shored up his position for good, news of the bribes that he had given Delphi suddenly leaked out. The scandal burst over Sparta. Outrage was universal. Cleomenes, caught red-handed for once, was forced to flee the city in disgrace. Not, of course, that exile was a fate he was remotely prepared to take lying down. Disdaining to beg his fellow citizens for permission to return, he sought to intimidate them instead. Cleomenes had always had a talent for setting the cat among the pigeons, but now it led him into blatant treachery. Reversing the policy of divide and rule that he had promoted to such effect throughout his reign, he sought to rally the northern Peloponnese to his personal cause—and to such effect that his jittery countrymen lost their nerve and hurriedly invited him back. But hardly in a forgiving mood; and Cleomenes, by returning to Sparta, was effectively sealing his doom. It began to be whispered that he was mad. The Spartans themselves blamed alcohol. The Argives preferred to see in Cleomenes' decline sure proof of the anger of the gods. Whatever the cause, though, virtually everyone agreed that the king who only a year previously had been hailed as the bulwark of Greece was now a lunatic. There were few complaints when his two surviving half-brothers, Leonidas and Cleombrotus, late in 491 BC, had him certified and locked up in the stocks. Nor were many eyebrows raised when his corpse was found the following morning, slices of flesh carved off his legs, hips and belly, a bloodstained knife dropped in the dirt by his side. The verdict, one that pushed plausibility to its outer limits but was nevertheless universally accepted: suicide.

So perished the Great King's most formidable enemy in Greece. With him also passed a style of leadership—unscrupulous, to be sure, but decisive and proactive—that the naturally cautious Spartans had never ceased to find alarming. Indeed, the squalid circumstances of Cleomenes' end did much to confirm them in their suspicion of strong leaders altogether. True, Leonidas, the new king, was his brother's successor in more ways than one, for he had married, with her father's blessing, Gorgo, Cleomenes' only child—as wealthy as an heiress as she had been precocious as a little girl. All the same, Leonidas remained, as a man new upon the throne and possibly tainted by fratricide, an unknown quantity: he was bound to take some time to find his feet. Who else was there, then, with the Persian hammer blow threatening, to take a lead? Leotychides? He was too busy crowing over the wretched Demaratus. The Gerousia? Or the Ephorate? Both were instinctively conservative bodies, far less likely to sanction a policy of forward defense than Cleomenes had been. Persian spies, feeding intelligence back to Sardis that winter, had much good news to report of Sparta. The turmoil in the city, the faction fighting that would have struck Darius' strategists as so inveterately Greek, appeared to offer them their perfect opening: the opportunity to strike at Athens and take her out while she stood alone.

A chance not to be missed. In the early weeks of 490 BC, the long-awaited invasion order was finally given. A large army, "powerful and well equipped," totaling perhaps some 25,000 men in all, marched out from Susa.[35] With Mardonius still recovering from his injuries, command of the expedition was entrusted to two other generals with detailed knowledge of the western front: Artaphernes, son and namesake of the satrap in Sardis; and, as effective supremo, Datis the Mede, the seventy-quarts-a-day veteran of the Ionian revolt, and a man who, unusually for a member of the imperial elite, had such a specialized understanding of the enemy that he could actually speak some faltering Greek. The strategy these two commanders were to follow had been mapped out for them directly by the Great King: cross the Aegean with an immense armada, bring the benefits of Persian rule and peace to all the islands, and then, that objective completed, "reduce Athens and Eretria to slavery, and bring the slaves before the king."[36] The conquest of the rest of Greece, including Sparta and the Peloponnese, was to wait; and yet, even as Darius' instructions stood, the planned expedition was an ambitious one. Certainly, as an amphibious operation, it promised to be on a scale not witnessed since the invasion of Egypt thirty-five years before. On top of that, the plan not to hug the coast but to island-hop directly to Greece was as bold and innovatory a strategy as any that even Darius had conceived.

Yet Datis and Artaphernes can have had little doubt as to their ultimate success. Every day's journey westward brought them fresh evidence of the barely believable scale of the Great King's resources: the labor gangs toiling to maintain the roads, whole populations sometimes, transplanted from the furthest reaches of the earth; the guards, stationed beside every bridge, every flotilla of pontoons, every mountain pass; the troops in their own rear, not merely Persians and Medes, but levies drawn from even further east, Bactrians, Sogdians and axe-wielding Saka. What was Athens to peoples such as these? Not even a name. Yet on they marched, directed by the will of their far-off, all-seeing king; and every evening, no matter where they halted, these men from the steppes, from the mountains, from the villages of Iran, they would be provisioned out of monstrous depots, supplied punctiliously with jugs of wine, and loaves of bread, and barley for their horses. And when at last, having passed through the Syrian Gates and descended into the plain of Cilicia, on the southeastern coast of modern-day Turkey, they found there waiting for them an immense fleet of ships, some built as weapons of war, others as horse transports. Up the gangplanks they climbed, men and horses alike; Datis gave the order; and the armada pulled out to sea.

Rumors of its approach were soon filtering through to Greece. No one there was unduly alarmed. Although the monstrous fleet was clearly bound for the Aegean, even to the jumpy Athenians it hardly seemed to be an imminent threat. Plenty of Persian fleets had been seen off Ionia before, after all—and they had always sailed northward, hugging the coast, on to the Hellespont. What reason to think that this fleet would take a different course? Onward the armada glided, past the ruined harbors of Miletus, toward the straits between Mount Mycale and the island of Samos—or so it appeared. But then, just by Samos, something wholly unexpected: the fleet suddenly changed its course. A shudder of disbelief passed through all those watching from the shore. The Persians were not continuing northward but heading west! There could be only one possible explanation: Datis and his task force were embarked for the open sea, for Greece—for Attica.

And as the Persian fleet fanned out across the Aegean, so its commander gave a master class in the arts of empire building. First: shock and awe. Gliding into the harbor of a startled Naxos, he took belated revenge for the debacle of the expedition there a decade previously by torching the city and rounding up the natives as slaves, dragging them onto his ships in chains as their homes and temples burned. Next: win hearts and minds. Arriving off his next port of call, the island of Delos, holy throughout the Greek world as the birthplace of Artemis and Apollo, Datis reacted to the news that the Delians had fled before his approach with injured innocence. "You men illumined by the sacred," he expostulated, "what a strange notion of me you must have, that you run away in this manner!"[37] This might have been thought a disingenuous complaint—for the Persians, after the fall of Miletus, had thought nothing of sacking the holy oracle of Didyma and carting off its great bronze statue of Apollo to Ecbatana. But the Delians were sorely mistaken if they imagined that this stern treatment of the rebels' shrine had in any way implied disrespect for great Apollo! After all, it was the rebels themselves who had shown the god of light the grossest disrespect, by turning to the Lie and thereby surrendering his holy oracle to the night-bred pollutions of the *daiva*. Datis, resolved that this theological subtlety should not be lost on the Greeks, duly staged a spectacular demonstration of his devotion to the Lord Apollo, standing before the god's altar and burning in his honor barrowloads of frankincense. Then, his point expensively made, he returned to the fleet to continue his tour of the islands, receiving their submission, taking hostages, press-ganging troops. None thought to resist him. The twin clouds of smoke—one belching black from the flames of burning Naxos, the other white and perfume-scented, rising to the nostrils of Apollo himself—had done their work. It was as though the armada, heading for Eretria and Athens, still sailed beneath their shadow—and as though that same shadow were drifting westward, inexorably, to plunge all Greece into darkness.

Sure enough, by late July, Datis had reached the easternmost tip of Euboea.[38] He was now within sight of Attica. Athens, however, would have to wait; for, rather than crossing directly to the mainland, Datis had decided that he would aim first for the smaller and less formidable of the two targets on Darius' hit list. Forty-five miles up the ever-narrowing straits that separated Attica from Euboea the Persian fleet sailed, until at last, well inland and framed against a backdrop of mountain peaks, the rebel city of Eretria could be made out, its acropolis a rugged hump set amid a narrow plain of fields and olive groves. Scanning the shore nervously, Datis was soon breathing a sigh of relief; for the Eretrians, rather than fighting his task force on the landing beaches, where it would have been most vulnerable, had opted instead to retreat behind their walls. The Persians duly started their assault. For five long days, the fighting was bloody and desperate; on the sixth, treachery handed the city to the besiegers. Two fifth columnists opened the gates. They both came, as Datis had surely known they would, from the aristocracy—indeed, were "the most respected men in all of Eretria."[39] Intimidate the masses, flatter the elite: once again, the Persians' favored policy had triumphantly proved its worth. As in Ionia, so now in Euboea, gutted ruins bore witness to the aptitude of the Greeks for treachery and class hatred.

And one man, turning from the spectacle of blazing Eretria and the coffles of slaves being readied for deportation, would surely have seen in it a foreshadowing of the fate of his own city and his own people, unless they could only be persuaded to see reason, to open their gates, to welcome him back. Hippias, the exiled tyrant of Athens, was more than eighty years old now. He had not seen his native land for two decades. Yet he devoutly believed himself the Athenians' last, best hope. Only he could divert the justified fury of the Great King from them; only he could hope to restore his wretched city to the sunlit uplands of Darius' favor.

It was with no sense of guilt, then, but rather through patriotism and a belief in his own destiny, that the aged Pisistratid boarded a Persian ship and guided Datis' fleet back the way it had sailed. Across the straits, on the far side of the Euboean Gulf, the coast of Attica rose rugged and steep from the water. There could be no landing there on its northern coast. But only round the headland, and the perfect spot was waiting: a scimitar-shaped bay wide and sheltered from the winds, with beaches where a whole fleet of ships might be drawn up, a plain beyond it, ideal for Datis' cavalry, and a choice of two roads leading onward round Mount Pentelikon to Athens. Hippias would have had good cause to remember the place. More than fifty years previously, he and his brother had landed there with their father, Pisistratus, when the would-be tyrant, at the third attempt, had finally succeeded in establishing his rule over Athens for good. Now, with the Persian fleet driving toward the same disembarkation point, Hippias knew that history, surely, was on the verge of repeating itself. Just as his brother's visions had once done, so now his own had offered a tantalizing glimpse of what was to come. The previous night he had dreamed that he was sleeping with his mother; and so, as the prow of his ship met slushy sand, the old man readied himself to disembark, to embrace his native land, to prove the omen true. He was home at last.

Meanwhile, all around him, the bay was black with ships, and men were clambering into the waters, and wading onto the seaweed-matted beach, thousands upon thousands of them, an armed multitude of an order never before seen in Greece; and already, far and wide, Persian outriders were raising dust across the plain of Marathon.

That Greece Might Still Be Free

The deadliest enemy that a hoplite had to face in battle was panic. All it took was for one man to despair of victory, to abandon his place in the line, to drop his shield and start shoving his comrades aside in a desperate scrabble to the rear, and a shudder of dread might pass through the whole phalanx, and that single soldier's flight become within seconds a general rout. An unsettling phenomenon—and one that the Greeks preferred to blame not on mortal fallibility but rather on some freakish supernatural event, the breath of a god, perhaps, sending a chill across the ranks, or the sudden apparition of an angered hero woken from his grave and striding across the battlefield. Yet even this theory, though it might provide balm to the injured pride of a routed army, still carried with it a disturbing implication: that to fight in a phalanx was always to be vulnerable to the faint-heartedness of a few. "Men wear helmets and breastplates for their own protection—but shields they carry for the good of everyone who forms the line."[40] March to war without perfect confidence in the stomach of one's fellows for the coming fight, and a hoplite might well reflect that he was marching to his doom.

So that when men in Athens, looking from their walls to Mount Pentelikon and seeing the blaze of a great beacon there, warning of the Persians' landing, knew that the moment dreaded for so many years had finally arrived, opinion on how best to meet the peril was by no means unanimous. Fabulous reports of the size of the Asiatic hordes were already swirling through the city, and it was evident even to the soberest Athenian strategist that any army the democracy could put into the field was bound to be horrendously outnumbered. Add to that the invaders' overwhelming superiority in cavalry and the numbing fact that no Greek army had ever, in fifty years, succeeded in defeating the Persians in open combat, and the arguments for staying put, manning the city's walls and hunkering down for a siege might have appeared irresistible.

Yet the decision to march from the city and confront the invaders had in fact already been taken. No sooner was it confirmed that the Persians had landed at Marathon than the hoplites of the democracy, all those citizens who could afford to arm themselves, perhaps some ten thousand in total, prepared "to take food with them and march."[41] They left under the command of the war archon, Callimachus—but the strategy was Miltiades', and it was one that had been adopted, after days of bitter debate in the Assembly, as an official resolution of the Athenian people. The judgment of the city's greatest Mede fighter was not one to be lightly set aside; and Miltiades, against the claims of everyone who had pushed for a defensive policy, had presented a compelling case of his own. Yes, the invaders had landed in overwhelming force; and yes, they had brought with them their fearsome cavalry; but that was precisely why they had to be met. Two roads led from Marathon round Mount Pentelikon to Athens: only let the Persians take command of one of these, and their horsemen would be granted the whole sweep of Attica. If the Athenians marched quickly, however, and secured the two exits from the plain, they might yet contain the Persian beachhead. True, they would almost certainly then be committing themselves to battle—but it was not only within a phalanx that fraying nerves might breed disaster. It had needed only two traitors to open the gates of Eretria, after all. Could a city such as Athens, one that had been rife for a decade with rumors of treachery, fifth columnists and profiteers from the Great King's gold, really hope to hold out during a siege? It beggared belief. Better, surely, if the worst came to the worst, to die in harness than to be stabbed ignominiously in the back.

Yet the Athenian people, despite having voted in favor of Miltiades' forward policy, still shrank from believing that they might have to stand and face the terrifying invaders on their own. Even as the army of the democracy, heading for Marathon, vanished from the sight of those left behind in Athens, one citizen was leaving in the opposite direction, south, into the Peloponnese. His name was Philippides, an athlete celebrated as his city's greatest runner, and a man of prodigious stamina and speed. By covering the staggering distance of 140 miles in under two days, he found himself, on the second evening of his epic run, descending the rugged northern hills of Lacedaemon into the Eurotas valley. As the sun sank behind the peaks of Mount Taygetos, Philippides reached the unwalled cluster of barracks and temples that constituted Sparta.

The scenes he found there could not have been in sharper contrast to those he had left behind in Athens. The whole of Lacedaemon was *en fête*. Philippides had arrived while one of the Spartans' holiest festivals, the Carneia, was in full swing, and all across the city young men were resting after a day spent playing brutal games of tag, while their elders feasted in field tents set up in deliberate imitation of a battlefield encampment. Far from signaling the Spartans' readiness to leap up and march off to war, this parody of their conventional campaigning style in fact displayed the precise opposite: the Carneia was a time of peace. There could be no question, the Spartans informed Philippides regretfully, of breaking such a sacrosanct period of truce. Only once the moon climbed full in the silver-lit August sky would they be able to march to Marathon. On the evening of Philippides' arrival in Sparta, that was still a week away. Add the marching time, and the Athenians could not expect to see a Spartan army for at least another ten days. Surely, had he still been alive, Cleomenes, that scoffer at taboos and inveterate enemy of Persia, would have insisted upon an immediate departure—but he was dead, and Sparta, in the wake of his violent end, was still in a state of shock. Of faction-fighting too. The bitterness between Leotychides and Demaratus, in particular, was continuing to poison public life, with the new king jeering at his predecessor as a commoner at every turn. With the Spartans embroiled in such turmoil, it would hardly do to anger the gods further—even though, as Philippides put it, "the Athenians beg you for your assistance, they beg you not to stand by idly while the most venerable city in the whole of Greece is crushed, they beg you not to let it be enslaved by gibberish-speaking invaders."[42]

Yet even if ten days must have struck the disconsolate runner as a perilously long time for the Athenians to have to hold out, he was not destined to return from his mission entirely empty-handed.[43] As he headed back to Athens, he was greeted by name on the heights beyond Tegea by a figure with the legs of a goat, two jutting horns and an enormous phallus. Perhaps it was a hallucination brought on by despair, exhaustion, or heatstroke—but Philippides himself had no doubt that he was being spoken to by a god. A potentially mischievous one as well—for Pan had a warped sense of humor, and was perfectly capable, if he bore a grudge against a city, of giving every citizen within its walls a raging erection. But on this occasion, appearing to Philippides, the god had only words of encouragement, reassuring the runner of his affection for the Athenians and promising to be of use to them very soon. Pan did not go into specifics; but since he was, as his name implied, the god of panic, whose very appearance on a battlefield could send a chill through one army and fire another with potent courage, his words must have struck Philippides as rich with hope and promise.

And all the more so when he finally arrived home and found not the smoldering pile of rubble that he might have feared but rather a city that was just about keeping its nerve. In fact, the news from the front appeared almost promising: the Athenian hoplites had marched with such speed to Marathon that they had been able to secure the two roads to Athens, then had promptly dug themselves in before the invaders could break out from the plain. On top of that, they had been joined in their camp by some eight hundred men from Plataea: every hoplite the tiny city had been able to dispatch. This was hardly a substantial reinforcement, but it was so bold a gesture of gratitude and so touching a demonstration of friendship that the Athenians had found themselves powerfully fortified by it. Perhaps, they now began to hope, as they listened to Philippides' news, the standoff at Marathon might continue until the Spartan relief force arrived. Perhaps their city might be preserved from the Persian firestorm, after all.

Not that the mood of optimism, among a people stripped of their fighting men, could be reckoned wholly unclouded, of course. Fearful imaginings, fearful questions still swept through the nervous streets. What if the Persian fleet, making its way round the coast of Attica while the Athenian hoplites were being held at Marathon, suddenly landed at Phalerum? What if traitors were in touch with Hippias? What if they had plans to open the gates? The darkest whisperings of all inevitably had as their focus the Alcmaeonids. But nothing could be proved against them; nor, despite all the rumors, was there evidence of overt treachery or defeatism from anyone else. The city gates remained barred. Philippides, heading on to Marathon, could report to the generals there not only the news from Sparta and his encounter with Pan, but that morale back in Athens was holding firm.

Yet the runner, when he arrived at the Athenian camp and had his first view of what his fellow citizens there were facing, must surely have felt his own resolve begin to waver. The spectacle of the plain of Marathon was fit to chill the blood; as terrifying, perhaps, as the sight that had greeted defenders on the walls of Troy, for when since those ancient times had there been any invasion force to compare with that of Datis? At the far end of the bay, sheltered by a long promontory known to locals as the "Dog's Tail," the Persian ships had been hauled onto the sand, and they now extended along the curve of the beach for miles. The Asiatics themselves, monstrous numbers of them, dressed

in their outlandish, brightly colored costumes and swarming over
the plain, trampled beneath their alien feet crops sprung from the
sweat of Athenian farmers and the holy Attic soil. Their horsemen,
galloping up to the Athenian lines, wheeled and turned, wheeled and
turned, mocking their adversaries' lack of archers with fast-dispersing
plumes of dust.

They did not yet dare to venture beyond the lines, however—for
the Athenians, camped as they were on raised ground, with steeper
ground rising sheer behind them, and a grove sacred to Heracles
screening them from the approach of the Persian cavalry, occupied a
formidable defensive position. Now, with the arrival of Philippides at
their base, they could gauge precisely how much longer they would
have to hold out until the Spartans arrived: a single week. Perfectly
feasible, in the opinion of a majority of the Athenian generals. When
others heard Philippides' news, however, they knew that it brought a
perilous moment of reckoning that much nearer. The Persians, as
Miltiades in particular had good cause to appreciate, had a sinister
mastery of the arts of espionage: there could be little doubt that Datis
was already factoring the vagaries of Spartan timetabling into his own
calculations; little doubt either that he would have realized that he
was running out of time. Since the Athenian holding force had—so
far—signally failed to disintegrate amid treachery and dissension, as
Datis had evidently been expecting it to do, the Persian commanders
would soon find themselves obliged to adopt a new strategy—and
Miltiades, for one, appears to have had little doubt what it would
prove to be. With the Athenians blocking the two roads south, there
was only one way for Datis to strike at Athens before the Spartans
arrived: by sea. If—when—the invaders began to embark, the
Athenian army would be confronted with a hideous choice: stay put
and risk seaborne enemy cavalry being welcomed into Athens by fifth
columnists; or advance into the open plain and offer the Persians
battle. Both were fearful prospects; but only the latter, Miltiades
argued, offered even the faintest hope of victory.

A day passed, then another, and another. Four days now until the

Spartans were due to arrive, and still the deadlock held. The Persian ships remained where they were, menacing but motionless, beached on the sand. The sun sank behind the mountains that rim the plain of Marathon. The moon, at last, shone full in the August sky. Far off in Lacedaemon, the men of Sparta would be preparing to march to war. And in the Persian camp? Illumined a ghostly silver the plain may have been, but it was hard, miles from the invaders' ships, to track what might exactly be happening within the shadow of the Dog's Tail. Something, certainly: for a great commotion, the sound of thousands upon thousands of tramping feet, could be heard faint, then louder, nearing the Athenian lines. The invaders, it appeared, were advancing in force at last. But was this a full assault or a diversion? The answer would come soon enough. Datis was not the only commander to have realized the vital significance of intelligence. Someone—and one can only assume that it was Miltiades, experienced as he was in all the Persian arts of war—had recruited spies from among the invaders. That night of the full moon, some Ionian conscripts, sneaking across the plain, crept into the grove that screened the Athenian camp. The news they brought could not have been more urgent. Hurriedly, it was conveyed to Callimachus and the ten tribal generals who together constituted the Athenian high command. "The horsemen are away!"[44]

Here was the moment that Miltiades had been waiting for. Clearly, if his spies' intelligence was accurate, the Persian task force had been split, with a holding force advancing to distract the Athenians' attention while far to the rear the cavalry was being clandestinely embarked.[45] A council of war was hurriedly convened; Miltiades implored his fellow generals to vote for immediate battle. Never, he urged, would there be a better chance of victory: the invaders' army was divided and all but a skeleton force of its cavalry had gone. Four of Miltiades' nine fellow generals agreed; five, appalled at the prospect of attacking the Persians on open ground, without archers, without cavalry, and still overwhelmingly outnumbered, did not. The casting vote now lay with the war archon, Callimachus, who had consistently shown that he felt it no shame to bow to the superior expertise of Athens' most famous Mede fighter. He did so again now, and sided with Miltiades. The order was given. Battle would be joined at dawn.

Throughout the Athenian camp men were woken with the news that within the hour they would be advancing against an enemy who had never before been beaten by a hoplite army in open combat, "and whose very name, when spoken, was sufficient to send a shiver down the spine of any Greek."[46] Yet if, by summoning every last reserve of physical and moral strength, and by screwing their courage to a truly excruciating pitch, there was a chance of averting their obliteration, and that of their families and their city, then the Athenian hoplites had to brace themselves now to seize it. Slaves, charged with the care of their precious armor, duly brought out the burnished panoplies. The naked Athenians were transformed into fearsome automata of bronze. Then, sheathed within their breastplates and their greaves, their shields and spears in their hands, their helmets propped back upon their heads, the hoplites took their places in the battle line, standing alongside their fellows from their demes, their thirds, their tribes. It was the custom among the Athenians to serry their phalanx in ranks eight deep; but Miltiades, fearful of being outflanked by the Persians' more mobile light infantry, and by what remained of their cavalry, ordered the center to be thinned out so that the Athenians' line exactly matched that of the invaders, now increasingly visible a mile away through the early glimmerings of the dawn. With the first rays of sun touching the gray Euboean hills in the distance, sacrifices were offered to the gods; the omens proving favorable, the generals then took up their positions directly in the foremost line. Calli-machus, as was customary for the war archon, took command of the right wing; the Plataeans were stationed on the left; Themistocles and a fellow rising star of the democracy, Aristeides, led their tribes in the center of the phalanx, at its perilously weakened heart.[47] Miltiades himself, allotted overall command for the day, stood where all could hear him, and at length raised his arm, pointed to the Persians, and yelled out: "At them!"[48]

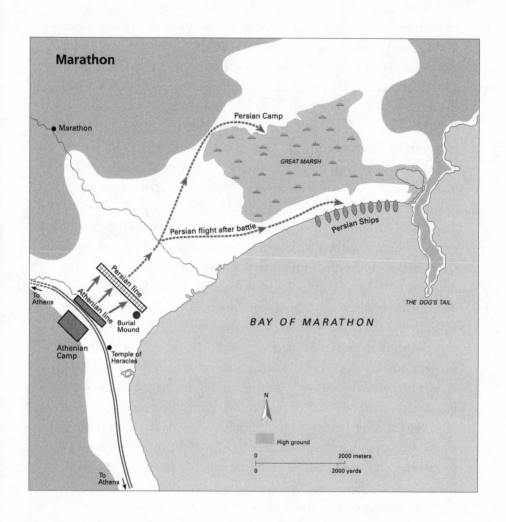

Marathon

Marathon

Persian Camp

GREAT MARSH

Persian flight after battle

Persian Ships

Persian line

To Athens

Athenian line

Burial Mound

THE DOG'S TAIL

BAY OF MARATHON

Athenian Camp

Temple of Heracles

N

High ground

To Athens

| 0 | 2000 meters |
| 0 | 2000 yards |

A shimmering of metal all along the line as the hoplites lowered their helmets, hefted their shields, shouldered their spears. Here, at last, was the moment of no return. His head encased now almost entirely within metal, every member of the phalanx found himself frighteningly cut off from the sights and sounds of the battlefield, barely able to see the enemy ahead of him, barely able to hear the braying of trumpets that instructed the Athenians to start their charge. Only the sudden jolting of his fellows on either side and the surging of the weight of men behind him appeared real. Downward, into the open expanse of the plain, the phalanx began lumbering, keeping its formation, not once threatening to break. All were borne on the dread and the intoxication of the moment—for while it was true that the faintheartedness of a few within a shield wall might prove fatal to the many, then so too was the converse, that even a hoplite shaking with terror as he advanced, wetting himself uncontrollably, streaking his cloak with shit, could know himself strong for being one with his friends and relatives, one with a mighty body of armed and freeborn men. How, indeed, without the self-consciousness of this, would any Athenian have dared to do what all in the phalanx did that August dawn: to move against a foe widely assumed to be invincible, to cross what many must have dreaded would prove to be a plain of death.

Extraordinary stories were later told of this advance. It was said that the Athenians ran the whole mile, as though men bold enough to attack the Persians for the first time must have been somehow more than human. In truth, no man wearing the full panoply of a hoplite, some seventy pounds of bronze, wood and leather, could possibly run such a distance and still have energy left to fight effectively. Even in the relative cool of the early morning, sweat rapidly began to mingle with the dust kicked up by ten thousand pairs of feet, half-blinding the advancing hoplites and stinging their blinking eyes, so that their vision of the enemy ahead of them—the outlandishly dressed archers reaching for their arrows, the slingers for their shot, the expressions of glee and disbelief in the Persian ranks—grew ever more obscured. Soon, as the Athenians crossed deeper into no man's land, the first arrows began to hiss down upon them; then, raising the monstrous weight of their shields to protect their chests, the hoplites did at last begin to run. Simultaneously, as though the phalanx were "some ferocious cornered creature, stiffening its bristles as it turns to face its foe,"[49] those in the front three ranks lowered and aimed their spears, in preparation for the coming collision. By now, with some 150 yards still to travel, a storm cloud of arrows and slingshot was breaking over them, thudding into their shields, bouncing off their helmets, striking the odd hoplite in the thigh or through the throat, but still the Athenians, braving the black rain, only quickened their pace. Those of the enemy directly in their path had already begun scrabbling to erect wicker defenses, as they realized, to their horror, that the wall of shields and iron-tipped spears, far from providing easy pickings for their bowmen, as they had at first imagined, was not going to be halted. A hundred yards, fifty, twenty, ten. Then, as the Athenians' war cry, a terrifying ululation, rose even above the thundering of their feet upon the dry earth, the cacophony of clattering metal and the screams of the panic-stricken enemy, the phalanx crunched into the Persian lines.

The impact was devastating. The Athenians had honed their style of warfare in combat with other phalanxes, wooden shields smashing against wooden shields, iron spear tips clattering against breastplates of bronze. Now, though, in those first terrible seconds of collision, there was nothing but a pulverizing crash of metal into flesh and bone; then a rolling of the Athenian tide over men wearing, at most, quilted jerkins for protection, and armed, perhaps, with nothing more than bows or slings. The hoplites' ash spears, rather than shivering, as invariably happened when one phalanx crashed into another, could instead stab and stab again, and those of the enemy who avoided their fearful jabbing might easily be crushed to death beneath the sheer weight of the advancing men of bronze. Soon enough, on the wings of the Persian army, men were breaking in terror, streaming back across the plain, as the Athenians, skewering and hacking, continued their deadly work. Only in the center, where the force of the phalanx's impact had been much weaker, did the invaders have the better of the fight, withstanding the collision and then slowly pushing the hoplites back. Here was where the invaders' best troops had been stationed: the Persians themselves, more heavily armored than most of the other levies, and the Saka, those brutal fighters from the far-off eastern steppes, their axes perfectly capable of cleaving a hoplite's helmet or smashing through his chest. Yet already the Athenian wings were wheeling inward, attacking them on their flanks, reinforcing the hard-pressed tribesmen of Aristeides and Themistocles, so that soon the Persian center too began to crumple and the slaughter grew even more incarnadine. It was then that the few Persians and Saka who were left joined the general rout, and fled for their ships, some miles back across the plain, stumbling in the sands. They were pursued by the Athenians, exultant in their triumph, but half disbelieving it too, thoroughly dazed by the manner in which Pan had kept his word.

Yet, if the battle was won, the victory was still far from decisive. The necessity of the two Athenian wings to finish off the battle in the center had given plenty of time to the sailors manning the Persian fleet to prepare their ships for departure, and to start hauling aboard the panic-stricken levies as they milled among the shallows. True, many of their comrades had been crushed in the general stampede, or else had floundered in a great marsh that stretched northward from where the Persian ships had been beached, drowning there in such vast numbers that it was estimated later "to have been the site of the deadliest slaughter of all."[50] Yet, while Datis and Artaphernes kept control of their fleet, they remained a menace; and Miltiades and his men, powerless to deal with those ships that had already embarked, were naturally desperate to capture or burn any still remaining on the sand. The fighting on the beach, then, was as ferocious as at any stage in the battle, and, for the Athenians, just as fatal: one hoplite, reaching up to seize the stern of a ship, had his hand hacked off by an axe, and fell back spraying blood from the fatal wound; Callimachus, the war archon, was also killed; so too one of the tribal generals. Seven ships were ultimately secured; but all the rest succeeded in pulling away. The road to Athens may have been blocked to the Persians—but not the sea.

And what of the ships containing the cavalry that had embarked before the battle? The question haunted the Athenian high command. Even as they waded back past the corpses bobbing in the shallows and gazed across the plain in the direction of their city, the weary hoplites could see, glinting from the slope of Mount Pentelikon, the flashing of a brightly polished surface, deliberately angled to catch the rays of the morning sun.[51] It was clearly a prearranged signal, and one that could only have been intended for the Persian fleet, somewhere out to sea. It was impossible to know its precise meaning—but every Athenian guessed at once that it spoke of treachery.

Consternation swept through the ranks. Twenty-six miles away, their families and homes still lay wholly undefended. Exhausted, sweat-soaked and blood-streaked, they had no choice but to head back at once for Athens "as fast as their legs could take them."[52] It was not yet ten in the morning when they left the battlefield; by late afternoon, in an astounding display of toughness and endurance, they had reached their city.* In the nick of time, too—for soon afterward the first ships of the Persian fleet began to glide toward Phalerum. For a few hours they lay stationary beyond the harbor entrance; then, as the sun set at last on that long and fateful day, they raised anchor, swung around, and sailed eastward into the night. The threat of invasion was over.

So it was that Athens escaped the terrible fate of Miletus and Eretria, and proved herself, in the ringing words of Miltiades, "a city fit to

---

*This was the march that inspired the French educationalist Michel Bréal to propose a "marathon race" for the 1896 Olympic Games, tracing the route taken by the Athenians from the battlefield to Athens. The legend that it was Philippides who brought the news of the victory, gasping out, "We have won!" and then expiring, is sadly no less spurious for being so poetic and fitting.

become the greatest of all in Greece."[53] At Marathon, her citizens had stared their worst nightmare directly in the face: not merely that the Athenian people might be transplanted far from the primordially ancient soil that had given them birth, from their homes, their fields, their demes, but, even worse, that their bloodlines, amid hideous scenes of mutilation, might be extirpated. Every hoplite fighting on that day must have known that the Great King, incensed by the Athenians' oath-breaking, had ordained for them that "most terrible of all known acts of vengeance":[54] the castration of their sons. Had the Athenians, perhaps, in their darkest imaginings, dreaded that the gods themselves might uphold this ghastly sentence? Athens had indeed betrayed her promises of loyalty to Darius; and it was the habit among the Greeks when they swore an oath to stamp upon the severed testicles of a sacrificial beast, and pray that their progeny be similarly crushed if they went back on their word. By charging the enemy at Marathon, the Athenians had, in effect, steeled themselves to put this most terrible of all their fears to the test—and had resolved it spectacularly.

And much more besides. Whoever had sent the signal to the Persians from Mount Pentelikon kept his silence now. When the news was brought that Hippias, dashed of all his hopes, had expired of disappointment en route back into exile, it merely confirmed what everyone already knew: that no one after Marathon should stake his future on there being a tyranny in Athens again. Everyone was in favor of rule by the people now. Or at least in favor of rule by the people who had won the famous victory: the farmers, the landed gentry, the armor-owning stock. 192 of them, it was discovered, had died in the battle—and to these heroes of Athenian liberty a unique honor was accorded. No tombs in the Ceramicus for them; instead, for the first and only time in their city's history, the dead were buried, "as a tribute to their courage,"[55] on the very field where they had fallen. A great tomb was raised over their corpses to a height of more than fifty feet, and marble slabs listing the names of the fallen were placed along its sides. Not even the haughtiest of noble dynasties could boast of anything to compare. Mingled with the dust they had fought so courageously to defend, the dead were to lie buried together, without class or family distinctions of any kind. They were citizens—nothing less and nothing more. What prouder title than that of Athenian could possibly be claimed? Athens herself was all.

Even the Spartans, when they arrived there after their grueling three-day march, regarded the men who had conquered the Mede unaided with a new and ungrudging respect. Marching onward to inspect the battlefield, they found at Marathon, rotting amid the dust of the plain or half sunk into marsh slime, evidence enough of the scale of the menace that had been turned back so heroically. Six thousand and four hundred invaders lay there, fattening the flies—and that was only a fraction of the task force that Datis had led. How many teeming millions more the Great King might have at his command, breeding and swarming within the fathomless hinterlands of Asia, neither the Athenians nor the Spartans much cared to contemplate. Every Greek, looking upon the Persian dead and reveling in the great victory, must nevertheless have felt just a tremor of apprehension. Yet the Spartans, methodically inspecting the battlefield, turning over the corpses, making notes, would have found much to reassure them as well. It was the first opportunity they had ever been given to study the armor and the weapons of the fabled masters of the East; and what they saw did not greatly impress them. Datis may have led a huge army to Marathon—but nothing that the Spartans would have recognized as their equal.

Meanwhile, even as they continued their tour of inspection, a great trench was being dug on the southern margins of the marshes. Into this makeshift refuse tip the invaders' corpses were flung unceremoniously. No memorial for the slaughtered Persian hordes.* Mute and inglorious as their grave was, what better was deserved by men who in

---

*Only when a German surveyor in the nineteenth century found a great jumble of bones on the plain was the location of the Persians' grave identified.

life had known nothing of the comradeship of a city, or of liberty from royal diktats, or of the discipline of a phalanx, but had instead milled like the merest herd of beasts, their voices animal screechings, full of sound and fury, signifying nothing? The Ionians had labeled the Persians "barbarians"; now, in the aftermath of their great victory the Athenians began to do the same. It was a word that perfectly evoked their fear of what they had seen that early morning on the plain of Marathon: an army numberless and alien, jabbering for their destruction, "gibberish-speakers" indeed. Yet "barbarian," especially on the tongue of a veteran of the famous battle, could also suggest something more: a sneer, a tone of superiority, or even of contempt—one, certainly, that few Greeks would have dared to adopt prior to that fateful August dawn.

Marathon had taught not only Athens but the whole of Greece a portentous lesson: humiliation at the hands of the superpower was not inevitable. The Athenians, as they would never tire of reminding everyone, had shown that the hordes of the Great King could be defeated. The colossus had feet of clay.

Liberty might be defended, after all.

6

THE GATHERING STORM

Weeds in Paradise

Marathon, trumpeted by the Athenians as the greatest victory of all time, was regarded by the King of Kings in an understandably different light. True, Persian propagandists were hardly in the habit of drawing attention to their master's setbacks—yet neither was it entirely stretching a point for them to dismiss the battle as a minor border skirmish. While it was certainly to be regretted that the pestilential Athenians had managed to wriggle free of their punishment, the failure to take their city detracted only mildly from an expedition that had otherwise been a great success. Anyone doubting this had only to watch the Eretrians as they were led cringeing through the streets of Susa. Darius, exceedingly gracious, responded to the spectacle of his captives' misery and submission by ordering their chains struck off and settling them just to the north of modern-day Basra. This region was already widely celebrated for the mysterious black liquid that bubbled up from beneath its sands, and the smell of what the Persians called "*rhadinake*" hung heavy in the air—a far cry from the salt tang of the Aegean. Just as the Judaeans had once wept beside the rivers of Babylon, so now the Eretrians mourned their homeland amid the oil wells of southern Iraq. "Farewell, famous Eretria, our country no more. Farewell, Athens, once our neighbour across the straits. Farewell, beloved sea."[1] Their exile, as Darius had recognized, was punishment enough.

Such magnanimity, of course, could only ever be the sunshine after the storm of the Great King's righteous anger. On Athens, that obdurate stronghold of *daivas* and the Lie, the death sentence still stood as immutably as before. But not on Athens alone. The sin committed by the Spartans in murdering the Great King's ambassadors had been neither forgotten nor forgiven, and Darius, reformulating his western strategy in the aftermath of Marathon, was now resolved that Sparta as well as Athens should be destroyed. By good fortune, his intelligence chiefs, always at the forefront of the Great King's military planning, had recently pulled off a particularly spectacular coup: the recruitment as an agent of none other than a former king from that closed and mysterious city. Demaratus, publicly insulted by Leotychides in the full view of the Spartan people, had finally snapped: making his way first by stealth and then in open flight to the court at Susa, he had been greeted there with lavish marks of favor—and pumped greedily for information.[2] The defector, already homesick for his city, had duly answered his interrogators with an unstinting and embittered relish.

Yet, for all that Demaratus found himself pushing at an open door when encouraging his patrons to consider an invasion of the Peloponnese, Darius' plans for conquest could not easily be hurried. Whereas Datis' expedition had been little more than a glorified razzia, the full-scale pacification of a land as remote and mountainous as Greece was a challenge of a wholly different order of complexity. The wheels of Persian bureaucracy ground both slowly and exceeding small. In June 486 BC, three years after Darius had first given orders for the mobilization of his empire, the Egyptians, oppressed by their master's ceaseless demands for grain and levies, rose in sudden revolt. From Athens, the gaze of the Great King swung abruptly southward. Egypt, so rich, so fertile, so golden, was far too precious a prize to be risked for the barren wilds of Greece. A task force that had imagined Athens its target was duly ordered to prepare itself instead for an assault on the land of the Nile. As summer shaded into the blessed cool of autumn, preparations were made for its departure from Persia. The King of Kings readied himself to ride in person at its head.

At court, everyone could recognize this as a potentially fateful moment. Darius had embarked on many expeditions before, but he was no longer, at the age of sixty-five, a young man, and rumors of his frailty were rife. Courtiers with painful memories of what had happened the previous time that a Persian king had set off for Egypt dared to contemplate the end of an era—and they dreaded it. Cambyses, after all, campaigning beside the Nile, had left behind him in Persia only a single brother; Darius, a serial wife-taker and proudly prolific, had bred any number of ambitious sons. War in the provinces, a looming succession: here, if the past offered any guide, was a recipe for disaster. Fratricide, its malignant effects threatening the foundations of Persian rule, had already brought one line of kings to extinction—who was to say it might not do so again?

The aged Darius himself, however, having labored all his reign to give to the world the fruits of truth and order, was hardly the man to regard the prospect of their ruin after his death with equanimity. An immense reservoir of able sons, far from threatening his empire, might, he preferred to believe, serve to buttress it. The Persian people could be reassured, rather than alarmed, by his fecundity. Not for nothing had it always been a fundamental principle of theirs that "the surest gauge of manliness, after courage in battle, is to be the father of a great brood of children."[3] Darius, scrupulous in all things, had certainly not neglected the education of his sons. Mollycoddling was hardly the Persian way. Even the Greeks, who liked to reassure themselves that a people who wore trousers as their national dress could only ever be hilariously effeminate, were obliged to acknowledge that. Sheathed in brightly colored patterns his legs might be, but a Persian prince was still raised to be very tough indeed.

Granted, he might well pass the first years of his life amid the silken comforts of the women's quarters—but only so that the eunuchs there could better mold him, "forming his infant beauty, shaping his toddler's limbs, straightening out his backbone."[4] From the age of five, he would find himself subject to a curriculum quite as exacting as the Spartan: woken before dawn by the blaring of a brass trumpet, a young prince would start his day with a brisk five-mile run, before embarking on a grueling round of lessons, voice-training, weapons practice, and immersions in icy rapids. To teach him the arts of leadership, he would be given the command of a company of fifty other boys. To teach him a properly regal facility with the lance and the bow, he would go hunting with his father. To teach him the principles of justice, of the glories of Persian history, and of devotion to Ahura Mazda, he would receive instruction from the Magi. Born into the lap of luxury he might have been—but luxury existed to dazzle the gaze of inferiors, not to soften the steel of the elite. Even a princess, although she might own whole towns with no function save to keep her shod in exquisite slippers, was expected not to loll around in vapid idleness but rather to study hard under her governesses, to practice her riding, and perhaps, like her brothers, to prove herself "skilled with bow and lance."[5] Much was expected of the children of the King of Kings. Awesome and splendid beyond compare as were the privileges of royalty, so too, and just as terrible, were the responsibilities that it brought. The inheritance of Darius' progeny, after all, was nothing less than the mastery of the world. No children in history had ever been born with quite such golden spoons in their mouths. Empire had become, under the artful and calculating management of Darius, a family concern—and it was in the interests of none of his children to scrap over the dazzling spoils. Prove themselves worthy of their father's favor, and they might all look forward to the rule of ancient kingdoms, of mighty satrapies, of splendid armies. The more deserving they were, of course, the more extravagantly they could hope to profit—with the supreme prize of Darius' own universal monarchy going, as was only fitting, to the most deserving prince of all.

Darius had decided who that should be years previously.[6] One son of his in particular shone out from the crowd: Xerxes was not the oldest of the royal princes, but he had long been the Great King's heir apparent. Many circumstances had combined to win him this title. Most crucially of all, perhaps, Xerxes, unlike many of his half-brothers, had the right mix of blood flowing in his veins—for his mother was the imperious Atossa, the best-connected woman in the kingdom, widow of both Cambyses and Bardiya, and daughter of Cyrus the Great. Yet such a pedigree, although certainly an advantage, would hardly have been sufficient to win Xerxes his father's blessing had he not possessed manifold other qualities, too. As a graduate of the most exclusive education in the world, he would have more than demonstrated his proficiency in riding, the handling of weapons, and the wisdom of the Magi—"for no man could be King of Persia who had failed to be instructed properly in that."[7] Likewise, in the hunt and on campaign, leading from the front, he would have given ample evidence of his personal bravery. Perhaps the clincher, however, was that Xerxes, tall and handsome, *looked* a king. This was a crucial consideration: the Persians were a people so obsessed by physical appearance that every nobleman kept a makeup artist in his train; the must-have fashion item was a pair of platform heels; and false beards and mustaches were so valued that the treasury ranked them as taxable items. Not even Xerxes' father could compare with the prince for good looks: for Darius, who was otherwise reckoned a strikingly handsome man, had arms like a gibbon's "that reached down to his knees."[8] Xerxes suffered from no such physical peculiarities: "both in his stature, and in the nobility of his bearing, there was no man who appeared more suited to the wielding of great power."[9]

So it was that when the ailing King of Kings, in the late autumn of 486 BC, and before he could set out for Egypt, finally "went away from the throne,"[10] as the Persians euphemistically put it, Xerxes was able to succeed to the monarchy of the world without opposition. Nothing, perhaps, became Darius' reign like the leaving it: in the contrast between the violent illegalities of his own accession and the stately smoothness of his son's lay striking testimony to the order he had brought to his wide dominions. Coated with wax, laid upon a magnificently ornamented chariot, pulled by horses whose manes had all been cropped, the body of the dead king was borne from Persepolis amid scenes of awful mourning. Led by Xerxes himself, the whole population of the city spilled out after the bier, wailing and hacking at their hair, stumbling in the ostentation of their grief toward a distant line of rugged limestone cliffs, out of which, high up on the rock face, had been carved the royal tomb. There the Great King was laid to rest; and all across Persepolis, and Persia, and every satrapy of the empire, wherever the blessings of Arta had been brought, the sacred fires kept alive for the thirty-six-year span of Darius' reign were solemnly extinguished, and the glowing embers left to fade away into dust.

The altars would not blaze into life again, and the reign of the new king officially begin, until Xerxes, proceeding northward to Pasargadae, had been inducted into certain secrets which only the wisest of the Magi, and the king himself, were permitted to know. As part of this initiation, Xerxes was obliged first "to divest himself of his own clothes, and put on a robe which Cyrus had worn before becoming king,"[11] and then to down various foul concoctions prepared for him by the Magi, necromantic brews of curdled milk and sacred herbs. A scepter was placed in his right hand; the *kidaris*, the fluted tiara of royalty, upon his head. Xerxes was then led into the glaring brightness of the Persian day. The satraps, the high officials, the expectant, swirling crowds, all of whom had assembled at Pasargadae for just this moment, now fell to the ground, prostrating themselves, as it was their duty and their honor to do, whenever graced by the presence of their king. Heir of Cyrus and chosen one of Ahura Mazda, Xerxes stood resplendent before the Persian people as both.

Not that he lingered long to enjoy the acclaim. Urgent business awaited him. Taking up the reins of Darius' command, Xerxes was soon leaving his still festive capital for Egypt. Descending on the rebels, he briskly demonstrated that he was indeed, just as his father had hoped he would prove to be, a chip off the old block: not only was the revolt summarily crushed, but Xerxes, showing that same eye for constructive nepotism that his father had always practiced to such advantage, installed there as satrap one of his numerous brothers. The Great King himself, even more militantly than Darius would have done, regarded this as a triumph not merely over mortal adversaries but over the far more sinister forces of cosmic evil. That countries where *daivas* were worshipped should be attacked and brought low; that their sanctuaries should be obliterated; that territories once given over to the Lie should be reconsecrated to the cause of Truth: this, throughout Xerxes' reign, was to be the guiding manifesto of the Persian people. Just in case there should be any doubt, inscriptions set up at Persepolis proclaimed it sternly to the world, reminding Xerxes' courtiers that there was no path of righteousness save for that set out by their king: "The man who respects the Law given by Ahura Mazda, who worships Ahura Mazda and Arta with the reverence that they are both due, he will find happiness in life, and become one with the blessed after death."[12] King of Kings though he was, "King of Persia, King of the Lands," Xerxes never forgot that all his unexampled power had been entrusted to him for a holy and momentous purpose. The obligations laid upon his broad shoulders were hardly of the kind that might be shrugged off casually. Those who had chosen him to bear their heavy weight could not be disappointed. "Darius had other sons," Xerxes freely confessed, "but Darius my father made me the greatest one after himself." And this, in turn, had been done as the expression of an even higher purpose: "For all was done in accordance with the wishes of Ahura Mazda."[13]

Certainly, once Egypt had been successfully pacified, there could be no question of neglecting the other great business left unfinished by Darius' death. No sooner had Xerxes returned to Persia than any number of different interest groups, clamoring for the Great King's attention, began urging him to set in motion a new expedition, to push deeper into Europe, to punish Athens, to conquer Greece. Most insistent of all in the royal ear was Xerxes' cousin, Mardonius, long since recovered from the wound he had received in Thrace, and spoiling for a return to the Aegean, which he regarded as very much his personal sphere of expertise. Nor was he the only glory hunter: one brother might have been installed in the pharaoh's palace, but there were any number of the Great King's other relatives eager to prove their mettle, to revel in the glamour of high command. After all, conquering far-distant *"anairya"* was what being a Persian was all about.

Turning to his intelligence chiefs for information on the western front, Xerxes was gratified to be informed that all stood fair. Yes, Athens and Sparta remained implacably opposed to his ambitions, but the aristocracy in other areas of Greece—including, not least, the vital territory of Thessaly, just to the north of Boeotia and Thebes—would, so the intelligence chiefs reported, welcome any Persian invasion with open arms. Once Thessaly had fallen, Thebes herself and a host of other cities further south were bound to collaborate. Indeed, even Sparta and Athens might not be utterly lost causes—for Demaratus, comfortably ensconced at Susa, and the Pisistratids, now well into their third decade of life on the Persian payroll, could guarantee the support of a few clients still. The admirably proactive sons of Hippias, indeed, ventured to offer the Great King the support of the heavens themselves—"describing to Xerxes how it was fore-ordained that a native of Persia should bridge the Hellespont, and expounding in detail on the triumphs that were bound to follow."[14] Source of these confident assertions was none other than Onomacritus, that same charlatan who had once been an intimate of the tyrants back in Athens, until falling out with them over accusations that he had been doctoring prophecies. Perhaps he was not the most reliable source of information—but the Pisistratids had an exile's desperation to see their homeland again and had returned desperately, pathetically, to trusting his every word.

It is doubtful that the Persian high command had quite the same level of confidence in Onomacritus, but that hardly mattered. Already, within months of Xerxes' return from Egypt, the drive to war had become unstoppable. Those few doves opposed to the invasion found themselves powerless to halt it. If they did speak out, they were labeled cowards. Their warnings, however, despite impatient snorts from the war party, could not so easily be swept aside. That the Athenians, as they had proved at Marathon, were no pushover; that the provisioning of any task force was bound to prove onerous even for the Persians' practiced bureaucrats; that the mountainous terrain of Greece was notoriously inhospitable: concerns such as these could hardly be dismissed as defeatist scaremongering. Yet even the perils of the venture, for all that they might inspire the occasional spasm of hesitation in Xerxes, served in the end only to stiffen the royal resolve. To have shrunk from risk, to have confessed that Persian power might be susceptible to overstretch, to have abandoned Athens and the continent beyond her forever to the Lie, such would have been an abject betrayal of Darius and, even more unforgivably, of the great Lord Mazda. Yes, the invasion was ripe with hazard—but then again, if it had not been, it would hardly have been a challenge worthy of the attentions of the King of Kings.

How best to meet it? Deep within the innermost sanctum of Persepolis—beyond the looming entrance halls carved in the form of colossal bulls with human heads and the wings of eagles, beyond the brightly painted courtyards manned by officious eunuchs, beyond even the thousand bodyguards stationed on perpetual duty outside their royal master's door, their long robes gem-studded, the butts of their spears adorned with delicate apples of gold—Xerxes' most trusted advisers assembled before the royal throne to offer their opinions. Although they were sequestered within the nerve center of Persian power, what was spoken there would in due course come to be shrewdly guessed at, thanks to rumor and to the progress of events.[15] At issue, of course, once it had been resolved that the war should go ahead, was a single question: what kind of task force should be marshaled for the invasion and conquest of Greece?

It seems that Mardonius urged that only elite fighters—Persians themselves, Medes, Saka and East Iranians—be conscripted. Such a strike force, he argued, would be able to move like lightning, outpace any foe, descend upon the lumbering infantrymen of the enemy with the same murderous speed that had always proved so lethal to the Greeks of Ionia.[16] Yet this strategy, although modeled on glorious precedent, did have a major, indeed, an insuperable drawback. Times had changed: how could an army drawn from so few satrapies possibly be considered sufficient for the dignity of the man who was to command it? What might have served Cyrus in the days of his mountain banditry was hardly adequate for his grandson, who ruled the world. Xerxes, when he conquered the West, would do so not merely as the King of Persia, but as king of all the dominions that lay beyond it, too. The people of even the obscurest frontier had a sacred duty to pay him the tribute of their sons. And in their obedience would be reflected the peerless glory of their master, the King of Kings.

So it was settled. And perhaps, very faintly, above the issuing of the royal commands, could be heard from the great courtyard outside Xerxes' audience hall the chiseling of sculptors as they adorned a nearby staircase wall.[17] Just like the steps themselves, which swept gracefully upward at a height sufficiently shallow to permit a nobleman in his voluminous robes to ascend them without any impairment to his dignity, the work had to be delicate in the extreme—for the workmen had been commanded to portray, in row after finely detailed row, lines of subject peoples presenting treasure to the king. This, so far, was the most that Xerxes knew of many of his subjects, remote from Persia and savage as the majority of them were; yet now, as his messengers prepared to gallop to every corner of the empire, to rouse the satrapies and summon them to battle, he could look forward to seeing all the fabulous diversity of his tributaries gathered before him and armed for war. Indians in their cotton dhotis, with their tall bows made of cane; Ethiopians draped in leopard skins, armed with arrows tipped with stone; Moschians wearing wooden helmets; Thracians with fox skins wrapped around their heads; Cissians in turbans; Assyrians in linen corselets, wielding their studded clubs. All, as though they had emerged from the stone of Persepolis into exotic flesh and blood, would assemble before their master, and march with him against the West.

Admittedly, this swelling of his task force with a vast babel of poorly armed levies would generate any number of headaches for the Great King's harassed commissariat. Transporting an army of the size envisaged by Xerxes across the Aegean was clearly out of the question: the only possible way to Athens was by land. This in turn would require wonders of preparation: the Hellespont would somehow have to be bridged; roads driven through the wilds of Thrace and Macedonia; harvests planted, garnered, stored. Burdensome demands on the logistics teams appointed to deal with them, of course—and yet, for the Great King himself, as glorious a manifestation of his power as any number of victories in battle. To tame a wilderness, to conjure from the living earth scenes of order and ripening plenitude: what more perfect image of his global mission could be conceived? The Persians, hemmed in all around by mountains and barrenness, had always regarded the ability to make a desert bloom as the surest mark of any statesman. The satrap who could demonstrate to the Great King's satisfaction "that he had fostered the cultivation of his province, planted it with trees, and seeded it with crops,"[18] was invariably marked down as a highflyer. Present the Great King with a prize vegetable, and even the humblest gardener might be fast-tracked on the spot. As one of Xerxes' heirs was supposed to have said, when given a monstrous pomegranate, "It should be no problem for someone who can grow fruit of this size, it seems to me, to make a small city just as correspondingly great."[19]

Even the Great King himself boasted of green fingers. Justifiably, too—for the young Xerxes, when not practicing with his bow or fording icy streams, had spent happy afternoons out in the garden, "planting trees, cutting and collecting medicinal roots."[20] Indeed, perhaps only the hunt could rival gardening as a passion of the court. To combine the two was, for a Persian, true fulfillment. Rare was the satrapal capital that did not have its own park, well stocked with game, but also, planted beside lakes and murmuring streams, pavilions and lovingly manicured lawns, plants of every description, herb gardens and flower beds, pear and apple trees, pines and cypresses, sunk into the soil and perfumed with the scents of exotic blooms. Empire, not for the last time, had fostered a mania for botany. Darius, even amid the labors demanded of any conscientious universal monarch, had always kept himself abreast of the latest horticultural innovations, tirelessly encouraging his satraps to experiment with cuttings and collect rare seedlings. Mardonius, it was said, eager to stoke his cousin's war fever, had assured Xerxes that Europe was one vast garden center, "the nursery of every kind of tree."[21] As news began to spread through Persepolis that the invasion of Greece would be going ahead, the royal gardeners could begin rubbing their hands with as much glee as anyone at the prospect of rich pickings.

"*Paradaida*," the Persians called their exquisitely beautiful parks, a word transcribed by the Greeks as "*paradeisos*"—"paradise."[22] Entering one, walking beside the coolness of a crystal-watered stream, surveying natural wonders transplanted from every corner of the empire—rare beasts, rare trees, rare flowers—the Great King might indeed imagine himself in heaven. And yet, a paradise offered him more than merely a sanctuary, a refuge from all the miseries and banalities of mortal life. Everything that he could delight in, "the beauty of the trees, the perfect accuracy with which they had been planted, the straightness of the lines they formed, the regularity of their angles, the multitude of exquisite scents that mingled together and filled the air,"[23] had been ordered according to his pleasure. Similarly, for he was the King of Kings with the whole world at his fingertips, might he command nature to be ordered anywhere.

For just as he could illustrate with a sweep of his hand to his gardeners how a line of cypresses should be planted, so also, by laying his finger on a map, might he redraw the sea and the land. Where the waters of the Hellespont flowed, brushwood and tightly packed soil, spread out over an immense pontoon, were to unite Asia and Europe; simultaneously, further west along the Aegean coast, a great canal, hacked out from the isthmus below Mount Athos, was to free the Persian fleet from having to round the treacherous peninsula from which the mountain rose. There, two years before Marathon, Mardonius had lost his fleet, a disaster rendered all the more horrific, so it was claimed, by strange prodigies of nature: for sea monsters, thrashing amid the boiling waves, were said to have gorged themselves on the drowning sailors, while white doves, born out of the spray, had risen and fluttered above the carnage, "this being the first time these birds had appeared in Greece, never before having been witnessed there."[24] No further such eruptions of the bizarre were to be permitted: as surely as a panther caged within a paradise was no danger to those who looked at it through the golden bars of its pen, so the sea monsters off Mount Athos, no matter how many Persian ships were to pass them on their way toward Athens, would be left to salivate in vain.

And all of Greece would quake. To build a canal wide enough to permit two warships to pass, deep enough so that their hulls would not scrape the bottom, and one and a half miles long, here was a commission beyond the scope of any mortal man—saving only one. As the labor gangs toiled, their hammer blows echoed far beyond Mount Athos, beating out a message of insistent and clamorous terror. All of Asia was stirring. The Great King was drawing near.

Clearing the Decks

The notion that any man had only to clap his hands to have a canal dug, a bridge built or a whole continent summoned teeming into arms was, to the Athenians, profoundly alien and alarming. The dust-swept columns of the great temple of Zeus, left abandoned by the Pisistratids when they were forced into exile, loomed as a sobering memorial to the city's distaste for looking up to any leader. The automatic reflex of the Athenian aristocracy, whenever confronted by a tall poppy, had always been to reach for a scythe. "For people do not find it pleasant to honor someone else: they suppose that they are then being deprived of something themselves."[25] This was a sentiment common among Greeks everywhere, in any time. Democracy, in that sense, had changed little. Themistocles' father, it was said, hoping to dissuade his son from a career in politics, had pointed out the rotting hulks of warships hauled onto the sand at Phalerum, and warned that such was the fate of every high-flying politician. "For in Athens, this is how leaders are always treated, when they have outgrown their usefulness."[26]

Certainly, rivalries among the elite remained quite as carnivorous and unforgiving as they had been prior to the establishment of the democracy. Even the towering figure of Miltiades had been speedily dragged down to his ruin. In 489 BC, barely a year after saving his city from annihilation, he had suffered a wound to his thigh while leading an expedition against a city of collaborators in the Aegean and had been obliged to return to Athens, his reputation in sudden tatters. The Alcmaeonids, nostrils twitching as ever, had sniffed blood. Unleashing the talents of an ambitious young politician named Xanthippus, to whom they had already married Cleisthenes' niece, they had brought a prosecution against Miltiades, accusing him, with typical effrontery, of "deceiving the Athenian people." Carried in before a baying Assembly, Miltiades had duly been convicted, and would have been hauled out of his stretcher, dragged through the "Hangman's Gate" and flung down a pit had not the jurors, reluctant to deal with the victor of Marathon as they had previously treated the Great King's ambassadors, voted instead for a crippling fine. Not so crippling, however, as the gangrene that had begun rotting the fallen hero's leg, and which would, within a few weeks of the sentence, finish him off for good. His young son Cimon, somehow scraping together sufficient cash to pay off the fine, had duly inherited the leadership of the Philaid clan, together with a much-depleted fortune, and—it went without saying—an ongoing feud with the Alcmaeonids.

Yet, if the Athenian people, fearful of any situation "in which one man is able to exercise a wholly disproportionate power over his fellows,"[27] had been content to see the great Miltiades humbled, that hardly spelled enthusiasm for his rivals. Who, precisely, had been the stooges in the prosecution brought by Xanthippus: the voters in the Assembly or the Alcmaeonids? The answer would not be long in coming. Two years after the death of Miltiades, citizens began flocking into the Agora, where a large voting pen had been erected especially for the day, with officials carefully scrutinizing all those who passed through it to ensure that no man voted twice. By the ten entrance-ways, one for each tribe, lay piles of broken pottery. Each Athenian, as he bent to pick up a shard, knew that he was laying claim to a feared and fearsome right. Once, in the time before the democracy, exile had been a fate inflicted by armed menaces at the whim of faction leaders, ruinous and brutal in its effects; now, for the first time, it was to be imposed as a measured sentence of the sovereign people. Every citizen, registering his vote on the back of a piece of pottery, was obliged to choose a prominent politician's name. At the end of the day, all the shards—"*ostraka*," as the Greeks called them—were to be sorted into piles and counted. The citizen with the largest number of nominations would then have ten days to leave Attica. He would not, as exiles had once done, suffer the loss of his property or his civic rights—but nor, for ten years, would he be permitted to return home. He was to remain, as the Athenians put it, "ostracised."

This, a deadly weapon against the ambitions of any over-mighty family, had remained untested in the democracy's arsenal ever since Cleisthenes had first provided for it, twenty years before.[28] That the Athenians had voted to unleash it in the aftermath of Miltiades' downfall suggests how resolved they were not to become the patsies of feuding clans. A people who had seen off the Great King certainly no longer felt obliged to live in the shadow of turbulent aristocrats. First to be cleared from the deck was Hipparchus, the notorious pro-Pisistratid, who, as archon in the previous decade, had been widely suspected of collaborating with Hippias and Artaphernes. The follow-ing year, 486 BC, it was the turn, not surprisingly, of an Alcmaeonid to get the push. Two years later, Xanthippus himself, reaping the due reward of his rise to prominence, was likewise dispatched. Philaids, Pisistratids, Alcmaeonids: all, in the years following Marathon, had effectively been decapitated. If the establishment of democracy had been a velvet revolution, then ostracism was a guillotine that cut off heads but spilt no blood.

And naturally, as in all revolutions, the elimination of an elite of power brokers left the field clear for more agile, more adaptable, more opportunistic rivals to take their place. The Alcmaeonids were not the only citizens to have felt themselves diminished by the blaze of the victor of Marathon; nor was it only grandees who hankered after a place in the sun of the Assembly's favor. One man in particular, who had found the glory won by Miltiades a peculiar agony, suffering sleepless nights as a consequence, to the extent of being put right off his drink, was already moving adroitly to take advantage of the cull. Themistocles, who certainly did not lack for enemies himself, was aware that by continuing to pursue his political ambitions he was risking his own ruin. But even though, from the first ostracism, he had been a popular candidate for exile, with mounds of *ostraka* cast against him every year, he possessed one crucial advantage. The abuse that might be scrawled angrily against the names of other candidates for exile—"traitor," perhaps, or "Datis lover," or even, roughly sketched on to the occasional shard, the figure of a bowman with a Median cap—could hardly be leveled against Themistocles. Unlike most of those actually condemned to ostracism, he had always been consistent in his opposition to the King of Kings. The great harbor complex of Piraeus, begun during his archonship, and now, almost a decade later, the largest and best-fortified port in Greece, stood as bristling evidence of that. Indeed, as Themistocles had now begun arguing openly, all that was needed to complete the transformation of Athens into a naval power of the top rank was a fleet.

A tempting prospect for the poorer classes, perhaps—but hardly for the landowners and farmers who had so recently triumphed at Marathon. Themistocles was pressing for some two hundred ships to be built: the manpower required to propel such an immense navy would leave few citizens to fight on land, as was traditional, with shield and spear. Was the hoplite class really expected to vote itself into liquidation? And who, perhaps even more pressingly, was to fund Themistocles' extravagant naval program? Warships did not come cheap: a fleet of them was perhaps the most expensive status symbol to which any city could aspire. Listening to Themistocles' proposals, the rich could have a shrewd idea as to who were likeliest to be stung for the bill. No wonder, then, with the elimination of those traditional spokesmen for reaction, the heads of the great families, that the upper classes had to cast around desperately for an alternative champion. They did not have far to look. Aristeides, the general who had stood alongside Themistocles in the weakened center at Marathon, had begun to emerge by the mid-480s BC as his bitterest and most effective opponent. Even in their characters the two men appeared formed for rivalry. While Themistocles was labeled a chancer, a man of superlative duplicity and cunning, Aristeides was hyped by his followers as the ultimate model of upright, homespun virtue. Whereas Themistocles was notorious for pocketing bribes at any opportunity, his rival had a reputation for poverty so stern and honest that when, after Marathon, the Athenian army had set off on its desperate foot slog to Phalerum, it was Aristeides who had been left behind on the battlefield, entrusted with the loot. "The Just," his admirers liked to call him: a moniker which the great man, without the faintest embarrassment, had made his own.[29]

For to this seeming paragon of virtue belonged a potent and momentous discovery: that image, in a democracy, might take a statesman just as far as substance. Irrespective of his nickname, Aristeides was, in truth, no less proficient at political machination than Themistocles. Far from "avoiding the entanglements of faction, and cleaving to his own path,"[30] as he pretended, he was in truth a networker of consummate ability. While Themistocles had been obliged to rely on obscure parvenus for his political education, for instance, Aristeides had aimed right for the very top, and made himself an intimate of Cleisthenes. Nor was his pose of rugged poverty any less a work of spin: he may not have been as keen on having his palm greased as Themistocles was, but then again, as the owner of a large estate at Phalerum and a close relation of some of the richest men in Athens, he hardly needed to be.

How, then, to explain Aristeides' peculiar hold on the electorate? His opponents, pointing out that he was a demesman of Alopeke, a village just to the south of Athens, made much play of how it echoed "*alopex*"—the Greek word for a fox. But this was, perhaps, to push the charge of deceit against Aristeides too far. Hypocrisy, it might even be argued, was the very lifeblood of the democracy. To be sure, the city's increasingly radical egalitarianism had done little to dim its traditions of snobbery. Aristeides, who mixed wealth with thrift, ambition with public service, the privileges of breeding with a resolve to trust the will of the people, offered to the Athenians a supremely comforting reassurance: that the ideals of their past might be squared with their new regime. Old certainties, he appeared to promise, sprung from the soil of Attica, as deeply rooted as the sacred olive tree that rose from the Acropolis, might still serve to guide the Athenian people through all the perils and insecurities that lay ahead. Set against the Just One's reassuring hoplite virtues, it was hardly surprising that the flash and dazzle of Themistocles' call to build a navy should have seemed to many as un-Athenian as the surge of the sea itself.

But this, perhaps, was to mistake the city's destiny. High on the Acropolis, right next to Athena's primal olive tree, could be found a cistern filled with salt water. Kneel down beside it and a citizen might hear from its depths "a sighing like that of waves when a south wind blows"; look at the rock, and he might see "a mark in the form of a trident,"[31] branded there in the distant past by Poseidon, the god of the sea. Once, it was said, he and Athena had competed to be preeminent in the city; Poseidon, although bested by the goddess, had left behind the well as a mark of his continuing patronage, driven into the rock of the holiest shrine in Athens.[32] Nor was the Acropolis the only site where the Athenians might ask the god for favors. At "holy Sunium, Athens' headland,"[33] which every ship had to round when leaving Attica for the open sea, a temple had recently been raised to Poseidon on the edge of the teetering cliff. Datis, commanding his horse transports on their desperate dash for Phalerum, would have seen its columns rising above him as he sailed his ponderous flotilla past the headland. Perhaps

219

Poseidon, stirring the currents with the tip of his trident that fateful day, had slowed down the progress of the Persian ships as they strained for Athens? Certainly, there was no god likelier to favor Themistocles' plans for saving his city from a second barbarian onslaught than the lord of the sea. Themistocles himself, since Sunium lay only eight miles south of his deme, would have found it an easy matter to travel to the headland, and maybe he often did. With the shadow of the sea god's shrine on his back and the murmuring of the swell below him, there would certainly have been no better place to pray for a miracle.

And were one to materialize, the likeliest spot for it, as Themistocles would have known, lay within easy walking distance of Poseidon's temple. The cliffs which formed the tip of the promontory did not extend far. North of Sunium stretched the bleak and blasted flatlands of Laurium, unrelieved by any of the breezes that kept the cape fresh. The air along this stretch of coast was baking and acrid, and filthy with poisonous fumes, yet thousands of people, women and children as well as men, lived here, their shacks clustered meanly around factory complexes. These were not citizens but slaves, unfortunates condemned to labor amid the dust and the pollution so that the democracy might be rich. As the pockmarked slopes which rose beyond the sea and the ceaseless din of picks bore witness, Laurium was an area so rich in silver that there were still fresh seams to be found in the rock, even though it had been mined since before the Trojan War. Over the previous couple of decades, the quarries had benefited from a substantial upgrade: stone tanks had been hollowed out of the rock face, for the washing of extracted ore, so that all extraneous elements, of which there were invariably plenty, might be sluiced away before smelting. This simple innovation had enabled the silver to be refined to an unprecedented degree of purity. It had also opened up a tantalizing prospect: a productive lode, if a new one could be found, would be more exploitable than any in Laurium's history. It just needed a single, lucky strike. And that, in 483 BC, was exactly what was made.

"A fountain of silver, a storehouse of treasure buried within the earth."[34] So the seam appeared to the dazzled Athenians. What to do with this windfall? No sooner had Themistocles received news of it than he was up on his feet in the Assembly, demanding a fleet. His proposal was greeted with cries of outrage. Aristeides, his blend of conservatism and demagoguery as inimitable as ever, rose in immediate opposition. It was the custom, he pointed out smoothly, for bonanzas from the mines to be divided equally among the Athenian people: an appeal to the voters' self-interest that managed to be both blatant and hedged about edifyingly by tradition. Themistocles, meeting it head on, chose not to scaremonger, nor even to mention the Persian threat at all. Rather, harping on an enemy far more immediate than the Great King, squatting as she did directly on the Athenians' doorstep, he began "whipping up the voters' dislike and jealousy of Aegina."[35] The Assembly, pulled in opposite ways by the rival temptations of avarice and jingoism, settled eventually on compromise. The profits from Laurium would be spent on warships, but only one hundred of them. Themistocles, who had been campaigning for double that number, refused to back down. So too did Aristeides. Neither man was able to force an advantage. Autumn turned to winter, and the democracy, riven by the dispute, found itself paralyzed. By January, when the Assembly met to vote on whether an ostracism should be held that year, the result was a foregone conclusion. The logjam had to be broken: either Themistocles or Aristeides would be going. The pottery shards, it was settled, would be brought out when winter turned to spring.

It may not have been framed as such, then, but the ostracism of 482 BC was, in effect, the first referendum in history. Perhaps the most fateful, too: for on its result would hang the future not only of Athens but of an independent Greece, and of much more besides. As the date appointed for the ostracism neared, the Athenians themselves appear dimly to have woken up to this. Rumors of the massive construction project on the Athos peninsula were by now hardening into menacing fact; and talk of the Great King's preparations for war, whispered in horror-stricken tones, must surely have begun swirling through the anxious streets. That Themistocles' enemies, even as they opposed giving the city a fleet, should still have hyped Aristeides as "the Just" appears increasingly to have grated on people's nerves—as Aristeides himself would soon discover. Standing by the voting pens on the day of the ostracism, he was approached by an illiterate peasant who, failing to recognize the great man, handed him a pottery shard and asked him to write "Aristeides" on it. Nonplussed, Aristeides asked the peasant why. "'Because,'" came the answer, " 'I am fed up with hearing him called the "Just" all the time.' And Aristeides, when he heard this, did not reply, but merely took the shard, wrote his name on it, and then handed it back."[36] An inspiring story—and one that could have derived only from the Just One himself, of course. As such, it had the palpable whiff of damage limitation. Even as he watched the *ostraka* stacking up against him, Aristeides was looking to salvage something from the ruin. Perhaps he had even seen what was written on some of the shards: "Datis' brother." Certainly, once the result had been confirmed and it was announced that he would be heading into exile, Aristeides knew that, whatever else he was obliged to leave behind, he had to keep his reputation for honesty. The time might come when he would need it again. Ostracized Aristeides may have been; but even before he had left, he was preparing the ground for his return.

Meanwhile, however, the vote had served its purpose. The air was cleared and Themistocles had triumphed. Athens would have her two hundred ships. More than two hundred, in fact—for the Athenians, after all their prevarications, appeared suddenly possessed by a quite contrary spirit of nervous energy, as though, having finally grasped the situation, they dreaded that they were doing too little, too late. Agents armed with Laurium silver fanned out urgently across the Aegean, buying timber wherever they could obtain it. Day and night, the shipyards of Piraeus rang to the din of saws and hammers. Warships had been gliding down the slipways since the vote the previous summer, but now they began to do so at the astounding rate of two a week. Nothing but the best would do, and the deadliest and most up-to-date model, the trireme, a slim, ram-headed killing machine equipped with three separate banks of oars, required workmanship of the highest precision.

Themistocles, indeed, hands on as ever, had personally insisted on experimenting with a new design, aimed at enhancing "speed and ease of turning":[37] for while high productivity was essential, so too was quality. "A terror to her enemy, a cause of joy to her friends": such had to be the benchmark for every trireme launched by the democracy.[38]

Yet soberingly, all the challenges of constructing a fleet were as nothing compared to those of learning how to power and maneuver it. The effective pulling of an oar on a trireme was a notoriously difficult skill to master. "Seamanship, after all, like so much else, is an art. It cannot merely be dabbled with in one's spare time. Indeed, it allows for no spare time at all."[39] Particularly when time itself, as seemed increasingly likely, might be in short supply. The whole population of Attica needed to be broken urgently to the rowing bench—and even then, Themistocles fretted, there might not be enough citizens to man the swelling fleet. Day after day, as the summer of 482 BC slipped by and darkened into winter, farmers from the remotest olive groves, potters who might never before have left the Ceramicus, "steadfast men of the hoplite class,"[40] their armor left behind to gather cobwebs in stable lofts, all practiced, practiced, practiced, enduring the blisters, the perpetual weariness and the aches in strange muscles they had never known they had, only to take out their rowing cushions, lay them on their benches, and set to practicing once again. A brutal crash course—but so it had to be. There were few who still believed, as spring came to Athens in 481 BC, that the enemy they were training to meet was the fleet of Aegina. Rumors of what was being planned for their city by the Great King were by now flooding in from all directions. It was even said, alarmingly, that Xerxes and his army were preparing to leave from Susa that very spring. Foreboding gripped the Athenians—and a longing, amid all the uncertainty and confusion, to know the worst. Then at last, from a most unexpected quarter, there came some definite news.

It was the Spartans who had received them: a pair of blank writing tablets. Much perplexity had greeted this cryptic delivery until the ever bright-eyed Gorgo, wife of King Leonidas, had suggested scraping

223

away the wax—and a message had been found inscribed on the wood that lay beneath. It had been written by Demaratus: a warning of the plans of the King of Kings. The Spartans confessed that they did not know if this tip-off revealed "a benignant care for his people or a malicious sense of joy";[41] and yet how strange it was, and how alarming, that there was any doubt at all as to the defector's motivation. A message that had mysteriously made it past every checkpoint on the Royal Roads, that was calculated to chill the blood of its recipients, that had boosted the image of the puppet king in waiting: this had the fingerprints of the Persian dirty-tricks department all over it. The Spartans, although they lacked the Athenians' enthusiasm for broadcasting their differences in public, were not lacking their own internal divisions. Demaratus' message could only have been written with the intention of widening these, between the hawks, confident of victory against any opponent who might dare to challenge them, even the King of Kings himself, and the more pessimistic, those who quietly dreaded that the gods had sentenced them to ruin, and that the hour of their doom was drawing near.

Both Demaratus and his controllers in Persian intelligence would certainly have been well aware that the latter group was no small minority in Sparta. The ghosts of Darius' heralds, murdered a decade previously by Cleomenes, were widely feared to be haunting Lacedaemon, calling to the heavens for vengeance—as, of course, was their right. So conscience-racked were some Spartans, indeed, that two prominent Heraclids, frantic to expiate their city's sacrilege, had adopted the desperate expedient of traveling to Susa and offering themselves up to the King of Kings as a sacrifice. Xerxes, far too shrewd to take up this startling offer, had graciously spared them—for why should he deign to relieve the Spartans from the debilitating burden of their guilt? Demaratus' news, as it was designed to do, served only to compound their dread. Most cursed the traitor: dredging up old scandal, they smeared him as the bastard of a helot, the fruit of his mother's rolling with a stinking stable hand, fit to be an Asiatic's slave. Others, however, realizing that Demaratus might be the only man who stood between them and total ruin, and acknowledging that he had opposed Cleomenes and his impious excesses at every turn, began whispering differently. They too repeated rumors of Demaratus' paternity; but they called him the son, not of a slave, but of the phantom of a legendary hero, halfway to a god.[42]

Naturally, it still went without saying that the Spartans, if the Great King did invade the Peloponnese, would stand and block his way. But if even they, the bravest warriors in the world, were racked by self-doubt, how were the men of lesser states supposed to steel their nerves? As spring turned to summer the choice for every city in Greece became unavoidable: resistance or appeasement. No longer could the prospect of a Persian invasion be dismissed as an alarmist fantasy of ambitious politicians such as Themistocles. It was now evident even to the most obdurate skeptic that all the rumors of Xerxes' departure from Susa had been true: he was indeed heading west. By early autumn, so it was reported from Ionia, he had arrived at Sardis— and still, flocking to his banner, his vast dominions continued to empty themselves upon his command. The Great King and all his hordes were coming. By the spring of the following year, it would have begun: the advance of the largest army ever assembled, over the Hellespont, into Europe, and then down, like a wolf upon the fold, on to Greece. Those who lived there, in what might easily prove to be their last winter of freedom, could now shudder with a dreadful certitude as to whom the Great King's target was going to be.

And the Persian high command, as adept as ever at psychological warfare, neglected no opportunity to turn the screws. Envoys, just as they had done a decade previously, before the Marathon campaign, began crisscrossing Greece, demanding earth and water. Every city was visited, with two exceptions: Athens and Sparta. The message of intimidation to the rest of Greece could hardly have been clearer. Frantic not to be earmarked in a similar manner for destruction, many cities scurried to oblige the imperial emissaries. Even those who openly refused the demand for earth and water had their pro-Persian factions, or were patently equivocating. It did not seem beyond the bounds of possibility, during that bleak and dread-shadowed autumn, that the whole of Greece might simply drop like overripe fruit into Xerxes' lap.

Which was, of course, for the Spartans and the Athenians, who had no choice but to fight, the ultimate nightmare. Hoping to stiffen the sinews and summon up the blood, they too hurriedly sent out ambassadors, calling their fellow Greeks to arms and to a conference of war to be held at Sparta. This was a logical location, perhaps, since it was the Peloponnesian League that would provide any allied army with its muscle; and yet the Spartans, nervous of alienating cities that did not belong to the League, and displaying an unwonted care for their sensitivities, were careful to title the conference center the "Hellenion"—"the united nations building of Greece."[43] Nor was this merely an empty flourish. Many of the cities who had chosen to send delegates to Sparta were still at war with one another; yet, startlingly, when it was proposed that all such feuding should be resolved, everyone agreed then and there. Aegina, for instance, having decided this time round to throw in her lot against the invaders from the very start, found herself burying the hatchet with Athens; and with the very real prospect, furthermore, of her ships being combined in a single fleet with those of her erstwhile bitter foe.

Not that this new spirit of harmony was entirely without limits. When Themistocles, pointing to the disproportionate contribution that his city would be making to any allied navy, laid claim to its command, the Aeginetans joined delegates of other cities with ancient maritime traditions, such as Corinth and those of Euboea, in howling down the upstart. Heroically, and ever the pragmatist, the Athenian admiral managed to swallow his pride. His vanity may have been immense, but his determination to be the savior of Athens was even greater. Themistocles was never the man to let his ego cloud either his intelligence or his uncanny ability to enter other people's minds. He could see, with the penetration that came naturally to a born infighter, that the Greeks had only one hope of survival: "to put an end to their feuding, to reconcile the various cities with one another, and to persuade them to join together in the cause of defeating Persia."[44] Recognizing the danger that no city's fleet would ever tolerate accepting orders from the admiral of another, he made the masterly suggestion that leadership of the allied fleet be given to a people without a drop of sea blood in their veins. So it was that the Spartans, who had already laid claim to the land command by right, won command of the sea as well. A bitter expedient for Athens—but, as Themistocles well knew, there were far worse blows that could befall a city than a bruising of her *amour propre*.

With a command structure, however vague, now successfully established, the allies could start to lay their plans. Two major challenges faced them. One, self-evident to all the delegates at the Hellenion, was the need to boost their numbers. Of the seven-hundred-odd cities in mainland Greece, barely thirty had sent delegates to Sparta. Notable absentees, such as the Argives, would somehow have to be persuaded to join the common cause; pro-allied factions in fence-sitting cities, such as Thebes, would have to be bolstered. The solution finally adopted was a carrot and stick approach. On the one hand, it was settled, ambassadors should be sent to Argos, and to all the other cities that had so far remained aloof from the alliance; on the other, a proclamation warned any would-be medizers that they could look forward to having a tenth of their income tithed as punishment for their treachery. Furthermore, since the allies would undoubtedly require divine as well as merely mortal assistance in order to achieve this, all the proceeds of the tithing, it was piously agreed, would be given "to the god at Delphi."[45]

In this desperate hope that Apollo might be bribed, and his oracle with him, there was nothing remotely naïve. Rather, it betrayed one of the allies' best-founded fears. They were all hard-nosed men. They knew that Persian spies were everywhere, secreting gifts of gold here, whispering promises of the Great King's favor there, working stealthily to rot the Greeks' resolve from within. Somehow, in the face of this espionage campaign, the allies had to find a way to strike back. Here, then, was the second challenge facing the allies: to infiltrate the camp of the King of Kings.

For the Greeks, as yet, despite all the wild talk, had little idea as to the true scale of what they were facing. Only with hard intelligence could they start to formulate their strategy—and for that, under-cover agents would be needed. Three spies were duly chosen and given their mission: to travel to Sardis and make notes on all they saw. Do this without being captured, and they would enable the allies to have an infinitely better sense of the odds facing them, and to plan accord-ingly come the spring, when they had agreed to meet once more.

Their conference now concluded, the delegates began exchanging their farewells and leaving for home. The three agents were mean-while heading for the nearest port, and a ship to Ionia. Spring, and the campaigning season it would herald, was still months away; but at least the Greek allies could now feel that the first blow against the King of Kings and his invasion was being struck.

The Rape of Europa

Once, before the coming of the Persians, the Aegean had been a Greek lake. That winter of 481 BC, however, with a crippled Ionia still count-ing the ruinous cost of rebellion, with Miletus a blackened shell of her former greatness, and Naxos and the other islands having submitted a decade previously to Datis' armada, the journey of the three Greek spies from the Peloponnese was very much a voyage into enemy waters. The nearer they drew to Asia, the more unsettling it became. Evidence of the terrifying scale of Xerxes' preparations was every-where. Winter was drawing in, but the Aegean sea-lanes were still unseasonably busy. Along the Ionian coast, vessels that had swarmed there from every corner of the eastern Mediterranean crowded the harbors. The Greeks, even in their own backyard, were being swamped. Thirteen years previously, at Lade, the last fleet of a free Ionia had been swept off the sea. Now, with the invasion of Greece itself only months away, the contingents that had contributed most notably to that crushing victory for the King of Kings were back in

Ionian waters. Any Greek would have recognized them with a sinking heart. Slim, shield-hung and sublimely maneuverable, the triremes that would constitute the shock force of Xerxes' fleet had a deadly reputation. The sailors who manned them were universally acknowledged as the most proficient in the world. "Your borders," as the Judaean prophet Ezekiel put it, "are in the heart of the sea."[46] He was addressing the city of Tyre, but he might just as well have been speaking to her even wealthier neighbor Sidon, or to Byblos, or to any of the great merchant strongholds that stood on islands or abreast of double harbors along the seaboard of what is now Lebanon. Proudly independent of one another each city may have been, but this, to many outsiders, was a wasted subtlety. The Greeks, certainly, lumped all their citizens together as one single, perfidious crew: *Phoinikes*—Phoenicians.

This name, deriving as it almost certainly did from *"phoinix,"* the Greek word for "purple," reflected that same blend of admiration and contempt with which they tended to regard any people whom they found threatening. Admiration—because the violet dye which the Phoenicians manufactured from shellfish was definitively the color of refinement and privilege, an internationally desired luxury product that had helped to fill the coffers of Tyre and Sidon to overflowing. Contempt—because how vulgar it was, after all, how crashingly and irredeemably vulgar, to be defined by an item of merchandise! "The love of lucre, one might say, is a peculiarly Phoenician characteristic."[47] So Athenian aristocrats liked to sniff. Yet this characterization of Phoenicians as oily money-grubbers, universal Greek prejudice though it was, might just as easily inspire resentment as disdain. The merchants of Tyre and Sidon were not the only people who had a taste for turning a profit. There were many Greeks who shared it, and who profoundly resented the competition that the Phoenicians gave them. No matter how far they traveled, no matter where they sought new markets, or raw materials, or land for a trading post, "those celebrated sea-rovers, those sharp dealers, the holds of their black ship filled up with a hoard of flashy trinkets,"[48] seemed always to have got there first.

This rivalry, stretching back centuries, extended to the outer limits of the known world. The Phoenicians, their cities quite as hemmed in by mountains as were those of the Greeks, had always set their sights upon the open horizons of the sea. As far back as 814 BC, it was said, the Tyrian princess Elissa, leaving her homeland, had led a great party of colonists along the coast of North Africa until, arriving opposite Sicily, she had founded there a "new city"—"*qart hadasht*," or Carthage—destined to become the greatest metropolis of the West. By the time that Euboean colonists, a few decades later, began nosing their own way westward, the tentacles of Phoenician trade had already reached to Spain. Soon they were extending even further, into the Atlantic and toward the Equator, to beaches fringed by jungle, where the Carthaginians would trade with impassive natives: gewgaws and baubles for gold.

The Greeks, listening to these travelers' tales with an envious gleam in their eyes, had found themselves, by and large, too late on the scene to gatecrash the African market; and yet, although frozen out of Africa and Spain by the sophistication of their rivals' commercial networks, they too had discovered in the West a frontier ripe with opportunity. Although their first colony, on the island of Ischia in the bay of Naples, had initially courted Phoenician investors, partnership with the old enemy had not come naturally. Soon enough, throughout Italy and Sicily, it had degenerated into open confrontation. As ever more Greek settlers arrived looking for a new beginning, so the sheer weight of their numbers had begun to tell. On and on they had come, from Euboea, from Corinth, from Megara, from Ionia, a flood of maritime colonization, unsurpassed in scale until the discovery of America more than two thousand years later. By the turn of the eighth century BC, a new city was being founded in Italy or Sicily virtually every other year. Even the natives had begun to talk of "Great Greece."

Certainly, by the time that mass colonization had finally trickled to a halt in the mid sixth century BC, the wild West was semi-tamed. Determined to overawe the natives where they could not enslave

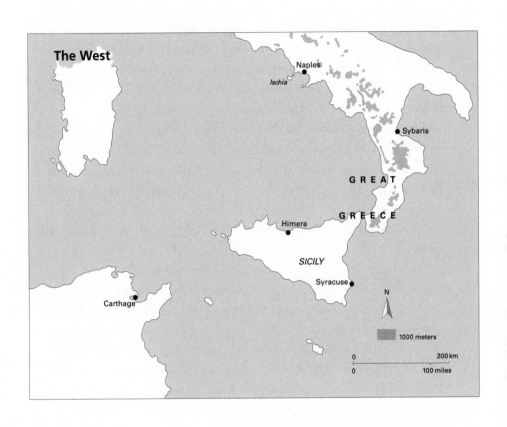

them, the colonists had adopted a self-consciously swaggering style. Everything they did was on a monumental scale: walls loomed far vaster in the Greeks' new world than in the old; temples sprawled more grandiosely; colors gleamed brasher and more polychrome. Even the pleasures that men took in the West smacked of intimidation. In Sybaris, a town on the instep of southern Italy and an object of appalled fascination even to her neighbors, dandies would sprawl languidly on beds of rose petals and then complain in a drawl of suffering blisters. In war, their horses had only to hear flautists piping an enemy phalanx into battle and they would start shimmering together in a perfect synchronicity, practicing their dance steps. Even the ruin of Sybaris, when it ultimately came, had been spectacular. Captured by a coalition of its enemies in 510 BC, the city had been obliterated, razed from the face of the earth, so that not a trace of it remained. Success and failure in the West were both lit by a lurid and extravagant glow.

No wonder that the allies meeting at the Hellenion had resolved, even as they dispatched their three spies eastward, to send a mission in the opposite direction as well. Enthusiasts for rose petals and late-night dancing the western Greeks may have been, but they could be fearsome soldiers when the mood took them. A tyrant by the name of Gelon, a ruthless and exuberant adventurer who had seized power in the great Sicilian port of Syracuse four years previously, appeared particularly well qualified to play the role of Greece's savior. His credentials as a man of action were so impressive as to be unsettling. Already, rather as an Assyrian might have done, he had annihilated three neighboring cities, transplanting their populations to Syracuse when not selling them into slavery, and raising fleets and armies on an almost Oriental scale. Just the brand of militarism, in short, that might seem to promise much against the King of Kings.

Except that there was, that same winter of 481 BC, the shadow of a looming crisis over Syracuse as well. Gelon, crashing and swaggering ever further westward in a bid to expand his supremacy over the whole of Sicily, had found himself colliding with a rival power bloc on the other side of the island, one largely comprised of Phoenician set-tlements. These, looking around frantically for an ally, had turned for help, as was only natural, from the most powerful Phoenician settle-ment of all: the city of Carthage. There, the subtle and calculating merchant princes who guided its affairs had been watching Gelon's progress with mounting alarm. Their Sicilian kinsmen were wel-comed with open arms: the opportunity to overthrow the troublesome tyrant of Syracuse while simultaneously indulging in some expansionism of their own was far too good to let slip. During the autumn of 481 BC, even as the triremes of Tyre and Sidon were gliding northward into the Aegean, the Carthaginians had begun equipping a fleet and recruiting a fearsome army of mercenaries, ready for a showdown with Gelon come the spring. In the West as well as in the East, it seemed, the Phoenicians were massing. And west and east, it was the Greeks who were to bear the brunt of their drive to war.

Coincidence? No one in Greece could quite be sure. The spies sent to Sardis, for all that they might be able to nose around a few harbors on their way, had not the slightest hope of tracking down communica-tions—even if they existed—between the Carthaginians and the King of Kings. Nevertheless, suspicion of the long reach of Phoenician cun-ning came naturally to most Greeks. After all, if the Carthaginian high command had indeed been liaising with Xerxes, attempting to synchronize their twin invasions, then the likeliest suspects as middle-men were agents from the mother city of Tyre. Some conspiracy theorists, though, fretted that even this might not be the limit of Phoenician malignancy. What if the entire expedition of the King of Kings, the massing of the hordes of Asia, and the extermination of Greek freedom that it threatened, were merely the climax of a feud infinitely more ancient and inveterate? "Persians in the know," it would be asserted with bald confidence after the war, "put the blame for the quarrel squarely on the Phoenicians."[49] The hatred between East and West, Asia and Europe, barbarian and Greek: all, according to this theory, welled from a single perfidious source.

It was stretching paranoia to extremes, of course, to imagine Xerxes the mere tool of a fiendish global conspiracy masterminded from Tyre. The King of Kings went to war on no one's behalf save his own. The Phoenicians, just like any other subject people, were his slaves. They were obliged to pay him tribute, to host a satrap and even, when they sailed to war, to submit to the authority of a lubberly Persian courtier. But that is not to say that the Phoenicians lacked all influence with the imperial high command. The Medes aside, there was perhaps no group of people in the Persians' entire dominion with such ready access to the royal ear. The kings of Tyre and Sidon were perfectly aware that the Great King's expedition would be holed below the waterline without the enthusiastic participation of their fleets. So it had always been. Cambyses, when he founded the imperial navy, had soon discovered the limits of what he could achieve with his new toy. Ordering a task force prepared for the conquest of Carthage, he had been astounded to have his plans vetoed by the Phoenicians, "on the grounds that it would be an unnatural deed for them to go to war with their own children."[50] The lesson of this startling display of lèse-majesté was one that Persian strategists had been quick to absorb. While the levies of other subject nations could be dragooned into war, it was wise to handle the Phoenicians more diplomatically. Slaves though they were, it might sometimes prove counterproductive to rub their noses too brutally in the fact. Better to have them sailing not merely as conscripts but as eager partisans for the cause of the King of Kings. Better, in short, to have them believe that their own interests were also at stake.

And, of course, in the enterprise of Greece, they certainly were. The Phoenicians, who had provided the Persians with the bulk of their fleet at Lade, had already profited hugely from the destruction of Miletus—a city once quite as much of a commercial hub as Sidon or Tyre. Were Athens to be flattened in a similar manner, and the neutralization of Corinth and Aegina secured, then the prospects for Phoenician business would glitter promisingly indeed. As a result, enthusiasm in the chanceries of Tyre and Sidon for the Great King's war was unstinting. The Phoenicians brought three hundred ships with them to the Aegean: more than the entire fleet of Athens. Nor had these been patched together in a hurry: Sidon, which competed with Corinth for the title of birthplace of the trireme, had been at the forefront of naval innovation for centuries. The Athenian oarsmen, often with only a few months' practice under their belts, would find themselves, in their first true taste of battle, going head to head with the very best.

Horrendously outnumbered too. The Phoenicians were far from the only people to have sent a fleet in answer to the Great King's summons. Some, notably the Egyptians and the Ionians, were almost the equals of the Sidonians with an oar. True, both came from satrapies with a track record of rebellion; and perhaps, as they snooped along the harbor front, the three Greek agents found some hope in this fact. If so, they were clutching at straws. The Persian admiralty, having been caught napping in the early days of the Ionian Revolt, knew better now than to neglect their backs. Command of the Egyptians and Ionians had been placed directly in the hands of two of Xerxes' brothers, and every ship in the armada manned with marines of proven loyalty. Why, then, would anyone in the Great King's fleet risk mutiny and their own annihilation for the sake of the Athenians, who were clearly doomed anyway? No one crowded into the ports of Ionia that winter could have had much doubt on that score. The mammoth fleet would soon start sweeping along the Aegean coastline, and all who stood in its way were bound to be destroyed. The Greek spies totted up 1207 triremes: a figure of suggestive precision.[51] Whether all that vast number would embark for Greece and, if they did, whether they would all survive the summer storms unscathed were questions that only the campaign to come would answer. But the odds, even if the Great King lost a quarter of his fleet, even if he lost a half, would still be far from balanced. One simple, brutal fact, to the Greek spies, was menacingly clear. The allies, come the summer, would be facing a force greater than any that had ever been seen at sea.

And by land? Only a visit to Sardis could answer that question. The Greek agents hurried on. By their third day of travel from the coast, they could see ahead of them, obscuring the silver mountains that loomed to the east, an ominous pall of smoke. Soon, nearing their destination, they began to make out great humps of earth, the cemetery of the ancient Lydian kings; then, dimly through the haze, Sardis itself, the red cliffs of the acropolis framed by steepling walls and surmounted by Croesus' monumental palace. The banners that flapped over the city's battlements, however, one adorned with "an image of the sun enclosed in crystal," and the other, the royal battle standard, embroidered with the image of a golden eagle,[52] were those of a monarch mightier by far than Croesus had ever been; and the evidence of his greatness, there before the dumbfounded agents' gaze, stretched for miles far across the plain. The smoke they had seen from the far distance was pluming up from campfires: thousands upon thousands of them. Whether huddled in tents, or practicing with their outlandish weaponry or jabbering in their impenetrable tongues, the multitudes of the Great King's army seemed conjured from a world stranger and more barbarous than most Greeks had ever cared to imagine. All the spies' darkest forebodings appeared fulfilled. The remotest reaches of Asia and of Africa had emptied themselves. Millions upon millions would be pouring, in barely a few months, into Greece.

Or so it seemed. In truth, to count—or even to estimate—such monstrous hordes was no easy matter; and the spies, before they could even start their calculations, were unmasked and apprehended. The men who had arrested them were soldiers, not intelligence officers, and so it never crossed their minds not to have their captives tortured, then put to death. Just as the sentence of execution was about to be carried out, however, captains from the Great King's personal bodyguard came rushing up, frantically ordering that the prisoners must be spared. Led stumbling up the acropolis into the inner depths of the palace, the three spies found themselves, to their astonishment, being personally interrogated by the Great King himself, then escorted on a full tour of the imperial camp. Only once they were laden down with copious notes were they finally sent packing back to Greece.

And the reports they took with them, just as the Great King had intended they would be, dealt only in terrifying superlatives. What the spies had been shown was nothing less than a panorama of his world-spanning dominions. At its heart the Great King himself and his crack corps of bodyguards: the thousand who attended him personally and bore golden apples on their spear butts, and then a further nine thousand, also hand-picked, with silver apples on their spears, a shock force of warriors known collectively as the "Immortals"—"for if one of them were killed or fell sick, a replacement would immediately step forward to fill the gap in the ranks."[53] Then elite contingents of cavalry, from Persia and various subject nations: Media, Bactria, India, the steppes of the Saka. Finally—for the Great King lacked heavy infantry fit to measure against the bronze-clad hoplites of Sparta or Athens—teeming brigades of spear fodder: exotically armed levies who might not, under normal circumstances, have appeared to a Greek observer as anything other than contemptible foes, but who, rolling forward in a great torrent of humanity, might be expected to sweep away any shield wall standing in their path. This, at any rate, was how it was reported back in Greece—for the three spies, reliant on their own dazzled estimates of the Great King's troop numbers, and no doubt on records helpfully provided by their Persian minders, did indeed find themselves talking in terms of millions. One million, seven hundred thousand to be precise—and even that total took no account of the levies that the Great King was planning to recruit as he advanced through Thrace and into Greece.

Such figures, so colossal as to be virtually meaningless, were almost certainly a grotesque exaggeration. Most historians, forced to make an estimate, would put the army under Xerxes' command closer to 250,000.[54] Even that, however, translated into an invasion force vaster than any previously assembled; and it was hardly a surprise that the Persian propaganda machine, looking to panic the Greeks into despair and perhaps even outright surrender, should have pumped their agents full of disinformation. Statistical sleight of hand the muster lists may have been, of the kind that a talented bureaucracy could pull off in its sleep; but they were not—to the Great King's way of thinking, at any rate—a total fraud. Rather, in the message they proclaimed— that the whole world stood united beneath his banner, and that only the most inveterate of terrorist states could possibly presume to defy it—they expressed the simple truth.

And Truth, after all, was what Xerxes sat on his throne to defend. Strongly though considerations of geopolitics had weighed with him, and a sense of duty to his father, and personal ambition, yet Athens was to be burned, and Greece conquered, for a reason profounder than any of these. "All I do, I do by the favor of Ahura Mazda." So it pleased Xerxes, as it had pleased Darius before him, to proclaim. "When there is a task to be done, it is Ahura Mazda who gives me aid, until that task is completed."[55] To the imperial army, then, as it embarked upon the supreme challenge of its master's reign, there clung a nimbus of the divine. The Lord of Light was to be regarded as a constant presence on the campaign. Not, of course, that Ahura Mazda could be represented as other people chose to portray their gods, in the form of some vulgar idol or painted image; yet vacancy, mystery-hedged and awful, might serve instead. So it was that an exquisitely decorated war chariot, guided by a charioteer following it on foot, was to accompany the army into Greece, wholly empty—"for the mortal does not exist who may take his place upon that chariot's throne."[56] To pull it, eight white horses, of marvelous size and beauty, had been brought specially to Sardis. Others, when the army left for Greece, were to lead the way; still others were to pull the chariot of Xerxes himself. These creatures, as was only fitting, were touched by the sacred themselves—for they came from the plain of Nisaea. There, on that fateful first day of Darius' reign, when the assassin of the false Magus had emerged from the fort of Sikyavautish holding aloft his bleeding dagger to pronounce Persia and all her dominions purged of the Lie, the white horses had whinnied in salutation. Now, far from Nisaea, horses of the same breed, pulling the chariot of Darius' son, were to witness the dedication of demon-racked Athens, and all of Greece with her, to the Truth.

For if, as Xerxes had been raised to believe, the world was his to conquer, it was also his to mend. Keen horticulturalist that he was, he knew that a paradise, before it could be considered completed, first had to be cleared of weeds, set in order, beautified. Significantly, even embarking on a brutal campaign of destruction, Xerxes' love of the natural world and his eye for its glories never left him. Nearing Sardis, for instance, he had come across a plane tree of such surpassing loveliness that he had halted the entire march of his army in admiration. One of the Immortals had even been detached from the company and ordered to serve as its guard. Golden jewelry brought out from the expedition's mobile treasure trove had been festooned from its sweeping branches. To be sure, the Great King took—but he also gave away.

And not just to trees. Xerxes, tending the garden that was the world of his enormous empire, delighted in servants who served him loyally, and loaded them down just as he had loaded down the plane tree, with lavish rewards. "For what robes are there that can compare in beauty to those the King hands out to his friends? Whose gifts—whether bracelets, or necklaces, or horses in harnesses studded with gold—are so distinctive?"[57] Xerxes' Europe-bound expedition, while it was certainly intended to demonstrate the folly of scorning the Great King's favor, also had a more pacific intent. Remote satrapies, hitherto cruelly denied the royal presence, might now enjoy the supreme privilege of paying homage to the King of Kings in person. His subjects, as he rode through their towns, would line the roads, tossing flowers before the clattering hooves of the Nisaean horses, and prostrating themselves in the dust; attendants, following in their master's wake, would gather up gifts and petitions; guards, lashing the moaning, sobbing crowds with whips, would ensure that they retained, even in their ecstasy, a sense of their proper place. Naturally, there was nothing that any of the Great King's subjects, whether peasants or plutocrats, could offer their master that was not already his; but Xerxes, turning the light of his royal favor upon those who humbled themselves, might be munificent as well as gracious. "Generously," he boasted, "do I repay all those who do well by me."[58] Even the Greeks, if they would only submit to the majesty of the Great King, might hope to win, as Demaratus already had, extravagant honors and gifts. This, at its heart, was the symbiosis of global monarchy. Even Xerxes had to plant as well as reap.

Which was not to deny that blooms, for the good of the garden, might sometimes need to be pruned. Servants, unlike plants, could on occasion grow presumptuous. Xerxes, shortly before passing the plane tree that had so astounded him with its beauty, had been entertained by Pythius, the Lydian reputed to be the richest commoner in the world. Some thirty years previously, this same plutocrat, sensitive to the tastes of his Persian masters, had presented Darius with a plane tree made of gold. Now, greeting Xerxes, he had not only fed the Great King's entire army, but vowed to bankroll it. Xerxes, breezily dismissing this offer, had nevertheless been charmed. All that winter, Pythius and his five sons stood high in the royal favor. Pythius himself had been lavished with gifts; his sons all confirmed in prominent military posts. Then, with the coming of spring to Sardis, and the time at last for Xerxes and his task force to depart upon their great enterprise, there was sudden consternation. An eclipse, blotting out the sun, had cast the world into shadow. Although the Magi were quick to reassure their anxious master that this portended the ruin not of his expedition but of the rebel Greeks, Sardis remained racked by a sense of foreboding. The aged Pythius, as "alarmed by the sign from the heavens"[59] as anyone, even went so far as to beg the Great King for his eldest son to be spared from going to Greece. A terrible, a fatal mistake. At a time when Xerxes himself was preparing to ride into danger with all his "sons, and brothers, and relatives, and friends,"[60] no more scandalous a request could possibly have been imagined. While the Great King, mingling mercy with the stern dictates of justice, did somehow bring himself to spare his former favorite's life, it was clearly out of the question to pardon the Lydian's impertinence altogether.

Pythius' precious eldest son was duly apprehended, killed and sawn in two. Then, with the army massing to march northward for the Hellespont, the two halves of the corpse were exhibited on either side of the Sardis highway. "And the army, everyone in it channelled between the two halves of the young man's body, embarked on its advance."[61]

A less than cheery send-off, it might have been thought. In fact, grisly though this blood offering certainly was, and an increasingly fly-blown one at that, yet it broadcast to the jumpy levies passing between it a potent message of reassurance. The demands of ritual as well as justice had doomed the son of Pythius. The sacrifice of a human life was an act pregnant with fearful magic, a magic that Xerxes, hoping to purify his army, had now dared to harness. The Great King himself, trusting in the judgment of the Magi that the eclipse had been a favorable portent, had his private doubts whether there was in fact any evil that needed keeping at bay; but he also knew, with Sardis so shadow-haunted, that it was better to play things safe. Certainly, as his troops prepared to venture into the wilds of a new continent, they could do so confident that there was nothing their royal master would not countenance in his drive for victory.

Nor, as the Great King neared Europe, did he neglect to toy with the superstitions of his foes. Devout in the worship of Ahura Mazda he may have been—yet Xerxes had the traditional Persian genius for turning the religious sensibilities of alien peoples to his advantage. This was why, having closed in on the Hellespont, he took the opportunity to break his journey and explore a site that to him would have appeared merely a grass-covered series of bumps, but to the Greeks meant infinitely more: Troy. By ordering the Magi to pour libations upon the site, Xerxes was self-consciously laying claim to the role that the Greeks, in their terror, had already given him: that of nemesis for the carnage wrought by Agamemnon. Vengeance, on behalf of all the men of Asia slaughtered in the Trojan dust, was to be the King of King's. Just as Troy had once done, Athens and Sparta were shortly to burn.

Then, with the Pisistratids no doubt whispering helpful encouragements from the side, a thousand oxen were driven up the hill, and the whole lot immolated on the summit as an offering to Athena. This, since the goddess had always been notorious for her loathing of the Trojans, might have been thought a maladroit gesture—except that Xerxes, by displaying his respect for the protectress of Athens so extravagantly, was sending the Athenians a very public message. The Athena worshipped in their city was no Olympian, but rather a demon who had taken on her form, one of the *daivas*, a servant of the Lie. The King of Kings, pledged though he was to burn the Acropolis, was no enemy of the true goddess, whose worship, in the company of the Pisistratids, he would shortly be restoring. Only with Athens under Persian rule could Athena return to her ancient home—and that moment, in the spring of 480 BC, was drawing ever nearer.

For the Great King, from the summit of Troy, could see at last, beyond the plain on which so many Greeks and Trojans had once fought and died, the fateful glittering of the Hellespont. Further along the straits, where Asia and Europe stood separated by barely a couple of miles of sea, twin pontoon bridges were awaiting him, their immense cables chaining together the two continents, proof against the currents and the raging of the winds. That winter, it was true, a particularly ferocious gale had swept away two prototypes of the pontoon, but the Persian high command, having decapitated a few engineers *pour encourager les autres*, and with plenty of ships and manpower to spare, had quickly made good the repairs. Even the Hellespont appeared to have been taught to behave itself: a few symbolic touches of the whip, a set of fetters dropped into its waters, and the sea had been peaceable ever since. Now, as Xerxes descended from the grass-covered hill of Troy, all was ready for him: his army massed along the beaches and plains of Abydos, the city nearest to the bridgehead; his fleet, gliding into the straits, cramping the fish with beating oars. The locals, having correctly gauged the kind of welcoming gift that might prove acceptable to a world monarch, had erected a throne of white marble on a promontory overlooking the awe-inspiring scene. When he arrived, the Great King duly took his seat to admire the view.

"And from where he sat, gazing out across the bay, he could take in the spectacle of his army and his navy in a single sweep . . . And when he saw the whole of the Hellespont covered with ships, and all the beaches and plains of Abydos filled with men, Xerxes counted himself truly blessed."[62] The world was all before him: a spectacle of outright global dominion such as no king had ever staged before. Of intimidation, too. The extravaganza may have been flamboyant, and self-consciously theatrical in its mustering of levies from around the world, but the parade, beneath its flummery, bared fearsome teeth. The Great King, concerned even amid the ecstasy of the moment to demonstrate his enthusiasm for quality as well as quantity, sent messengers to the various naval contingents, instructing them to demonstrate their proficiency in a rowing match. Only once the regatta had been staged—and won, inevitably, by the Sidonians—did he decree that preparations for the crossing should commence.

All afternoon they took, all evening, all night. Finally, with the horizon lightening to their right, the Immortals, wearing wreaths in their hair and holding their spears upside down, assembled in serried formation beside the eastern bridge, while distantly, from the other, there drifted the sound of pack animals, the braying of donkeys, the complaining of camels; and over them all, from glowing braziers, perfumes of incense billowed upward to meet the dawn. The King of Kings himself, emerging past the Immortals and treading over boughs of myrtle, walked to the edge of the bridge. By now, beyond the straits, the silhouette of Europe was growing clearer by the minute—until, from the east, the first ray of sunlight touched the Hellespont, and Xerxes, pouring wine from a golden cup into the sea, raised a prayer of supplication to the heavens for the success of his great enterprise. When he was done, he dropped the cup into the black currents, then a golden bowl, and finally a sword. The ceremony was over. The crossing could begin. And the sun, touching the ranks of the Immortals as they advanced onto the creaking bridge, caught the gold and silver apples on their spears, so that they seemed, as they advanced, to be moving points of light.*

Seven days in all it took the task force to pass from Asia into Europe. The army crossed the eastern pontoon; the baggage trains the western. No one knows for sure when Xerxes himself rode onto the bridge: some said that it was on the second day; others that he was the very last man to make the crossing. What is certain, however, is that the expedition made it over the Hellespont without mishap—and that the achievement, to those who witnessed it, appeared to be the work less of a man than of a god. "Why, O Zeus," one local is said to have exclaimed, watching the King of Kings ride by, "have you gone to the bother of disguising yourself as a mortal from Persia, and giving yourself the name of Xerxes, and summoning the world to follow you, all for the purpose of annihilating Greece? Surely that was something that you could have done more simply on your own!"[63]

Drawing a Line

At around the same time as Xerxes was leaving Sardis, a delegation from Sparta was heading north to attend a congress of the allies at the Isthmus. Its mood would have been a good deal less cheery than the Great King's. Spartans tended to be bad travelers at the best of times, and the spring of 480 BC was decidedly not the best of times. The news that almost two million barbarians were making for their city might have

---

*No detail better proves the authenticity of Herodotus' sources for Xerxes' crossing of the Hellespont than this: that the Immortals marched to war with their spears held upside down. Assyrian frescoes, which no Greek could possibly have seen, show exactly the same scene, evidence both of the continuity between Persian traditions and those of earlier empires, and of Herodotus' remarkable scrupulousness as a historian.

been thought sobering enough. Yet not even the ultimate in invasion scares could entirely eclipse for the Spartans a more traditional source of paranoia. Crabbed and provincial in their anxieties as in so much else, their supreme dread remained, as it had always been, revolt in their own backyard. The helots, kept ignorant of anything beyond the brute facts of their serfdom, could be counted upon to have heard little, even by that spring, of the Great King's approach; but few others would have been similarly oblivious. In cities long subordinate to Sparta, and resentful of it, the prospect of swapping a local superpower for a global one was prompting gimlet-eyed calculations. Even en route to Corinth, the Spartan delegation to the congress at the Isthmus would have passed cities darkly rumored to be rife with medizers. One of these, just inside the border with Tegea, was Caryae—a town so intimately linked to the rest of Lacedaemon that girls from Sparta would regularly travel there to go dancing. Tegea herself, in recent years, had also shown a worrying tendency toward insubordination—even going so far as to indulge on occasion "in open spats with Sparta."[64] These, however, were mere pinpricks of concern compared to the city that remained Sparta's bitterest and most poisonous foe, crippled, maybe, since the slaughter at Sepeia, but hungry still for revenge and for what she saw as her ancient birthright: dominance of the Peloponnese. The Spartan delegates, as they headed north for Corinth, could hardly have failed to cast an uneasy sideways glance in the direction of Argos.

Admittedly, the Argives, playing hard to get, had not yet openly committed themselves to the cause of the Great King. Nor, however, as the Spartans were all too painfully aware, had they pledged themselves to the allies. When representatives from Sparta, arriving in Argos that winter, had invited them to do so, the Argives had responded with what they knew were impossible demands: a thirty-year truce and a share of the command. The negotiations had collapsed on the spot. The Spartan ambassadors, frog-marched to the border, had been warned that any repeat of their mission would be interpreted as a hostile act. "For rather than concede so much as an inch to them, the Argives would actively prefer barbarian rule."[65]

A statement of neutrality that appeared, to the Spartans, quite as menacing as a threat. Even before the allies' first conference at the Hellenion, they had suspected the worst of Argos—and with good cause. While the Argives, in justification of their inglorious fence-sitting, could brandish a warning from Delphi advising them to "look after yourselves and keep your spears locked away,"[66] the Spartans, "at the first stirrings of the war," had also applied for a long-range forecast from Apollo. The Pythians, returning from the oracle, had brought their royal masters, Leonidas and Leotychides, a most alarming message.

> *Your fate, O inhabitants of the broad fields of Sparta,*
> *Is to see your great and famous city destroyed by the sons of Perseus.*
> *Either that, or everyone within the borders of Lacedaemon,*
> *Must mourn the death of a king, sprung from the line of Heracles.*[67]

Food for thought indeed. It was not merely that either Leonidas or Leotychides appeared to have been given a death sentence; there was also, in the description of the apocalypse that would otherwise over-whelm Sparta, a sinister, and typically Delphic, ambiguity. Who precisely were the "sons of Perseus"? The Persians? The Argives? Both? That the allies' spring conference was being held at the Isthmus, midway between the Peloponnese and northern Greece, would only have served to make the question more alarming and pressing yet. Ahead of the ambassadors, far distant on the frontiers of Asia but drawing ever closer by the day, the Persians; behind them, eyes pre-sumably fixed brightly on their backs, the Argives: sons of Perseus both. It was scarcely surprising that the Spartan delegates were jumpy.

Whether Leonidas and Leotychides were among them, we do not know. It was not normally the practice of Spartan kings to act as their own ambassadors, but Leonidas, in particular, as representative of the senior royal line and therefore the allied supreme commander, would surely have wished to keep track of new intelligence in person. If he did attend briefings at the Isthmus, however, he would have found it a singularly discouraging experience. Despite the high hopes of the previous autumn, no new allies had committed themselves. Just as Argos had done, many of the states that had been approached had explained that Apollo was advising them to keep their heads down. The biggest disappointment of all was the man who had attracted the giddiest hopes: the tyrant of Syracuse. Gelon, who desperately needed every last ship and soldier for his own looming showdown with Carthage, but did not wish to lose face by admitting as much, had extricated himself from his commitments to the old world by trumping even the Argives for impudence. First, he had demanded exclusive command over all the Greek forces; then, making a great show of compromise, over either the army or the fleet. When the allied ambassadors, just as they were meant to, had refused these terms indignantly, Gelon had snorted in contempt: "You seem to have no lack of leaders, my friends—all you need now is to find some men for them to lead."[68]

A withering put-down—and one that appeared to have dealt a fatal blow to any notion the Greeks might have had of staging an amphibious holding operation. While an army of hoplites, if they could find a suitable mountain pass to blockade, might still conceivably hope to keep the barbarian hordes at bay, most delegates felt the allied fleet, deprived of Gelon's two hundred triremes, had no hope now of engaging the Persians on equal terms. Themistocles, of course, profoundly disagreed; but he was having trouble, that spring, in keeping even his own fellow citizens on board. The Spartans were not the only people to have passed a twitchy winter. The Athenians, having spent a fortune on their new fleet, and much time and effort, were having second thoughts about their whole strategy. Many were steeling their nerves for the ordeal ahead with a renewed nostalgia for Marathon. The closer the Great King drew, the more the veterans who had triumphed in that celebrated victory—the doughty, obdurate, conservative hoplite class—itched to smash their oars over Themistocles' head and have another crack at the barbarians on land. Themistocles himself, who had hoped this particular chimera had been slain with Aristeides' ostracism, had almost been dismissed from his command. Only by bribing his rival for office to stand down had he scraped through in the annual elections to the board of generals. His authority was ebbing—and his enemies in Athens knew it. So too did his fellow delegates at the Isthmus. Themistocles, for the moment, was in no position to throw his weight around.

Instead, amid all the drift and despondency, it was left to a posse of cattle barons, sun hat–wearing bull-wrestlers from Thessaly, to seize the initiative. Arriving unexpectedly at the conference, they urged the downcast allies to look to the north. Alarmingly flat and spacious though Thessaly was, and therefore ideal for the Persians' cavalry, its rolling fields were surrounded on every side by mountain ranges, superlative natural bulwarks looming upward from the dusty plain. Of these, the most imposing by far lay to the north, along the border with Persian-held Macedon. Here, the Thessalian barons urged, the allies should make their stand. The delegates were intrigued. To many of them, instinctively parochial as most Greeks were, Thessaly was *terra incognita*, not merely remote but positively sinister, as famous for its witches as for its livestock or corn—yet everyone had heard of Mount Olympus, of course, and its immediate neighbor, Mount Ossa, two of the mountains that defined its northern border. Many delegates would also have heard of Tempe, the narrow five-mile pass that separated Olympus from Ossa, its walls so sheer that only Poseidon's trident, it was generally assumed, could possibly have shivered the cliffs apart. The Thessalians assured the allies that any army heading south would have to pass through this gorge: all the Greeks needed to do to halt the Great King in his tracks was dispatch a force to Thessaly and stopper Tempe up. It appeared a foolproof argument. Even the Spartans were convinced; and this despite the fact that the plan would oblige them to send troops perilously far from their comfort zone of the Peloponnese. Ten thousand hoplites, from a variety of cities, were marshaled for the journey: the same number, perhaps significantly, as had seen off the barbarians at Marathon. A Spartan, naturally, one

Euainetus, was put in overall command. The Athenian contingent was led by Themistocles.

A few weeks later and the whole expedition had been humiliatingly aborted. The smooth-talking Thessalians who had persuaded the allies to embark upon it had, it proved, skated over a number of inconvenient details. First: a rival faction in Thessaly had already signed up to the Persians. Second: Tempe was not in fact the only pass through the northern mountains. Third: the whole area was already swarming with enemy agents, and had been for years, ever since the dominant faction in Thessaly, looking to finish off their rivals for good, had first made contact with Xerxes' spy chiefs and suggested their master launch an invasion. The allied task force, far from securing an impregnable position for itself, had walked into a trap. With a civil war brewing in their rear, and no chance of securing all the mountain passes into Thessaly, Euainetus and Themistocles had no sooner dug themselves in at Tempe than they were deciding to cut their losses and make a dash for it back home. It was undoubtedly the correct decision, and one that saved the lives of ten thousand men—but the ignominy of the withdrawal could hardly help but send a shudder through the rest of Greece. All the rival factions in Thessaly, now that they had been abandoned to the barbarians, began to medize frantically; collaborators in cities further south felt confirmed in their own view of themselves as realists; those still committed to the fight sank into a paralyzed despair. Before the rising tide of menace, growing darker by the day, it appeared that the allies had only one policy: retreat. Whisperings that the Persians were invincible grew louder. Such was the talk even in those cities committed to resistance when, in late May, news that the Great King and his army had safely crossed the Hellespont broke like a thunderclap over Greece.[69]

It was in Athens that the shock was felt most keenly—and there that the impasse over strategy appeared most ominous and fateful. Facing the prospect not merely of defeat, like the citizens of other cities, but of obliteration, the Athenian people, in their extremity, turned for guidance to Apollo.[70] Leaving Attica, skirting warily past Thebes, climbing the foothills of Mount Parnassus, the Athenian emissaries were soon on the winding and increasingly lonely road that led between jagged peaks and past walls of fissured rock to Delphi. Once they had arrived there, they were led first through the cluttered gaudiness of the shrine to the Castalian spring, and then, having purified themselves in its freezing waters and offered up a sacrifice before the flames of the eternal fire, back to the temple itself. At the far end of the inner sanctuary, obscured by a jumble of ancient treasures, the Pythia waited for them, sunk within deepest shadow. Compared to the net-covered stone of the Omphalos, or the sacred laurel tree, or the lyre of the god, all of them crammed into the tiny chamber alongside her, the Pythia, an old woman in a young girl's dress, appeared almost a thing of grotesquerie, ill suited, certainly, to be the vessel of golden Apollo. Already, however, as vapors from the cauldron she was perched upon caressed her parted thighs and curled beneath the skirt of her virgin's tunic, she was shuddering with mantic ecstasy: the trance had come upon her. The Athenians, guided by the priests, took their seats beside the doorway; and at once the Pythia, without even waiting to hear their question, began to spasm with the urgency of her possession by the god. "Why sit down, you wretches?" she cried, her accent distorted and terror-stricken. "Get out of here, flee, flee, flee to the ends of the world!" Words spewed out in horror soared and stumbled in a savage rhythm, conjuring up images of carnage, and fire, and annihilation. The god of war was coming, the wheels of his Syrian chariot rattling, towers crumbling in his wake. The temples of Athens would burn. Black blood would drown the city. "Go, go, leave the sanctuary, surrender to your grief!"[71]

Tottering out weakly into the sunlight, the Athenian emissaries found themselves with little option but to do as the Pythia had instructed, and slump down in despair. So all was settled, then: the hour of their city's doom was at hand. Or was it? A priest, seemingly as shocked by the Pythia's vision as the Athenians themselves had been, hurried after the emissaries, and urged them to approach the oracle a second time. To a skeptic, this might have seemed suspiciously like bethedging. And so indeed, perhaps, it was; the priesthood, after all, had to consider its own future. While understandably anxious not to antagonize the Great King, it could not afford to stake all its chips on a Persian walkover. Every eventuality—even one as improbable as a Greek victory—had to be covered. It would have been only politic, then, for the priests to have allowed their Athenian guests at least a glimmering of hope.

Yet cynicism, as the fatal example of Cleomenes had demonstrated, might well be pushed too far. Not every ambiguity uttered by the oracle could be dismissed as mere calculation. To sneer at Delphi was to sneer at the divine. The assumption behind the priest's advice to the Athenians—that Apollo, having delivered them a forecast of unmitigated pessimism, might somehow be persuaded to temper it with a rosier one—was not necessarily far fetched. A god's wisdom, by its very nature, was something mysterious and infinite. Matters were rarely, with Apollo, altogether as they seemed. If Delphi, as most Greeks took for granted, did indeed open a portal to the supernatural, then the glimpses of the future that this afforded might well appear to flicker and change like fire.

The Athenians, then, following the priest's advice, were not wholly nonplussed when the Pythia, seeing them a second time, did indeed fall into a renewed frenzy and start chanting fresh prophecies. "Athena cannot mollify the power of Olympian Zeus," she warned, "although she begs him with all her eloquence and subtlety." So far, so depressing—but then, abruptly, a flash of hope: "*And yet,*" the Pythia moaned:

> And yet—*this word I give you, adamant, a promise:*
> *Everything within the borders of Attica shall fall,*
> *Yes, and the sacred vales of nearby mountain ranges,*
> *But the wooden wall alone, the wooden wall shall stand,*
> *That much Zeus grants to Athena, as an aid to you and all your children.*
> *Men on horses, men on foot, sweeping they come from Asia:*
> *Retreat, for soon enough you will meet with them face to face.*
> *Divine Salamis—you will be the ruin of many a mother's son,*
> *When the seed is scattered, or the harvest is gathered in.*[72]

251

And with these final, cryptic phrases, the Pythia woke abruptly from her trance; and all fell silent in Apollo's shrine once again.

What on earth had she been talking about? The Athenian emissaries, without really having the faintest idea, were just relieved that her second batch of verses sounded cheerier than the first, and gratefully took the transcript back to Athens. There it was exhaustively dissected. Debate and perplexity were general. One phrase, in particular, served to polarize opinion: "the wooden wall." Themistocles' opponents, displaying a prodigious capacity for lateral thinking, proposed that this was a reference to the wattle fence that in the time of Erechtheus had ringed the summit of the Acropolis. Themistocles himself, with more plausibility, argued that it referred to ships. Why else, he argued, would the Pythia have mentioned the island of Salamis? Yes, retorted his opponents, but she had failed to mention which mothers—Greek or barbarian—would mourn their sons. True enough, Themistocles hit back: but had not Salamis been hailed by her as "divine"? And so the arguments raged on.

Only the votes of the Assembly could ultimately serve to settle them. Such was the wisdom of Apollo: to have given Athens an oracle that did not merely hold up a mirror to her innermost doubts but obliged her to resolve them on her own. It was as the citizens of a democracy that the Athenian people were facing their supreme test; and it was as the citizens of a democracy that they would decide how best to meet it. A date was set in early June for the formal debate on the oracle, which would also, of course, serve to determine once and for all how they were to fight the looming war. With the Great King now only weeks away from their city, the Athenian people could no longer afford to prevaricate. At long last, they would be obliged either to back Themistocles and his strategy, or to reject them both for good.

Venue for the momentous debate was that first and most imposing of monuments raised by the democracy to itself: the great meeting-place hollowed out two and a half decades previously from the hill of the Pnyx. As they took their seats there amid the dust and scent of thyme, the voters could see before them an unrivaled panorama of their city, and of that blessed landscape from which, in the beginning, the first Athenians had sprung. In the distance, almost bleached of color by the purity of the Attic light, the outline of Mount Pentelikon and the roads that led to Marathon. In the foreground, the Agora, with its great twin nudes of the tyrannicides and its gleaming new civic monuments. Rising just to its right, and most imposing of all, the holy rock of the Acropolis. Cluttered as its summit still was with the detritus of aristocracy—family shrines, statues, votive shields and bronzes—there were, even on this most sacrosanct of sites, imposing marks of the new order. The venerable but shabby temple of Athena Polias, for instance, once a showcase for Boutad exclusivity, was long gone, replaced, during the first decade of the democracy, by an imposing structure infinitely better suited to the dignity of the goddess, and of the Athenian people themselves. The flamboyantly decorated sanctuary raised by the Alcmaeonids midway through the previous century had also been demolished, torn down even as ostracism was destroying the family's political base. In its place, work had begun on a magnificent new temple, conceived as a celebration of Marathon and an expression of gratitude to Athena for her protection. Looking across from the Pnyx, the voters could see the scaffolding that covered its half-finished shell. Such a labor of love, on such a site, in such a city: this could not be abandoned, surely? Not to the barbarians. Not to their impious fire.

Yet abandonment of the city, on that fateful day of the most decisive debate in Greek—and perhaps all European—history, was precisely what Themistocles was indeed proposing. No longer, if they ever had been, could the implications of his naval policy be whitewashed. Even if every able-bodied citizen were to take his place upon a rowing bench, the Athenian fleet would still be seriously undermanned. No man of fighting age could be spared to garrison a "wooden wall" on the Acropolis, or anywhere else in Athens come to that. Women, children, old men, all would need to be evacuated, and the city itself entrusted "to Athena, the mistress of Athens, and to the other gods."[73] It was possible, of course—as Themistocles would no doubt have argued—that the barbarians might be fought to a standstill north of Attica. That, however, with every Athenian committed to the fleet, would require the Spartans and their allies to hold the line by land. Whether the Peloponnesians could be persuaded to venture beyond the Isthmus a second time, far from their own cities, only time would tell. Yet the Athenians, if they were to have any hope of convincing the Spartans not to abandon Attica, had little choice but to show themselves prepared to do so. Themistocles could certainly offer blood, toil, tears and sweat to his fellow citizens. What he would not give them was any promise to fight the invaders on the beaches. Surrender Athens but pledge themselves never to surrender: such was the policy, bold and paradoxical, that Themistocles urged on the Athenians.

What precise heights of oratory he attained, what memorable and stirring phrases he pronounced, we have no way of knowing: not a single account of his speech has been preserved. Only by the effect that it had on the Assembly can we gauge what must surely have been its electric and vivifying quality—for Themistocles' audacious proposals, when put to the vote, were ratified. The Athenian people, facing the gravest moment of peril in their history, committed themselves once and for all to the alien element of the sea, and put their faith in a man whose ambitions many had long profoundly dreaded. Few Athenians seemed any longer to doubt that Themistocles had "a supreme talent for arriving at the correct solution to a crisis at precisely the correct moment";[74] yet, perhaps it was only on the very brink of catastrophe that they could bring themselves to acknowledge the exceptional quality of his foresight. Under normal circumstances, the democracy had little tolerance of genius. The circumstances of that summer, however, were decidedly not normal; and so the Athenians, rather than punish Themistocles for having been right all along about the Persian threat, decided instead to give him his head. Suspicion of talent, at a moment of crisis such as Athens faced, was no longer an indulgence that she could afford. So it was, on Themistocles' own insistence, that the various victims of ostracism were summoned urgently back to Attica, "in order that all Athenians might be of one mind in the defence against the barbarian."[75] And Cimon, the son of Miltiades, who was, perhaps more than anyone, the heir to the tradition of Marathon, led a procession of the Athenian *jeunesse dorée* through the Ceramicus to the Acropolis, and there, with great ostentation, dedicated the bridle of his horse to Athena, before picking up a shield and heading with his companions down to Piraeus. "And this he did to broadcast to the whole city a simple message: that what was needed now was not prowess on horseback, but rather men to fight at sea."[76]

With Athens united at last, all that remained was to persuade her allies to play their parts. Themistocles, returning to the Isthmus, did so with his hand immeasurably strengthened; nor did he find the Peloponnesians necessarily hostile, despite the debacle at Tempe, to the drawing of a second forward line. After all, the Athenian fleet was pledged to the defense of their coastline as well as that of Attica; and Themistocles, for whom the expedition to Thessaly had clearly not been a complete waste of time, had already identified the perfect spot for an attempt to keep the Persian fleet at bay. Between the northern tip of Euboea and the mainland there was a narrow strait barely six miles across, ideally suited to being plugged; furthermore, it was only some forty miles east of the even narrower pass of Thermopylae. A fleet and army, operating in tandem, might well hope to hold both the straits and the pass—even in the face of monstrous odds. The Athenians, prompted by Themistocles, had already voted to send a hundred ships to Euboea; and now the allied delegates at the Isthmus—again, no doubt, at Themistocles' urging—voted to back this strategy. Corinth, Aegina, Megara and other, lesser, naval powers all agreed to dispatch squadrons in support of the Athenian fleet; Sparta to lead a task force to Thermopylae. At last, it seemed, in spite of everything, a resolution had been reached. Now, in the lull before the storm, there was nothing to do but wait for the barbarian.

And to wait—and to wait some more. June turned to July and still the Great King did not come. Rumor fanned prodigious reports of his advance: of how his army was drinking rivers dry; of how all who lay

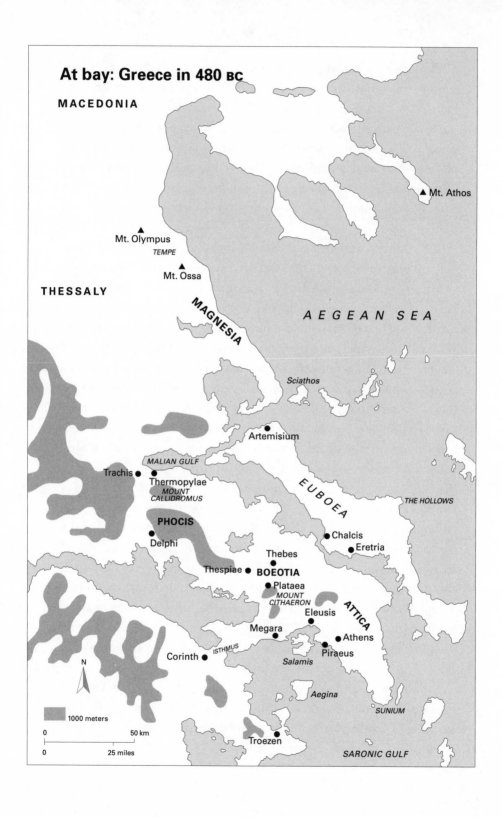

At bay: Greece in 480 BC

MACEDONIA

▲ Mt. Athos

▲ Mt. Olympus
TEMPE

THESSALY

▲ Mt. Ossa

MAGNESIA

AEGEAN SEA

Sciathos

Artemisium

MALIAN GULF

Trachis ●
● Thermopylae
MOUNT
CALLIDROMUS

EUBOEA

THE HOLLOWS

PHOCIS
●
Delphi

● Chalcis
Thebes ● Eretria
●
Thespiae ● BOEOTIA
● Plataea
MOUNT
CITHAERON

Eleusis ●
ATTICA
Megara ●
● Athens
Corinth ● ISTHMUS
● Piraeus
Salamis

N

Aegina
SUNIUM

1000 meters

0   50 km
Troezen
0   25 miles
SARONIC GULF

on his path were scurrying to offer him earth and water; of the gilded splendor of his regattas and feasts and entertainments. So far, it appeared, his progress through Europe had been less an invasion than a leisurely procession—and already, as July turned to August, the best conditions for campaigning were slipping away. Soon enough, with the Aegean heated to sweltering levels and colder air turning turbulent to the north, the season for summer gales—northeasterlies, or, as the Greeks called them, "Hellesponters"—would arrive. "Pray to the winds," the priests of Delphi advised, in a final message to the allies. "For they will prove good friends to Greece."[77] A message that all preparing to sail with the Greek fleet took to heart.

Yet, among the people of one city, the dilatoriness of the Great King was starting to prompt sentiments altogether less enthusiastic. For the Spartans, the prospect that they might have to defend Thermopylae during August was a truly excruciating one. Four years had passed since the previous games at Olympia; now, with the moon already waxing, the new games were destined to start when it was full. So too, to compound the agony, was the Carneia. The conjunction of these two festivals portended a period of more than usually sacrosanct truce. How could the Spartans possibly break it? Haunted already by the specters of the murdered Persian ambassadors, the notion that they might offend the gods with even more impieties was too hideous to contemplate. With the Peloponnese full of potential medizers, and the Argives as ever sniffing the air, the Great King was hardly the only agent of divine retribution ready to hand. No, the Spartans could not possibly march north in August. To do so would be both criminal and lunatic. The Carneian truce could not be broken.

But who were barbarians to respect such scruples? Sure enough, no sooner had August arrived than the news that all Greece had been half dreading and half anticipating duly arrived at the Isthmus: the Persians had begun clearing roads along the foothills of Olympus. The conference broke up at once. In Athens, where the docks were already in turmoil with the demands of the evacuation, any consideration of truces was the last thing on people's minds. Rather—literally—it was all hands on deck. The city's fighting men were frantically scrambled. Some ships—the most disposable—were even entrusted to volunteers from loyal Plataea, "whose courage and spirit, it was hoped, might serve to compensate for their total ignorance of the sea."[78] Thus, even leaving behind a substantial reserve fleet to guard their home waters, the Athenians succeeded in dispatching to Euboea, not the 100 ships they had originally agreed upon, but 127. Other cities— Corinth and Aegina prominent among them—sent all they could as well. To anyone watching the allied fleet as it rounded the headland of Sunium on its journey north, trireme after trireme, oars churning the water, flashing in and out, the spectacle would have been a stirring one. There were 271 front-line warships in total sailing for Euboea: no doubt only a fraction of the fleet at the command of the Great King, but a brave effort all the same, and inspirational.

Sent in command of it, as had been agreed the year before at the Hellenion, was a Spartan, an aristocrat named Eurybiades. Here, for his countrymen, was a bitter irony. Haunted although they may have been by their dread of breaking the Carneian truce, the contemplation of what other cities were committing to the war effort could hardly help but serve to prick their sense of honor. To man the land approaches as others were to guard the sea lanes: this was hardly a duty that the Spartans could now shrug aside. Somehow, a compromise had to be found, one that might spare them the fury of the gods while simultaneously enabling them to hold true to their sworn commitments. Why not, then, since it was still clearly out of the question for a full army to be dispatched until the Olympic truce was over, send an advance guard to secure the pass? If other cities, lying on the two-hundred-mile road that wound from Lacedaemon to Thermopylae, could be persuaded to swell it with contingents of their own, then even a small force of Spartans might hope to hold out. Particularly if that force were to be drawn from the very sternest, the very toughest of the elite. And particularly—since the message broadcast to the world of Spartan resolution would then be unmistakable—if it were led by a king.

Leonidas it was who took the perilous commission. As representative of the senior royal line, he would have felt that it was his duty to do so, no doubt—but he may have had a more personal motive, too. The ghosts of the murdered Persian ambassadors were not, perhaps, the only phantoms abroad that summer in Lacedaemon. More than a decade had passed now since Cleomenes, his legs and stomach fretted by a carving knife, had been found twisted in the stocks. What remained mysterious was whether he had perished by his own hand—just punishment for his oracle-bribing, god-baiting impiety—or had been the victim of a brutal conspiracy, one possibly orchestrated by the Spartan high command itself. Either way, Leonidas must have felt himself implicated in his predecessor's horrific end. Cleomenes had been his own kin, after all. The blood had long since been scrubbed away, but the sense of a curse, oppressive, menacing, as close as the August heat, still lowered over Sparta. Leonidas, preparing for his desperate mission, would hardly have forgotten the menacing terms of the oracle: either his city was to be wiped out "or everyone within the borders of Lacedaemon / Must mourn the death of a king, sprung from the line of Heracles." It would surely not have escaped his attention either that it was on a peak above Thermopylae that Heracles himself had perished, consigning his mortal flesh and blood to fire that he might then ascend to join the gods. Well, then, might Leonidas have dismissed the Hippeis, that crack squad of three hundred young men who customarily served in battle as the bodyguard of the king, and replaced them with older veterans—"all men with living sons."[79] A ringing statement of intent. Whatever might happen at the pass—whether glorious victory or total defeat—Leonidas would stay true to his fateful mission. One way or another, he would secure the redemption of his city. There was to be no retreat from Thermopylae.

7

AT BAY

Epic Preparations

Hipparchus, the playboy tyrant whose murder in a lovers' tiff back in 514 BC had been commemorated by the Athenians as a blow struck for liberty, had himself, throughout his reign, always delighted in invention. An ardent patron of architecture, as princes so often are, he had also possessed a rare passion for literature. Travelers could still read, inscribed beneath the erect phalluses that were a somewhat startling feature of way-markers in Attica, pithy and improving verses, composed by the murdered Pisistratid himself. In other ways, too, the Athenians had benefited from Hipparchus' bookish brand of tyranny. It was thanks to his enthusiastic backing, for instance, that the cream of Greek literary talent, who would once have sniffed at Athens as a backwater, had come to regard the city as a cultural powerhouse, and flocked to settle there. So determined had the tyrant been to ferry celebrity poets to his court that he had even laid on a luxury taxi service for them, in the form of a fifty-oared private galley.

Even more than for modern literature, however, Hipparchus' true enthusiasm—and it was one shared throughout the whole Greek world—had been for two peerless epics: *The Iliad* and *The Odyssey*, composed centuries previously, and set during the time of the Trojan War. Little was known for certain of their author, a poet named Homer— but he was, to the Greeks, so infinite, so inexhaustible, so utterly the wellspring of their profoundest presumptions and ideals, that only the Ocean, which encompassed and watered all the world, was felt to represent him adequately. No wonder that Hipparchus, looking to put his city on the literary map, had been keen to brand Homer—who was generally, and frustratingly, agreed to have been a native of the eastern Aegean—as somehow Athenian. Pisistratus, Hipparchus' father, when he sponsored an edition of the poet, was even said to have tried slipping a few surreptitious verses of his own into the texts, hymning Athens and her ancient heroes; Hipparchus himself, less vulgarly, had introduced recitals from the epics to the Panathenaea. Not that these were performed in any refined spirit of *belle-lettrisme*, however, being rather, like the athletic contests that also featured in the festival, ferociously competitive—which was only fitting. "Always be the bravest. Always be the best." Maxims, it went without saying, from *The Iliad* itself.

And regarded by Greeks everywhere, despite Hipparchus' best efforts, as the birthright of them all. The Spartans, for instance, those countrymen of Helen and Menelaus, hardly needed to stage poetry readings in order to parade their affinity with the values of Homer's epics. If the letter of their military code derived from Lycurgus, then its spirit, that heroic determination to prefer death and "a glorious reputation that will never die,"[1] to a life of cowardice and shame, appeared vivid with the fearsome radiance of the heroes sung by the "Poet." And of one hero more than any other: Achilles, greatest and deadliest of fighters, who had traveled to Troy, there to blaze in a glow of terrible splendor, knowing that all his fame would serve only to doom him before his time. True, the pure ecstasy of his glory-hunting, which had led him to squabble with Agamemnon over a slave girl, sulk in his tent while his comrades were being slaughtered, and return to the fray only because his beloved cousin had been cut down, was a self-indulgence that could hardly be permitted a Spartan soldier.

Nevertheless, that death in battle might be beautiful, that it might enshrine a warrior's memory, even as his spirit gibbered in the gray shadows of the underworld, with a brilliant and golden halo, that it might win him "*kleos*," immortal fame: these notions, forever associated with Achilles, were regarded by the Greeks as having long been distinctively Spartan, too. Others might aspire to such ideals but only in Sparta were citizens raised to be true to them from birth.

When Leonidas, leading his small holding force, arrived in early August at the pass of Thermopylae, then, the example of the heroes who had fought centuries previously in the first great clash between Europe and Asia could hardly have failed to gleam in his mind's eye. From Homer, he knew that the gods, "like birds of carrion, like vultures," would soon be casting invisible shadows over his men's positions—for whenever mortals had to screw their courage to an excruciating pitch of intensity, whenever they had to prepare themselves for battle, "wave on wave of them settling, close ranks shuddering into a dense, bristling glitter of shields and spears and helmets," they could know themselves passing into the sphere of the divine.[2] Certainly, it would have been hard to imagine a more eerie portal to it than Thermopylae—the "Hot Gates." Steaming waters rose from the springs that gave the pass its name; the rocks over which they hissed appeared pallid and deformed, like melted wax; a tang of sulfur hung moist in the August heat. All was feverish, dust-choked and close. So narrow was much of the pass that at two points either end of it, known as the East and West Gates, there was room for only a single wagon trail. On one side of this road there lapped the marshy shallows of the Gulf of Malis; on the other, "impassable and steepling,"[3] the cliffs of Mount Callidromus, tree-covered over the lower crags, then rearing gray and bare against the unforgiving azure. It was a strange and unearthly spot—and one seemingly formed for defense.

As the locals had long appreciated. Men from Phocis, the valley-scored country that lay between Thermopylae and Delphi, had once built a wall across the pass, blocking off not one of the two bottlenecks at either end but rather a stretch some sixty feet wide, the so-called

"Middle Gate." Here the cliffs rose at their sheerest and most unflank-able. Leonidas, bivouacking beneath them, immediately set about having the Phocians' wall repaired: no great challenge, for he had brought with him, in addition to his bodyguard, some three hundred helots and five thousand further troops.[4] These, alternately cajoled and bullied into joining him, had come mostly from the Peloponnese—but not all. Seven hundred were volunteers from Thespiae, a city in Boeotia that, like Plataea, had long been resentful of Theban weight-throwing and had willingly donated manpower in support of the allied cause—and four hundred had come from Thebes herself. Leonidas, uncomfortably aware that central Greece was rotten with medizers, had made a point on his way to Thermopylae of calling in on the chief conspirators and bluntly demanding their support. The Theban ruling classes, not yet bold enough to refuse a Spartan king, had responded with silken evasions. Confident, however, that Leonidas was embarked on a suicide mission, they had cheerfully per-mitted "men from the rival faction,"[5] those opposed to their medizing, to leave with him; and Leonidas, desperate for every reinforcement, had received these loyalists gratefully. Even so, he could have had no doubts, as he gazed out at the shimmering emptiness of the flatlands beyond Thermopylae, scanning the horizon for smears of dust, await-ing a first glimpse of the Great King's monstrous hordes, that there were plenty to his rear who were willing him to fail.

Nor was that the limit of his anxieties. Even as his men were busy digging themselves in, a delegation from the nearby city of Trachis, in whose territory Thermopylae lay, came to Leonidas with some most unwelcome news. The pass, it appeared, was not quite as secure as the strategists back on the Isthmus had cared to presume. There was, skirting the mountainous heights of Thermopylae, a trail. While hardly suited to cavalry or heavy infantry, it was, the Trachians reported, perfectly negotiable by anyone lightly armed. If the barbar-ians discovered this route, they would surely take it. There was no choice for the defenders of the Hot Gates, but to plug it. Simple enough, it might have been thought—except that Leonidas, with the full strength of the Great King's army about to hurl itself against his position, could ill afford to spare so much as a single hoplite. In the event, as he had little choice but to do, he compromised. A thousand men from Phocis, whose loathing for the medizing Thessalians had prompted them to side enthusiastically with the allies, volunteered to guard the trail. Leonidas, banking on their local knowledge and on the likelihood that only light infantry would be sent against them, accepted their offer. No Spartans, not so much as a single officer, were sent to leaven their inexperience. Bracing himself for the coming storm, Leonidas wanted all his elite alongside him. Understandable, perhaps—but a hideous gamble, even so.

Not that the Spartan king was the only commander having to make some awkward calculations. Forty miles to the east, across the Malian Gulf and beyond the narrow straits that separated Euboea from the mainland, the allied admirals were fretting over the state of their own flank. True, the station they had chosen appeared, like Thermopylae, to be a strong one. In contrast to the bleak aspect of the facing coastline, where scrub-covered slopes loomed up from the sea like olive teeth set in gums of naked rock, the northernmost tip of Euboea consisted largely of pebbles and dirty sand. Level and long as this beach stretched, it had been a simple matter for the Greeks to haul their warships onto the shingle, hundreds upon hundreds of them; and since there were no shoals or reefs offshore, only a sudden, pre-cipitous deepening of the sea, it promised to be an equally simple matter, once the Persian fleet was sighted, to launch the fleet again. Where, though—and this was the question gnawing at the self-confidence of the Greeks—would the barbarians be heading? If westward, toward the straits that led to Thermopylae, then the allied battle line, pivoting like a door upon a hinge, would be well placed to block their access; but if eastward, down the outer coast of Euboea, either to strike onward at Attica and the Isthmus or to swing back up the opposite side of the island and aim for the Greek fleet's rear, then the danger would be grave indeed. The Great King commanded so many triremes that he could easily afford to divide his armada in two and still bring overwhelming force to bear on separate fronts. The allied admirals therefore risked finding themselves, not barring the straits that separated Euboea from the mainland, but bottled up inside them. As in the pass, so on the beach, forward defense carried the risk of obliteration.

The first two weeks of August slipped by. Still the approaches to the north remained empty. There stretched, across the sea from the increasingly jittery Greeks, a mountainous peninsula known as Magnesia, forested and monster-haunted; and all knew that it was down this inhospitable coastline that the invaders were bound to come, hidden from the sight of all on Euboea, until, funneling past the island of Sciathos, just off the southern limit of the mainland, they would at last heave into view. Only from Sciathos itself did there appear any prospect of receiving advance warning of their approach, and so three patrol ships were duly stationed on the island, and beacons readied on its hills. Still the sea remained empty of vessels, however—and still, crunching up and down the shingle, wiping sweat from their stinging eyes, the sailors of the Greek fleet kept an anxious watch on Sciathos, and waited for the war to begin. Only at dusk, when the sun set behind the distant peak of Callidromus, could they afford to relax: for no one in the Aegean, where to navigate was to island-hop, presumed to sail across the open sea at night. Then, perhaps, the Greeks could feel themselves transported back to a different age, one in which their forefathers had similarly camped beside their ships on a lonely beach: for although, on a low hill behind them, there stood a temple to Artemis—from which the headland took its name of Artemisium—the strand was otherwise theirs alone.

> *And so their spirits soared,*
> *as they took positions down the passageways of battle*
> *all night long, and the watchfires blazed among them.*
> *Hundreds strong, as stars in the night sky glittering*
> *round the moon's brilliance blaze in all their glory*
> *when the air falls to a sudden, windless calm . . .*[6]

Then, one morning in mid-August, at the most unexpected time of the day, just after dawn, a blaze of fire rose suddenly on Sciathos. The enemy had been sighted. A first battle had already been fought. The result had been, for the Greek patrol ships, a humiliating rout. As though from nowhere, and even as the stars were still glimmering, a squadron of ten Sidonian triremes had swooped down upon Sciathos—for the Phoenicians, unlike their rivals, had learned to navigate the open sea by night.[7] Comprehensively ambushed, the Greek patrol ships had then been outpaced as well. One had surrendered almost immediately, and the throat of the best-looking prisoner had been ritually cut above the prow as a dedication to the gods: first blood to the Sidonians. The second, by contrast, had been captured only after furious fighting. Indeed, the enemy had been so impressed by the prowess of one particular Greek marine that, having finally overwhelmed him, they had treated his wounds with myrrh, wrapped them up in bandages, and feted him as a war hero. The third ship, an Athenian trireme, had successfully evaded its pursuers only to run aground on a mud flat off an estuary. Not the most glorious start to the defense of Greek liberty.

Meanwhile, back at Artemisium, all was alarm and consternation. Unclear whether the fire beacon on Sciathos heralded the approach of the entire barbarian fleet, crews stumbled over pebbles and waded through shallows in a frantic struggle to launch their ships. As the hours passed, and no enemy reinforcements appeared, it became evident that the Sidonians, rather than forming an advance guard, were engaged only on a reconnaissance mission. Despite its spectacular early successes, this was not going entirely to plan: Greek patrol vessels, skirting the gap between Sciathos and the mainland, watched as three of the enemy triremes foundered on a hidden reef. Nevertheless, back at Artemisium, the Greeks continued to launch their own ships, and then, once they were afloat, to aim for the straits off Euboea and the mainland, as though in headlong panic. Nor, giving even more of an impression of craven-heartedness, was any attempt made to secure the capture of the Sidonians; not even when, with a brazen display of coolness, they began to build a way marker on the hidden reef. It was as though the Greeks, flaunting their own demoralization, were positively looking to have it reported back to the Persian high command.

And perhaps they were. Of course, bearing in mind the full force of the hammer blow that was about to fall on them, a certain twitchiness was only to be expected. It may even have spread to the very top. Eurybiades, the high admiral, was hardly the most inspiring of leaders. As a Spartan, he appears to have felt doubly uncomfortable at finding himself on board a ship so far removed from the Peloponnese. His main contribution to allied strategy was to moan repeatedly that "the Persians were invincible at sea."[8] Yet Eurybiades, although the commander, was hardly in command. Effective leadership of the Greek fleet lay instead with the admiral of its largest contingent—and Themistocles had always argued for holding a forward line. Why, then, would he have sanctioned a withdrawal from Artemisium? His nerve, at any rate, could hardly be doubted: he had fought at Marathon; he knew what it was to face the barbarian and not turn tail. He would also have remembered how the celebrated victory had been won. He and his comrades in the weakened center, forced back by their enemy's advance, turning the barbarians' own onslaught against them, so that their flanks could be rolled up, had suckered the Persians into a lethal trap. Arrogance, the arrogance of an enemy who believed himself invincible, could, if manipulated with due cunning, transform even a seemingly overwhelming weight of numbers into a liability: such appears to have been the lesson that Themistocles had absorbed from his previous engagement with the enemy. Hence, it may be, his opting to retreat from Artemisium. Withdraw before the Persian battle fleet, tempt it into the narrow straits off Euboea, cramp it for room, attack it—and finish it off, perhaps. A long shot—but long shots had worked before against the Mede.

Not on this occasion, however. The trap had been sprung—but there was no one to take the bait. The day passed, and still the lookouts on the heights of Euboea reported the sea lanes from Magnesia empty. The Greek warships, rather than return to Artemisium, withdrew instead further south. Chalcis, where the weary oarsmen finally paused for breath, lay midway down the western coast of Euboea. From there, dependent on the news brought to them by their lookouts of the Persian fleet's intentions, the Greeks would be well positioned either to make a dash for the comparative safety of the Attic coastline or return the way they had come, back to the defense of Leonidas' flank. The oarsmen themselves, with the great ridge of Euboea now positioned like a shield between them and the open sea, and the heat growing ever more sweltering, could certainly feel a measure of relief at being away from the exposed beaches of Artemisium—for sweltering heat in late summer invariably portended a Hellesponter. It was mariners' lore in the Aegean never to trust the weather after August 12—and August 12 had already come and gone. Still the days slipped by. Still there were no fresh sightings of the Persian fleet. Still there was no easing of the heat. The Greeks, hunkered down at Chalcis, kept their eyes fixed on the warning beacons atop the high Euboean hills, dabbled their toes in the cooling currents of the sea, and did as Apollo had advised them: offered up prayers to the winds.

They also serve who only stand and wait. If Leonidas, on his lonely sentry duty at Thermopylae, was primed for death, then Themistocles, just as surely, had his heart set on survival. Glorious as it was, having left home and family behind, having journeyed to war in a distant land, having staked one's life in a supreme contest of valor and endurance, then to fall in battle, yet so also, in Greek tradition, might a hero display an instinct for self-preservation and be no less a hero. Achilles, offered by his mother the alternatives of a happy but obscure old age or an early death and undying glory, had not hesitated; but Homer, in his second great epic, had sung the exploits of a man who made a very different choice. Odysseus, as barrel-chested as Themistocles and quite as much a "man of twists and turns," had wanted nothing more, having sacked Troy, than to return home to his wife. In the cause of achieving that, he had held no ploy, no deception, no ruse beneath him. This was why Athena had admired him and honored him above all her favorites: for "here among mortal men," as she told Odysseus, "you're the best at tactics, spinning yarns, and I am famous among the gods for wisdom, cunning wiles, too."[9] So it was that she loved the Athenians, who were held to be the most intelligent of the Greeks; and so it was, too, whenever the impossible appeared suddenly possible, and the solution to a seemingly insuperable problem began to glimmer into view, that a mortal could know Athena stood by his side. Themistocles, weighing up the odds of battle, turning fresh stratagems over in his mind, would surely not have confined himself to raising prayers to the north wind alone.

"In league with Athena set your own hand to work": so the proverb went.[10] For the moment, however, the initiative had slipped from Themistocles' grasp. His next move would depend on what others did first: the Persians—and the gods of the winds. Still there were no new developments—and still the temperature rose. Then, at last, some ten days, perhaps, after the Greek fleet had abandoned its station at Artemisium, there was a sudden wake-up call. A thirty-oared cutter, captained by an Athenian, a crony of Themistocles named Abronichus, came speeding down the straits to Chalcis. Appointed at the start of the campaign to serve as the liaison officer between Leonidas and the Greek fleet, Abronichus brought his friend alarming news. The phony war, it appeared, was over. The Great King's army was approaching Thermopylae. The Mede was at the Hot Gates.

The Storm Breaks

Lookouts were hardly needed to warn of the approach of the King of Kings. Well before the first Persian reconnaissance units began spilling out over the flatlands along the shore of the Malian Gulf, Leonidas would have known that a force beyond computation was closing in on him. Cloudless the August sky may have been, but the horizon to the north was lost behind a haze of dust. Ever filthier, thicker, more swirling it grew; and then the earth itself, trampled beneath thousands upon thousands of kicking feet, began to tremble. Such,

269

rendered literal, was the power of the Great King: that he could shake the world. For years, his agents had inflicted on the Greeks a strategy of creeping terror; and now, at last, the terror was at their gates.

For the defenders of Thermopylae, gazing in horror across the bay, the spectacle of the Great King's hordes was of an order beyond their darkest imaginings. On and on, the din of their progress now thunderous, shimmering in and out of view, borne upon rolling breakers of choking dust, the barbarians advanced. To the Greeks, wiping grit from their watering eyes, feeling the earth beneath them shiver for hour after ceaseless hour, the reports of the three spies sent to Sardis, who had spoken of Asia being emptied, and of millions being mustered against them, must have seemed horrifically confirmed. Panic began to grip the tiny army. All except the Spartans, that is, who maintained their customary composure; and Leonidas, even as he sought to steady nerves among the allies, ordered his bodyguard to hold a position beyond the wall. Soon enough, clattering up through the West Gate, there came a Persian outrider. None of the three hundred looked up. Some combed their long hair, as was the Spartan habit when preparing to face death. Others, their naked bodies slippery with oil, ran or grappled with one another; not strenuously, however, for "on campaign, the exercising required of the Spartans was always less demanding than normal . . . so that for them, uniquely, war represented a relaxation of military training."[11] The Persian scout, having surveyed this scene in astonishment, then wheeled round and galloped away. No attempt was made by the Spartans to stop him.

Later in the day, a formal embassy from Xerxes approached the Hot Gates. Leonidas, who would surely have met it beyond the wall so that the ambassadors could not see how few men he had under his command, was informed of the Great King's terms. The defenders, if they laid down their arms, might have a free passage back to their homes; the title "Friends of the Persian People" would be granted them; "and on all the Greeks who accepted his friendship, King Xerxes would settle more lands, and of better quality, than any they currently possessed."[12] To many of the Peloponnesians, already itching to scuttle back to the Isthmus, these proposals only confirmed them in their sudden enthusiasm for a retreat from the pass; but the Phocians, for whom the Isthmus might as well have been in Egypt for all the protection it afforded them, responded with fury to the prospect of abandoning Thermopylae. So too, unsurprisingly, did Leonidas; and since he was the commander in chief, and a Spartan king to boot, his resolution was sufficient to sway the waverers. The allies would stay where they were. The pass would be held. When the Great King's embassy, returning to the Hot Gates, demanded that the Greeks hand over their arms, Leonidas' defiance was aptly laconic: "*Molon labe*"; "Come and get them."[13]

His countrymen had always prized such gems of cool. The bleaker the circumstances, the more imperturbable a Spartan was trained to be: and Leonidas, perfectly aware that sangfroid was the best morale booster that he could offer his wavering allies, naturally looked to his bodyguard to back him up with some steely nonchalance of their own. They did not disappoint. When the barbarians fired their arrows, one of the locals pointed out tremulously, so many would hiss through the air as to blot out the sun. The Spartans, who were in the habit of dismissing arrows as mere spindles, womanish and cowardly, affected to be colossally unfazed. "What excellent news," one of them drawled. "If the Mede hides the sun, then so much the better for us— we can fight our battle in the shade."[14]

Yet, inspiring though such witticisms surely were, they must have struck Leonidas as perilously close to gallows humor. He knew that in truth the situation facing his men was even graver than most of them appreciated. Themistocles and the Greek fleet, still praying for storms, remained at Chalcis. With Artemisium abandoned, there was nothing now to stop the Persian fleet, once it arrived off Euboea, from heading directly for the shallows off Thermopylae. Such a moment, with the Great King already installed beyond the Hot Gates, could hardly be far off. As Leonidas scanned the eastern horizon, searching for distant masts, he would have watched the deepening of twilight over the Malian Gulf and the blazing of campfires in the pass with profound relief. Night had come—and the Persian fleet had not. The allies still held Thermopylae. But for how much longer? Nervously, men glanced above them. The moon, almost full, gleamed in a cloudless, windless sky. So it would also be gleaming over distant Olympia, and Lacedaemon too. Even though Leonidas had sent messengers to the Isthmus earlier that afternoon with a desperate appeal for reinforcements, he knew that there was little chance of it being answered—not for another week or so, at least, until the games at Olympia and the Carneia were over. And time was running out.

Dawn broke. Still there came no hints of an imminent assault upon the pass. Along the coastal road, straggling units of the Great King's army and his baggage train picked their way toward his camp. Beyond the Malian Gulf itself, the straits remained empty of Persian shipping. The imperial fleet was surely out there somewhere, closing in from the north, making for a rendezvous with the King of Kings—but where? Perhaps the new day would bring the answer. The sea, touched by the rays of morning, stretched away calm and clear, framing the blue silhouette of Euboea. Far distant, to the northeast, rose the peaks of Magnesia. All was still: curiously, brightly, menacingly still. A sailor, bred to recognize the moods of the Aegean, might have read what the moment portended; but there were few sailors at Thermopylae. The change in the weather, then, coming abruptly as it did, on a sudden howling of wind, must have struck them as something eerie and unearthly, as the breath of the gods indeed. Seemingly from nowhere, a gale began to sweep across the bay, whipping up the waves, lashing the defenders of the Hot Gates with plumes of spray. The light of the dawn darkened to blackness, and thunder rumbled distantly over the Aegean.[15] The Hellesponter, much yearned for, long prayed for, had come at last—"and all the sea began to boil with it, like water in a pot."[16]

Two days the storm raged. Two days the allies remained huddled beside the Middle Gate, the Spartans with their scarlet cloaks wrapped tightly about them, as the gales swept in from the sea. Two days the barbarians bided their time, making no assault on the pass. Instead, both sides watched the weather, scanned the eastern horizon, and

272

sweated on news of their missing fleets. By the third morning of the storm, with the winds at last starting to ease, flotsam, drifting in from the straits off Euboea, could be glimpsed across the Malian Gulf, bobbing on the choppy waters. Then, distant across the gray sea, squadrons of ships began emerging into view, straining against the winds, bearing north. The Greek fleet had survived the storm; and now it was returning, to the immense relief of the small army at Thermopylae, to its station at Artemisium. The links in the chain had been reforged. The front, for the moment, at any rate, could be held. And still no certain sighting of the enemy fleet.

Reports brought that evening by the liaison officer serving at Artemisium suggested why. Heading for the Sciathos gap, the barbarians had been caught on the open sea. The coast of Magnesia, battered by the full force of the gale, was said to be littered with corpses, spars and gold. The precise number of ships lost to the storms was as yet a matter of conjecture, but there were some among the Greek fleet who dared to claim "that there would be only a few left to oppose them."[17] Hardly, of course, a forecast that Leonidas himself could echo: on the plain beyond the West Gate, the barbarian campfires still blazed numberless. There too the carnage off Magnesia would have been reported. The failure to outflank Thermopylae by sea would have been digested. A new plan of attack would have been ordered, and urgently, for the Great King, with hundreds of thousands of mouths to feed, could hardly afford to kick his heels. The implications for Leonidas and his tiny army that evening appeared self-evident— and menacing. Four days they had waited for the Great King to make a frontal assault on their position, and on the following morning, the fifth, all the multitudes of Asia would surely be hurled against them. Their resolve and courage would be put to a test such as few men had ever had to face before; not even in the days of song; not even on the fields of Troy. Combing their hair, sharpening their weapons, burnishing their shields to a dazzling brightness, the Spartans prepared for the dawn, and for what, all their lives, they had been raised to give: a display of the art of killing.

And sure enough, sunrise coming, the barbarian came as well. It was the Medes who had been given the task of clearing the pass. These were men skilled in all the requirements of mountain warfare, well armored too, their mail coats glittering like the scales of iron fish, and their very name had long been a terror to the Greeks. Leonidas, however, had chosen his position carefully, and the Medes, practiced though they may have been at climbing the defiles of the Zagros, found it impossible to scale the cliffs of the Middle Gate and outflank the defenders' line. Nor, in the closeness of the pass, was there sufficient space for them to unleash what might otherwise have proved an equally lethal strategy: the firing of a rain of arrows so heavy as to serve the sweltering Spartans as a sunblock. Instead, breasting the pass, hurrying to the attack, the Medes found themselves with little choice but to charge directly at the shield wall and attempt to batter it aside. But this was the form of warfare in which all hoplites, supremely, were battle trained; and the shields of the Medes were fashioned of wicker, while their spears were much shorter than those of the Greeks.

So it was that their weight of numbers, although it might have appeared overwhelming, failed to tell. Never before having tested themselves against the barbarian, the Spartans would have known within seconds of the first impact that they had the measure of their assailants. There could be no doubting the bravery of the Medes, men prepared to throw themselves against a line of bristling spears and shields, but they provided, even in their fish scales, easy prey for a wall of bronze-clad professional killers. Within minutes, the front had taken on the character of a charnel house. The Spartans employed their spearheads and swords to eviscerate, and their skill in "fighting close to their enemies"[18] was a thing of horror to their fellow Greeks. Now, in the hellish closeness of the Hot Gates, the Medes learned to share in that dread. Those who fell did so with gaping wounds; those still on their feet found themselves soused with blood, slithering over entrails, stumbling over the growing piles of the dead.

For the Greeks too, though, straining to hold their positions against the seething crush of the enemy, the fight was desperate. Butting back their assailants with their heavy shields, jabbing, slashing, hacking all they could, feeling the sun steadily heating up the bronze of their armor, soaked in sweat and blood, those in the line of battle could hardly be expected to hold their position all the day. Nor were they: for Leonidas, with cool efficiency, ensured a regular transfusion of fresh troops to the front. Those withdrawn could remove their armor, have a drink, and bandage their wounds. Even a Spartan might sometimes need to catch his breath.

And particularly so because Leonidas, uncertain what further tactics the King of Kings might employ, needed his elite corps primed to cope with any sudden emergency. All day the battle continued to rage, until the Greeks, having seen off the Medes, and then reinforcements from Susa, found themselves, as the shadows lengthened, facing precisely such a moment of crisis. A glittering of jeweled weaponry, a shimmering of exquisite colors, and the Immortals, the most proficient and dreaded of all the Great King's regiments, as supreme among the Persians as the Spartans were among the Greeks, advanced into the pass. To meet them, Leonidas ordered all his bodyguard back to the front line—"and there the Lacedaemonians fought in a manner never to be forgotten."[19] Courage, strength and resolution they displayed, as was only to be expected; but also a murderous talent for the tactical maneuver. At a signal, they would turn, stumble, appear to flee in panic; and then, as the enemy surged forward in triumph, their discipline momentarily forgotten, the Spartans would wheel round, reform their line with a fearsome clattering of shields, and hack down their pursuers. This tactic was doubly demoralizing to their assailants: for, apart from the casualties that it inflicted, it served to rub their noses in the brute fact of the Spartans' continued battle worthiness, even after a whole day's fighting, even amid the heat, and the blood, and the stench and the flies. Reluctant to squander his best troops fruitlessly, the Great King at length ordered their withdrawal, and the Immortals retreated back through the West Gate. The pass was left to the evening shadows, the carnage and the Greeks.

That night, amid the distant rumbling of thunder over Magnesia, rain started lashing down over the battlefield, slowly turning it into a mulch of gore and mud. In the piles of tangled corpses, the jewelry around the necks of Xerxes' slaughtered guardsmen, sparkling in the light of the sentries' guttering torches, would have appeared to mock the filth of slaughter. And the pretensions of the King of Kings as well? So Leonidas would have wanted desperately to believe. But he would have known better than to surrender to complacency. Though his position had demonstrated itself impregnable to a frontal assault, it still remained only as strong—or as weak—as its flanks. Messengers from the Phocian camp high on the slopes of Callidromus, having slithered and stumbled their way down to Thermopylae, reassured Leonidas that the mountain approaches were empty; but communication with the fleet at Artemisium that night, so violent had the weather turned again, was out of the question. Just as during the previous storm, Leonidas could only listen to the screaming of the winds, hug his red cloak about himself, and hope for the best.

And perhaps, for his peace of mind, this was just as well—because a day that could be viewed by the defenders of Thermopylae as a triumph of obduracy had been passed by the admirals at Artemisium in a very different spirit.[20] Unpleasant surprise had followed fast on unpleasant surprise. The Persian fleet, far from being almost utterly destroyed, as optimists among the Greeks had hoped, had proved very far from finished. It may have been storm-battered—but throughout the early afternoon, as squadron after squadron, having limped past Sciathos and rounded the headland of Magnesia, began massing on the shore opposite Artemisium, the Greeks had watched with a mounting sense of despair. Never before had any of them seen the sea quite so black with shipping. Even after the havoc wreaked by the storms, the Persians could still muster perhaps eight hundred triremes, sufficient to outnumber the allied fleet by almost three to one. Not even the accidental blundering into their base of fifteen enemy ships and the capture of their crews had done much to cheer the Greeks. Now that they could see the Persian fleet before them, a bare ten miles away across the open sea, there were many who began to argue for a second withdrawal, and urgently, before the barbarians could complete their repairs. This talk had grown louder and louder—to the consternation of the locals, who were already twitchy at the prospect of being abandoned to the Mede. Soon they had sent a frantic delegation, first to Eurybiades, and then, when he turned down their request, to Themistocles, begging the allies to stay. Themistocles, who was as appalled as the Euboeans at the prospect of evacuating Artemisium, had nevertheless cheerfully demanded a backhander for his services. Having salted most of it away for himself, he then used the surplus to grease the palm of Eurybiades. This was hardly the style of backbone-stiffening favored by Leonidas, but it was just as effective. Eurybiades and the other admirals duly agreed that the allied fleet would stay at Artemisium and hold the line.

No sooner had the high command resolved this, however, than it was thrown into renewed panic. In the late afternoon, at around the same time as the Immortals were advancing against the Hot Gates, and while the Persian squadrons, with all the ostentation they could muster, were staging an intimidatory review off the opposing coast, the allies hauled a Greek deserter from the enemy fleet, one Scyllias, out of the sea. A professional diver, who claimed to have swum the ten miles to Artemisium entirely underwater, the news he brought with him had a credibility that his boasting maybe lacked; certainly, it was sufficient to chill the blood of the listening admirals. The enemy, Scyllias reported, while the main body of their fleet was being repaired, had detached two hundred seaworthy vessels to make their way unseen down the eastern coast of Euboea, round its southern tip, and then back up its western side. Here, raising its head again, was the Greeks' worst-case scenario: that they might find themselves bottled up, with the barbarian both ahead of them and blocking off their escape. A moment of mortal peril, to be sure—and yet, as Themistocles was quick to point out, Scyllias' intelligence spelled opportunity as well as danger. Detach a sizable squadron from the fleet at Artemisium, send it down the straits between Euboea and the mainland, trust to the gods that the patrols off Attica would pursue the two hundred Persian ships when they caught sight of them, and it might be the barbarians who found themselves trapped in a vise.

All a massive gamble, of course—but the Greeks, if they were to have any hope of halting the Persian advance, had little choice but to trust occasionally to audacity and luck. A resolution was duly passed: "to put to sea and meet the enemy ships that were sailing round Euboea."[21] Naturally, since it was essential not to alert the barbarians on the opposite shore to any thinning of the main fleet at Artemisium, the detachment would be able to leave only after nightfall—and after the Greeks, if they possibly could, had demonstrated to the enemy that they had no intention of cutting and running. This they did by boldly venturing out from their positions into the open sea, challenging the Persians to attack them—which the Persians, confident in the crushing weight of their numbers, and the greater skill of their crews, duly did. Even as the sun began to set behind the western peaks of the mainland, their fleet was sweeping down hungrily across the open channel, swamping the much shorter line of the Greeks, looking to envelop it, crush it and end the war there and then. The Greeks, however, anticipating this tactic, had prepared a maneuver specifically designed to counter it: forming themselves into a circle, their rams pointed outward, like the spines of a hedgehog rolled up tightly into a ball, they then moved out suddenly to the attack. The Persians, in the close fighting that followed, found their superior speed and agility negated. Some thirty of their ships were captured, and when twilight, deepening over the Aegean, at length brought the fighting to the end, it was the Greeks, to their astonishment and delight, who could claim the honors of the engagement. Barbarian seamanship, it appeared, might be countered, even defeated, after all. No better fillip could have been imagined for those crews facing a perilous nighttime voyage.

Then, of course, came the gale. As rain drummed down on the ships of the Greek fleet, so the winds, screaming in from the southeast over the bleak strand of Artemisium, quickly shredded any prospect of a midnight getaway. Fortunately for the allies, however, that was not the limit of the storm damage: for wreckage from the evening's battle soon began to be swept up-channel toward the enemy positions, where it fouled the oars of the rolling patrol ships and filled the harbors with bobbing spars and corpses. Buffeted by yet another storm, and still licking their wounds from the unexpected mauling they had received at the hands of the Greeks, it was now the turn of the Persians to be thrown into a panic—"for they imagined that the hour of their doom had come."[22] As it proved, they imagined wrong: the harbors in which the fleet had taken sanctuary the previous day served to shelter it from the worst depredations of the gale. No such refuge, however, for the two hundred ships sent south around Euboea, for the savage eastern coast of the island, with its jagged rocks and cliffs, was a miserable place to be caught off during a storm. The armada, it is said, "running blind before the wind and rain," was shattered upon a notorious black spot known as the "Hollows"; and certainly, irrespective of whether all the ships were lost, as the Greeks would later crow, the gale had spelled their mission's end.[23]

By the following afternoon, reports of the shipwreck were reaching Artemisium, and the Greek admirals, confident that their lines of retreat were no longer threatened, could afford to breathe a huge sigh of relief. Not that they had any intention now of abandoning their forward position. Prospects for holding the front suddenly appeared as rosy as they had looked bleak the day before. Good news was coming in from everywhere: reinforcements, fifty-three ships fresh from Athens; the destruction, in an evening hit-and-run raid, of a squadron of Cilician ships; the briefing, brought by Abronichus, the liaison officer, that Leonidas and his men had withstood a second day of hard pounding at the Hot Gates. If the Great King could not make a breakthrough soon, his army would start to starve. It was already late in the campaigning season, and the barbarians were far from home. If they could merely avoid defeat, and keep the Mede at bay, that, for the Greeks, would surely prove victory enough.

But the true test, for the allied fleet and its ability to hold off the enemy, was still to come. The Persians, laboring desperately to make their remaining ships fully seaworthy again, had not yet attempted to smash the linchpin of the whole Greek line that, if forced, would open the way to Thermopylae: the straits between Euboea and the mainland. The third day of battle dawned and the Greeks, watching from Artemisium, could have had little doubt that the moment of truth was coming at last. Squadron after squadron of the barbarian fleet— Phoenician, Egyptian, Ionian—began massing in the open channel. Now, after all the skirmishing, all the shadowboxing, it was to come: the first full frontal assault by the Great King's navy on the Greek positions. Rowing out to block its passage, men who had first pulled on an oar just months—or, in the case of the Plataeans, weeks— before braced themselves for the fight.

Less mobile than its enemy, the Greek fleet, having plugged the straits, then opted to wait for the Persians to force the attack. Rowers, their knuckles whitening as they gripped their oars, their noses wrinkling against an overpowering stench of sweat and loosening bowels, sat crouched on their wooden benches, straining to hear above the creaking of timbers, the lapping of the water, and the nervous talk of their comrades the approaching tide of battle. Soon enough, from the marines on deck, the cry went up: the barbarians were closing in. "Overwhelming numbers; gaudily painted figure-heads; arrogant yelling; savage war-chants":[24] such were the sights and sounds of the Persian advance as it fanned out across the channel. The impact, when it duly came, was pulverizing. All day the Greeks fought desperately to keep the enemy at bay, "yelling out to one another that the barbarians should not break through, even as the Persians, looking to sweep the passage clear, sought to annihilate them."[25] Somehow, despite the fearful battering they received, the Greeks managed to hold the straits—but only just. Numerous ships were sunk or captured, losses which the smaller allied fleet could ill afford; many others were disabled. The Athenians, who had borne the brunt of the enemy assault throughout the battle, had a full half of their fleet put out of action.

Prospects of holding the straits the following day looked bleak. Disconsolately, the Greeks began gathering wreckage from the battle, piling it up on the sand to serve as pyres for their dead, while their admirals, anxious faces lit by the funeral fires, debated what to do next. By now, the locals, who had seen the shattered state of the Greek fleet and already drawn their own conclusions as to its prospects, were driving their livestock down to the seafront, in the hope that they might be included in any evacuation. Themistocles, recognizing that the abandonment of Artemisium might indeed be a necessity, and not wishing his already battle-weary men to have to row through the night on empty stomachs, ordered the cattle barbecued.

Yet the mood along the fire-dotted beach that night, even amid all the weariness and disappointment, was not entirely one of despair. The Greeks had faced the Great King's armada in open battle and lived to tell the tale. Great things had been achieved at Artemisium—and not all of them owing to the winds. The allied fleet remained intact as a fighting force; and withdrawal, if it did come, would be strategic and orderly. Not that any final decision could be made either way until news had arrived from the Hot Gates—for synchronization with Leonidas and his army remained the key to the whole campaign. And none of the navy knew what had happened at Thermopylae. As dusk turned to night, the admirals had to play a waiting game. Up and down the shore they crunched, breathing in the mingled scents of beef and burning human flesh, casting their gaze across the channel to the distant lights of the Persian positions, and waiting for Abronichus to deliver his daily briefing from the Spartan king.

His small galley arrived that night off Artemisium in good time. The sailors, gathered around their campfires, were still at their supper. The ships had not yet been readied for departure; no sense of crisis gripped the camp. One glimpse of Abronichus' face, however, as he came stumbling through the shallows, and all that changed. Everyone who saw him knew, even before he spoke, that something calamitous had occurred at Thermopylae.

King's Dinners and Spartan Breakfasts

Even road-blocked on a dusty plain, beside the shore of the Bitter Sea, in a remote and savage land, the Great King remained the hub around which the spokes of his world empire turned. Unable to direct the invasion of Greece from Persepolis, Xerxes had simply ordered Persepolis to be brought with him to Greece. Night after night, no matter where the Great King halted, servants would scurry to unload mountains of luggage from trains of mules and camels, to level out a huge expanse of ground, and then to raise on it a tent so splendid as to put most palaces in the shade. Since Persian royalty was inveterately restless, migrating from capital to capital depending on the season, the Great King's engineers, with their long experience of providing for royal road trips, knew precisely how best to prefabricate luxury. As a result, even in the bleak surroundings of the approach to Thermopylae, the imperial dignity, cocooned in rugs and cushions, leather awnings and colored hangings, was never under any threat: chamber after chamber led away from the royal presence, while the Immortals, stationed by every doorway, stood as surety against any assassination attempt by veterans of the Crypteia.* The contrast with conditions inside the Hot Gates could hardly have been more brutal: while Leonidas was obliged to camp out amid stench and putrescence, the Great King could direct the battle from within the perfumed cool of his audience hall; or, at night, looking to conserve his energy, retire to a silver-footed couch, where the coverings would have been pre-pared for him by a specialist bed-maker, a slave trained to "make linens beautiful and soft, for the Persians were the very first people to have regarded this as an art."[26]

---

*It is possible that such an attempt was made. Several sources claim that Leonidas, on the eve of the Spartans' last stand, launched a raid on the royal tent and was killed. It is hard to know what to make of this story — since Leonidas himself certainly died in battle — unless it hints at a garbled memory of a foiled mission to assassinate Xerxes.

The Greeks, clutching at straws, presumed to attribute the extrav-
agances of such a campaigning style to effeminacy: a woeful betrayal of
their own lack of sophistication. Having given ample demonstrations
of his courage while still a young man, Xerxes had no intention of risking his life in battle now, not with a great army and fleet both looking
to him for leadership, and a campaign of unprecedented complexity to
direct. The royal tent may have been monumental, but it had to be if
it were to provide an adequate nerve center for a global superpower.
As at Persepolis, so on the wayside of the road to Thermopylae, the
Great King did not disdain advice but rather demanded it, having recognized that the wisest master is the one who makes best use of his
slaves. Xerxes, whose subordinates were rarely short of obedience and
courage, evidently had a talent for inspiring devotion in them: not for
nothing did his name mean "He Who Rules Over Heroes."

No less than the Spartans, then, the Great King's followers were
steeled by a rigorous discipline. Protocol, even on campaign, even for
heroes, was rigid and sacrosanct. No matter how violently the gales outside the tent might rage, or how alarming the news from the front
might prove to be, the Great King, seated in due magnificence upon a
throne of solid gold, conducted his councils of war precisely as though
presiding at Persepolis. Only in the degree to which the royal ear might
bend itself to foreigners did the very different circumstances of
Thermopylae intrude upon proceedings. Filled by the Great King's relatives and intimates though the top ranks in the military were, not
everyone honored with a summons to the royal presence was necessarily a Persian. There were two sons of Datis, for instance, in
command of the cavalry; and then, of course, the key adviser on everything Greek, there was Demaratus. Even as Xerxes, periodically
dispatching his troops into the Hot Gates, continued to probe the
defenders of the pass for any suggestion of weakening, he pumped the
exiled king for insights into Spartan psychology. Overwhelming force
and a mastery of data: the twin characteristics, as they had ever been, of
the Persian way of making war. To synthesize these adequately, in order
to neutralize a problem such as the one presented by defenders of

Thermopylae, was a challenge that could only really be met in the tent of the King of Kings, where princes of the royal blood, and intelligence agents, and logistics chiefs, and Greek renegades, all might equally be summoned and have their reports and judgments pooled.

And Xerxes, though enraged by the defense of the Hot Gates, did not surrender to his frustration, but rather consulted his briefings, made calculations, gave orders and kept his patience. The king of a mountain people, it hardly came as any great revelation to him that a narrow pass might be rendered impregnable to a frontal attack. The Syrian Gates, for instance, through which Datis and his army had snaked on their way to Marathon, bristled with fortifications far more imposing than those of Thermopylae: a tourniquet ever ready to be applied, in case of emergency, to the flow of the Royal Road. Yet even when "a natural gateway exactly imitates the defences raised by human ingenuity,"[27] it will invariably, as the Persian military well knew, betray a fatal weakness—for there are few gorges that cannot somehow be bypassed by a path across their heights. The Syrian Gates, and the Cilician Gates, and the Persian Gates: all were vulnerable to being outflanked by mountain roads. Why not the Hot Gates, too?

With the Greeks holding out against all that could be thrown directly at them, this became, hour by hour, an ever more pressing question. There can be little doubt that Persian agents, even before the arrival of the Great King, would have been fanning out over the foothills of Oeta and Callidromus, scanning the lie of the land, waving gold before peasants, appealing for native guides. None had been forthcoming: Trachis, perched above the fissure of the nearby, boulder-strewn Asopus gorge, was openly hostile to the Great King, and most of the locals had fled either into the mountains or to Leonidas. Some were left, however, and all it would take was for one Greek, just one, intimidated by the spectacle of the Great King's magnificence, to crack; and magnificence, of course, was something that the Great King did surpassingly, superlatively well.

In particular, colossal in the middle of the sprawling camp, the imperial war banners decorated with eagles flapping imperiously above it, there was Xerxes' own tent. This was not merely a campaign headquarters, but, thanks to its careful reproduction of the layout of Persepolis, right down to the very last detail, a mobile master class in the dynamics of royal power. Oblivious to these as only savages on the outer rim of the world could be, the Greeks were to be dazzled, over-awed and terrified out of their lamentable ignorance. Attempting to explain to Xerxes the significance of the Lycurgan code, Demaratus had boldly asserted that the Spartans feared it "more than your sub-jects fear you"[28]—at which the King of Kings, "showing no anger," had merely laughed, "and then with great gentleness dismissed him."[29] Perhaps the bristling provincialism of a homesick exile was altogether too pathetic a joke to anger the master of a superpower. And perhaps—for the Spartans were a people who had dared to kill his father's ambassadors, and had sent their king with only three hun-dred men to oppose the whole might of his army—their arrogance was something that Xerxes could hardly doubt. "The typical Greek: a man who envies the good fortune of others, and resents the power of those stronger than himself."[30] This, delivered with crushing but not inaccurate condescension, was the considered judgment of the Persian high command on the psychology of their enemy. Precisely the same profile, however, could once have been applied to the Medes, the Babylonians, or the Egyptians—and all those ancient peoples had been sternly shown the error of their ways.

That the Great King felt a solemn obligation to open the eyes of Europe to its future in the new world order could be gauged from the leisurely pace of his advance from the Hellespont. This had left him arriving at Thermopylae perilously late in the campaigning season; but it had been important to Xerxes to instruct his new subjects very pre-cisely in the character of the submission that they owed to him. While a succession of parades, regattas and horse races had continued to flaunt the global scale of the Great King's resources, so the contribu-tion that the natives themselves were to make to this magnificence, and the abasement that they would graciously be permitted to display to their master, had been similarly driven home. Over the winter, every city on the expedition's path had been instructed to prepare a feast fit for a king. For months, the natives had done little except panic over menus. To be charged with preparing a dinner party to the opulent standards of Persepolis would have been headache enough for any hosts, but that was almost the least of their obligations. There were also the Great King's soldiers to be fed, and his horses, mules and camels. Wood had to be provided for the fires of the royal cooks. The cups on the Great King's table had to be fashioned of silver and gold, the fittings of finest linen, the rugs and carpets of the softest and most luxurious materials that the wretched citizenry could afford. Nor, once these had been used, was there any prospect of then selling them off to help recoup expenses, since the Persians, like the worst kind of houseguest, were in the habit of crating up all the furnishings "and marching off, leaving not a single thing behind."[31] No wonder that one wag, bled white by the "honor" of hosting the imperial army, had called on his fellow citizens to offer up thanks to the gods "that King Xerxes was not in the habit of demanding breakfast as well."[32]

No wonder either that Alexander of Macedon, back in May, when confronted by the prospect of a Greek holding force bedding down at Tempe on the southern borders of his kingdom, had sent it a frantic message, warning its commanders that their position was untenable. Perfectly true, of course—and a conclusion that the Greeks had already begun drawing for themselves—but the security of the task force had been, from Alexander's point of view, merely incidental. Rather, his principal concern had been to ensure as short a stay for the Persian army in Macedonia as possible. Vassal of the King of Kings that he was, Alexander had been painfully aware that his master regarded the whole empire as his larder—that "the various delicacies of the countries over which he ruled, the choicest first-fruits of each,"[33] were all his due, a tribute to be skimmed for the exclusive benefit of the royal table. The feasts scraped together with such expense and agony by those on Xerxes' path had been portrayed as the gifts, not of those who had provided them, but of the Great King himself, magnanimously bestowed upon his followers: the "King's

Dinner." It was also said, conversely, that Xerxes had refused any Greek specialities, and ordered them taken away if they were ever served—for only the fat of his own subjects' lands could be permitted to pass the Great King's lips. Time enough for Attic figs once Xerxes sat in conquered Athens.

The prospect, then, that his army might starve, or even—perish the thought—that the royal table itself might stand empty, was a crisis of far more than mere logistics: for at risk were the very foundations of imperial prestige. Deprive the Great King of his pudding, and morale might start to plummet. Not that it was an easy matter to catch out a bureaucracy so attentive to detail that it was in the habit of issuing travel chits to ducks. Extensive preparations had been made for just such a moment of crisis as was brewing at Thermopylae. Waterfowl would certainly have been brought in the imperial baggage train, but so also would any number of the other delicacies to which the royal palate had grown accustomed: acanthus oil from Carmania, dates from Babylon, cumin from Ethiopia. Even the Great King's drinking water had been transported in great jars from a river near Susa.

All the same, the supply of ingredients—and particularly fresh ingredients—had its limits, even for the peerless logistics chiefs of Persia. By the sixth day of the enforced halt at Thermopylae, the situation beyond the gilded confines of the royal tent, out among the teeming multitudes of the rank and file, was turning serious. The appetites of Iranians, in particular, did not readily lend themselves to belt-tightening. The Greeks, who tended to eat only the meat of animals that had first been sacrificed to the gods, told wide-eyed stories of their enemy's carnivorous tastes. A Persian, it was said, would think nothing of baking a whole donkey by way of a birthday celebration; or even, if he were particularly well off, a camel. Soldiers on campaign took a regular supply of "oxen, asses, deer, smaller animals, ostriches, geese and cocks"[34] as their daily right. The approaches to Thermopylae, never abundant in ostriches at the best of times, were proving an alarming culinary letdown to the men of the Great King's army. Persian cooks, celebrated though they were for the inventiveness of their recipes, could hardly magically produce meals out of fields stripped wholly bare.

Yet Xerxes, though anxious about the rumbling in his soldiers' stomachs, knew that there were others who would be feeling the pinch even worse. The presence of the Persian army on their doorstep threatened local landowners with ruin. Since responsibility for this regrettable state of affairs clearly stopped with Leonidas and his pestilential little army, the obvious—indeed, the only—way for the natives to spare themselves utter destitution was to help the Great King flush the Hot Gates clear of its obstruction. Surely, then, Xerxes had to trust, where the spectacle of royal invincibility had so far failed to recruit a guide, self-interest was bound to succeed?

And so in the end it did, as, amid the dust and disappointments of the second day's fighting, the Greek capacity for backstabbing came to the rescue of the Persian high command. For almost a week the imperial army had been encamped before Thermopylae—and now, at last, an informant was brought cringing into the royal tent. His name was Ephialtes, a native of the plain on which the Persian army was camped, and he it was who revealed to his interrogators that Callidromus did indeed possess a secret. "In the hope of a rich reward, he told the king about the trail which led over the mountain to Thermopylae"[35]— and even offered, in the truly fatal act of treachery, to serve the invaders as their guide.

Immediately the fearsome machinery of the imperial army was set into smooth and deadly motion. Late in the day though it already was, further delay was clearly out of the question: the ascent of Callidromus was ordered for that very night. Nor was it to be attempted by the light infantry that Leonidas had presumed would be the only troops capable of making such a journey. The Immortals, their toughness bred amid the uplands of Iran, were a squad made for such an adventure. Bloodied the previous day in the pass, there was not a man among them who would not have relished his chance of revenge. For their commander, in particular, the mission had a particular piquancy. Hydarnes was son and namesake of the coconspirator with Darius who, forty-one years previously, had held the Khorasan Highway against a vast army of rebel Medes. Now, given the perfect opportunity to add to his family's battle honors, Hydarnes would serve Darius' son, not by holding, but by clearing a vital pass.

He and his ten thousand men left at dusk. Their route began several miles west of the Hot Gates, west too of Trachis and of the Asopus gorge above which it stood.[36] Behind them, as they began their ascent, watch fires were already starting to dot the plain, but soon the view of the camp was lost. Fortunately, just as Ephialtes had said it would be, the trail was easy to follow, and the moon, the fateful Carneian moon, full in a cloudless sky, outshone even the brilliance of the August stars. For hours the Immortals marched, through silver light and shadow, swinging left across the broad plain which stretched beyond the high cliffs of Trachis, down into a valley and then over the River Asopus. Here, beyond the far bank, the way at last grew steeper. Even now, however, despite being weighed down by shields and armor, the Persians could still make their ascent without zigzagging, and after an hour or so, breasting a fringe of oaks and pines, they reached the edge of another wide plateau. Ahead of them, past more woods, and over occasional stretches of open grass, the path wound on, still climbing, but gently once more, and the Immortals, picking up speed again, began to round the peak that now loomed between them and Thermopylae. Between them and their view of the eastern horizon, too. But gradually, as the stars began to fade, so the marching Persians could sense the coming of morning, and that the sun, bright with the eternal beauty of Ahura Mazda, would soon be rising over the Hot Gates. The gradient began to flatten out. The Immortals passed into a wood of oaks. Even beneath the trees, however, the way ahead of them remained perfectly visible, for not only was it growing lighter by the minute, but the recent gales had swept bare the trellis of branches above them. The leaves, already dry, crackled underfoot. Then, above the rustling and the tramping of ten thousand pairs of feet, there came a sudden ringing: the sound of metal.

Stepping forward to the edge of the trees, the Immortals'

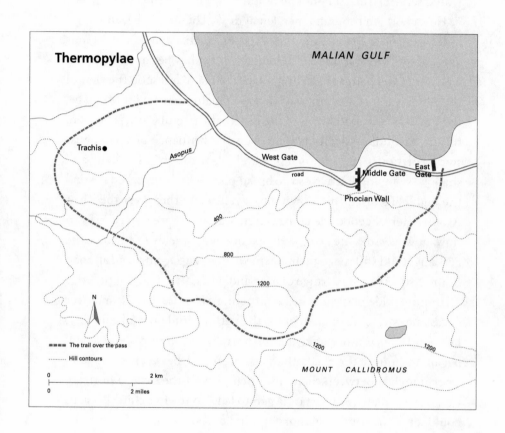

Thermopylae

MALIAN GULF

Asopus

Trachis ●

West Gate

road

Middle Gate

East Gate

Phocian Wall

400

800

1200

1200

1200

N

The trail over the pass

Hill contours

0   2 km

0   2 miles

MOUNT   CALLIDROMUS

commander saw, to his consternation, a garrison of hoplites block-ing his path. He had clearly taken them by surprise, for the Greeks were still struggling to pull on their armor; but Hydarnes, who had learned the hard way not to underestimate the Spartans, wanted his rematch with them at the Hot Gates, not on the heights above the pass. When Ephialtes, however, pointing to the lack of scarlet tunics and cloaks among the enemy, reassured his master that he was not facing Leonidas' men, but the soldiers of another city, most likely Phocis, Hydarnes immediately gave his men the order to attack. Drawing their bows, the Immortals duly fired a withering volley at the half-formed phalanx. The Phocians, lacking the strate-gic good sense that would have been supplied to them, perhaps, by the presence of a Spartan officer, and taking it for granted that the barbarians had marched through the night with the specific goal of wiping them out, retreated chaotically to the top of a nearby hill. Here they steeled themselves to make a heroic final stand—only to see the Immortals sweep contemptuously past them, and continue along the open path.

Hydarnes, as he began his descent toward the Hot Gates, now had to presume that there was a Phocian runner on the trail ahead, hur-rying to alert Leonidas. It is unlikely that this reflection greatly unsettled him; it may even have been Persian strategy to give the Greeks warning of their doom. Shortly before sunrise, and the Immortals' clash with the Phocians, a deserter from the Great King's camp had slipped into the Hot Gates. He was an Ionian, one Tyrrhastiades—motivated, he insisted, purely by concern for his fellow Greeks. Perhaps he was—except that there appears to have been more than a whiff of the Persian dirty-tricks department about his arrival. Quite apart from the fact that it is unusual for rats to join a sinking ship, the timing of his appearance in the Greek camp had shown every sign of the most careful calculation. Too late to enable Leonidas to reinforce the Phocians, it simultaneously tempted him with the hope that there might yet be the chance of a withdrawal. Which was, of course, precisely what the Great King wanted him to believe: for the Greeks, if they opted to defend both ends of the Hot Gates against the pincer movement being deployed against them, might yet hold the pass for days. Catch them retreating on the open road, however, and the Persian cavalry would have no problem cutting them to pieces. The pass would be clear, five thousand Greek hoplites would have been eliminated from the military balance sheet, and the Great King's triumph would be complete.

But would Leonidas take the bait? The commander in chief of the Allied League, desperate not to see his whole army lost, but also pledged, as a Spartan king, not to abandon Thermopylae, had a third option. Once it had been confirmed that disaster could be read in the entrails of goats killed in sacrifice, he summoned the bleary-eyed leaders of the other contingents to a council of war. Confusion and alarm, not surprisingly, was general at this meeting, with some refusing to countenance evacuation, while the majority demanded that it begin at once. Leonidas, silencing the uproar, announced that it was the intention of his bodyguard to hold the breach against the enemy, no matter what was thrown against them. Then he not merely permitted but positively ordered the main body of the army to leave, and as fast as possible, to give itself every chance of surviving to fight another day. The Thespians, famously cussed, refused to abandon their posts; so too—for with their city now doomed to medize, they had nothing to return to, save the prospect of being purged—did the loyalist Thebans.[37] Leonidas ordered the helots to remain at the Hot Gates as well, to help the Spartans prepare for battle, to serve as light infantry and to die in the cause of their masters' freedom. Some 1500 men in all, then, fingering their notched and battered weapons with clammy fingers, feeling the sun's first rays against their faces, trying not to let their expressions betray their emotions, whether of scorn, resignation or envy, watched their comrades pack up their armor, leave the camp and head south.[38] A fading of the sound of marching feet, a dispersal of white dust on the morning breeze, and the tiny holding force was left alone to the reek and the closeness of the pass. Nothing to disturb the calm came from the westward slopes of Callidromus, down which

Hydarnes and his Immortals were even at that moment descending; nothing to suggest that the barbarians were drawing near. As yet, there was nothing from the West Gate, either. "Eat a good breakfast," Leonidas advised his men, "for tonight we eat in the underworld."[39]

Meanwhile, in the royal tent, breakfast was also being taken, but no doubt in a far cheerier mood. A more relaxed one as well: for Xerxes, although he had risen at dawn to pour libations to the sun, wished to give Hydarnes a chance to reach the pass before he launched his own attack. Finally, at around nine o'clock, he gave his generals the nod, and the colossal mass of his army began its advance. Even before they reached the pass, the stench of death, given sound by carrion flies, would have seemed to shimmer like the dust clouds and the heat; and when they entered the Hot Gates, they would have seen ahead of them the tangled limbs of their slaughtered fellows, bellies swollen, or else ripped apart, abdomens pale, the viscera spilled across the ground. The enemy, too, were in the open; for rather than staying behind the wall of the Middle Gate, as they had done during the two previous days' fighting, the Greeks had advanced beyond it, braced to fight, not in relays, but in a single, bristling mass. For a moment, appalled by the sight of these men of bronze and blood, the Great King's troops held back; then their officers, brandishing whips, began to lash them forward. Scorned as Greek propaganda though this detail often is, there seems no real cause to doubt it. Weight of numbers, now that it could more effectively be brought to bear against the enemy, was a crushing advantage that the Persian high command had every reason to exploit; and the use of untrained levies, at least during the hellish opening of the battle, must have struck them as the most cost-effective way of neutralizing the long spears of the Greeks. Trapped between their own military police and the fearsome, bronze-tipped, blood-bespattered Greek phalanx, the hapless levies had little choice but to shamble forward, to be crushed against the shield wall or else drowned in the shallows, falling in their hundreds upon hundreds, to be sure, but also, as they did so, gradually splintering the Greek spears into matchwood.

And then it was, it seems, when all the shafts had been snapped, that the Persian elite moved in for the kill. What followed was battle as *The Iliad* had described it: the clash of mighty champions, "screams of men and cries of triumph breaking in one breath."[40] Among those who fell were two sons of Darius, and a brother—and then Leonidas himself. A desperate struggle, fittingly Homeric, was fought over the dead king's body, until the Spartans, in the ferocity of their anguish and despair, hauled it back to temporary safety. But then, from behind them, just above the eastern exit from the Hot Gates, there came the glinting of spear tips amid the scrub of the slope: the Immortals had arrived. Menaced from all sides now, the surviving Greeks retreated back beyond the wall, aiming for a small hillock in the shadow of the Middle Gate. There—although the Thebans, separated from their fellows, and forced against the cliff face, never reached it—the Spartans and the Thespians made their final stand. Feathered with arrows, slathered with gore, they resisted to the end. Even when their swords shivered, they used the hilts as knuckle-dusters, or else fought with their teeth, their fists, their nails. Only when every last Spartan and Thespian lay dead, the dust blood-slaked, the corpses piled high, could the struggle be reckoned over, and the pass the Great King's at last.

Xerxes himself, entering the Hot Gates at around midday, was both elated by the sight of Persian banners fluttering over the battlefield, and revolted by the carnage. As was his duty to the men who had fallen in his cause, he gave instructions for trenches to be dug, and the bodies of his dead to be laid in them, then reverently covered with earth and leaves. He left the corpses of the Greeks to rot, while those few Thebans who had chosen to fling down their weapons rather than be slaughtered he ordered to be chained and branded. That he was in no mood for magnanimity was hardly surprising; for, despite his brilliant success in destroying, after only two and a half days' fighting, the Greeks' seemingly impregnable position, it had been no part of his battle plan that so many of the defenders should escape annihilation. Another pinprick was soon to come; for the Greek fleet, it was reported to him the following afternoon, had staged its own successful evacuation, having skulked away in the dead of night to safer waters. The Persian fleet, crossing to Artemisium in the morning, had found nothing of the enemy save for the smoking embers of campfires and the well-gnawed bones of cattle. Fugitives the Greeks may have been, humiliated by land and sea—but it seemed that they were still resolved to carry on the fight.

Yet surely now it would not be long before they would have their necks wrung like chickens. The Great King, sifting intelligence reports in the aftermath of Thermopylae, could not help but smile at the desperate attempts of his enemies to rival him in psychological warfare. It was reported, for instance, that a Greek admiral, pausing in his flight down the coast of Euboea, had carved messages along the seashore, appealing to the Ionians to desert—or at least to fight badly. A laughable stratagem! Why, when two great victories had just been won by Persian arms, when the cities of Boeotia were scurrying to open their gates to the conqueror, when the mastery of Europe lay within the Great King's grasp, would any of his subjects contemplate mutiny? His squadrons may have been storm-battered, possibly even disconsolate because the Greeks had slipped from their grasp—but a way to boost their spirits was conveniently close at hand. A formal invitation was issued to the fleet: "leave to go and see how King Xerxes deals with lunatics who think that they can beat him."[41] So many men took up this offer, it is said, that there were not enough boats to ferry them all to the Hot Gates.

More than the corpses of the Greeks, more than the piles of helmets with their horsehair crests, hacked and dented, more even than those badges of the Spartans' pride, their blood-red cloaks and tunics, now nothing but tattered rags, one trophy, shocking and hideous, would certainly have brought home to Ionian sailors the full awful scale of their master's power. Driven into the side of the road was a stake, and driven onto the top of the stake was a human head. Although it was normally the custom of the Persians, "more than any other people in the world, to honor men who distinguish themselves in war,"[42] no honor had been shown Leonidas. King of a city accursed, what better fate had he deserved? So did his conqueror, the King of Kings, deal with all servants of the Lie.

And the sightless eyeballs of the allied commander in chief, shrunken already and crawled across by flies, were fixed upon the road that led to Athens—now open and defenseless.

Ghost Town

One day every year, just as winter was thawing into spring, the Athenians became strangers in their own city. Their temples were roped off and placed strictly out of bounds. Their doors were smeared with pitch. Their relatives, their children, even their slaves were kept off the streets. In the privacy of their own homes, seated at separate tables, racing to drain separate jugs, forbidden to talk until their drafts had been drunk, the Athenians celebrated the Anthesteria: the festival of new wine. No occasion gave better opportunities for a joyous family riot. Children as young as three, crowned with wreaths of flowers and brandishing their own tiny jugs, would be allowed to join in the drinking contest and then to totter round unsteadily, gawking at the scenes of celebration. "Couches, tables, pillows, covers, garlands, perfume, whores, appetisers, they're all there, sponges, pancakes, sesame buns, pastries, dancers, good ones too, and all the favorite songs."[43] Whores aside, perhaps, no other festival in the Athenian calendar came quite as close to the spirit of modern-day Christmas.

Yet as the muffled sounds of merriment drifted out from behind glistening, black-painted doors, the streets were not wholly abandoned. Demons were believed to be abroad: spirits of evil, harbingers of disaster. People called them "*Keres*," specters from beyond the city walls. Only at sundown did the Athenians feel able to cry out in relief, "Away with you, *Keres*—for the Anthesteria is over!"[44] The pitch-coated doors were flung open, men spilled out onto the streets, and the ropes were taken down from around the temples. The rhythms of daily life returned to Athens.

But what if these rhythms were to vanish and never return? This was the question that had been haunting the city ever since

296

Themistocles, earlier in the summer, had persuaded the Athenian people to evacuate their homeland. Perhaps there were aliens more menacing even than ghouls. An unsettling ambiguity cast its shadow over the Anthesteria. "*Keres*," thanks to a peculiarity of the Attic accent, might easily be pronounced "*Kares*"—"Carians," or "the people of Caria." These, neighbors of the Ionians in the southwest corner of what is now Turkey, had been among the very first barbarians to intrude upon the consciousness of the Greeks. For centuries they were emblematic of foreignness, and of Asia. They had fought, it was said, in the first great war between East and West, on the side of the Trojans; and unlike their cousins in Ionia, they had never submitted to the rule of Greek settlers. Even though Halicarnassus, the great metropolis of Caria, had owed its original foundation to colonists from the Peloponnese, Greeks were only one ingredient in what had become, over the centuries, a complex melting pot. The city was, to Athenian eyes, at any rate, disturbingly mestizo. Peculiar customs, florid and exotic, flourished there. Why, it was even ruled by a woman: Queen Artemisia. So "masculine" was this alarming female's "spirit of adventure"[45] that it had prompted her to sign up with the imperial battle fleet. Decked out in golden jewelry, draped in purple robes and perfumed with expensive scents she may have been, but her proficiency as an admiral could hardly be doubted. So well captained were her triremes, indeed, that they had a reputation second only to the squadrons of Sidon. If the barbarians could not be halted before they reached Attica, then Artemisia and her warships might soon be gliding into Piraeus. "*Keres*" or "*Kares*," it would hardly make much difference which word was used: aliens would be walking the streets of Athens—and they would not be vanishing at sunset.

Perhaps it was only to be expected, then, that many Athenians, even as their countrymen fought and died at Artemisium to win time for the evacuation of Attica, dragged their feet. This was certainly no reflection on the quality of provision that had been made for them in exile. The gates of Troezen, a city safely in the Peloponnese, some thirty miles across the Saronic Gulf from Piraeus, had been open to refugees from Athens since the onset of the crisis. Miserable though it was to be homeless—and perhaps peculiarly so for an earth-born Athenian—the Troezenians had already proved to be remarkably generous hosts: every nervous mother arriving in their city was given public welfare, every child free education, and even carte blanche to pick fresh fruit from groves and orchards. Nevertheless, back in Athens, the very success of the evacuation provoked a renewed bout of anguish. The more that families could be seen boarding up their homes, trudging through the streets with their luggage, pushing overloaded handcarts down to the beaches and the docks, the more it struck those too upset or angry to join them that the world had been turned upside down.

And how ominous a sign of the times it was that wives and mothers—respectable Athenian matrons!—were on the streets at all. The opportunities for misbehavior that an international crisis might offer women had been preying on the minds of Greek husbands since at least the days of the Trojan War. In Athens, however, such anxieties had a particular resonance. "Brought up under the most cramping restrictions, raised from childhood to see and hear as little as possible, and to ask only a minimum of questions,"[46] Athenian women lived a life of seclusion without parallel elsewhere in Greece. The peculiar character of the democracy demanded nothing less. The capacity of women to stir up mischief in public life had been a cause of alarm to thoughtful reformers well before the revolution of 507 BC. Concerned to instruct the elite in the virtues of self-restraint, Solon had found any hint of female showiness particularly insufferable, and had made stringent efforts to rein it in. Rather than permit daughters of the aristocracy to flaunt their wealth and taste in public, he had taken the simple, if drastic, step of decreeing that any woman seen "walking the streets, out and about,"[47] should be regarded as a prostitute. Athenian husbands—or at least those with sufficient floor space to immure their wives in separate quarters—had seized the opportunities presented by this legislation with relish. Increasingly, over the decades, the law had ensured that only women whom no one ever saw could be regarded as respectable. Simultaneously, of course, it did wonders for the sex trade.

So much so that Solon, a century after his death, would be remembered gratefully by the Athenian citizenry as a man who had used state funding to subsidize brothels, on the impeccably egalitarian principle that whores should be available to all. This tradition—since the great reformer's attitude toward women was almost certainly one of stern indifference—was probably a distortion; but it does suggest how the right to cruise for prostitutes had come to be seen by many citizens as a foundation stone of democracy. Like the statue of the tyrannicides in the Agora, or the rows of seats carved out of the Pnyx, the Athenian red-light district, vibrant with riot, suffering and pleasure, served as one of the supreme monuments to the new order. Whores were to be seen everywhere in the Ceramicus, whether sunning themselves topless outside brothels, brawling in squalid back alleys or haunting tombs beyond the city limits. Menaced by this flamboyant visibility, their respectable sisters shrank and grew ever less visible before it, so that it had soon become the convention, under the democracy, not even to mention the name of a married woman in public. Indeed, the carnivorous nature of Athenian politics being what it was, the only real impact that even the most virtuous of wives could have upon the career of her husband was as a liability. For a politician, there was only one thing worse than not being talked about, and that was having his family talked about. Many citizens, watching matrons and whores jostling each other on their way down to the beaches, were so appalled that they flatly forbade their own wives to join the exodus.

As a result, when Themistocles, having led his battered fleet safely back from Artemisium, finally limped into Piraeus, he found to his horror that Athens was very far from evacuated. It was he, of course—ever "the man of twists and turns"—who had posted the appeals to the Ionian squadrons to mutiny; but he knew better than to bank on any implosion of the imperial battle fleet. Or on the Peloponnesians, for that matter. There were many in the upper reaches of Athenian society, trusting in private assurances from the Spartans, who clung to the desperate hope that an allied army might soon be marching to their rescue. Not Themistocles. In a pass far distant from the Peloponnese, a king of Sparta and all his bodyguard lay dead, and there was nothing the Athenians could say or do now that would persuade the Spartans to commit more of their troops to a foreign field. The response of the allied delegates at Corinth to the news from Thermopylae could hardly have made that clearer. Unanimously, the Peloponnesians had voted to look to their own backyard. Even as the Great King's outriders were closing in on Attica, an army of workmen, under the direction of Leonidas' younger brother Cleombrotus, was busy at work erecting a wall along the five-mile width of the Isthmus, "hauling blocks of stone, and bricks, and wood, and sandbags, not resting a minute, labouring night and day."[48] Others had already set to demolishing the road to Megara, a narrow and precipitous corniche hacked out of the flanks of coastal cliffs, and effectively the only land route that an army could follow to—or from—the Isthmus. With each landslide that crashed from the road into the shallow coves below, the Peloponnesians were abandoning Attica ever more surely to its fate.

Even the gods, it appeared, were despairing of Athens now. No sooner had Themistocles returned to the Assembly and frantically renewed the evacuation order than there came eerie news from the Acropolis. The sacred serpent, whose presence beside the tomb of Erechtheus had served generations of Athenians as an assurance that their city would never fall, was reported by its attendants to have left its honey cake uneaten, and disappeared. Word swept across the panicking crowds "that Athena herself had abandoned the city, and was pointing them the way to the sea."[49] All highly opportune for Themistocles, of course; as was, just as suspiciously, a second discovery, made even as refugees were surging to the coast with their luggage. The sacred serpent, it seemed, was not alone in having vanished from the Acropolis; so too, filched from around the neck of that holiest of statues, the self-portrait of Athena Polias, had a golden gorgon's head. Themistocles, loudly protesting his outrage at this sacrilege, immediately set to ransacking the bags of particularly wealthy citizens. When, as invariably he did, he found sacks of gold squirreled away among the luggage, he would impound them on the spot. These confiscations, combined with a whip-round among former archons, served to raise a substantial sum of money: a financial reserve that the Athenian people, now that they were passing into exile, might soon have little choice but to depend upon for their welfare.

And all the while, as sobbing children were shepherded through the shallows by their fathers, and mothers with wild, white faces clutched their head scarves tight about them and stumbled in their wake, and vessels of every description crowded the waters off Phalerum and Piraeus, time was running out. Six days had passed since the forcing of the Hot Gates. With Athens increasingly a ghost town, those thronging the beaches began to glance ever more anxiously over their shoulders, scanning the horizon for smudges of dust, a glint of metal, a dot of fire. Still nothing. By the evening, when Athens stood empty at last, the only movement in all the great expanse of the abandoned city was that of dogs, bewildered by the sudden quiet. Many, faithful to their owners, had followed them down to the beaches, running along the sands, howling at the boats as they disappeared. Xanthippus, it is said, having been summoned back to Athens along with all the other victims of ostracism, but now heading off into exile again, had looked behind him as he sailed away from the mainland, only to see his own dog paddling desperately in pursuit. Reaching dry land at last, the exhausted creature had scrabbled up onto the rocks, whined and then expired.[50]

Xanthippus' destination, and that of all his fellow citizens, was Salamis. Here, across the narrow straits from Mount Aigaleos, the Athenian people had resurrected a semblance, however ghostly and impoverished, of the city they had just abandoned. A few women and children—those laggards for whom the journey to Troezen had grown too perilous—were now camped out there. So too, symbols and guardians alike of the constitution, were the magistrates of the democracy. The elderly, whose wisdom in a time of crisis was rated an invaluable resource, had been settled on the island since the very start of the evacuation, along with the city's treasures and grain reserves. And now, most stirring of all, weather-beaten and battle-scarred though they were, their timbers bearing the marks of frantic labors in the shipyards, there lay in readiness off the bays of Salamis some 180 Athenian triremes: a wooden wall indeed. Well might Themistocles, pointing to the fleet, insist that his countrymen, even in exile, still remained citizens of "the greatest city in all of Greece."[51]

A claim which he would be obliged to cling to as though it were a life raft in the hours that followed his arrival on Salamis. Athenian ships were not the only ones visible from the island. For the past two days, as Themistocles and his men had ferried refugees from Attica, the other allied squadrons had been lurking in the straits. That the Peloponnesian admirals had agreed to wait there for the length of the evacuation said much of the bonds of fellowship forged at Artemisium. Both their orders and their personal inclinations would have urged them to head immediately for the Isthmus. From Salamis, distant across the blue of the gulf, it was just possible to make out a stub of rock framed against the sky: this tantalizing landmark was the acropolis of Corinth, the watchtower of the Peloponnese, and barely five miles south of the Isthmus wall. Perhaps predictably, then, it was a Corinthian, the young and fiery commander Adeimantus, who took the lead in the council of war that immediately followed the return of Themistocles to the allied fleet. Leave for the Isthmus at once, he demanded of Eurybiades and his fellow admirals. Concentrate naval and military resources together. Join with the army already massed along the Isthmus. There were bays and gulfs enough around Corinth to guard the flank of a battle line. And if disaster did overtake the fleet—well, at least the Peloponnesians "might then find a refuge among their own people."[52]

Hardly, of course, an argument designed to thrill an admiral from Athens—nor those from Aegina and Megara—and it might have been thought, since these men were in command of around three-quarters of the Greek fleet's total of 310 triremes, that their objections would prove decisive.[53] Not a bit of it. The risk facing Themistocles and his two colleagues was the same one that had haunted the war effort from the start: that the alliance might fragment and disintegrate. Outnumbered probably two to one as the Greek fleet still was, not even the Athenians could afford to go it alone. Any split among the allied squadrons would sink all hopes of victory.

And it was victory that Themistocles was aiming for—not merely a holding operation, as was envisaged by Adeimantus, but a decisive crippling of the Great King's whole naval capacity. To convince his colleagues that this ambition was more than just the fantasy of a desperate exile, he drew on the one thing that could unite them, and gloriously so: their joint memories of the Artemisium campaign. Themistocles knew that battle in open waters—which the Greeks would face if they made their stand off the Isthmus—favored the enemy. "But battle in close conditions," he urged, "works to our advantage."[54] This was the lesson he had drawn from the day of the fiercest fighting, when the allied squadrons—although battered—had successfully held the passageway between Euboea and the mainland against the full weight of the barbarian fleet. The straits in that battle had been some two or three miles across; at Salamis, if the barbarians could only be lured into them, the waters were half a mile wide at most. "If everything goes well—and the prospects for that are not unreasonable—then we can win."[55]

And here, for all the soaring self-confidence with which it had been delivered, was a judgment quite as rooted in the experiences of everyone who had fought at Artemisium—the Peloponnesian admirals included—as in the fertility of the Athenian's ever-scheming brain. Themistocles himself well appreciated this, for he had, to a degree that none of his opposite numbers could remotely rival, made a career out of persuasion. Democracy, in its first decades, had proved an exacting school. No one in the world was now better practiced at getting his own way than a successful Athenian politician. The effectiveness of Themistocles' pitch can be gauged from the fact that when, midway through the council of war, messengers arrived with the terrifying news that the barbarians had been seen entering Attica, "setting fire to the whole country,"[56] the meeting did not break up in panic. Nor, despite the blood-curdling realization that the Persian fleet might be gliding into Athenian waters at any moment, and perhaps blocking off the escape routes, did the Peloponnesians press their demands for an immediate withdrawal. Instead, all of the high command agreed that the fleet would stay where it was: off Salamis. Themistocles, for the moment at any rate, had convinced the doubters.

And this despite the fact that he was now, in the eyes of his fellow admirals, that most despised of all creatures—"a man without a country."[57] Such a label was not entirely accurate, of course—not while Salamis remained in Athenian hands. Nor, even with the Persian cavalry clattering fast toward the city, had Athens herself been wholly surrendered: one stronghold, the sacred heart of Attica, still held out. Not even the iconoclastic Themistocles had ever proposed that the Acropolis should be abandoned. Instead, by a vote of the Assembly, it had been agreed "that the treasurers and priestesses remain on it to guard the property of the gods."[58] Other Athenians as well, those too stubborn to go into exile, had taken refuge there. The defenders, having had weeks to provision themselves and to erect barricades— "wooden walls"—across the ramp, could now plausibly regard themselves as well braced for a lengthy siege.

Yet their spirits, all the same, must have quailed at their first sight of the enemy. No better view could have been had of the arrival of the Great King into Athens than from the heights of the sacred rock. Fire, incinerating the blessed fields and groves of Attica, heralded Xerxes' coming. Gazing from the western battlements, the defenders watched impotently as the royal banners were raised triumphantly over their city. The hordes of the Great King's army were already swarming everywhere, taking possession of the familiar streets, laying waste the defenders' homes. In the Agora and on the slopes of the Areopagus, the hill which rose between the Pnyx and the Acropolis, engineers could be seen sinking boreholes: evidently, the barbarians were too mistrustful of the Athenians even to drink their water. Other work parties busied themselves with looting and stripping the city bare.

Most horrifying spectacle of all for the defenders on the Acropolis to have to endure was that of the bronze tyrannicides, those potent symbols of the democracy, being lowered from their plinth, crated up, and readied for transport. No doubt the Pisistratids, back in their homeland at last, had explained to their masters the precise significance of the statues. A perfect trophy to adorn the halls of Susa.

Meanwhile, above the Agora, the Great King had established his command post on the Areopagus. Archers were ordered onto the hill, and instructed to shoot fire arrows at the barricades blocking the ramp of the Acropolis. The wooden wall—"betraying the defenders"[59]— was soon ablaze, but the defenses beyond it held firm. The Great King, anxious to send the good news to Persia that the nest of *daivas* had been smoked out, began to grow impatient. Summoned to the royal presence, the Pisistratids were duly dispatched up the ramp to negotiate with their obdurate countrymen. Their overtures were rejected. The assault on the ramp was renewed. Arrows fizzed, and boulders, levered over the side of the fortifications by the defenders, crashed and rolled. The chaos of battle was general.

But now, with the Athenians at full stretch, the Great King's officers began surveying the opposite end of the Acropolis. Here, where the drop was so sheer that not even a single guard had been stationed, elite forces finally succeeded in scaling the face of the cliff. As at Thermopylae, so now, talents honed in the Zagros enabled the Great King to stab a Greek garrison in the back. The Acropolis was stormed. Many of the defenders hurled themselves off the battlements in preference to waiting to be slaughtered. Others sought sanctuary in the temple of Athena. The Persians, naturally, massacred the lot. Then, as their master had ordered, they put everything on the summit of the rock to the torch. What would not burn they demolished, toppled or smashed. The great storehouse of Athenian memories, accumulated over centuries—the city's very past—was wiped out in a couple of hours.

Plumes of thick smoke, billowing up from the inferno, began to blacken the Attic sky. To the Athenians, standing frozen upon their ships, or on the slopes of Salamis, the message they advertised was one of purest horror. To their allies too, watching as evening turned to night, and still the silhouette of Mount Aigaleos was lit an angry red, the spectacle was barely less demoralizing. In others, however, also on the sea that night, it would have prompted very different emotions. The Great King's admirals, who had not wished to arrive off Athens until they could be certain that the city's harbors were secured, had taken their time to rendezvous with the army. Now, however, with the whole of the Attic coastline, from Sunium to the Acropolis, a blaze of burning temples, the Persian victory was being broadcast far out to sea. There was no need for any of the Great King's squadrons, if they were still making their way to port that night, to rely on the stars: their oars, beating the waters, would have churned up waves illuminated by fire.

Dawn showed the Acropolis a blackened, smoking ruin. Once a nest of demons, now purged by flames, it stood cleansed at last of the Lie. The principles of Arta had prevailed, and Xerxes, the Lord Mazda's servant, had performed his bounden duty to the Truth. In witness of this, the Great King, having summoned the Pisistratids to his presence again, gave them orders to ascend the Acropolis, "and there offer sacrifices according to their native custom"[60]—for they alone, of all the Athenians, had stood firm against the blandishments of the Lie. Gratefully, the returned exiles duly climbed onto the cinderscape. Over broken statues and toppled columns and the charred corpses of their slaughtered countrymen they picked their way, to that most sacred spot on the otherwise barren summit, where the primal olive tree, the city's gift from Athena, had always stood. The shrine built around it had been systematically flattened, but a blackened stump was soon unearthed beneath the rubble. Tenaciously, as they had always done, the living roots still clung to the rock.

And sprouting from the stump—a certain miracle—a long green shoot was rising up to meet the sun.

8

NEMESIS

Sucker Punch

And so it came to Salamis.

"You will be the ruin of many a mother's son." More menacingly than ever now, with the allied fleet moored off the island, and the Persians at Phalerum, the ambiguities of the oracle were weighing on people's minds. But it was not only among the Greek high command that Apollo's teasing words were being debated: the Persians too, ever assiduous in their intelligence work, would surely have learned of the prophecy. "He who revealed truth to my ancestors":[1] so Darius himself had described the archer god. Yet, respectful of Apollo though the Persians had often shown themselves, their faith in the pronouncements of Delphi was hardly, of course, as instinctive as that of their enemies. There must have been many on the Great King's staff, puzzling over the phrase "divine Salamis," who found themselves debating its precise authorship. Perhaps someone aside from the god had breathed a word in the Pythia's ear. A priest, for instance? Delphi was the center of a great web of international contacts, after all, and Apollo's servants, with their profound knowledge of current affairs, were as well qualified as anyone to forecast the likely progress of the war.

They would certainly not have forgotten the fate of the last Greek attempt to defeat an imperial armada. Fourteen years previously, some 350 Ionian triremes, outnumbered almost two to one by the Persian fleet, had rowed out to battle off the Milesian island of Lade and been annihilated. Just as Miletus had been the heart of resistance to the Persians then, so Athens was now. And the only potential equivalent to Lade off Attica was, of course, Salamis. Whether Persian strategists believed the Delphic prophecy to have derived from the heavens or from mere mortal calculations, it would certainly have buttressed them in their belief that the hand of a god infinitely greater than Apollo was guiding their affairs. The great wheels of time, turning as they did at the command of he who dwelt beyond them, Ahura Mazda, were clearly grinding with a quite merciless precision. Once already a fractious alliance of Greek squadrons, when menaced by a much larger Persian fleet, had disintegrated amid treachery and back-stabbing—and now, with a mysterious but no doubt divinely sanctioned symmetry, history appeared destined to repeat itself.

To be sure, there were some among Xerxes' entourage who urged their master not to depend upon this. Demaratus, for instance, with a hearty appreciation of what his countrymen would least like the Great King to do, had advocated the launching of an amphibious operation directly against Lacedaemon—"for you need hardly worry that the Spartans, if the flames of war are consuming their homeland, will bother themselves coming to the rescue of anyone else in Greece."[2] True enough; but so depleted had storms and enemy action left the imperial navy that the detachment of even a small task force from the main body of the fleet might leave the Greeks a match for either. The proposal was therefore vetoed. So too—although after more soul-searching—was the advice of the formidable Queen Artemisia of Halicarnassus. When the Great King, descending in state upon Phalerum, summoned his admirals to a council of war, hers was a lone voice raised in warning against the plan to force a second Lade. Battle, she insisted, was a pointless risk. Athens was captured, and autumn was closing in. Better by far, then, to maintain a standoff, and leave the Greek squadrons either to starve or to "scatter and sail for their homes."³ A shrewd analysis, as Xerxes himself was well aware; but time was running out, and he could not afford to adopt it. For the Great King to pass a winter on the remote frontiers of the West was clearly out of the question: a devastated Athens was no place from which to administer the world. Having graced the expedition against Europe with his royal presence, it was now imperative for him to finish the war before the close of the campaigning season. Only a thumping victory while the weather held would do.

How gratifying, then, that the imperial spy chiefs could report to their royal master that the enemy, squabbling and snarling in their camp, were behaving true to form. Just as hatreds, doubts and fears had once riven the Ionian squadrons off Lade, so now, across the straits off Salamis, a Greek fleet appeared to be on the verge of a similar implosion. The proofs of defeatism could hardly be doubted. Already, on the day of the burning of the Acropolis, several crews had stampeded in panic down to their boats and tried to raise their sails ready for flight. That same evening, it was reported, the high command itself had fragmented yet again into rival factions, Peloponnesians against Athenians and their supporters. The insults bandied had been the talk of the whole Greek camp. Adeimantus, it was said, had sneered at Themistocles as a "refugee," and warned him, when he spoke out of turn, that "athletes who start a race before the signal is given are whipped." "Yes," Themistocles was claimed to have retorted bitterly, "and those who are left behind never win the crown."⁴ Only by threatening to withdraw the entire Athenian fleet from the battle line and sail at once for Italy, and permanent exile, had he ultimately had his way. But it was impossible to say for how long. What if the Peloponnesians, panicking at the prospect of being bottled up in the straits, finally opted to call his bluff? What options then for the Athenians and their fleet?

Persian intelligence chiefs, with more than sixty years' experience of exploiting Greek fractiousness to draw upon, knew precisely how best to find out. In the wake of the conference at Phalerum, with the Great

King's wish to conjure up a second Lade now clear in his servants' minds, a contingent of Persian troops was ordered to take the road to the Isthmus. Since the corniche beyond Megara had been destroyed, and the Isthmus itself solidly fortified, the expedition had little prospect of storming the gates of the Peloponnese—but that was not its mission. Leaving Athens, rounding Mount Aigaleos, following the Sacred Way toward Eleusis, the soldiers marched along the southern reaches of the Attic coast. Their weapons glittered brightly. Their war songs could be heard for miles. Their feet, thirty thousand pairs of them, pounded the road. A great cloud of dust, rising in their wake, drifted on the breeze, and was borne across the straits toward Salamis.

Where the reaction was—just as Persian strategists had anticipated that it would be—one of consternation. Mutinous whisperings began to sweep through the Peloponnesian contingents yet again. Then, with afternoon fading into evening, and anxious sailors already besieging their captains with demands to sail for the Isthmus, the Great King gave instructions that the screws be tightened further. Squadrons of the imperial fleet, "bearing down on Salamis, and taking up their stations with a perfect show of leisure," began to patrol directly off the island—menacing the escape routes.[5] As the setting sun blazed its reflection across the sea from Salamis to the Isthmus, many Peloponnesians appeared on the verge of insurrection.

> For there they were, stranded on Salamis, obliged to fight in defence of Athenian territory, and certain, if they were defeated, to find themselves trapped and blockaded on an island. And all the while their own country stood defenceless, even as the barbarians, marching through the night, were advancing directly on the Peloponnese.[6]

This, since the very earliest days of contact between the two peoples, was how the Persians had always played cat and mouse with the Greeks. News of the wrangling on Salamis, brought to the Great King by his agents, confirmed him in his assurance that he had gauged the character of his enemies to perfection. Now, with the whole Greek fleet apparently at daggers drawn, it was time to bait the trap that he had laid with such cunning. It was almost sunset. The squadrons on patrol off Salamis were ordered back to base.[7] This withdrawal, performed in full view of the allied lookouts, left the escape route to the Isthmus very obviously—and very temptingly—open. As the Persian admiralty had discovered at Artemisium, Greek sailors were hardly reluctant to conduct a hurried nocturnal retreat if a sudden crisis appeared to demand it. The Peloponnesians, not knowing when the opportunity to bolt from their rat hole might present itself again, would surely feel themselves facing just such a crisis that evening. If so—and irrespective of whether the Athenians agreed to sail with them—they might very well take their chance and flee the straits. Just as had happened at Lade, a Greek fleet would then disintegrate into fragments.

But Xerxes, weighing the odds that evening, still had to know for sure. The ambush could be attempted only once. It was not enough merely to foster division; active treachery was needed, too. The ideal would be a double agent within the ranks of the Greek high command. Fortunate, then, that the Persian intelligence chiefs had long and fruitful experience of recruiting top-level moles. It was, after all, as the royal spymasters would hardly have needed to point out, the bribing of the Samian captains that had doomed the Ionian battle line at Lade. With that delectable precedent before them, it beggars belief that the Great King's agents, armed with gold and the promise of royal patronage, would not have been active in the allied camp on Salamis. And if so—who might their target have been? The Persians, in the war of nerves that they were waging with such proficiency against the various Greek divisions, would surely have been tempted to launch a two-pronged attack. Even as they menaced the Peloponnesians, pressuring them to flee, they would have been alert to the anxieties and resentments of those who faced being left in the lurch: the Aeginetans, the Megarians—and the Athenians.

"The man who co-operates with me, on him will I bestow rich

311

rewards."[8] This, baldly stated, had always been the manifesto of the Persian monarchy. What rewards, then, for the man who had it within his power to betray the whole Greek fleet, and win the war, and the West itself, for the Great King? Splendid and glorious beyond compare, no doubt. Little matter that Themistocles was the native of what for years had been a demon-racked stronghold of the Lie—not now that fire, having consumed the Acropolis, had purged Athens of evil. If they would only prostrate themselves with due contrition before the royal presence, the Athenians might certainly hope to be graced with a pardon—and perhaps even, if they gave good service, with marks of the Great King's favor. No man in the world, after all, had the power to be more gracious, more generous, more beneficent. "The rewards that I bestow—they are in proportion to the help that I am given."[9]

We are nowhere openly told of contacts between Themistocles and Persian agents. The murk that veils treachery and espionage is often impenetrable—and all the more so at a remove of two and a half thousand years. What we do know, however, is that shortly after the Persian squadrons had returned from patrol back to Phalerum, and while the various Greek commanders, digesting the day's alarming events, were reported to be at loggerheads with one another, a tiny boat was slipping out from the dark ranks of the Athenian fleet and making its way across the straits. On board was the trusted tutor of Themistocles' sons, a slave by the name of Sicinnus. It is possible, since his name derived from Phrygia, a satrapy to the east of Lydia, that he spoke some Persian.[10] It is also possible that his arrival on the mainland did not come as a total surprise to those who met him—for no sooner had Sicinnus set foot on dry land than he was being hurried into the presence of the Persian high command. Certainly, the message that he had to deliver was of the utmost urgency: the Greeks, Sicinnus reported, were planning a getaway that very night. "Only block their escape," came the advice from Themistocles, "and you will have a perfect chance of success." Meanwhile, the Athenian admiral himself, revolted by his allies' pusillanimity, was described by his slave as being "in full sympathy with the king, and earnestly longing for a Persian victory."[11] The imperial espionage chiefs, if they had indeed been fishing for a communication from Themistocles, could hardly have hoped to land better news.

A dazzling coup indeed. The Great King, who had no doubt been alerted to the prospect of an intelligence breakthrough coming that evening, was informed of it at once. Contingency plans, evidently prepared in the expectation of just such an opportunity, were put smoothly into action. The fleet was ordered to ready itself for battle. Rising from their suppers, oarsmen hurried to their benches, marines to their stations on deck. "Crew cheered crew, all the way down the length of the battle-line,"[12] and then, rank after rank, pulling out from Phalerum into the waiting darkness, they took to sea. No more cheering now—for the slightest sound might alert the enemy. Instead, with only the measured beating of their oars to mark their progress, the various squadrons glided through the night to the positions allotted them by their master. One, comprising the two hundred ships of the Egyptians, had been ordered to circle the entire south coast of Salamis, aiming for the narrow bottleneck of the westernmost strait, there to stopper it, in case the Greeks should attempt to escape that way. Others, serrying themselves in ranks of three, cruised into position off the eastern channel, out of which, so their captains had assured them, the panicking Peloponnesians would be bolting at any minute. Just beyond the exit, where it led out to the open sea, there was an island, sacred to Pan, known to the Athenians as Psyttaleia; here, setting the seal on the ruthless efficiency of his preparations, the Great King stationed a garrison of four hundred infantry. Come the midnight breakout, these troops would be "directly in the passage of the expected action, ready for all the men and shattered ships that would soon be swept onto the island's rocks."[13] Nothing had been left to chance. Not a single Greek was to be permitted to escape the Great King's deadly trap.

Meanwhile, Sicinnus, the slave whose message had led to all of these preparations, had returned to Themistocles. His courage had been astonishing. He would surely have expected to be kept for

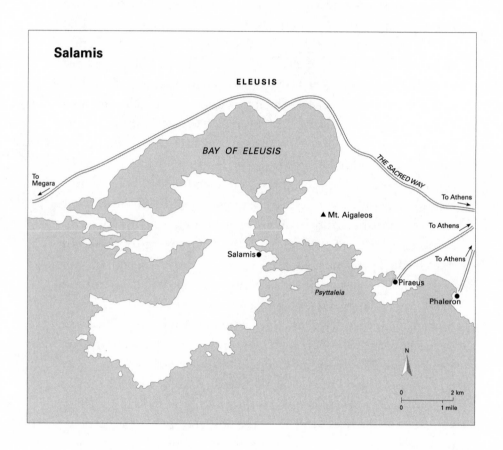

Salamis

ELEUSIS

BAY OF ELEUSIS

THE SACRED WAY

To
Megara

To Athens

To Athens

To Athens

▲ Mt. Aigaleos

Salamis●

●Piraeus

Psyttaleia

●
Phaleron

N

0   2 km

0   1 mile

further interrogation; indeed, it is hard to imagine why he was released, unless it was to carry a message from the Persian spy chiefs back to his master.[14] Nor is it hard to guess what the contents of this communication might have been: the Great King's final terms; the offer of an amnesty, perhaps, a chance for the Athenians to pick up their families before they sailed off into exile; or the assurance of a privileged future in Attica as favored servants of the King of Kings. Whatever the precise details, Themistocles must surely have breathed a sigh of relief when he read them, for he would have known that he had preserved his daughters from the slave market, his sons from the gelding knife, his fellow citizens from obliteration. Even were the Greek fleet to be wiped out in the morning, the Athenians, at least, would have a claim to the Great King's mercy.

But there was a second prospect, infinitely more glittering and glorious, that had also been opened up by Sicinnus' return. The Greek admirals, even as the imperial battle squadrons were embarking upon their secret maneuvers, remained in urgent session, "still quarrelling furiously," it is said.[15] At some point toward midnight, Themistocles—who had evidently been having a busy time of it, slipping in and out of the meeting—rose to his feet and made his excuses yet again. Stepping outside, he found waiting for him, cloaked in the shadows, an old enemy. Aristeides, the "Just," summoned back from exile along with Xanthippus and all the other victims of ostracism, had smoothly resumed his place at the very heart of the democracy's affairs. Returning that same evening from a mission to Aegina, he had seen, as he slipped back toward Salamis, the ominous silhouettes of the Persian fleet fanning out across the gulf to plug the exits from the straits. Themistocles, to whom this news naturally came as little surprise, confessed himself delighted, and told Aristeides that it was all his doing—"for our allies had to be forced into making a stand that they would otherwise have shrunk from, had it been left to themselves." Then, embracing his old adversary, he urged Aristeides to take the news in to the other admirals, "for if I report it, they will think that I am making it up."[16]

All of which, of course, was to cast the Peloponnesians as hapless stooges. No wonder that the Athenians, in the years to come, would enjoy harping on the story. Even so, there is something strange about it. Aristeides, although he did indeed inform the Greek commanders that their fleet was surrounded, neglected to mention, it appears, that this was courtesy of a trick pulled by one of their own colleagues. Understandably, it might be thought. Yet it is curious that the Spartans and the other Peloponnesians, even once the full details of Themistocles' stratagem had become public knowledge, betrayed not the slightest hint of resentment toward the man who was supposed to have out-smarted them so comprehensively, but, on the contrary, only lauded him for his cleverness and foresight. Nor, despite being ambushed, as we are told, by Aristeides' revelation, does it seem that the Greek admirals were thrown into a panic by it. Just the opposite—their dispositions for the morning appeared to reflect the minutest forward planning. Almost as though the news of the Persian blockade had come as no great sur-prise to them, either. Almost as though they had been complicit in Themistocles' scheme from the start.

And perhaps they had been. Details of the Salamis campaign only ever come into focus as though through a swirling fog, and then they are either lost, or are so confused that they can be interpreted in any number of ways. Frustrating, of course—and yet there is, in this very murk, a tantalizing glimpse of the contours of an otherwise hidden war, a shadowy counterpoint to all the din and crash and shove of battle. The Persians could legitimately claim to be the masters of the dirty trick, so it should be no surprise that their spy chiefs, arriving in Attica, brought with them the easy presumption of superiority that came nat-urally to members of the world's ruling class. Yet, just as the Great King's admirals should have been warned against any complacency by the performance of the Greeks at Artemisium, so his intelligence agents should similarly have been on their guard. The allies had already demonstrated their proficiency at feints and disinformation. At Salamis, there can be no question that Themistocles, displaying his customary pitiless grasp of psychology, had fed the Persian agents not merely what

316

their master wanted but what he desperately needed to believe was true. Even at his most eager, however, the Great King would surely have discounted the possibility of Athenian treachery, had it not been for the Peloponnesian admirals' very public flaunting of their own demoralization. Whether they were indeed a squabbling, incompetent rabble with no appetite for fighting in the straits, despite all the lessons they had learned at Artemisium, or rather coconspirators in a devastating sting, we can never know for sure. What is certain, however, is that the Peloponnesian admirals, if they truly had been desperate to make their escape that night, adjusted to the news that they were blockaded inside the straits with remarkable equanimity. Dawn rose on a day as fateful as any in human history—and found every squadron in the Greek fleet primed and nerved for battle.

And over the straits, men imagined, there glimmered a sudden sense of something uncanny, an almost palpable heightening of intensity upon the early morning light. To the Athenian marines, before they took their places on deck, Themistocles delivered an address that would long be remembered, urging them to consider "all that was best in human nature and affairs, and all that was worst—and to choose the former."[17] Yet not even these words, it may be, raised as many hairs upon the back of men's necks as did the assurance—one that seems suddenly to have swept the entire fleet— that the sons of gods who in ancient times had been the guardians of the rocks and groves and temples of Greece were present among them: so that men would later speak of seeing phantoms and even ghostly serpents gliding on the surface of the water, and of hearing unearthly battle cries echoing around the straits. That long-dead heroes would rise up from their graves to repel the barbarian invader was a conviction that had been sedulously promoted by the Greek high command. Indeed, it is probable that Aristeides, when he ran the gauntlet of the Persian blockade, had been sailing back with the relics of some Aeginetan heroes, sprung from Zeus himself. There could certainly have been no doubting the urgency of such a mission—and a measure of its success, perhaps, is the fact that the Peloponnesians, near mutinous the evening before, prepared for battle with as much conviction as anyone.

And, to be sure, there had been something eerie in the air for days. Even Greeks in the Great King's train appear to have sensed that the heavens might be turning against their master. Walking through the deserted fields beyond Eleusis on the day before the battle, Demaratus had seen a cloud of dust billowing up from the coastal road. This could only have been kicked up by the Persian division heading for the Isthmus, but an Athenian collaborator, strolling with Demaratus, had immediately identified the faint singing he could hear coming from the Sacred Way as the "*iacche*": the chant of joy raised by worshippers as they journeyed every September to Eleusis. This was impossible, of course, even though it was indeed the time of year for the annual pilgrimage—unless the *iacche* were being performed by a supernatural procession, in celebration of that great mystery of Eleusis, the return to life of what had appeared to be utterly and irrevocably dead. This, to the Athenian, as he trod the burned soil of his homeland, had proved a most unsettling thought. "I fear," he said at length, as he gazed towards the dust cloud, "that this presages some great disaster for the king's forces." And Demaratus, alarmed though he was by this judgment, had not disputed it. "Only keep quiet," he urged his companion. "For if your words should reach the ears of the king, then you will be sure to lose your head."[18]

Sensible advice—for Xerxes, in his determination to force a victory, was certainly in no mood to tolerate defeatism. That the failure to wipe out the Greek fleet at Artemisium had been due to a lack of backbone on the part of his servants appeared to him self-evident. Concerned to rectify this, he had issued his captains an uncompromising warning that "should the Greeks succeed in evading the terrible fate planned for them, and slip out through the blockade, then all those responsible would lose their heads."[19] Conversely, those who fought well would have the supreme honor of having their exploits personally noted by their master—an incentive that had been sorely lacking off Artemisium. So it was that even as the Greek oarsmen were hurrying to their benches, the Great King, followed by a mighty train of generals, officials and flunkeys, was riding out in his chariot past the southern spur of Mount Aigaleos, and round on to "the rocky brow / Which looks o'er sea-born Salamis." Here, above a temple of Heracles, he ordered his Nisaean horses reined in. As he descended, first onto a golden footstool and then—for the royal platform heels could hardly be permitted to touch bare earth—along a hurriedly unrolled carpet, servants were busy erecting a throne. The Great King had chosen his vantage spot well. Below him, becoming clearer by the minute, there stretched an unrivaled panorama: of Salamis, the straits, the gulf beyond them, and the distant Isthmus. But what, on the waters themselves, did Xerxes see that fateful morning, as the sun rose behind him, and the fateful moment of battle, long awaited, long maneuvered for, dawned at last?

Not what he had been hoping to see, that much at least is certain: not the spectacle of the Greek fleet shattered in his ambush, spars bobbing in the open sea, corpses twisted and heaped upon the rocks of Psyttaleia. The Great King would have been notified before his arrival above Salamis that the anticipated breakout by the Peloponnesians had failed to occur; even so, the spectacle of the Greek fleet drawn up in the narrows below him would still have come as a sore disappointment. And his own squadrons—where were they as dawn broke? A momentous question: for just as the allied strategy was dependent upon fighting a battle in the straits, so the Great King's admirals had all along been committed to facing the Greeks on the open sea. The resulting stalemate had already endured for three weeks. Only a conviction that their enemy was indeed a hapless rabble would ever have persuaded the commanders of the imperial fleet to break it, and advance with their squadrons into the channel. A decision as fateful as any in the history of warfare; for upon it rested the future course not merely of the battle, not merely of the war, but of Europe and of Western civilization itself. Infuriatingly, we are not told when or why it was made—only that battle, when it was joined, did indeed take place where the Persians had been most desperate not to fight it: within the straits of Salamis.

Historians have generally presumed that the Persians infiltrated these under cover of darkness. Yet this seems improbable.[20] The instructions given to the Great King's captains by their master had been perfectly clear: "guard the exits leading out to the sounding sea."[21] It is unlikely, with the threat of decapitation hanging over them, that there had been much enthusiasm that night for bold displays of initiative. The signal failure of the Greeks to come blundering out into the ambush that had been so carefully laid for them would only have confirmed the imperial admirals in their resolve not to budge from their station; for their oarsmen, rowing hard just to prevent their vessels from drifting and fouling the line, had hardly been given the ideal night's preparation for a battle. It may be that the Great King's dawn arrival above Salamis prompted some captains, eager for royal favor, to order their ships forward into the channel, and that the whole battle line then lurched and followed them. It is more probable, however, that the sight of its master served only to confirm the fleet in its discipline. While individual captains, no matter how desperately they peered from the prows of their triremes, could make out little of what was happening in the straits ahead of them, they could also see how well placed the Great King was to do it for them. And who better than Xerxes to make the final judgment? Who better to give the nod to a gamble on which so much had come to rest?

It seems likeliest, then, that the order to engage the enemy in the straits was given to the Persian fleet shortly after sunrise, and that it came directly from the King of Kings himself. We do not know how the signal was broadcast, nor whether Xerxes was able to communicate to his admirals a sudden and thrilling spectacle, clearly visible to him from his vantage point above the straits: the apparent disintegration of the whole Greek battle line. Some fifty triremes, veering off in the direction of Eleusis, looked to be in headlong flight, making for that narrow channel off the northwest of the island where, evidently unbeknown to their commander, the Egyptians were lurking. So it had happened at Lade, and so it seemed to be happening now—just as the traitorous Athenian admiral had said it would. Time, then, to close the twin jaws of the trap. Time to finish off Greek resistance for good. Time to enter the straits.

A fearsome din of trumpets, amplified by the closeness of the hills on either shore, and the great mass of the Persian battle fleet, breasting the island of Psyttaleia, rounding the southern spur of Salamis, began to quicken its oar strokes. Phoenicians on the right wing, Ionians on the left, Cilicians, Carians and other contingents in the center, they still, during these first minutes of their advance, had no clear view of the enemy, for the angle of the channel precluded it, and spray and the mists of an early autumn dawn would have veiled the waters. But then, rising from ahead of them as the front ranks closed in on the Greek positions, they heard singing, and the paean soared to such a pitch that "a high echo rolled back in answer from the island crags."[22] Hardly the sound of men in panicked retreat—but there could be no turning back now for the Great King's fleet, not even if certain captains in the front ranks of the battle line felt a sudden lurching in their stomachs, and a presentiment clammy like cold sweat across their brows that it was they who were sailing into the ambush. Already, stretching far behind them, an immense mass of shipping could be seen, crowding the channel, bobbing on the oar-churned waters, as the various squadrons sought to maneuver themselves into position, struggling not to foul one another in the narrowness of the straits. Hugging the mainland, where the shore was reassuringly thronged with their own troops, the Persian captains could hardly doubt now, as they looked toward Salamis, that the Great King had been well and truly conned. The Greek triremes, far from fleeing at their approach, were marshaled in a great battle line of their own along the bays and spurs of the island, from the Athenians on the northernmost wing to the Aeginetans in the south; and the ram of every ship was pointed directly at the Persian fleet.

Nevertheless, in the last, stomach-knotting moments before battle was finally joined, the imperial admirals must still have hoped that the enemy might prove a rabble: for the Greek warships, as though in trepidation, kept backing ever closer to the shore. But then, just when

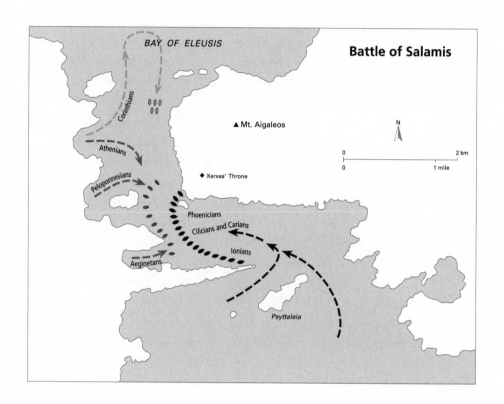

BAY OF ELEUSIS

Battle of Salamis

Corinthians

▲ Mt. Aigaleos

N

Athenians

0   2 km
0   1 mile

Peloponnesians

◆ Xerxes' Throne

Phoenicians

Cilicians and Carians

Aeginetans

Ionians

Psyttaleia

it seemed as though they would run themselves aground, a single ship came darting out of the ranks of retreating triremes. Men would later claim that those on board it had been stung by the words of a female apparition, a phantom who had materialized suddenly before the Greek line and asked, in ringing scorn, "Madmen, how much further do you propose to back off?"[23] Now the crew gave their answer: pulling hard on their oars, powering their vessel so that it sped across the open waters which still lay between the two battle lines, maneuvering it so that the bronze of its ram, glinting as it sliced through the sea, was aimed at the stern of a stray Persian ship. The rattling of a drove of arrows on the deck, then a crash and a splintering of wood: the first contact of the battle had been made. There was no clean kill, however, for the oars of the two triremes quickly became entangled, so that the vessels were locked together. Seeing this, captains of other ships brought their craft skimming forward in support of their comrades. Soon all were on the move, and the Greeks, as they advanced "with discipline and in perfect order,"[24] sang nevertheless with the joy and frenzy of the killing that was to come.

And in no time the battle was general along the whole course of the channel. It is a mark of the confusion of the engagement that even the identity of the first ship to engage the barbarians should later have been furiously debated: for both the Aeginetans and the Athenians laid claim to the honor. Proper adjudication was impossible. The two contingents were fighting at opposite ends of a line that stretched for upward of a mile—and no one in the straits had a view of the whole panorama of the battle. No wonder, then, that memories of that grim and glorious day should have been, not of strategy, nor of the performance of rival squadrons, nor of the ebb and flow of the fighting, but rather of stirring deeds of individual heroism, exploits that shone all the more brightly for being set against a backdrop of such clamor and carnage and chaos.

The greatest glamour of all attached itself to certain trireme aces. Most celebrated of these was an Athenian, Ameinias, from the village of Pallene. In the shock of the battle's opening, he dared to attack the flagship of the Phoenician fleet, a towering vessel commanded by one of the Great King's own brothers. The royal admiral, naturally infuriated by the impudence of his assailant, ordered missiles to be rained down upon the Athenians while he himself led a boarding party—but he was skewered by Ameinias as he made the jump, and pitched overboard. Altogether more ambiguous was the performance of a second of the Great King's commanders to be attacked by the same Athenian captain: none other than Queen Artemisia of Halicarnassus. Seeing Ameinias bearing down upon her, and panicking, she found her escape blocked by the trireme of one of her own vassals—and so resorted to the startling expedient of ramming it herself. Ameinias, presuming that the queen had deserted the Persian cause, duly abandoned his pursuit of her. And so it was that Artemisia made her escape.

And the Great King, seated upon the heights above the battle, saw it all, and was hugely impressed. As mistaken, in his own way, as Ameinias had been, he imagined that the ship sunk by Artemisia had been Greek; for the ferocity of the fighting was such that his aides found it hard to distinguish friend from foe. Yet, while it might certainly prove a challenge on occasion for the royal secretaries, busily scribbling down examples of particular prowess, to transcribe all the details with total accuracy, they and their master could have had few illusions as to the broader progress of the battle. "My men have turned into women," Xerxes is said to have cried, watching as Artemisia's warship pulled away from the wreckage of its victim, "and my women into men."[25] His bitterness was understandable—for the Great King, far more clearly than any of his captains embroiled in the actual fighting, could take in the full sweep of the catastrophe unfolding in the straits. He could see how his crack Phoenician squadrons, left leaderless by the death of their admiral, and hemmed in by the Athenians, were being progressively driven back onto the shore, or else into open flight. He could mark the chaos that was the result of his squadrons' attempts to withdraw, as rank after rank of them began to lose formation, cramping one another in the narrows, "their bronze rams smashing the sides of their neighbors, shearing off whole banks of oars."[26]

16. This watercolor of hoplites arming for battle is based on a vase that dates from the decade before the battle of Marathon. The Athenian victory over the Persian invaders in 490 BC was the first demonstration of how lethal Greek armor and weapons might be when brought to bear against the much more lightly armed troops of the East. *(akg-images/Peter Connolly)*

17. A view of the modern-day plain of Marathon, looking north from the position of the Greek camp to where the Persian camp would have been. *(Tom Holland)*

18. A bronze helmet worn by a Persian soldier who fought at Marathon. It was dedicated by the victorious Athenians to the temple of Zeus at Olympia. *(akg-images/John Hios)*

19. The King of Kings seated on his throne. This is probably a representation of Darius—in which case the Crown Prince standing behind the throne is Xerxes. Alternatively, the King may be Xerxes himself. Artists at the Persian court were employed to portray idealized representations of royal power, not to draw from real life. *(National Museum of Iran, Tehran/Bridgeman Art Library)*

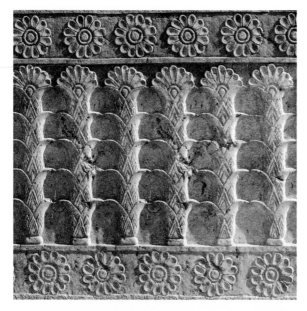

20. A frieze of palm leaves and sunflowers from Xerxes' private quarters at Persepolis. Gardens and the beauties of the natural world were a universal passion among the Persian elite.

21. The Great King, symbolically borne on the shoulders of his soldiers. The invasion of Greece was not merely a military expedition—it was also designed to demonstrate the full scale and reach of royal power. *(Sadie Holland)*

22. An ostracon cast in the 480s BC, when dread of Persia was starting to infect political life in Athens. This particular shard was cast against "Callias the son of Cratius"; the rough sketch on its reverse side, showing Callias as a Persian archer, makes clear the crime of which he was suspected. *(Deutsches Archäologisches Institut, Athens)*

23. Themistocles: "the subtle serpent of Greece." *(Werner Forman/CORBIS)*

24. A fragment of a relief from Persepolis, showing a chariot pulled by Nisaean horses. This was the form of transport that Xerxes used to cross the Hellespont. *(British Museum)*

25. Persian infantrymen, from a frieze discovered at Susa. The richness and beauty of their robes suggest that they belong to the Immortals, the elite squad of 10,000 who served the Great King as his shock troops. *(Gianni Dagli Orti/CORBIS)*

26. A view of the beach at Artemisium as it looks today. Back in 480 BC, the ships of the Greek fleet could easily be hauled up onto the shingle or launched back into the sea as the movements of the enemy demanded. *(Tom Holland)*

27. A coin from the fourth century BC, showing a Sidonian warship. Slim, shield-hung and sublimely maneuverable, Phoenician triremes moved faster than anything the Greek fleet could pitch against them. *(British Museum)*

28. This bust of a Spartan warrior has traditionally been taken to represent Leonidas, the king who lead the 300 men of his bodyguard to their heroic deaths at Thermopylae. Whether it is truly a portrait of Leonidas or not—and the overwhelming probability must be that it is not—it powerfully expresses the resolution and defiance that Spartans were trained all their life to attain. *(The Art Archive/Archaeological Museum Sparta/Dagli Orti)*

29. Thermopylae, seen from the heights above the East Gate. Back in 480 BC, the flatlands stretching away from the pass to the east would have been submerged beneath the waters of the Malian Gulf. Otherwise, this is essentially the view that Hydarnes and the Immortals would have had as they descended from the mountain pass to attack the Greek holding force in its rear. *(Tom Holland)*

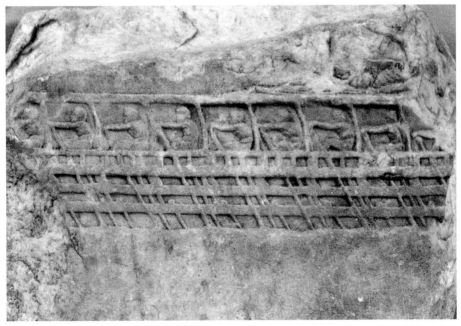

30. This relief, sculpted some eighty years after the battle of Salamis, shows the midsection of a Greek warship. Banks of straining rowers pull on oars. *(Bridgeman/Alinari Archives)*

31. Modern-day Salamis. The straits in which the Persian fleet were defeated are now crowded with tankers, warships and speedboats. The topography, however, has stayed essentially the same. This is the view from the entrance to the straits. A full view of them is only possible once a ship has advanced further into the channel. *(Tom Holland)*

32. Down, and almost out. The Persian defeat at Plataea finished off the Great King's hopes of conquering Greece for good. *(National Museums of Scotland)*

33. A view from the Pnyx, where Themistocles rallied his fellow citizens to defiance of the Persian juggernaut, looking eastward toward the Acropolis. On the summit of the sacred rock stand the ruins of the Parthenon: the most beautiful war memorial ever built. *(Bridgeman/Alinari Archives)*

He could observe in mounting disbelief how a deadly wedge of Greek ships, massing inward, was splitting his fleet in two, leaving the Phoenicians on the right wing of the battle line trapped like tuna fish in a net, there to be speared or battered or hacked to death. And he could reflect, perhaps, that the order to engage the Greeks had been his own.

That he had blundered in giving it would have been evident to him even before the battle had begun. The triremes which he had observed heading north up the channel toward Eleusis, and which the Greeks among his aides would no doubt have identified as Corinthian, had not, once they reached the northeastern cape of Salamis, continued their flight. On the contrary: after scanning the straits which lay between Eleusis and Salamis, the Corinthians had veered round, lowered their sails and masts, and headed back to the battle line. Clearly, far from panicking, they had been engaged on a reconnaissance mission, making certain that the Egyptian squadron, which had been sent around the island during the night, was not now advancing in the Greek fleet's rear. Which, of course, it was not. The Egyptian squadron, as Xerxes himself was painfully aware, was still eight miles from a battle in which its extra numbers might well have proved crucial, lurking by the westernmost straits, waiting for a Greek escape bid that was never going to come.

Unsurprisingly, the Great King, in his vexation, was testy in the extreme with any survivors of the fiasco. When a group of bedraggled Phoenician captains, attempting to excuse the loss of their ships, sought to lay the blame for it on the treachery of other contingents in the fleet, he had them decapitated on the spot. Naturally, it was out of the question for the Great King himself to accept any responsibility for the catastrophe; and the Phoenicians, now that their strength had been shattered upon the rocks below his throne, could serve him well enough as scapegoats. Yet Xerxes, as he followed the course of the debacle from his command post, must have felt an increasingly embittered consciousness that his own stratagems, devised with such care and with such confidence of victory, had been turned against him.

Midday turned to afternoon, and the Persians began to be swept out of the straits. Perhaps half of those triremes that had entered the deadly channel survived to leave it. Behind them, harrying them as they lurched and limped desperately back to Phalerum, came the Greeks, pursuing them across those same open waters on which, the day before, the Great King had planned to stage his ambush and secure his mastery of Greece.

Perhaps the cruelest cut of all came toward sunset. By now, excepting the "lamentations and screams that echoed across the sea" and the bobbing of Persian corpses as they snarled up the oars of the predatory victors, the straits had been cleared of the Great King's men. There was only one further deed of slaughter left for the Greeks to perform before the coming of "black-eyed night."[27] The four hundred troops stationed by the Great King on Psyttaleia the previous evening had been left stranded at their post, for there had been no opportunity, amid all the panic and desperation of the imperial navy's rout, to secure their evacuation. Now, having been ordered to serve as the executioners of any Greeks who might be swept onto the rocks, the unfortunate Persians found that they themselves had become the objects of an execution squad. Slingers, archers and heavily armored marines, debouching from allied warships, won bloody payback for the cornering of the Spartans at Thermopylae. Led by Aristeides, the Greeks "dashed over their enemies like a roaring wave, their voices raised in a single cry, hacking at the limbs of the wretched men until the life had been butchered out of them every last one."[28] The rocks were left slippery after the slaughter, and Aristeides' men, slithering over the corpses, hacked at them with their knives, harvesting their rings and bracelets, or else waded through the red surge of the shallows, scavenging from the dead that they found drifting there. And the sea for miles was filled with the timbers of countless warships, and they slowly drifted and were dispersed upon the swell of the darkening gulf.

And so ended the attempt of the Great King to force the straits of Salamis.

So Near, So Far

In 484 BC, while Xerxes, back from suppressing the revolt in Egypt, was drawing up his first plans for the conquest of the West, the Mesopotamians had unexpectedly launched an insurrection of their own. Decades had passed since Darius, impaling the man he had contemptuously arraigned as "Nidintu-Bel," had disposed of the last native "King of Babylon, King of Lands." These titles, imbued with all the ancient glamour of the city between the two rivers, had been among the more splendid honorifics that the usurper had bequeathed his son. Not, of course—as Darius himself had well appreciated—that titles alone a King of Babylon could make. The Persian grip on Mesopotamia, during the long years of his reign, had become increasingly a matter of securing real estate. Vast swaths of it, confiscated from the hapless natives, had ended up as the personal property of the King of Kings. Other holdings, parceled out to favored servants, had been granted on the understanding that they be settled with colonies of reservists from the distant reaches of the empire. As a result, the mudflats of Mesopotamia, like the huge metropolis that they fed, had begun to fill with immigrants. Walking along the course of a palm-tree-fringed canal, one might pass through whole villages of aliens: Egyptian archers, Lydian cavalrymen, axe-wielding Saka. This, under the rule of the King of Kings, was to be the future of the world: a universal melting pot.

When rebellion erupted on the banks of the Euphrates, Xerxes had therefore moved speedily to crush it. An expedition to the West could hardly have been risked while Babylon, the largest and richest city in the Great King's dominions, was in ferment. The great capital still held a crucial significance in the Persian order of things. It was not only bureaucrats in the imperial treasury who could testify to that. Just as both Cyrus and Darius had discovered in the ancient city a mirror held up to all their proudest pretensions, so too Xerxes, with his invasion of Europe, was making manifest a vision of global monarchy that had first been dreamed of long previously in Babylon—the original cosmopolis. The camp of the Great King's forces, thronged with soldiers from every corner of the world, brought to Attica more than a touch of far-distant Mesopotamia. The Athenians too, and the Peloponnesians, and all the Greeks, reaching even to the islands of the far West, were expected soon to add their own numbers to the mix. Once they had been conquered. Once they had only been conquered.

But how to secure that submission was now, after Salamis, a sudden and unanticipated headache. Mardonius, in the council of war that followed the battle, cheerfully dismissed the whole debacle as being of sublime unimportance. "What are a few planks of wood?" he sniffed dismissively. "So what if a shamble of Phoenicians, of Egyptians, of Cypriots, of Cilicians have messed things up? It is not as though the Persians had any hand in it. No, my Lord, it was hardly a defeat for us."[29] Ringingly stated—and an expression of the chauvinism that came naturally to every Persian aristocrat. To the Great King, too, of course—for Xerxes was hardly the man to dispute his countrymen's bravery and prowess. All the same, he had marched on Greece as more than just the King of Persia: he was, literally, "King of Lands." The rout of the various squadrons he had summoned to his banner had stung his pride. It was all very well for Mardonius to sneer at the ragbag character of the imperial navy—but that was precisely what had made it, in the opinion of the Great King, such an effective embodiment of his global power.

Nor, despite the mauling that it had received, could Xerxes initially bring himself to accept that his reach might have been reduced as a consequence of the defeat. No sooner had his fleet been swept out of the straits than he was attempting to impose his mastery in a fresh and suitably imperious manner: by erecting a causeway across to Salamis. Rocks were dropped into the shallows, merchant ships lashed together in a desperate attempt to bridge the central depths of the channel. But it was the Greek archers, not the straits themselves, that ultimately posed the insuperable obstacle to the attempt. The imperial engineers, harassed by predatory warships, provided easy pickings for enemy fire, until the Great King, bowing to the inevitable, was forced reluctantly to abandon the project. For a man who had bridged the

Hellespont and split the peninsula of Mount Athos, this was an ago-nizing frustration. Having dreamed only days previously of conquering an entire continent, the Great King now found himself defied by a mile-wide stretch of water.

And by further grim tidings, too. Reports were starting to come in from Sicily, a theater crucial to the Great King's hopes of extending his power ever further westward, of a second Greek victory.* Gelon, the precocious tyrant of Syracuse, was said to have inflicted a sensational defeat on the Carthaginians. The destruction of their army had been bloody beyond compare. Below the walls of Himera, a city in north Sicily, 150,000 Carthaginians lay butchered; the survivors had all been enslaved; their general, surprised while making a sacrifice, had immo-lated himself in the flames. For the Great King, as he pondered his next move in an increasingly autumnal Athens, the implications of this news were sobering in the extreme. His ambitions, once so grandiose, seemed suddenly diminished and circumscribed. Dreams of extending the limits of Persian greatness to the setting of the sun counted for little against the reality of a blockaded Isthmus, an unpaci-fied Peloponnese. What had previously been represented as a campaign of universal conquest appeared to have shrunk to the status of an awkward border war.

And as such, of course, to have become hardly worthy of the Great King's personal attention. Mardonius, recognizing this, was quick to seize his chance. "Head back to your regional headquarters in Sardis," he urged his cousin, "and take the greater part of the army with you, and leave me to complete the enslavement of Greece with men whom I will personally choose to finish off the job."[30] Such a commission was

---

*The precise date of the Battle of Himera is uncertain. Gelon's propagandists, keen to foster the notion that their master had been fighting in defense of Greek liberty, rather than merely his own interests, liked to claim that it had been waged on the same day as either the last stand of the Spartans at Thermopylae or the Battle of Salamis.

precisely what Mardonius had been angling after for years; and the Great King, reluctant to pass a second summer on campaign in Greece, no longer had any reason to oppose his cousin's strategy. The scale and flamboyance that had characterized the expedition under his own leadership would be scandalously inappropriate once he was no longer at its head. As the task force's new commander, Mardonius would be judged by only one measure: whether he succeeded in bringing the new satrapy to heel. Against the Spartans and their allies it was quality, not quantity, that would count. The lessons of Thermopylae, bruising though they were, had been well learned. As the Great King, having left a still-smoking Attica behind him, began leading his troops northward, through Boeotia and then into Thessaly, so Mardonius, given a free hand by his cousin, began to cherry-pick the elite.

Top of his wish list was cavalry: mobile, heavily armored, and, in the case of the Saka, able to fire a rain of arrows at any ponderous lines of infantry they might happen to be galloping past. The virtual helplessness of Greek hoplites against such opponents had been demonstrated repeatedly over previous decades and there seemed little reason to doubt that it soon would be again. Nor was Mardonius alone in this opinion. What neutrals made of his prospects can be gauged from the fact that the Great King, despite his failure to subdue Greece, completed a leisurely and unscathed retreat.[31] To be sure, the allies spun any number of far-fetched anecdotes—claiming that his army had been reduced to eating grass, that it had been virtually wiped out after crashing through an ice-covered river, that Xerxes himself had crossed the Hellespont huddled alone in a fishing boat—but these were all lies. Any tribe or city that dared to betray its oath of submission could expect to meet with an immediate and blistering response. Most opted to play things safe. Thrace, Macedonia and Thessaly all stayed loyal to the King of Kings. So, too, did Thebes and central Greece. Even the imperial fleet, although certainly down, was far from out. The carnage of Salamis notwithstanding, it still outnumbered the allied navy. There appeared every prospect, come the summer, that Mardonius would indeed "finish off the job."

Or perhaps he would be spared the need. Embarrassing though the intelligence failure at Salamis had been, and devastating in its consequences, the Persian high command still looked to divide and rule. Remarkably, channels were even kept open to Themistocles. After all, it had not been on the Athenian's recommendation that the Great King had chosen to fight in the straits—a detail with which Themistocles appears to have made considerable hay. Only days after Salamis, in a startling display of cheek, he had sent Sicinnus back over the straits with a second message for the Persians: a reassurance that he remained "eager to be of service to the royal cause" and was acting as a restraining influence on the rest of the allied fleet.[32] Mind-boggling claims, it might have been thought—but the spy chiefs had not, as they must have been itching to do, put Sicinnus to a long and agonizing death. Instead, just as on the eve of Salamis, they had opted to send the slave back to his master. We do not know what message they gave him to carry, but there must surely have been one: an amplification of the Great King's peace terms, no doubt. The Athenian people, still buoyed by their victory at Salamis, could hardly have been expected to accept them—but that was not the point. Just as Themistocles was obviously shadowboxing, so too was the Persian high command. Each side was indicating to the other their appreciation of a guilty secret: that the moment might yet come when it would be in their mutual interests for Athens to be granted a privileged surrender.

But why would Themistocles, at the moment of his greatest triumph, be prepared to send such a treasonous message? The answer, for those skilled in the dark art of interpreting Greek diplomatic maneuvers, had not been long in coming. Several weeks after Sicinnus' second mission, the Spartans had sent an embassy of their own to the Persian camp. Arriving in Thessaly, where the Great King was preparing to depart for the Hellespont, they had bluntly demanded reparations for the death of Leonidas. The Great King, bursting into laughter, had suddenly fallen silent, as though making private calculations. "You will get all the reparations you deserve," he had said at last, gesturing to his cousin, "from Mardonius here."[33] Witty enough—but Xerxes had surely been mulling over more than a menacing *bon mot*. He would have recognized that behind the Spartans' seemingly brutish demand there was an intriguing hint: that they just might, if offered a hefty enough bribe, be prepared to tolerate the status quo. A comical notion, of course: the Great King did not negotiate with anyone. Nevertheless, it was, in its implications, full of interest. It would, after all, oblige the Spartans to wash their hands of the whole of central Greece—including Attica. Well might the Great King have paused and furrowed his brow.

And well might the Spartans, their embassy rebuffed, have loudly insisted that they had only sent it in the first place because they had been instructed to do so by Apollo. The Athenians, and everyone else, were happy to take their word for it. None of the Greeks who had triumphed at Salamis had any interest in destabilizing the alliance if they could possibly help it. Even as the campaigning season drew to a close amid autumnal storms, the afterglow of the famous victory still lit the lengthening evenings. To celebrate their achievement, the various Greek squadrons, returned from a profitable few weeks spent touring the Aegean, and extorting money from the islanders, all assembled off the Isthmus. Here, at the temple of Poseidon which had served the alliance as its headquarters throughout the summer, a great jamboree of mutual backslapping was held. Sacrifices were offered to the gods, and prizes given. The sense of relief was immense. "A black cloud," as Themistocles put it, "has been swept away from off the sea."[34]

But not, unfortunately from off the land—with implications for the alliance that might prove ominous, as the shrewder Athenians and Spartans had already begun to appreciate. The Isthmus, even as it hosted the great festival of unity, served as a fracture line. If a delegate tired of the celebrations, he could have this brought home to him while paying a call on the neighborhood's most obvious alternative source of entertainment. There stood, two thousand feet above Corinth, on the summit of the city's steepling acropolis, a temple dedicated to Aphrodite, the goddess of love. Here, complementing the marble statuary, could be found an altogether less chilly brand of votive offering: prostitutes. Donated to the goddess by grateful Olympic champions and other such luminaries, these had a reputation so superlative that in Greek "*korinthiazein*"—"to do a Corinthian"—meant to fuck. Patriotic as well as proficient, Aphrodite's temple whores had spent the weeks before Salamis raising urgent prayers to their divine mistress, imploring her to inspire the allies with a love of battle. Any war hero who did take time off from the celebrations at the Isthmus to visit them could look forward to a particularly enthusiastic reception. Then, shattered by the climb as well as by all of his subsequent exertions, he could slump down, admire the matchless view, and see for himself why the alliance that had won at Salamis might be in imminent danger of fissuring.

For from nowhere else could the opportunities and the dilemmas presented by the Isthmus be more readily appreciated. To the south stretched the Peloponnese—now, thanks in large part to the Athenian fleet, secure from invasion. To the north curved the coast that led to Attica—still wide open to Mardonius. Hardly surprising, then, that the Athenians, even as they began returning across the straits from Salamis to their ruined homeland, should have kept a nervous eye on the road to Thessaly. Resentful of the monstrous unfairness of geography, and hardly able to restrain themselves from blaming it on the Peloponnesians, they pressed loudly for a commitment from their allies to send an army north against Mardonius come the spring. The Peloponnesians stonewalled; and the more that the Athenians, attempting to shame them into action, harped upon their role as the victors of Salamis, the more their partners, snug and smug behind their wall, dug in their heels.

The result, bubbling away beneath the facade of amity presented at the Isthmus, was a toxic brew of resentment and spite. The Peloponnesians, infuriated by Athenian cockiness, made sure that the prize for civic achievement was awarded to Aegina. Then, rather than endure the spectacle of Themistocles strutting around wearing the crown for individual achievement, they split the vote among nominees from their own cities, so that no one won the prize at all. The

Athenian response was to start flinging around slanders like mud—including, choicest of all, an accusation that the Corinthians at Salamis had headed north up the channel, not to confront the Egyptians, but because they were fleeing like cowards. Well might the delegates at the Isthmus have reveled in their sense of deliverance from the barbarian menace. Pettiness, envy, backbiting: it was just like old times.

But the Spartans at least, tempted though they may have been to join in the fun, had recognized it as a self-indulgence that their city could ill afford. Their security had to come ahead of even the pleasure to be had from baiting Themistocles. The Athenian fleet, as the Spartan high command was naggingly aware, remained the key to the security of the Peloponnese. Only if Mardonius could somehow win Athens round to the Great King's cause would he have a hope of breaching the Isthmus. So that the Spartans, displaying the coarse pragmatism that invariably marked their understanding of human nature, opted not to insult the Athenian admiral, but rather to stroke and pet his ego.

Themistocles, his pride still bruised by the small-minded humiliations inflicted on him at the Isthmus, was duly invited to Lacedaemon. There, having crossed the frontier of that ordinarily crabbed and suspicious land, he was greeted with a veritable orgy of flattery. The crown that had been denied him at the Isthmus was now awarded to him at Sparta—"in recognition of his ability and cleverness."[35] He was also presented with a splendid chariot. When he left, he was escorted as far as Tegea by the three hundred members of the Hippeis. No foreigner had previously been given such an honor; but it is likely that the bodyguard was granted to Themistocles for a much more pointed reason as well. His route home took him past Caryae, the city that had been darkly suspected of being in the pay of the barbarians all summer: evidently, the Caryaeans were still in a medizing mood. Beyond their borders there lurked in turn a much more threatening beast: Argos, the dog that had so far signally failed to bark. But it might yet: for the Argives were reported to be in direct contact with Mardonius, and to have promised him "that they would do all they could to stop the Spartans from marching to war."[36] Clearly, then, the Spartans themselves, by bestowing on Themistocles his three hundred escorts, were aiming to remind him not only of the sacrifice that they had made at Thermopylae but of the dangers that still menaced them in their own backyard. By the time that the Hippeis, arriving at Tegea, came to salute their guest and bid him godspeed, the point would have been rammed well and truly home: the Spartans had not the slightest intention of sending an army north of the Isthmus.

Which was hardly, from Themistocles' own point of view, the ideal boost to his career. Reports of the honors paid to their admiral did not greatly console the Athenian people as they shivered and went hungry amid the blackened ruins of their city. Nor did the suspicion that their fleet, even as it stood guard over the stay-at-home Peloponnesians, was offering minimal protection to the farms and families of the men who were crewing it. Anger and resentment began to grow in the squatter camps that now dotted the city. The hoplite class, whose loathing of Themistocles had only been fueled by his crowing after Salamis, could suddenly smell his blood. Already, over the winter, there had been a concentrated effort to spin the slaughter of the Persian garrison on Psyttaleia as the key turning point of the battle, with Aristeides as its star. Now, as winter began to turn to spring, and the campaigning season of 479 BC drew near, the maneuvering against the hero of Salamis turned increasingly vicious. Voters, as had been proved time and again in the brief history of the democracy, might have lethally short memories. Come the February elections, Themistocles' reward for having saved his city was to be removed from the command of his precious fleet.[37] The admiralship was awarded instead to Xanthippus, the adopted Alcmaeonid. Command of the land forces went to—who else?—Aristeides.

The impact of these changes on Athenian policy was immediate and far reaching. Energies that had previously been devoted to the fleet were now diverted toward preparations for a second Marathon. In spring, when the allied squadrons assembled at Aegina, the Athenians were noticeable by their absence. The Spartans, who had signaled their own enthusiasm for a naval campaign by sending royalty, in the not altogether inspiring person of King Leotychides, to command it, found the Athenians obdurate: no ships would be contributed to the allied fleet until the Spartans had committed manpower to an expedition north of the Isthmus. The Spartans, calling the Athenians' bluff, refused to buy the deal. The result was stalemate. Leotychides, with barely a hundred triremes under his command, skulked around off Delos, too nervous of the Persians to sail any further eastward. Meanwhile, the Persian fleet, correspondingly nervous of the Greeks, skulked around off Samos. The Peloponnesians skulked behind their wall. Mardonius, knowing that he had no hope of winning his satrapy unless he could lure the Spartans north of the Isthmus, or somehow secure the Athenians' fleet, skulked in Thessaly. The Athenians, trapped impotently in the middle, had little option but to skulk as well. And so the deadlock continued, all the way into May.

It was Mardonius who finally moved to break it. Wearying of secret diplomacy, yet reluctant to jeopardize its potential fruits, he decided to place the Great King's terms openly on the table before advancing south from Thessaly. Having ostentatiously consulted a slew of Greek oracles in his effort to reassure the Athenians of his good intentions, he sent as his ambassador that unctuous bet-hedger, King Alexander of Macedon. As the brother-in-law of a Persian general and an official "Friend and Benefactor of the Athenian People," the smooth-talking monarch must have struck Mardonius as the ideal go-between; and Alexander certainly had a rare talent for making a plausible pitch. With the rubble-strewn panorama of the Acropolis and the Agora stretching behind him, and oozing honest concern, he warned the Athenian people that their city, of all those that had set themselves in opposition to the Great King, "stood most directly in the line of fire." Two options therefore confronted them. The first was to see their country become "a no-man's land, trampled underfoot by rival armies." The second was to become not merely the friends of the Great King, but friends such as would have few rivals for the royal favor throughout the whole dominion of the Persians. A full pardon, a guarantee of self-government, their temples rebuilt at royal expense, an expansion of their territory could all be theirs. "What earthly reason, then, can you have," Alexander exclaimed, "to stay in arms against the king?"[38]

Cunningly framed as Mardonius' offer was to play upon all their darkest suspicions of Sparta, the Athenians must have felt in their hearts that they would be perfectly justified in accepting such generous terms. They had fought longer than the people of any other city in Greece, and at a far greater cost—and yet the Peloponnesians, as Alexander had suavely pointed out, appeared content to abandon them to their fate. Of course, the Athenians themselves, before permitting Alexander to deliver the Persian peace offer, had made sure that there was a high-ranking delegation from Sparta on hand to hear it as well; but still the Spartans, when their turn came to address the Assembly, opted to prevaricate. An offer to take in refugees was not remotely what the Athenian people had been hoping to hear, nor high-minded lectures on the perfidious character of barbarians. "You know that there is neither truth nor honor in anything they say."[39] An aphorism that the Athenian people might well have flung back in the Spartans' faces.

And perhaps once they would have done. Perhaps once they would have chosen to forsake all their dreams of independence, accept that there might indeed be submission with honor, bow their necks to the King of Kings. But much had changed. A sense of the preciousness of freedom, instilled in the Athenian people by the thirty-year experiment that was their democracy, and by the experience of having fought to defend it against the most terrifying odds imaginable, had left the Assembly unwilling now to barter it for peace. "The degree to which we are put in the shadow by the Medes' strength is hardly something that you need to bring to our attention," they told Alexander. "We are already well aware of it. But even so, such is our love of liberty, that we will never surrender."[40] Brave words indeed: for the Athenian people, having uttered them, once again faced the prospect of their city's annihilation.

And the Spartan ambassadors? It is hard to believe that they were not moved by such defiance. Even as they left Athens, the squatter camps were starting to empty, as evacuees, for the second time in ten months, began pushing their handcarts down to the beaches. Not that admiration of Athenian spirit necessarily implied any sense of obligation on the part of the Spartans themselves—and yet the ambassadors, on their return, would surely have warned the ephors that the crisis brewing in Attica did indeed imperil Sparta. Stirringly though it had been proclaimed, the Athenians' love of liberty might yet be pushed to breaking point. Only their illusion that the Spartans were pledged to cross the Isthmus in their defense was serving to keep the talk of appeasement at bay. "Get your army into the field as soon as you can." Such had been the parting words of Aristeides. "Quickly, before Mardonius appears in our country, you must join with us, and confront him in Boeotia."[41]

So it was that when the barbarian, sweeping southward into Attica, occupied a deserted Athens for the second time, Peloponnesians everywhere felt a sudden tremor of alarm. King Leotychides, still cruising off Delos with the allied fleet, saw, on the western horizon, a distant pinprick of fire, then another, then another in turn, as beacons, linking Attica directly to the imperial information network, broadcast to distant Sardis the news of Athens' fall. Meanwhile, in Lacedaemon, the ephors had been brought an even more unsettling communication: Mardonius, it was reported, had sent his envoys across the straits to Salamis and repeated his peace terms to the Athenian evacuees. This time, a prominent nobleman, Lycidas, had dared to speak out openly in favor of accepting them. A straw in the wind, surely—despite the fact that his fellow citizens, cornered and despairing as they were, had promptly stoned the would-be medizer. Lycidas' wife and children too, surrounded by the women camped out on Salamis, had been similarly pulped to death. Athenian defiance, it appeared, was turning pathological. The more savage it became, and the more suspicious, the greater the risk that it might buckle.

By now it was June. The Spartans, inevitably, were celebrating yet another festival, this time the Hyacinthia, a great spectacle of songs and feasting held in honor of a dead lover of Apollo. Once again, just as had happened in the dark days before Marathon, an Athenian embassy arrived in Lacedaemon desperate for military assistance, only to find everyone having a party.[42] Behind the scenes, however, wheels were already turning. Ten days the Athenian ambassadors were kept in Sparta. Ten days they cooled their heels. On the eleventh day, their patience finally cracked. They delivered an explicit ultimatum: either the Spartans abandoned their festivities and went to war or the Athenians would be obliged to accept Mardonius' terms. The ephors, far from panicking, or working themselves up into a fit of righteous indignation, merely smiled, then revealed all. Why, they exclaimed blandly, had the ambassadors not heard? The Spartan army was already on the march.

A true *coup de théâtre*—and the Athenians were far from the only ones to whom it came as a bolt from the blue. The Argives, having vowed to obstruct any Spartan expedition before it could reach the Isthmus, suddenly woke to find themselves bypassed. "The whole fighting force of Lacedaemon is on the march," they reported frantically to Mardonius, "and we are powerless to stop it."[43] Mardonius himself, still camped out in Attica, promptly abandoned his attempts to woo the Athenians and put what remained of their city, "walls, houses, temples and all," to the torch.[44] Then, determined to lure the Peloponnesians as far north from the Isthmus as he could, he withdrew from Attica into Boeotia. Here, having been guided along the safest paths by enthusiastic Theban liaison officers, he finally halted. He was now in prime cavalry country. The perfect spot to build his camp. The perfect spot to fight a battle.

Four miles south of Thebes, on the bank of the broadest river in Boeotia, the Asopus, Mardonius duly ordered the construction of a palisade. Again he had chosen his position well. Beyond the river there stretched the gently undulating territory of Thebes' old enemy, Plataea. Beyond the fields of the Plataeans there rose foothills, and beyond them, the heights of a mountain with extensive spurs and ridges, Cithaeron. The allies, if they wished to bring Mardonius to battle, would first have to cross a host of barriers—and cross them knowing that defeat would mean their certain annihilation. There could be no easy retreat back to the Isthmus from Plataea. Nor, equally, for Mardonius, if he lost, back to Thessaly. If the allies came, then the moment of truth would come as well.

The Dorian Spear

Long delayed it may have been, but there were no half measures about the advance of the Peloponnesians from their bunk hole when it came. Making good their demolition work of the previous summer, engineers had already repaired the land route to Megara, and it was just as well that they had not botched their responsibility, for the Isthmus road, shuddering under thousands of tramping feet, had never before had to bear the weight of such an army. Indeed, a Greek expeditionary force to rival it had not been seen since the fabled times of the Trojan War. From Corinth to Mycenae, from Tegea to Troezen, an immense coalition of Peloponnesians had answered the Spartans' call. Naturally, the Spartans themselves, five thousand of them, almost three-quarters of their city's total manpower, provided the task force with its most menacing spear thrust. With five thousand further hoplites recruited from the outlying townships of Lacedaemon, and thousands of helots rounded up to serve as orderlies and light infantry, it was almost certainly the largest army that Sparta had ever committed to the field.[45]

Even cowards had been mobilized; or rather—which was not necessarily the same thing—men whom the Spartans had labeled cowards. One of these, an unfortunate veteran by the name of Aristodemus, was particularly grateful to have been given a chance to redeem his honor, for this was not the first time that he had marched to war against the barbarians. Less than a year previously, he had been one of the three hundred who had accompanied Leonidas to Thermopylae. Arriving at the pass, he and a fellow Spartan had fallen sick with an eye inflammation, and the two men had been dismissed and ordered to recuperate. Come the fateful morning of their king's last stand, however, Aristodemus' partner, rising from his sickbed, had instructed a helot to lead him, blind as he still was, into the thick of the fighting. Aristodemus, preferring to obey Leonidas' direct orders, had invalided himself home. There, on his arrival, he had been greeted with revulsion. His fellow citizens had branded him "trembler": the single most shameful word in the Spartan lexicon.

Harshly unfair—but it was only to be expected, in a city where courage was reckoned the greatest virtue, that the slightest hint of cowardice in a citizen would doom him to ignominy. The life of a "trembler" in Sparta was signally wretched. Patches sewn onto his cloak would alert the whole city to his disgrace. Whether sitting down at his mess table or attempting to join in with a ball game, he would be icily ignored by all his former friends. At festivals, he would have to stand up or make way for anyone who demanded it—even the most junior. Cruelest cut of all, his daughters, if he had any, would find it impossible to secure a husband: a typically Spartan eugenicist measure designed to prevent the taint of cowardice from being inherited by future generations. Unable to endure these humiliations, the only other survivor of Thermopylae, a liaison officer sent by Leonidas on a mission to Thessaly, had ended up hanging himself. "For after all, when cowardice results in such shame, it is only to be expected that death be preferred to a life of dishonor and obloquy."[46]

And for Aristodemus, the man who had spurned the chance to die in battle beside his king, the long months following his return from Thermopylae had been particularly bitter. The shadow cast by Leonidas' end had proved impossible to escape. Mourning in Lacedaemon was not, as it was in, say, Athens, the responsibility only of women. Every man too, whether ephor or helot, was obliged to wail and beat his brow when a king descended to the underworld. To other Greeks, indeed, Spartan lamentations appeared so excessive as to verge on the barbarian. Officially, the obsequies that accompanied a royal funeral lasted for ten days, but Leonidas was no easy ghost to

341

lay to rest. His mutilated corpse, left as food for kites and dogs in a far-distant pass, had never been recovered.* Adding to the pathos of his fate, and a constant reminder to the Spartan people of the loss they had sustained, was the fact that his son, the new king, was just a boy. Cleombrotus, Leonidas' younger brother, had been serving ably as regent but he, too, during the course of the winter, had died. When the Spartans, then, having resolved to give battle at last, marched out from the Isthmus, they did so under the generalship of a young man barely in his twenties: Pausanias, the son of Cleombrotus. Since he was, as the Regent of Sparta, also the supreme commander of the allied forces, this was a startling weight of responsibility for one so young to bear—but Pausanias himself, whose qualities as a general never entirely outpaced his conceit, shouldered it with insouciance. Even so, the brute fact of their general's youth must have kept Thermopylae, and Leonidas' death there, all the more firmly in the Spartans' minds. Marching to liberate Greece, they were also after revenge. And Aristodemus especially—for it was due to the barbarians that he wore his trembler's patchwork cloak.

And there were others, too, of course, who wanted payback—men whose losses had been infinitely greater than the Spartans'. At Eleusis, thirty-five miles along the coastal road from the Isthmus, Pausanias waited while Aristeides and eight thousand other Athenians ferried themselves across from Salamis. Also joining the expedition were six hundred exiles from a second city occupied and torched by the invaders: Plataea. Now at last, a year after fleeing their homeland, the cherished moment of return had finally arrived. It was time for the Plataeans, and for everyone else committed to meeting with the barbarian, to take the road to Boeotia.

Heading northward, the allies duly left Eleusis. Soon enough, dusty ridges of limestone and slopes of mangy brushwood began to obstruct

---

*His remains were finally brought back to Sparta for reburial in 440 BC.

any backward glances at the sea. As the advance progressed, so the way ahead of the tramping hoplites turned increasingly rugged, the valleys lonely, the fir-dotted slopes of Mount Cithaeron even more so, the haunt not of men but of wild beasts, deer and bears and lions—and sometimes, for he loved all such deserted spots, of the great god Pan himself. In happier times, the Boeotians had been accustomed to celebrate an eerie festival, wheeling colossal idols of wood from the banks of the Asopus, hauling them all the way up the side of the mountain, and then, at the very summit, incinerating them, so that the conflagration might be seen for miles around, a beacon lit for the gods. The Plataeans, surely, passing beneath the austere heights of Mount Cithaeron, would have pressed ahead now with particular eagerness, for they were just hours away from their city; and the road, after winding past spurs and jagged crags, suddenly opened out, giving them, away to their left, a view at last of their beloved homeland.

But not as they had left it. Their fields were overgrown and their city a blackened shell. Trees for miles around had been leveled. Stripped and raw, the timbers now formed the barbarians' palisade. Meanwhile, the barbarians themselves, their numbers appearing to slur together in the shimmering heat, swarmed across the plain, and everywhere, it seemed, there were horses, whether hobbled, or in corrals, or else being ridden across the parched dirt of Boeotia, plume-shadowed as they flaunted their speed and proficiency. There could have been few among the Greeks who did not feel a tremor of consternation at such a sight; and Pausanias himself, who was arrogant but certainly not foolhardy, had not the slightest intention of crashing down directly to confront the enemy on ground so favorable to their cavalry. Instead, sternly ordering his men to keep to the foothills, he then maneuvered them into a position roughly opposite Mardonius' forces—not only above but some seven miles to the east of Plataea. For the city's six hundred hoplites, the return to what remained of their homes was evidently going to be delayed.

Yet, though Pausanias was proving himself to be cautious, it is unlikely that his first sight of the Persian forces had prompted anything like the alarm that Mardonius must have experienced when he looked up from the banks of the Asopus and saw the full scale of the army snaking across the foothills above him. His agents had certainly brought him some reports of the allied preparations. For days, the mood among the high command had been jittery. At a dinner party hosted by a prominent Theban collaborator, for instance, a Persian officer had turned to his Greek neighbor and whispered that of all the guests around them, and of all the troops camped beside the river, "you will see, in a short time, only a very few left alive."[47] Mardonius himself would never have admitted to such defeatism; but neither, not even at his most pessimistic, would he have imagined the ever-fractious allies capable of coordinating a task force such as was now being brought to bear against him on the lower slopes of Mount Cithaeron. On and on, throughout the day, the Greeks descended from the pass, taking up their positions, until, by the time that they were finally embedded, Mardonius found that he was staring at the largest hoplite army ever assembled in a single place: almost forty thousand men.[48]

Against these fearsome numbers, he himself could muster perhaps twice as many again; but he would have had no illusions that his infantry, only lightly armed and armored, could hope to overrun the Greek positions.[49] Instead, only two options appeared to give him any real prospect of victory. The first was somehow to lure the allies down to the plain, and then to trust that their various contingents, unaccustomed as they were to fighting side by side, would blunder apart and prove easy meat for his cavalry. The second was to sow divisions among the enemy ranks with a strategic deployment of bribes, and then to wait for the endemic rivalries that afflicted all Greek coalitions to take hold. Horsemen and spies: the deadliest weapons, as they had ever been, in the Persian armory.

And Mardonius, looking to coordinate their deployment, decided that his first move should be to resume the war of nerves that he had been waging all summer against the Athenians. The Spartans, it would soon emerge, had been right to suspect a canker of medizm in the refugee camps on Salamis. The murdered Lycidas had not been alone in his pro-Persian views. Other prominent citizens, ruined by the war, resentful of the democracy, hungering to restore their lost fortunes, had also been plotting; and not merely appeasement, but naked treachery. Mardonius, who had lost contact with these collaborators following his withdrawal from Attica, would surely have looked to reestablish communications with them as a matter of urgency; simultaneously, hoping to concentrate the traitors' minds even as he dispatched agents to infiltrate their camp, he ordered his cavalry to launch a hit-and-run raid on the allied lines.

A cunningly crafted pincer attack—except that it did not go entirely according to plan. First, far from demoralizing the Greeks, the cavalry raid served only to boost their morale: for the Persian commander, a hulking dandy who had ridden into battle sporting a purple tunic and an eye-catching cuirass of golden fish scales, had his Nisaean horse shot from under him and ended up dead and exposed on a wagon, being paraded before the gawking allied troops. Shortly afterward, the treachery in the Athenian camp was uncovered by Aristeides, who, deciding that he could hardly ignore the plot but not wishing to stick his nose too far into the ordure, contented himself with arresting only the eight most prominent conspirators.[50] Two of these fled; the other six, ordered to redeem themselves in the coming battle, were released without charge. Aristeides, who had himself been labeled a Mede-lover when ostracized, knew perfectly well what it was to be given a second chance. There was no more talk of treachery, from that moment on, in the Athenian camp.

Yet these setbacks, rather than crippling Mardonius' strategy, served ironically to give it a second wind. Pausanias, his spirits much boosted, felt sufficiently emboldened to take up a new position, much closer to the Asopus, and therefore to the enemy. Mardonius, hoping to catch the Greeks on open ground, immediately began to hurry along the opposite bank, shadowing them, waiting for a chance to strike. It never came. Pausanias, even as he inched onto the plain, had been sure to move sideways into the territory of Plataea, and there was not a spur along the route he took, not a stretch of elevated ground, but the Plataeans were able to guide the allies along it. By the time that their dispositions had been completed, the Spartans were dug in along a broken ridge on the right of the battle line, and the Athenians were installed on a hillock on the left. The remaining contingents, led by men whose clout could hardly compete with that of Pausanias or Aristeides when it came to securing the safest billets, had to be content with occupying the lower—and therefore more exposed—ground in the center. Mardonius, eyeing up his opportunities from the opposite side of the Asopus, must have felt a quickening of excitement. He may not yet have been in a position to launch a frontal attack—for the fields of Plataea, even at their flattest, still undulated menacingly—but if he could just tempt Pausanias to continue his advance across the river, the Persian cavalry would have him. Mardonius was a practiced Greek-fighter; he knew that the instinct of a hoplite army was always to seek out battle. So when the heavens themselves, speaking through incontrovertible omens, warned the Persian high command not to go on the attack, Mardonius was more than content to listen. Time appeared to be on the side of a policy of wait-and-see: barely five miles away, in Thebes, "food was in abundance, including fodder for the animals"[51] and Mardonius had reserves of treasure enough to flood the whole Greek camp with gold. He did as the gods had advised: he kept to the north bank; he did not cross the river.

But nor did Pausanias. Instead, blunting all Mardonius' expectations of how a Greek general would behave, he kept grimly to his position. The Spartans clung to their ridge, the Athenians to their hill, everyone else to the fields in between. Although squabbles would periodically erupt between the various contingents—and particularly when the Athenians started throwing their weight around—the feuding never escalated so as to threaten the alliance itself with disintegration. Indeed, far from fracturing, the Greek battle line grew ever stronger: for as first a day passed, and then another, and ultimately a whole week, reinforcements kept trickling in. Eventually, on the eighth day of the standoff, Mardonius lost his patience. His cavalry were ordered to make a raid on the Cithaeron passes. A huge wagon train, loaded down with provisions from the Peloponnese, was successfully ambushed. The drovers and mules alike were massacred. Then, leaving the corpses to litter the foothills where they would be clearly visible to the Greeks down on the plain, the Persians, "once they were sated of slaughter," drove the wagons back in triumph to their camp.[52]

Now it was Mardonius' turn to be emboldened. His cavalry, buoyed by their victory, began to launch raids directly on the enemy positions across the Asopus. Closing in on the Greeks whenever they ventured to approach the river, the wheeling horsemen would leave the shallows a havoc of drifting, feathered corpses, and the allied lines increasingly thirsty. A few hours of this, and the Asopus was abandoned entirely to the Persian cavalry. The only source of water left to the Greeks was now a single spring. As the sun blazed in the pitiless Boeotian sky, jostling lines of parched men began to crowd around the well, armed with buckets, jars and wine sacks. For the Athenians, in particular, the task of keeping themselves supplied with water was grueling: the spring, which rose just behind the Spartans' encampment, lay a full three-mile trudge away from their own. Yet at least it ensured that they could hold to their hill—and a strong defensive position, with the Persian hit-and-run tactics now being deployed directly along the whole Greek line, was one that the Athenians were reluctant to abandon. A day passed, however, and then a second; and the immobile Athenian infantry, stung and tormented by the ceaseless buzzing of the enemy, began to have second thoughts. Indeed, the bolder the Persians showed themselves, the more infuriated their stationary targets became: "for none of the Greeks could get to grips with the mounted archers."[53] Still the galloping, wheeling horsemen continued to test the limits of their own mobility until, on the third day of their harassing of the allied line, a contingent of Persians succeeded in outflanking it altogether. Rounding the ridge of broken hills on which the Spartans had embedded themselves, the cavalry erupted into the phalanx's rear. Ahead of them, directly in their path, lay the precious—and, it seems, unguarded—spring. Quickly, before the Greek reserves could arrive to stop them, the horsemen smashed the wells, choked the spring itself, and then withdrew in triumph. A hugely enterprising blow—and one fatal, of course, to all Pausanias' hopes of maintaining his forward line.

At a hurriedly convened council of war, the Greeks weighed the unappetizing options that now lay before them. To abandon their positions by daylight would clearly be tantamount to suicide: the Persian cavalry would cut them to ribbons. Yet to postpone a withdrawal would be just as disastrous: thirsty already, the Greeks were also starting to go hungry, as the barbarians, raiding the Cithaeron passes, continued their policy of plundering the allied food convoys. The obvious solution, despite all the monstrous risks of confusion that it would entail, was a retreat by night. Pausanias therefore instructed the various allied contingents that, come darkness, they were to withdraw two miles to a new line directly east of Plataea. Here, everyone agreed, their position would be infinitely stronger. The foothills would offer them excellent protection against cavalry. They would be well placed to secure the passes over Cithaeron. They would have plentiful supplies of water. Indeed, there was only one real drawback: the Greeks had to reach their new line first.

And that was no simple matter. In the center, where the soldiers of a whole host of different cities, stumbling through the night, were obliged to pick their way over thoroughly unfamiliar terrain, the retreat soon veered badly off course. Thirsty, hungry and nervous as they were, it was hardly surprising, perhaps, that they should have missed the appointed rendezvous and ended up instead over a mile to the west, almost directly before the ruins of Plataea, where "they scattered and pitched their tents at random."[54] Meanwhile, on the wings, the confusion was worse still. As the sky began to lighten, neither the Athenians nor, at the opposite end of the battle line, the Lacedaemonians and Tegeans had even begun their retreat. The three contingents, mandated to serve as rear guards, seem to have found themselves, due to the general chaos and the delay of their allies' withdrawal, stranded at their outposts throughout the night. And now birds were starting to sing along the river, and the enemy camped out on the opposite bank to stir.

The Athenians panicked. A horseman was sent galloping over the fields to the Spartan camp, to demand what was going on. Arriving there, he found Pausanias and his staff officers engaged in a furious discussion. What precisely was being debated would later be a matter of much controversy. Some would claim that Pausanias was facing direct insubordination: a Spartan officer by the name of Amompharetus was said to have insisted that retreat was no better than cowardice, and refused to obey his general's orders. A second tradition, however, commemorated the same officer as one of the three Spartans who fought with most distinction at Plataea: hardly an award that suggests a record of mutiny. Far from disobeying Pausanias' orders, then, it appears likeliest that Amompharetus had been demanding for his men the honor of a uniquely perilous mission: for with the sun about to rise, and the withdrawal of the Lacedaemonians and Tegeans still to begin, a division was desperately needed to hold the ridge until as late as possible. So it was that Amompharetus and his men, even as Pausanias gave the order for their Spartan comrades and the Athenians to start their retreat, remained where they were, shields and helmets at the ready, grimly resolved to hold their position for as long as they could. And already, fanning out from the far bank, horsemen could be seen splashing across the river and cantering toward their camp.

Carefully, the Persian scouts reconnoitered all the deserted allied positions. News of the enemy withdrawal, brought back to Mardonius where he waited with the infantry, was soon confirmed for him, as the sun rose, by the dramatic evidence of his own eyes. The fragmentation of the Greek battle line, the task that he had set himself from the start of the campaign, had been spectacularly achieved—and without his once having had to fight the enemy on their own terms. Most gratifyingly of all, the Spartans, the supposedly invincible, iron-souled Spartans, were still in open retreat, isolated from their allies, and as vulnerable as they would ever be. Risky, of course, to engage a phalanx in open battle—especially a Spartan phalanx—but Mardonius knew that he would never have a better chance to tear out the heart of the allied army. Already the window of opportunity was closing fast. Fail to seize the moment, and the Spartans would complete their rendezvous. So that Mardonius, climbing into the saddle of a towering white Nisaean stallion, gave the elite squads of infantry massed around him the fateful order to advance. They began to wade through the shallows of the Asopus. As they did so, all along the Persian battle line, banners were raised amid great cheering, and every unit in Mardonius' army, moving in disordered eagerness whether it was with their general's permission or not, surged forward down the riverbank.

And now, as the haze of dawn glimmered and was burned up by the rising sun, there shuddered through the Lacedaemonian ranks that "dense, bristling glitter of shields and spears and helmets" which had always served to alert warriors that a time of slaughter was approaching, and that the gods themselves were near. From beside the temple grove where he had ordered his men to halt and prepare for battle, Pausanias could see Amompharetus and his division retreating uphill with measured discipline, even as the Persian horsemen, massing behind them, came wheeling in pursuit. Pausanias had heard the savage cries of the barbarians from the river, and then watched them cross it in a monstrous, banner-swept tide. He knew that soon not only cavalry but the whole weight of Mardonius' elite infantry battalions would be assaulting his shield wall. Frantically, while he still had the chance, he sent a messenger to the Athenians, begging them to join him—but the message arrived too late. Even as Aristeides turned and began leading his men crab-wise toward the Lacedaemonian positions, he felt the earth shaking, and saw over his shoulder the battle line of the Thebans drawing down upon them. The clash of the two phalanxes rang across the battlefield; and confirmed Pausanias, a mile away to the east, in all his apprehensions of the worst.

True, there was some relief to be had in the breathless arrival of Amompharetus and his men; but there could be no hope now of any

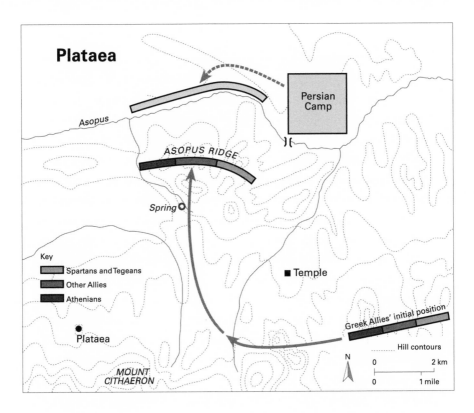

Plataea

Asopus

Persian Camp

ASOPUS RIDGE

Spring

Key
- Spartans and Tegeans
- Other Allies
- Athenians

Temple

Plataea

Greek Allies' initial position

MOUNT CITHAERON

N

Hill contours

0 — 2 km
0 — 1 mile

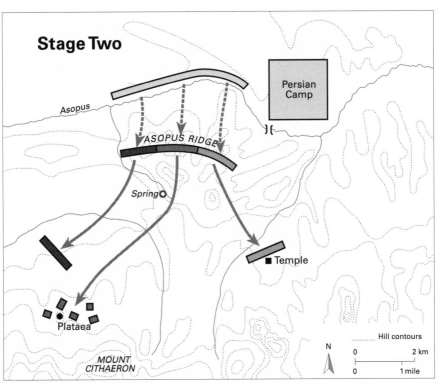

Stage Two

Asopus

Persian Camp

ASOPUS RIDGE

Spring

Temple

Plataea

MOUNT CITHAERON

N

Hill contours

0 — 2 km
0 — 1 mile

other reinforcements coming to swell the phalanx's numbers. Alone, then, the Spartans and the Tegeans would have to face Mardonius: 11,500 men against the elite of a superpower. Already, fired by the wheeling, darting Saka, arrows were rattling down upon their shield wall. Then, from behind the horsemen, barely visible through the hail of missiles, and all the more terrifying for it, the measured, thunderous approach of the barbarians' crack infantry divisions could be felt. Mardonius' cavalry withdrew; his infantry, maintaining their distance from the bristling phalanx, planted a wall of wicker shields; the rain of arrows began to thicken.

Still the cornered Greeks maintained their discipline. Holding up their shields, they listened from within their helmets to the eerily dimmed hiss and thud of ceaseless missiles all about them. Men began to stumble and fall, the arrows protruding from groins or shoulders bloody to the fletching; and now, every Lacedaemonian and Tegean began to think, was the time for the phalanx to make its charge across no man's land, to crash into the wall of flimsy wicker, to stab and trample its tormentors underfoot. But still Pausanias held back his warriors. Only once the approval of Artemis for the great enterprise of combat ahead of them had been clearly discerned in a blood sacrifice could he give the order to advance; and the goddess, no matter how many goats were slaughtered in her honor, refused to grant the Greeks her blessing. At last, in despair, Pausanias raised a prayer directly to the heavens, "and a moment later the victims, when they were sacrificed, promised success at last."[55] Just as well: for even as Pausanias was ordering the phalanx to advance, the Tegeans had already begun running toward the Persian lines—and a single Spartan with them. Of the Tegeans, who lacked the authentic Lycurgan discipline, such intemperance might, perhaps, have been expected; but not of Aristodemus, that graduate of the "*agoge*." And yet the "trembler"—even though he could hardly be honored for breaking from his place in the Spartan shield wall, for throwing himself single-handed upon the barbarians, for killing and being killed in a frenzy so berserk as to be barely Greek— had nevertheless, his messmates agreed later, redeemed his name.

Indeed, his courage would long be remembered by the men of other cities as something truly exceptional. To that extent, at least, it could be reckoned that Aristodemus had died a Spartan.

All the same, true glory in Sparta went to those who fought not in the cause of their own selfish honor but as links in a single machine; and great glory, that terrible morning, was won by every member of the phalanx. Only "Dorian spears, clotting the earth of Plataea with the butchery of a blood-sacrifice,"[56] could possibly have secured the victory; for only the men who grasped them had been steeled from birth to fight, to kill and never to yield. Descending the arrow-darkened slope of no man's land, smashing into the enemy's front line, the Spartans faced a test for which their whole lives had been preparation. Other men, perhaps, shoving against an enemy as teeming, as celebrated and as courageous as the Persians, would have found their spirits failing, their shield arms wearying, their bodies aching; but not the Spartans. Long though the battle appeared to hang in the balance, they did not cease to grind implacably forward. No matter that the Persians, in their growing desperation, sought to impede their enemy's advance by taking hold of the Spartans' spears and splintering them; swords were not so easily snapped, nor the weight of bronze-clad bodies stopped. Still Mardonius, "as brave as any Persian on the field,"[57] sought to rally his troops; but by now the Spartans were closing in on the elite that formed his bodyguard, and Mardonius himself, resplendent on his white charger, made for an easy target. A Spartan, picking up a stone, flung it at him, and the missile smashed into the side of his skull; and down from his saddle tumbled the cousin of the Great King, the man who had thought to be Satrap of Greece.

And the Persians, watching him fall, knew the battle lost. Mardonius' guardsmen, holding their ground heroically, were wiped out where they stood, but the remainder of the divisions, demoralized by the death of their charismatic general, began to run, and soon the rout was general over the battlefield. Forty thousand men, led by a quick-thinking officer, managed to escape northward onto the road to Thessaly, but most, stampeding in their panic, made for the fort, and the Lacedaemonians and Tegeans pursued them there. Soon enough, Pausanias was joined before the gates of the fort by the Athenians, whose bitter grudge match against the Thebans had ended with the medizers breaking and fleeing for their city. Now, together at last, the victorious allies forced the palisade. The massacre that followed was almost total: of the shattered remnants of Mardonius' army, barely three thousand were spared. And so ended the enterprise of the Great King against the West.

Gawking at the wealth and luxury displayed in Mardonius' camp, the Greeks again found themselves wondering why he had felt such a burning desire to conquer their land, when, self-evidently, he had more than enough already. One trophy, in particular, served to bring home to them the full, improbable scale of their victory: the King of King's own tent. Xerxes, it was said, leaving Greece the previous autumn, had granted to Mardonius the use of his campaign head-quarters; and so Pausanias, parting its embroidered hangings, walking over its perfumed carpets, took possession of what the previous year had been the nerve center of the world. Gazing in astonishment at the furnishings, the Regent pondered what it would be like to sit where the death of his uncle had been plotted; and so he ordered Mardonius' cooks to prepare him a royal dinner. When it was ready, he had a second dinner of Spartan black broth laid out beside it, and invited his fellow commanders to come in and admire the contrast. "Men of Greece," Pausanias laughed, "I have invited you so that you could appreciate for yourselves the irrational character of the Mede, who has a lifestyle such as you see here laid out before you, and yet who came here to our country to rob us of our wretched poverty."[58] A joke; and yet, of course, not wholly so. Freedom was no laughing matter. Few of the sweat-stained Greek commanders, gazing at the obscene luxury of the Great King's table and then comparing it with the bowls of simple soup, could have doubted to what the barbarians owed their defeat, and their own cities their liberty.

Meanwhile, beyond the tasseled doorways of the tent, the helots were hard at work, grubbing through the camp. Ordered by Pausanias to make a great pile of the loot, they lugged furniture out of tents, shoved golden plate into sacks, and pulled rings off the fingers of corpses. Naturally, they refrained from declaring all that they found; what they could, they salted away. With these scavengings, the helots hoped to secure their own liberty; but they were ignorant and backward, and so proved easy meat for con men. A consortium of Aeginetans, smelling an easy profit, managed to persuade the helots that their gold was brass, and paid for it accordingly. The helots, comprehensively ripped off, appear not to have won their freedom; but the Aeginetans, it is said, made a killing.

Hubris

Two stories were told of the parentage of Helen, the woman whose beauty had first plunged Europe and Asia into war. The best known claimed that she had been a Spartan, hatched from an egg after her mother, the queen, had been raped by Zeus in the form of a giant swan. A second, however, claimed that the queen of Sparta had only ever been the incubator, and that the egg itself had originally been laid by a quite different victim of Zeus' attentions: a goddess, no less, as solemn as she was mighty, as calm as she was fatal. In one hand, she held a bowl containing what was destined to be; in the other, a measuring rod, employed to gauge the scale of mortal excess. Those guilty of "overweening boastfulness" she would bring low.[59] None could withstand her, and the mightiest least of all. It was her habit, when she walked, to tread corpses underfoot. Her name was Nemesis.

Provoke her, and the world itself might be turned upside down. As evidence, the Greeks had always pointed to the career of Croesus, once so prosperous and smug that he had dared, until Nemesis took a hand in his career, "to suppose himself the happiest of men."[60] Yet not even that offense, rank though it was, could compare on a scale of horror with that of the Great King, the King of Kings, the King of Lands: the man whose goal it had been to make himself the master of all mankind. In Greek, only one word would serve to describe such lunatic behavior: "*hubris.*" "For this is the crime committed by any man who gains his thrills by trampling on other people, and feeling, as he does so, that he is proving himself pre-eminent."[61] An all too human failing, perhaps; and yet one to which barbarians, by their intemperate nature, and monarchs, by their rank, were peculiarly prone. The Greeks, who had always suspected this to be the case, now had, in Xerxes, their clinching proof. What had been the fruit, after all, of the Great King's staggering ambition, his unprecedented power, his armies, his fleets, his greatness? A record without parallel of offenses against Nemesis.

Her vengeance had been swift and sure. "This exploit is not ours," Themistocles, a man hardly given to modesty, and with much to be immodest about, had piously averred after Salamis.

> The gods, the heroes who guard our cities, they resented the impious presumption of the king: a man who was not content with the throne of Asia but sought the rule of Europe, too; who treated temples as though they were mere assemblages of bricks and mortar; who burned and toppled the statues of the gods; who even dared to whip the sea, and bind it up with chains.[62]

Treading the blood-manured fields of Plataea, surveying the tangled corpses of the Great King's finest fighting men, stripping his splendid tent bare, the conquerors of Mardonius could assert the same. All knew to whom the victory was owed. The goddess's handiwork was clear.

But she was not finished yet: one final twist remained. It had always been the practice—and the delight—of Nemesis to cause offenses to ricochet back upon their perpetrator. Now the Great King, far away in Sardis, was about to learn this lesson for himself. The previous summer, having torched the holy temples of the Acropolis, he had dared to vaunt his unspeakable crime by ordering beacons to blaze the news of it across the sea; Mardonius, capturing Athens a second time, had done the same. The beacons still stood; but now securely in Greek hands. Pausanias, ordering them lit, could ensure that the news of his victory would reach the coast of Ionia within a matter of hours. And this, it seems, is precisely what he did.[63]

It is hard otherwise to explain a haunting coincidence. Well over a hundred miles away from Plataea, on the far side of the Aegean, on the same day as the great victory, "a rumour suddenly flew through the ranks of the Greek fleet that their countrymen had beaten Mardonius in Boeotia."[64] The resulting surge of confidence among the crewmen could hardly have been better timed: for they too, that afternoon, faced an army of barbarians. Leotychides, after months of inactivity, had finally, a few days previously, ventured eastward out of his head-quarters and was now anchored in the great harbor of Samos, directly opposite the ridge of Mount Mycale. It was there, on the mountain's slope, that the Panionium stood, the ancient communal shrine of the Ionians; south, along the coast, lay devastated Miletus; and just off-shore from her harbors, in the bay, rose the island of Lade. Fateful scenes all, and clear evidence of Nemesis' hand: for in the war's beginning was its end.

Nor was it hard to discern the goddess's hand in the fact that the odds which had so favored the Persians fifteen years previously had now been dramatically reversed. The imperial war fleet, once the terror of the seas, had been sadly reduced from its wonted pomp. Its ships were battle scarred, its crews demoralized, its squadrons near mutinous. The Phoenicians, once its mainstay, had been dismissed from its ranks altogether. Leotychides, by contrast, had recently received a huge reinforcement in the form of the Athenian battle squadron: for Xanthippus, having kicked his heels on Salamis throughout the first half of the summer, had cheerfully set out for Delos the moment that Pausanias was confirmed to have left the Isthmus. As a result, the Allies—in a startling turnaround from the previous summer—now possessed the advantage of numbers. Scanning the horizon nervously, the Persian admirals had only had to glimpse the Greek fleet bearing down on them to jump ship. Landing directly in the shadow of Mount Mycale, they had hauled their triremes onto a beach, frantically improvised a stockade out of boulders and apple trees, and barricaded themselves inside it.

And it was this same stockade that Leotychides, on the day of the Battle of Plataea, decided to attack. Noon, and a wisp of smoke began to rise on the western horizon, soon to be answered by a beacon blazing into life on the heights of Samos. Meanwhile, marines—Athenian, Corinthian and Troezenian—were landing on the beach near the Persians' makeshift fort. The defenders, cheered by the small size of the allied assault force, emerged from behind their palisade; and the Greeks immediately charged them. A desperate fight ensued, with the Persians fighting bravely from behind a makeshift wall of shields; but in the end, as at Marathon and Plataea, the hoplites rolled them over. Meanwhile, Leotychides, having disembarked with the Peloponnesians in the rear of the palisade, gained sweet revenge for Thermopylae by emerging suddenly from a foothill of Mount Mycale and completing the rout. Only a fraction of the Persian garrison escaped to Sardis. The fort and all the ships lined up inside it were abandoned. Leotychides, having been sure first to pillage everything he could, torched the Persian fleet that same evening. No longer fighting in defense of their own soil, the Greeks had now gone successfully on the attack. Dusk settled over Ionia, and fires lit on the edge of Asia flickered throughout the night.

"Many are the marks of evidence which prove the hand of the goddess in the affairs of mortal men."[65] To the Greeks, it seemed a miracle that they should have prevailed twice on the same day over what was still, after all, the world's superpower. Leotychides himself could barely credit it. Even back on Samos, having left the Persian fleet to burn across the straits, he and his fellow admirals continued to dread the wrath of the King of Kings. Surely, they imagined, his vengeance was bound to strike at any moment. But it did not. Instead, some weeks after Mycale, it was reported that Xerxes, "in a state of bewilderment,"[66] had left Sardis altogether, and was taking the long road back to Susa. With him was going most of his army. A raiding party, dispatched from Sardis, did manage to land a blow on that favorite Persian punching bag, the holy shrine at Didyma, and once again cart off a statue of Apollo; but otherwise there was little action from the barbarians. A year passed, and then another; and still the Great King did not return.

This inactivity led to much conjecture among the Greeks. Cowardice, effeminacy and softness were all adduced as plausible explanations. The notion of the barbarians' decadence, which would have struck everyone as preposterous before Marathon, now began to be regarded by most Greeks as a simple fact. Nor was it merely the failure of the Persians to launch a third invasion which increasingly nourished this comforting prejudice. Everything about Xerxes' invasion which had struck the Greeks as so terrifying at the time—the teeming numbers of the Great King's hordes, the limitless resources at his fingertips, the wealth, the show, the spectacle, the extravagance of his train—all, in hindsight, appeared merely to have marked him out as effete. Conquerors of Asia the Persians may have been; but they might as well have been women when measured against the free-born, bronze-clad men of Greece.

Some even began to wonder if the bloody repulse that the Great King had suffered had doomed his regime altogether. One of these optimists was an Athenian by the name of Aeschylus—a man who had every reason to nurture such a hope. A veteran of both Marathon and Salamis, he had also suffered a bitter personal loss at the hands of the barbarians: for it was his brother who had clung to one of the ships moored off Marathon, and had his wrist hacked off by an ax. Well might Aeschylus have dreamed of the implosion of Persian power. In 472 BC, eight years after Salamis, he gave his optimism a truly visionary rendering at the City Dionysia, the Athenians' annual drama contest. As the audience, assembling in the shadow of the Acropolis, milled into the theater, they would have seen, wherever they gazed, scars and reminders of their city's recent ordeal. Behind them, on the sacred rock, the silhouette remained one of devastation still: for the allies—Athenians included—had vowed before taking the field against

Mardonius that any temple burned by the barbarians was to be left forever as a ruin, "to serve as witness for generations yet to come."[67] The bleachers on which the audience took their seats had been fashioned, almost certainly, out of timbers salvaged from the shattered barbarian fleet; while on the stage itself, it has been plausibly suggested, there may have stood that most spectacular of all battle trophies: the captured royal tent.[68] If so, then the leather that had once sheltered the King of Kings now provided an awning over the stage of the Dionysia—and the perfect backdrop for the tragedy that Aeschylus had titled *The Persians*.

Set in Susa, it offered, for the delectation of the Athenian people, a dramatic reconstruction of Xerxes' return home from Salamis. The king who had left Persia in the full pomp of his majesty was portrayed limping back in rags; the courtiers who had thought to hail a conquering hero were heard wailing in misery. All most enjoyable—and comforting—for the audience, of course. The Great King was indeed cowed, Aeschylus reassured his fellow citizens; and Athens, the city which had defeated him, was now a beacon of liberty to nations everywhere. "For the people of Asia will not endure to remain the slaves of Persia for long; to be strong-armed into paying tribute to their master; to prostrate themselves before him on the ground. Kingship itself and all its power are dead."[69] The world, in other words, had been made safe for Athens—and for democracy. No wonder that Aeschylus should have scooped first prize.

Even as he celebrated his victory, though, his fellow citizens would not have been left entirely purged of a residual fear. It was all very well for Aeschylus to claim that Salamis had left the Great King "denuded of men capable of defending him,"[70] but why, in that case, were Persian garrisons still in Thrace and beside the Hellespont? What were they doing in Sardis? How could they be in every capital of every satrapy, to the limits of the rising of the sun? Far from tottering, the empire of the Great King in truth remained on foundations as solid and formidable as ever. That the mighty edifice had received the odd chip to its western facade was indisputable, but few within the vast extent of the empire would have realized even that. The Great King, after all, was hardly in the habit of broadcasting his failures. If his subjects had ever heard of Athens, then it was only as a city that their master had put to the torch. If they had ever heard of the Spartans, then it was only as a people whose king their master had killed in battle. "May Ahura Mazda, and all the gods, protect me. And may he protect my kingdom. And may he protect all that I have laboured to build."[71] So Xerxes was in the habit of praying. And who was to say that Ahura Mazda did not listen to him still?

But Aeschylus, imagining "the people of Asia" restless beneath the Persian yoke, had not been indulging entirely in wishful thinking. Why, after all, had the Great King hurried away from Sardis—and why exactly had he failed to return? The solution to the mystery lay far distant from Greece, in that cockpit of the Near East, Babylon. There, late in the campaigning season of 479 BC, even as Xerxes was being brought the disastrous news of Plataea and Mycale, a fresh revolt had broken out.[72] The Great King, to his horror, had found himself caught between two fronts. Abandoning his campaign on the fractious periphery of his empire, Xerxes had sped back to its heartland—where the insurrection, sure enough, had been easily suppressed. Babylon, taught its lesson once and for all, had remained quiescent from that moment onward. But Xerxes himself, it appears, despite the successful pacification of the rebellion, had also absorbed a painful lesson. Cyrus, Cambyses and Darius had all taken it for granted that the frontiers of Persian dominion would prove infinite. Darius, in particular, that devout and cynical autocrat, had proclaimed that he was entrusted not merely with the right but with a sacred duty to subdue the Lie wherever he found it, to the very limits of the world. At least as pious in the worship of Ahura Mazda as his father, Xerxes had inherited this sense of global mission along with the imperial tiara. This, after all, was why he had led the invasion of the West. But that invasion had failed; and the chariot of the Lord Mazda, ridden with such awful ceremony along the pontoon over the Hellespont, had ended up stolen by a gang of Thracian brigands and dumped in a field.

To the Greeks, the bridging of Asia and Europe, and the desire to rule both continents, had always seemed the most fatal of the Great King's follies; and perhaps, in his heart of hearts, Xerxes had come to agree. Certainly, there would be no more attempts to conquer Europe following his return from Sardis. It was Xerxes, of all Persia's kings, who had been obliged to accept an uncomfortable truth, and one that for once was not synonymous with his own country's order: that even the mightiest empires can suffer from overstretch.

Imperial forces had not given up the fight in the Aegean—but they were no longer in the vanguard of a scheme of global conquest. The Great King's defeat in the West had dealt a fatal blow to that vaunting dream. Persian ambitions were now infinitely more modest: merely to stabilize control of Ionia. Even when basking in the afterglow of the victory at Mycale, Leotychides had recognized that this would be the Great King's policy, and he dreaded the inability of the Greeks to stand in its way. But when he had proposed the transplanting of the Ionians from their cities and their resettlement on the mainland, Xanthippus had exploded with indignation. He had protested that it was not for the Spartans to propose the dissolution of what were, originally, Athenian colonies; and he had pledged his city eternally to the defense of Ionian freedom. "And after he and his fellow citizens had expressed themselves with great vigour, the Peloponnesians at length gave way."[73]

So it was that the ethnic cleansing of the Greeks from Asia was postponed for 2400 years, until the era of Atatürk; and the claim of Athens to the command of the continued war against Persia was made explicit. One year later and it was formalized as well. An alliance was legally constituted, with its treasury on Apollo's sacred island of Delos, and subscription fees measured in either ships or cash. The Ionians, the islanders, the Greeks of the Hellespont: almost all signed up. With the added muscle that this new Delian League provided them, the Athenians could now take the attack directly to the barbarian. Throughout the 470s BC, Persian garrisons in Thrace and around the Hellespont were systematically reduced. The following decade witnessed even more spectacular successes. Led by Cimon, the dashing son of Miltiades, the Athenians swept the enemy from the Aegean, and fostered rebellion throughout Ionia and Caria. The climax of these triumphs came in 466 BC, when Cimon, confronted by the largest concentration of Persian forces to have been marshaled since the year of Salamis, won a sensational double victory. First, gliding into the mouth of the Eurymedon, a river in the south of what is now Turkey, he wiped out an entire Phoenician fleet. Next, landing his weary marines on shore, he inflicted the same treatment upon the imperial army. It was this battle, once and for all, that destroyed any lingering prospect of a third Persian invasion. Security had been won for Greece at last. The great war, in effect, was over.

But Athens, the city that had secured the victory at the Eurymedon, appeared to shrink from a sense of her own achievement: as though she could not bear to abandon a struggle that had served for thirty long years to define her. So that Persia, in the prayers offered up by the Assembly, continued to be named as the national enemy. So too that the Athenians, having run the Persians out of the Aegean but still addicted to making war on them, voted to hunt them down in foreign fields. In 460, a huge armada was dispatched to Cyprus and Egypt. Six years of fighting later, it had been comprehensively wiped out. The Athenians, in a panic that the barbarians might now come sweeping back into the Aegean, hurriedly removed the headquarters of the league from Delos to their own city. Even when the Persians failed to materialize in Greek waters, the treasury remained on the Acropolis. Naturally, just as they had always done, the Athenians required that subscriptions to the league be paid in full. Liberty, as they pointed out, did not come cheap. But many of the increasingly disgruntled allies began to mutter that Athenian-sponsored freedom was proving a good deal more expensive than slavery to the King of Kings had ever been.

That a Greek pledged to the overthrow of Persian despotism might himself start to ape the manners of a Persian was not, in the decades that followed the great invasion, a wholly novel paradox. Pausanias, for instance, giddy with conceit, had become a notorious enthusiast for barbarian chic. His countrymen, appalled to see a general of the Spartan people swanning around on campaign sporting the trousers of a satrap, had grown increasingly suspicious of their erstwhile hero. A mere decade after Plataea, the ephors accused him of plotting to overthrow the state. Pausanias, taking sanctuary inside the bronze-walled temple on the Spartan acropolis, was walled up there to starve; only at the very last moment was his emaciated body hauled out, so that his death would not pollute the shrine. The man who had laughed at the wealth of the Great King's table only himself to develop a gluttonous taste for Persian haute cuisine duly expired of hunger.

Nemesis, as ever, had proved herself both merciless and witty; and just to emphasize that hubris might prove a failing of Greeks as well as of barbarian kings, she had dragged down, in the weeks that followed Pausanias' wretched end, a hero greater even than the Regent. Themistocles, hated ever since Salamis for having been so persistently and spectacularly right, had already, by 470 BC, been ostracized by his resentful fellow citizens. Now, implicated in Pausanias' treachery, he had fled Greece altogether. After wanderings and adventures worthy of Odysseus, he had finally ended up in Susa, where Xerxes' son, the new Great King, had exulted in the capture of his father's most formidable enemy. "The subtle serpent of Greece,"[74] now that he was defanged, had proved a great favorite of his new master; and all the brilliant qualities of his intellect, once so fatal to Persian ambitions, had been put to the Great King's service. Dispatched to the western front, Themistocles had settled just inland from Miletus, where he had issued coins and run an army, just like any satrap. He passed his final days advising the court in Sardis on how best to resist the encroachments of his own countrymen. And so it was, as a royal servitor and as a traitor, that Themistocles, in 459 BC, finally breathed his last.

An unsettling precedent: that the savior of Greece should have ended up the enemy of liberty. Even in exile, it seemed to many, Themistocles continued to serve as a model to his city. For increasingly, throughout the 450s BC, cities freed from barbarian rule found their sense of gratitude toward Athens darkening into envy, suspicion and dread. They could see little difference between the tribute that they had once paid to Susa and the subscription that they were now obliged to send to the Acropolis. Already, in the 460s BC, cities that had attempted to secede from the league had found themselves being visited by the Athenian fleet. So too, in the following decade, had cities not even in the alliance. In 457, for instance, the Athenians put paid to half a century of rivalry by investing their old rival Aegina, dismantling her walls, confiscating her fleet—and then inviting her to join the league. An offer which the wretched Aeginetans could hardly refuse—and of which even the most imperious Oriental despot might have been proud. Men began to recall the first arrival of Athens to her empire as a moment both ominous and fateful: for Xanthippus, it was said, having sailed north from the Battle of Mycale, had moored off the Hellespont, seized the cables from Xerxes' bridge as plunder, and then nailed a captured Persian alive to a plank. This crucifixion, looming ever larger in people's memories, began to seem sufficient to cast all Greece into its shadow.

And yet the Athenians themselves knew better. Great though their city had become, and powerful, and rich, they never forgot for a moment what she had passed through, what braved, to win such preeminence. "Bulwark of Greece, famous Athens, city of godlike men": the world that she put in her shadow she also illuminated with her glory. Literally so: for a sailor rounding Cape Sunium might look toward "the shining city, violet-crowned, famous in song,"[75] and see, at a distance of thirty miles, a brilliant flash of light. This was the reflection of the sun upon a burnished spear, held in the grip of a colossal Athena, some thirty-five feet tall, who stood, heroic and beautiful, on the summit of the Acropolis, guarding the entrance to the rock, her gaze serenely fixed in the direction of Salamis. Fashioned out of plunder seized from the barbarians, funded by members of the league and crafted by Phidias, the greatest Athenian sculptor of his day, the bronze rendered physical the whole triumphant course of the democracy's history. A statue of liberty indeed.

And why not, the Athenians began to wonder, of Greek brotherhood as well? In 449 BC, a direct accommodation was reached at last with the barbarians, bringing to a conclusive end, after half a century of warfare, all hostilities between the Great King and his greatest enemy.[76] In the same year, an invitation was issued by the Athenians to the cities of Greece and Ionia, requesting them to send delegates to a congress on the Acropolis.[77] The ostensible purpose of this proposed conference was to discuss whether the temples burned by the barbarians might now acceptably be rebuilt. But there was also, hovering over it, an altogether more elevated goal. "Let everyone come and join in the debate on the best way to secure peace and prosperity for Greece,"[78] the invitation declared. An idealistic appeal—and one that invoked, in the first months of the peace with Persia, the spirit of the Athenians' finest hour. "We are all Greeks," Aristeides had proudly asserted to the Spartan ambassadors, back in 479 BC, when countering the accusation that his city might side with Mardonius. "We all share the same blood, the same language, the same temples, the same holy rituals. We all share the one common way of life. It would be a terrible thing for Athens ever to betray this heritage."[79] And the Athenians, rather than do so, had lived up to Aristeides' stirring words, and seen their city burn. The evidence of their sacrifice could still be seen cracked and blackened across the Acropolis. Why, the Athenians demanded now, did it require the barbarian to remind the Greeks that they were all Greek? Why could not their own example serve to inspire an era of universal amity and peace?

The Peloponnesians, led by Sparta, responded with scorn. Who exactly, they sneered, was to lead the cities of Greece into this promised golden age? The answer envisaged by the Athenians had been implicit in their invitation: cities that sent delegates to the Acropolis would effectively be ceding the primacy to Athens. Sparta, inevitably, refused point-blank to do so. Her allies in the Peloponnese dutifully did the same. The conference was aborted. Shrugging off this setback, Athens responded by tightening the screws on those that she could force to do her will. The war with Persia might have been brought to a close, but the Athenians were in no mood to see the league dissolved just because peace had come to the Aegean. Any hint of recalcitrance from a member state, still more open rebellion, and their crackdown would be merciless. The subscriptions sent to the Acropolis, now nakedly revealed as tribute, continued to be extorted every year. The very word "allies," having become hopelessly outdated, was replaced by the phrase "cities subject to the Athenian people"—a description that at least had the merit of accuracy. Far from being united, the Greek world found itself divided instead into rival power blocs, each one led by a city that put her dependants humiliatingly in the shade, and justified her hegemony by boasting loudly of her record in the defense of liberty.

For Athens was not the only city which laid claim to the title of savior of Greece. In the balance, Sparta, her former ally, and now increasingly bitter rival, could set Plataea and—above all—Thermopylae. To the rest of Greece, the Spartans remained peerless as models of heroism and virtue; and nothing, not even their most splendid victories, had done more to cement this reputation than the memory of the three hundred and their exemplary defeat. "Go tell them in Sparta, O passer-by / That here, in obedience to their orders, we lie."[80] These lines, carved on a simple stone memorial, could be read on the site of the famous last stand: an epitaph as laconic and stern as Leonidas himself. As immortal as well—for Thermopylae, of all the battles fought against the armies of the Great King, was the one most gloriously transfigured into legend. Yet the Athenians—as brilliant, as eloquent, as quick-witted as their Spartan opposites were sober—would nevertheless trump its memory. Late in 449 BC, a portentous motion was brought before the Assembly. Only a few months previously Sparta had refused to send her delegates to Athens and agree that the burned temples could be reconstructed; now the Athenians voted on the issue without reference to the opinion of the rest of Greece. The proposal to rebuild the monuments on the Acropolis was thunderously passed. Plans for a spectacular makeover of the sacred rock were put into immediate effect.

Such a scheme had been long in the preparation. The mover behind it was a Eupatrid grandee by the name of Pericles, a seasoned political operator who had first demonstrated his passion for eye-catching cultural projects by sponsoring, back in 472 BC, Aeschylus' celebrated tragedy on the Persians. Pericles certainly brought an unrivaled pedigree to his taste for *grands projets*: the son of Xanthippus, he was also, on his mother's side, an Alcmaeonid. This meant, of course, that he was the heir to a long family tradition of sponsoring monuments on the Acropolis; but no Alcmaeonid had ever been presented with an opportunity such as Pericles was grasping now. The barbarian holocaust had ravaged the entire summit of the rock, so that it was not a single temple but the whole Acropolis that Pericles was planning to rebuild. By employing the cream of Athenian talent, including the great sculptor Phidias, he aimed to raise, as he put it, "marks and monuments of our city's empire" so perfect that "future ages will wonder at us, as the present age wonders at us now."[81] In 447 BC, work began on a temple designed to be the most sumptuous and beautiful ever built. Subsequent generations would know it as the Parthenon.*

However, bold and original though all the new monuments on the Acropolis were destined to be, they still had their foundations deep in the bedrock of what had gone before. The Parthenon, for instance, that daring monument to the new age of Athenian greatness, was being raised on the scorched base of an older, unfinished building: the great temple that had been begun in the 480s BC as a celebration of the victory at Marathon. Now, with his plans for the Acropolis, Pericles was looking to enshrine the memory of Marathon for all eternity. Remembrances of the battle were to be everywhere on the sacred rock. Whether in the ground plan of the Parthenon itself, or in trophies raised to the victory, or in friezes illustrating the fighting, the greatest moment in Athenian history was to be celebrated with a brilliance that would proclaim Athens not merely the savior of Greece, but her school and mistress, too.

---

*What the temple was called in the time of Pericles is unknown.

For those who had fallen at Marathon were not altogether dead. Leave behind the dust and din of the building site on the Acropolis in the morning, and an Athenian might reach the battlefield by nightfall. There, silhouetted against the stars, he would see the great tumulus which had been raised over the honored ashes of the slain, and beside it a more recent monument, lovingly crafted out of white marble, barely a decade old. The most potent, and the eeriest, memorial, however, could not be seen—only heard. Every night, it was said, ghostly across the plain, strange sounds of fighting would disturb the midnight calm: the ringing of metal, the hiss of arrows, war cries, trampling, screams. No other field of battle that had been contested with the barbarians could boast of such a visitation; and an Athenian, although he would have dreaded to approach the phantoms, would perhaps have found in their presence a certain source of civic pride. They had been actors, after all, in the greatest drama in history—when Athens had stood alone and preserved the liberty of all Greece. "For they were the fathers not merely of children, of mortal flesh and blood, but of their children's freedom, and of the freedom of every person who dwells in the continent of the West."[82] Everything stemmed from Marathon; everything was justified by it, too.

Beyond the plain, with its monuments, graves and ghosts, the road wound on northward, leading over empty hills to a single temple on a slope above the sea. This was Rhamnus, where it was said that Zeus, having pursued Nemesis across the whole world, had finally brought her to earth. From that one rape had been hatched Helen, the Trojan War and all the long, violent story of hatred between East and West. It had brought Datis the Mede and his great armada to Marathon, barely five miles to the south; "and so sure was he that nothing could stop him from taking Athens that he had brought with him a block of marble, from which he intended to carve a trophy in celebration of his victory."[83] After the defeat of his expedition, the block of marble had been found abandoned on the battlefield; and so the locals had hauled it off to Rhamnus. No better place for it could have been imagined—for the temple that stood there above the slope that led down to the sea was sacred to Nemesis herself. It was clearly her anger that had doomed the barbarians' expedition; and so plans had been made to build a second temple to her, and as a memorial to Marathon. It was intended to fashion the marble into a likeness of the goddess. The great Phidias had been asked to carve it. As on the Acropolis, so at Rhamnus, an Athenian might aim to glimpse the future. If he arrived where the marble block stood, waiting to be carved, he might easily imagine that he could see within the spectral purity of its whiteness a foreshadowing of the sculpture that was to be; that he was catching a glimpse of the face of Nemesis herself.

Envoi

In 431 BC, the growing tensions between Athens and Sparta finally erupted into open hostilities. The ensuing struggle, which the Athenians called "the Peloponnesian War," lasted on and off for twenty-seven years. It ended in 404 BC with the total defeat of Athens. Her empire was dismantled, her fleet destroyed and her democracy suspended. Although in the following century she would stage a spectacular recovery, Athens would never again be the predominant power in Greece.

Nor, after 371 BC, would Sparta. One hundred and eight years after Pausanias had won his great victory over Mardonius, the Spartan army was brought to sensational defeat by the Thebans at the village of Leuctra, barely five miles from Plataea. The Thebans, pressing home their advantage, then invaded Lacedaemon. The Peloponnesian League was abolished. Messenia was freed. Sparta, deprived of her helots, was reduced overnight from being the hegemon of Greece to a middle-ranking power.

Over the following decades, the Greek cities would continue to tear themselves apart. Meanwhile, to the north, a new predator was readying itself for the murderous struggle to be the greatest power in Greece. In 338 BC, King Philip II of Macedon, following in the footsteps of Xerxes, swept southward into Boeotia. An army of Athenians and Thebans, attempting to bar his way, was cut to pieces. "We lie here because we strove to give freedom to Greece." So it was written on the tomb of the fallen. "The glory we enjoy will never age."[1] Proud words—but not even the most stirring epitaph could obscure the grim reality that Greek independence had effectively been brought to an end. Four years later, and Philip's son, Alexander, crossed the

371

Hellespont to assault the Persian Empire. Now it was the turn of the Great King to have his power humbled into the dust. Three great battles in succession were lost to the invader. Babylon fell. Persepolis was burned. The last King of Kings suffered a squalid and thirst-racked death. Alexander laid claim to the *kidaris* of Cyrus, and to an empire that stretched from the Adriatic to the Indus.

For the first time, Greece and Persia acknowledged the rule of a single master.

Even Nemesis, perhaps, might have permitted herself a smile.

Timeline

All dates are BC.

c. 1250: The Trojan War.

c. 1200: The destruction of the royal palaces at Mycenae and Sparta.

c. 1200–1000: The migration of the Dorians into the Peloponnese.

c. 1000–800: The migration of the Medes and Persians into western Iran.

814: The foundation of Carthage.

750–700: The Assyrian kings establish their control over the Medes of the Zagros.

c. 750–650: Sparta invades and conquers Messenia.

c. 670: The loss of Assyrian control over Media.

632: The failure of Cylon's attempt to become tyrant of Athens.

612: The Medes and Babylonians sack Nineveh.

608: The final collapse of the Assyrian Empire.

600: The exile of the Alcmaeonids from Athens.

594: Solon becomes archon.

586: Nebuchadnezzar sacks Jerusalem.

585: Astyages becomes King of Media. A peace treaty is signed with Lydia after an indecisive war.

566: Inauguration of the Great Panathenaea.

560: The first tyranny of Pisistratus. The return of the Alcmaeonids to Athens.

559: Cyrus becomes King of Persia.

556: Nabonidus becomes King of Babylon.

555: The second tyranny and exile of Pisistratus.

550: Cyrus conquers Media.

546: Cyrus conquers Lydia. The "Battle of the Champions" between Sparta and Argos. The Battle of Pallene: the third tyranny of Pisistratus; the Alcmaeonids return into exile.

545–540: Cyrus pushes into Central Asia.

539: Cyrus conquers Babylonia.

529: The death of Cyrus. Cambyses becomes King of Persia.

527: The death of Pisistratus. Hippias and Hipparchus become the tyrants of Athens.

525: Cambyses invades and conquers Egypt.

522: Bardiya revolts against Cambyses. The death of Cambyses. Darius and six accomplices assassinate Bardiya. Darius becomes King of Persia and puts down a revolt in Babylon.

521: Darius suppresses widespread rebellions across the empire.

520: Cleomenes becomes King of Sparta.

519: Athens at war with Thebes in defense of Plataea.

514: The assassination of Hipparchus.

513: Darius invades Scythia.

512–511: The Persian conquest of Thrace.

510: The expulsion of Hippias from Athens.

508: Isagoras becomes archon. Cleisthenes proposes democratic reforms.

507: The exile of Cleisthenes from Athens. Cleomenes and Isagoras are besieged on the Acropolis. Cleisthenes returns from exile and implements his reforms. Athenian ambassadors give earth and water to Artaphernes.

506: The defeat of Cleomenes' invasion of Attica. Athens is victorious over Thebes and Chalcis.

499: The failure of the Persian attack on Naxos. Aristagoras leads an Ionian revolt and travels to Greece in search of support.

498: The Ionians, with Athenian and Eretrian support, burn Sardis.

497: The death of Aristagoras.

494: The Ionians are defeated at the Battle of Lade. Argos is defeated by Cleomenes at the Battle of Sepeia. The sack of Miletus.

493: Themistocles becomes archon. Miltiades escapes from the Chersonese to Athens.

492: The trial and acquittal of Miltiades. Mardonius conquers Macedonia.

491: Darius' ambassadors tour Greece to demand earth and water; those who visit Athens and Sparta are put to death.

490: Datis and Artaphernes lead an expedition across the Aegean. Eretria is sacked. The Battle of Marathon.

487: The first ostracism in Athens.

486: Rebellion in Egypt. The death of Darius. Xerxes becomes the King of Persia.

485: Gelon becomes the tyrant of Syracuse.

484: Xanthippus is ostracized. Rebellion in Babylon.

483: A rich vein of silver is found in the mines at Laurium.

482: Aristeides is ostracized. Athens votes to build two hundred triremes.

481: Xerxes arrives in Sardis. A congress of Greek cities determined
   to resist the Persian invasion meets at Sparta. Envoys are
   sent to Gelon. Spies are sent to Sardis.

480: Envoys return empty-handed from Gelon. Xerxes crosses the
   Hellespont. The Athenians vote to evacuate their city.
   The battles of Thermopylae and Artemisium. The Battle
   of Himera. Athens is occupied and burned. The Battle of
   Salamis. Xerxes retreats to Sardis. Mardonius remains in
   Thessaly.

479: Athens is occupied a second time. The battles of Plataea and
   Mycale. Revolt in Babylon. Xerxes leaves Sardis.

472: Aeschylus stages *The Persians*.

470: Themistocles is ostracized.

469: The death of Pausanias. The flight of Themistocles to Susa.

466: The Battle of Eurymedon.

460: Athens sends an expedition to Cyprus and Egypt.

459: The death of Themistocles.

457: Aegina is forced to join the Delian League.

454: Destruction of the Athenian expedition to Egypt. The treasury
   of the Delian League is moved from Delos to the
   Acropolis.

449: Peace is signed between Athens and Persia. The Peloponnesians
   refuse an Athenian invitation to a pan-Greek conference.
   The Athenians vote to rebuild the burned temples on the
   Acropolis.

447: Work begins on the Parthenon.

Notes

Unless otherwise stated, author citations refer to the following texts: Aelian, *Miscellany*; Aeschylus, *The Persians*; Aristides, *Aelius Aristides Orationes*, ed. W. Dindorf (Leipzig, 1829); Athenaeus, *The Learned Banquet*; Cicero, *On Divination*; Ctesias, *Fragments*; Diodorus Siculus, *The Library of History*; Diogenes Laertius, *The Lives and Doctrines of Eminent Philosophers*; Herodotus, *Histories*; Pausanias, *Description of Greece*; Polyaenus, *Stratagems*; Quintus Curtius, *The History of Alexander*; Strabo, *The Geography*; Thucydides, *History of the Peloponnesian War.*

Preface

1 From bin Laden's "Declaration of war against the Americans occupying the land of the two holy places," quoted by Burke, p. 163.
2 Gibbon, Vol. 3, p. 1095.
3 Herodotus, 1.4.
4 Ibid., 1.5. Literally, "the Persians and the Phoenicians."
5 Herodotus has long been derided as a fantasist: the father not of history but of lies. The past few decades have brought about a fundamental reappraisal of his accuracy: again and again, archaeological discoveries have demonstrated the reliability of his claims. A brief but excellent survey can be found in Stephanie Dalley's article "Why did Herodotus not mention the Hanging Gardens of Babylon?," in Derow and Parker (eds.), *Herodotus and His World*. For the counterview, still not entirely routed, that Herodotus invented much of his story, see Fehling.
6 Herodotus, 1.1.
7 J. S. Mill, p. 283.
8 G. W. F. Hegel, *The Philosophy of History*, 2.2.3.
9 Herodotus: 7.228.
10 M. de Montaigne, "On the Cannibals," in *The Complete Essays*, p. 238.
11 Lord Byron, "The Isles of Greece," l. 7.
12 W. Golding, "The Hot Gates," in *The Hot Gates*, p. 20. It was reading this essay

at the impressionable age of twelve that first inspired me with a passion for the story of the Persian Wars.

13 Quoted by David, p. 208.
14 Aeschylus, 104–5.
15 Curzon, Vol. 2, pp. 195–6.
16 "The historical record of the Imperial visit to India, 1911" (London, 1914), pp. 176–7.
17 Green, p. xxiii.
18 Murdoch, p. 171.
19 Starr (1977), p. 258.
20 Ehrenberg, p. 389.
21 Or, to be strictly accurate, since the author, François Ollier, was French, *Le Mirage Spartiate*.
22 Plutarch, in his youthful and uncharacteristically splenetic essay "On the malignity of Herodotus."
23 Davidson (2003).

I The Khorasan Highway

1 The annals of Ashurnasirpal, Column 1.53, trans. Budge and King, p. 272. The phrase refers to Ashurnasirpal's campaigns in the mountains north of Assyria.
2 Quoted by Kuhrt (1995), p. 518.
3 That the Aryans arrived in the Zagros from the east is almost universally accepted, although hard proof is hard to come by. A minority view asserts that the Medes and Persians entered the Zagros from the north, over the Caucasus.
4 From the campaign records of Shalmaneser III (843 BC); see Herzfeld, p. 24.
5 The precise geographical limits of Media between the ninth and seventh centuries BC are unclear. According to Levine (*Iran* 12, p. 118), it was most likely "a narrow strip restricted to the Great Khorasan Road."
6 Nahum, 3.3.
7 This account of the Median Empire depends heavily—and inevitably—on the testimony of Herodotus, who wrote more than a century after the events he was describing. The broad outline of his narrative appears to have been confirmed by contemporaneous Babylonian records, which make mention of both Cyaxares (Umakishtar) and Astyages (Ishtuwigu), but nothing is clear cut. The archaeology of key Median sites shows a precipitous drop in living standards following the overthrow of the Assyrian Empire—precisely when the Medes were supposed to have flourished. This seeming discrepancy between written and material evidence has led some scholars (most notably Sancisi-Weerdenburg in *Achaemenid History* (hereafter

Ach. Hist.) 3, pp. 197–212, and *Ach. Hist.* 8, pp. 39–55) to doubt the existence of a Median Empire at all. Of course, lesser empires built on the ruins of greater ones can often appear impoverished in comparison—the history of Europe in the Dark Ages provides an obvious analogy. All the same, even if one does accept—as most scholars do—that Herodotus got his basic facts right, the details of Median history remain frustratingly vague.

8　The accounts of the two expeditions are to be found in Xenophon and Ctesias, respectively. While neither historian is renowned for his accuracy, there seems no particular cause to doubt them on this occasion. True, there is a tradition preserved by Aristotle (*Politics*, 1311b40) that Astyages was soft and self-indulgent, but this is flatly contradicted by all the other sources, to say nothing of the evidence of the length of his reign: weak kings, in the ancient Near East, rarely lasted for long.

9　The precise date of Ecbatana's foundation is unknown, but there is no record of it in Assyrian sources. This supports Herodotus' claim that the city was first established as an expression of Median royal power.

10　See Herodotus, 1.98.

11　Diogenes Laertius, 1.6.

12　The current scholarly consensus is that they were not.

13　Persian rule over Anshan was established shortly after 650 BC. The last native king of Anshan can be dated to this period, and the first Persian to claim the title did so a generation later. Anshan itself had been shored against the ruin of the even more ancient kingdom of Elam.

14　The main source for legends about Cyrus' upbringing is Herodotus, who claimed to have learned them from Persian informants (1.95); variants are recorded by Nicolaus of Damascus—who derived his account from Ctesias—and Justin. It seems probable that the elements of folklore in the story do derive from the Near East: a very similar upbringing is ascribed to Sargon of Akkad, a proto-King of Kings from the third millennium BC (see pp. 42–3). Only the tradition that Cyrus was the grandson of Astyages can really be considered historically reliable: Xenophon and Diodorus Siculus, as well as Herodotus, insist upon it, and we know from Babylonian sources that Astyages was indeed in the habit of marrying off his daughters to the princes of neighboring kingdoms. For the inevitable counterview, however, see Sancisi-Weerdenburg, *Ach. Hist.* 8, pp. 52–3.

15　From the so-called "Dream of Nabonidus" (Beaulieu, p. 108). It is from another contemporary source, the *Nabonidus Chronicle*, that we know it was Astyages—and not, as Herodotus claims, Cyrus—who began the war.

16　Darius, inscription at Persepolis (DPd 2).

17　Herodotus, 1.129.

18　*Nabonidus Chronicle*, II.17. The applicability of this verse to Lydia is almost certain; damage to the inscription prevents it from being incontrovertible.

19　Diodorus Siculus, 9.35.

20 Darius, inscription at Persepolis (DPg).

21 Herodotus, 1.164.

22 Xenophanes, Fragment 22.

23 Our ignorance of the details of Cyrus' campaigns in the east is almost total. While there is no doubt that a vast swath of provinces to the northeast of Iran were brought under Persian control, the likely dates of these conquests have to be argued for from virtual silence. We do know that Cyrus was in Babylon in 539 BC, but for the eight years preceding that date, and the nine years following it, the records are effectively nonexistent. That said—and although historians have argued for both—an earlier date for Cyrus' conquest of the east seems more plausible than a later. It certainly makes better strategic sense—and Cyrus was nothing if not a master strategist. Moreover, the apparently successful integration of the eastern provinces into the Persian Empire by the time of Cyrus' death is more readily explicable if one assumes a longer rather than a shorter period of pacification. Finally, there is the evidence of Herodotus, whose knowledge of eastern affairs was inevitably hazy, but who does state categorically that "While Harapagus was turning upside-down the lower, or western part of Asia, Cyrus was engaged with the north and east, bringing into subjection every nation without exception" (1.117). Berossus, a Babylonian scholar who lived shortly after the reign of Alexander the Great, but who would have had access to records unknown to the Greeks, corroborates this assertion.

24 *Mihr Yasht*, 14–15.

25 Ibid., 13.

26 Tentatively identified by some scholars as the Volga.

27 In Persian, "Kurushkath." The Jaxartes is the river now known as the Syr Darya, which runs through Kazakhstan.

28 Cyrus Cylinder, 11.

29 This account of Cyrus' death derives from Herodotus (1.204–14), and seems to make the best sense of the many different versions of it that have survived. According to Xenophon, for instance, Cyrus did not even die in battle, but in his own bed, back in Persia: such are the contradictions that plague the sources for Persian history. That Cyrus was seventy when he died is recorded by Cicero (*On Divination*, 1.23)—again, with what accuracy it is impossible to say for sure. Three score years and ten might perhaps be considered a suspiciously rounded age.

30 Xenophon, *Cyropaedia*, 1.4–5.

31 The practice of *khvaetvadatha*, or endogamous marriage, had been approved by Zoroaster as a positive religious duty, and it is possible—maybe even likely—that Cambyses' incestuous marriages reflect the influence of the Prophet's teaching. As with most things Zoroastrian, however, this must be speculation. The philosopher Antisthenes, an associate of Socrates, claimed that a Persian male habitually "enjoyed intercourse with his

mother, his sister, and his daughter"—maybe a garbled retelling of a genuine tradition.

32 Some of the sources appear to contradict this reading. According to Ctesias, Bardiya was summoned twice by his brother to court, but only came on the third command, and even then reluctantly. According to Herodotus, he was briefly present with Cambyses in Egypt, but then sent back to Persia in disgrace. Neither story seems likely. Bearing in mind what happened subsequently, Bardiya must have been in the eastern half of the empire for most—if not all—of the period that Cambyses was in Egypt, and his role there could only have been as his brother's lieutenant; anything else would have been politically inadmissible. Evidently, Cambyses felt that he had reason enough to trust Bardiya, and for four years, at least, he was not let down.

33 This story is found in the seventh book of Polyaenus' *Strategies*, written in the second century AD—perhaps a suspiciously late date.

34 The town of Anthylla. See Herodotus, 2.98.

35 Herodotus, 3.89.

36 According to Herodotus, it was his ability to draw a bow that no one else in the court had been able to string that had prompted his expulsion from Egypt in disgrace.

37 Herodotus, 3.20. The Egyptians and Persians knew Ethiopia as Nubia. According to Herodotus, Cambyses' invasion of Ethiopia was a catastrophe, but this again seems to reflect his reliance upon Egyptian sources. Persian records make it clear that at least northern Nubia had been brought into the empire.

38 Specifically, in Babylon.

39 Precisely when is not clear. This is a considerable frustration, for it is possible that Cambyses died *before* Bardiya proclaimed himself king, in which case it is also possible that there was never, strictly speaking, an attempted usurpation at all. Some of the later sources imply this, but they should probably be discounted. The tradition that labeled Cambyses the victim of an attempted coup is very strong, and it is hard to make sense of the chaos that engulfed the Persian world on Cambyses' death if one does presume an orderly succession from brother to brother. Also in favor of this argument is the fact that the last known document from Cambyses' reign is dated April 18, while the earliest known document which mentions "King Bardiya" is dated the 14th of the same month. This may not be conclusive evidence of a coup, but it is suggestive, at the very least.

40 It is nowhere explicitly stated that Bardiya was in Ecbatana during the summer months, but since it was the favored summer residence of the Persian monarchs, and we know that the king was definitely in Media in September, it seems a safe assumption.

41 Darius, the Bisitun inscription (DB 14).

42 Aeschylus, l.774.
43 One other scrap of evidence—albeit faint—has been used as evidence against Darius. In his own account of the events of the summer of 522, he employs the curious circumlocution "Afterwards, Cambyses by his own death was dead" (DB 11). As Balcer has pointed out, "It may well be that Cambyses had not simply died, but that for a specific reason his death had caused the framers of the Bisitun texts to emphasise that he had 'died a death of his own' when perhaps he had not. Thus, the framers may have left us with the hint that something peculiar had happened to cause Cambyses' death" (*Herodotus and Bisitun*, p. 98).
44 For the active presence of foreign merchants and bankers in Iran, see Zadok.
45 Strabo, 11.13.7.
46 This account of Bardiya's murder is a conflation of Darius' own and those of various Greek authors. Even though he mislocates the site of the assassination, Herodotus appears on this occasion to have had unusually precise information. Historians have long suspected that the source was Zopyros the Younger, the great-grandson of Megabyzos, one of the seven conspirators. In the 440s BC, Zopyros was an exile in Athens, where he may have met Herodotus, and given him a full account of the coup. The details of Bardiya being with a concubine and defending himself with a stool come from Ctesias (14–15)—and are typically tabloid touches. The claim that it was Darius' brother who slew Bardiya comes from Aeschylus (776), and is altogether more convincing, since Artaphernes would subsequently become a major player in the affairs of Athens, and his biography must have been widely known. Certainly, the presumption of most historians, that "Artaphernes" is a misspelling of "Intaphernes"—listed by Herodotus as one of the seven conspirators—seems mistaken, particularly since Herodotus' contemporary, the Ionian ethnographer Hellanicus of Lesbos, also fingered Artaphernes as the man who had struck down Bardiya. Sikyavautish, the site of the assassination, has never been precisely identified, but it was somewhere near modern-day Harsin, just to the south of the Khorasan Highway.
47 DB 11.
48 DB 55.
49 Herodotus, 1.136.
50 *Mihr Yasht*, 2.
51 Herodotus, 3.84.
52 *Yasna*, 43.4.
53 *Amesha* is generally translated as "immortal," but *Spenta* is an altogether more untranslatable word: its definitions include "strong," "sacred," "possessed of power," "beneficent" and "bounteous." See Boyce (1975), 1.196–7.
54 *Yasna*, 30.2.
55 For Persian opinion, we have to rely on the evidence of the Greeks:

Zoroaster was dated by Xanthus of Lydia (fifth century BC) to six thousand years before the time of Xerxes, a number which almost certainly reflected Zoroastrian notions of the cycle of world ages. The first Greek to date him to Astyages' reign was Aristoxenus, in the fourth century BC, who also cast the Prophet as the teacher of Pythagoras. Both traditions appear to be worthless, although the fact that they could coexist suggests the degree to which Zoroaster was a figure of mystery and myth. The confusion has continued to plague contemporary scholarship. The current consensus— arrived at by dating the most ancient Zoroastrian texts—places Zoroaster in or around 1000 BC, but wide divergences of opinion remain. Some (notably Boyce) date him to 1700–1500 BC; others (notably Gnoli) to the end of the seventh century BC. As Gnoli (p. 5) himself ruefully acknowledges, though, arguing about the date of Zoroaster is, for Iranianists, "the favorite pastime of scholars."

56 Although the Median city of Ragha, near what is present-day Tehran, would one day promote itself as the birthplace of the Prophet.

57 The phrase "fire-holder" is Boyce's (*Zoroastrianism*, Vol. 2, p. 52), as is the identification of the three Pasargadae structures as such.

58 Clemen, pp. 30–1.

59 DB 63.

60 In Old Persian, Bagastaana.

II Babylon

1 "Enuma Elish," 6.5–6.

2 Jeremiah, 28.14.

3 Ibid., 5.16–17.

4 Quoted by Leick, p. 96.

5 Nabonidus, inscription 15.

6 Cyrus Cylinder.

7 George, p. 41.

8 Herodotus, 1.191.

9 "Instructions of Shuruppak," 204–6.

10 Darius, inscription at Naqsh-i-Rustam (Dna 2).

11 Cyrus Cylinder.

12 Haggai, 2.6.

13 DB 25 (Babylon).

14 DB 1.

15 DB 4.

16 Byron, p. 43.

17 DB 70.

18 DB 72.

19 DB 73.
20 The origins of this title are obscure. The kings of Urartu, in what is now Armenia, employed it, but quite how, and if, it gravitated from them to the Persian monarchs is a puzzle. The kings of Assyria did sometimes lay claim to it, but only rarely; the kings of Babylon not at all.
21 Darius, inscription at Persepolis (DPf).
22 Herodotus, 3.89.
23 Darius, inscription at Susa (DSf 3e).
24 Ibid., 3h–i.
25 Ibid., 3f.
26 Darius, inscription at Persepolis (Dpg 2).
27 This is a logical presumption. "The Persian kings," we are told, "had water fetched from the Nile and the Danube, which they laid up in their treasuries as a sort of testimony of the greatness of their power and universal empire" (Plutarch, *Alexander*, 36.4). The list of rivers surely reflects the historian's Greek perspective: it seems improbable that the Indus would not also have been included.

III Sparta

1 Herodotus, 1.153.
2 Ibid., 1.4.
3 *The Iliad*, 3.171.
4 Cicero, *On Duties*, 2.22.77. Hans van Wees, in his essay "Tyrtaeus' *Eunomia*," has conclusively demonstrated the archaic origins of this anonymous proverb. See Hodkinson and Powell, pp. 1–41.
5 Herodotus, 1.65.
6 Phocylides, Fragment 4. These lines almost certainly postdate the fall of Nineveh, and probably reflect fears of the growth of Persian power in the 540s BC.
7 Who precisely the Dorians were is one of the great imponderables of a period known even by ancient historians, who are well used to sifting minute fragments of evidence, as the Dark Ages. As with the migrations of the Medes and the Persians, the precise details of the Dorian invasion are irrecoverable. Inevitably, a minority of historians dispute whether it was ever anything more than a myth.
8 Plato, *Hippias Major*, 285d.
9 Tyrtaeus, 5.2–3.
10 Ibid., 5.4.
11 Ibid., 5.10.
12 Plutarch, *Lycurgus*, 2.
13 Herodotus, 1.65.

14 Plutarch, *Lycurgus*, 29.

15 Thucydides, 1.6.

16 Tyrtaeus, 7.31–2.

17 Plutarch, *Lycurgus*, 29.

18 For the best discussion, see Hodkinson, p. 76.

19 For instance, Ephorus, quoted by Strabo (8.5.4). An alternative—and etymologically more convincing—theory equated "helot" with a word for "captive."

20 Tyrtaeus, 6.1.

21 Herodotus, 1.66.

22 Xenophon, *Agesilaus*, 2.7.

23 The earliest reference to the Spartans' scarlet cloaks does not occur until as late as 411 BC—in Aristophanes' comedy *Lysistrata*—and there is no way of knowing precisely when they first began to be worn. It seems likeliest, however, that they were introduced as part of the increasing standardization of the Spartan military that was a feature of the mid-sixth century BC. A further complication lies in the ambiguity of the Greek words used to describe the cloak: it may be that the Spartans' tunics, as well as their cloaks, were scarlet.

24 Lysias, *In Defence of Mantitheus*, 16.17.

25 Thucydides, 1.10.

26 *The Iliad*, 21.470. Her shrine by the Eurotas was originally dedicated to an obscure goddess named Ortheia. The Spartans worshipped Artemis there as Artemis Ortheia, probably from the sixth century BC, although the name is not attested before the Roman period.

27 The masks date from the seventh and particularly the sixth centuries BC.

28 Pindar, quoted by Plutarch, *Lycurgus*, 21.

29 According to Plato, only the elderly were permitted to criticize aspects of the state. See *Laws*, 634d–e.

30 Pindar, quoted by Plutarch, *Lycurgus*, 21.

31 Xenophon, *The Constitution of the Spartans*, 10.3.

32 Plutarch, *Lycurgus*, 16.

33 Ibykos, Fragment 58.

34 Plutarch, *Lycurgus*, 14.

35 Herodotus, 6.61.

36 The king was Charilaus, but since he was supposed to have lived in the eighth century, before the Lycurgan revolution, the saying is surely apocryphal. It was recorded by Plutarch, and is grouped in his *Sayings of the Spartans*.

37 Plutarch, *Lycurgus*, 16.

38 It is only fair to point out that both these details derive from late sources, Aelian and Athenaeus (both *c.* second century AD), respectively.

39 The precise origins of this practice are obscure—some scholars date it to as late as the fifth century BC.

40 Xenophon, *The Constitution of the Spartans*, 2.9.
41 There is an ambiguity here in the sources. It is claimed that Spartans married in secret, but how a bride could keep her new status a secret when she had just been cropped is unclear. In Sparta, it was only married women who were veiled in public.
42 Critias, 88B37 D-K.
43 Herodotus, 7.105.
44 Tyrtaeus, Fragment 2.
45 *Homeric Hymns*, 3.214–15.
46 When precisely this occurred is unclear. The story that the Pythia had originally been a young girl was much repeated, but all the writers of the classical period took it for granted that she was old. The state of our knowledge of the history of archaic Greece being so patchy, it is perfectly possible that she always had been.
47 *Homeric Hymns*, 3.538.
48 The so-called Sacred War is traditionally dated 595–591 BC. There is an eeriness about the details as they are found in the sources that has suggested to some historians that the entire episode may be legendary.
49 Pausanias, 10.5.
50 Ibid., 10.4.
51 Heraclitus, quoted by Plutarch, *Why the Pythia No Longer Prophesies in Verse*, 404E.
52 *The Odyssey*, 17.323–4.
53 Plutarch, *Agis*, 11.
54 Thucydides, 1.70.
55 The date is approximate. Cleomenes was certainly king by 519 BC, at the latest.
56 Herodotus, 5.42.

IV Athens

1 From Pericles' famous funeral speech (Thucydides, 2.36). The sentiments here derive from the golden age of Athenian self-confidence, in the mid-fifth century BC, but the Athenians' belief that they were earth-born seems to be genuinely ancient, and can be traced, albeit vaguely, at least as far back as Homer.
2 From the Acharnes Stele, a copy of the oath sworn by the ephebes, young Athenians who were obliged by the city to undergo two years' military training. The formal nature of such a program was a fourth-century BC innovation, but the words of the oath are traditional, and date back at least to the time of the Persian Wars.
3 The precise name of the Athenians' earliest hero is beset by one of those confusions so typical of archaic Greek history. The Athenians of the late fifth

century called him Erichthonius, and identified Erechtheus with his grandson. The close similarity of the two names and the fact that "Erechtheus" is much the older one, however, strongly suggest that grandfather and grandson were originally one and the same. A further layer of confusion comes from the fact that Cecrops, another Athenian king, and sometimes held to be Erechtheus' son, was also earth-born and snake-tailed. Erechtheus himself long continued to be worshipped as a god on the Acropolis. His legend is a further fragment of evidence that the Athenian belief in their own earth-born status was ancient. As Shapiro (p. 102) has pointed out, "Generally, myths involving the legendary Kings of Attika are genuinely old."

4   *The Iliad*, 2.549–51.

5   Herodotus, 7.161.

6   The question of when Attica was formally unified, so that the citizens of communities beyond Athens came to be identified as "Athenian," has never been answered definitively. Orthodox opinion would accept that the process was completed, at the latest, by the end of the seventh century BC, although Greg Anderson, in a brilliant if controversial book, has argued that it was completed only by 500 BC, as part of the reforms that also helped establish the democracy.

7   The evidence for the backward-looking nature of Athenian exceptionalism during the seventh century BC derives principally from archaeology. See Morris (1987), in particular.

8   Sappho, 58.25.

9   Ibid., 1–13.

10 Alcaeus, 360. A poet from Lesbos, in the Aegean, he is quoting Aristodemus of Sparta.

11 The most commonly accepted date. See R. Wallace. Some historians have speculated that Solon's reforms postdated his archonship.

12 Solon, 3.

13 Ibid., 36. It is likely that the lifting of the boundary stones signaled less a straight cancellation of debt than a reform of the system of sharecropping, whereby tenants paid a sixth of their produce to their landlords.

14 Ibid., 5.

15 Ibid., 4.

16 Aristotle, *Politics*, 1274a16–17.

17 *The Iliad*, 6.208.

18 Pindar, *Fifth Isthmian Ode*, 12–13. The poem was written in 478 BC, when noblemen could still be described in terms that evoked the gods on Olympus, but only with stern caveats. Pindar's poem, having described the glory won by a victor in the games at Corinth, next gives him a stark warning: "Do not try to become Zeus."

19 Plutarch, *Table Talk*, 2.5.2.

20 Although, according to the uncorroborated evidence of Thucydides (1.126), Cylon and his brother managed to escape.

21 For the dating, see Rhodes (1981), p. 84.

22 Such, at any rate, is the traditional story. The chronology is a trifle awkward.

23 Herodotus, 6.125.

24 Whoever inaugurated the Great Panathenaea, with its grand procession to the summit of the Acropolis, must surely also have been responsible for the construction of the ramp. Other names have been proposed (see Shapiro, pp. 20–1), but Lycurgus, with his responsibilities toward the cult statue of Athena, to say nothing of his clearly attested political dominance in the 560s BC, appears overwhelmingly the likeliest candidate.

25 This description of Athena's statue derives from Pausanias (1.26.7), who appears to be implying that the holy image was a meteorite. Confusingly, however, it is also described in a speech by Demosthenes (*Against Androtion*, 13) as being fashioned out of olive wood. The truth has been lost.

26 At issue is the question of whether the so-called "Bluebeard Temple"— named after a figure found among the rubble of its pediments—was built as a replacement for the seventh-century temple of Athena Polias or in competition with it. If the former, then the Boutads were probably responsible for its construction; if the latter, the Alcmaeonids. The scholarly consensus, having originally favored the first hypothesis, has now swung in favor of the second. See Dinsmoor, for the archaeological evidence, and Greg Anderson (pp. 70–1), for the part played by the Alcmaeonids.

27 Such, at any rate, on the principle of *cui bono*, appears the likeliest explanation of the muddled descriptions of the episode that have survived.

28 Almost certainly. The epitaph comes from the "Anavyssos Kouros," a memorial statue raised to a young man named Croisos, who is conventionally assumed to have been an Alcmaeonid killed at Pallene.

29 Aristotle, *The Constitution of the Athenians*, 15.5.

30 Solon, 36.

31 Aristotle, *The Constitution of the Athenians*, 16.2.

32 Ibid., 16.5.

33 Ibid., 16.7.

34 The exact date is unknown. It would later please the Alcmaeonids to pretend that they had never reached an accommodation with the tyrants, but had always remained in obdurate and principled exile. Only the discovery in 1938 of an archon list from the late fifth century BC gave the game away.

35 Plutarch, *Solon*, 29. He is said to have made the comment to Thespis, who was held by the ancients to have been the inventor of tragedy. Since Solon died around 560 BC, and Thespis was said to have produced the first tragedy in 535, the tradition is clearly unreliable in the extreme.

36 Herodotus, 5.93.

37 Thucydides, 6.54.

38 Ibid., 6.57.
39 Aristotle, *The Constitution of the Athenians*, 19.3.
40 Herodotus, 5.63.
41 Ibid.
42 Aristotle, *The Constitution of the Athenians*, 20.1.
43 We are nowhere told explicitly that Cleisthenes made his proposals to the Assembly, but such is the almost universal presumption.
44 Whether Cleisthenes ever used the word "*demokratia*" is much debated. The consensus is that he didn't, and that it was not coined until the 470s BC, more than thirty years later. In a sense, however, the argument is sterile: later generations of Athenians certainly recognized the form of government established by Cleisthenes as a democracy, and so too has almost every modern historian. In this book, I will refer to it, and post-Cleisthenic Athens generally, as a democracy. For the reasoning of a classicist who would argue that this is no anachronism, see Hansen (1986).
45 Herodotus, 5.66.
46 Aristophanes, *Lysistrata*, 279.
47 Such, at any rate, is the implication of a phrase in Herodotus (5.78), where he associates the sudden rise to greatness of democratic Athens with the benefits that derive from "*isegoria*"—literally, equality in the *agora*, the place of assembly in a Greek city, but with a specific subsidiary meaning: that of the right of every citizen to address the people. Some scholars argue that *isegoria* was introduced to Athens by later reformers.
48 Plato, *Protagoras*, 9.82.
49 Herodotus, 5.74.
50 In Greek, the Eteoboutadai.
51 Herodotus, 5.78.
52 Ibid., 5.77.
53 For the best account of the earlier *agora*, see Robertson.
54 Herodotus, 5.73.

V Singeing the King of Persia's Beard

1 Xenophon, *Cyropaedia*, 8.2.11–12.
2 Darius, inscription at Naqsh-i-Rustam (DNb 8a).
3 Such, at any rate, is what the archaeology suggests. See Dusinberre, p. 142.
4 Isaiah, 45.1. "Christ"—"*christos*"—is the Greek translation.
5 Ibid., 45.2–3.
6 Xenophanes, 3d.
7 Heraclitus. From Diogenes Laertius, 9.6.
8 Diogenes Laertius, 1.21. The saying was also attributed to Socrates.
9 Hipponax, 92.

10 The dating is not absolutely certain.

11 Herodotus, 4.137.

12 Ibid., 5.28.

13 For this interpretation of Herodotus, 5.36, see Wallinga (1984).

14 Herodotus, 5.49.

15 Ibid., 5.51.

16 Ibid., 5.97.

17 Ibid.

18 Aelian, 2.12.

19 Plutarch, *Themistocles*, 22. Plutarch does not otherwise describe Themistocles, but his assertion that lifelike portrait busts of the great man could still be seen under the Roman Empire makes the survival of exactly such a portrait bust at the Roman port of Ostia all the more intriguing. Conventionally dated to the second century AD, the bust is judged by most—though by no means all—scholars to derive from an original sculpted between 480 and 450 BC, and therefore almost certainly drawn from life.

20 Thucydides, 1.138.

21 Herodotus, 6.11.

22 Precisely when is unclear.

23 Herodotus, 6.76.

24 Ibid., 6.21.

25 Ibid., 6.104.

26 Ibid., 5.105.

27 Strabo, 15.3.18.

28 Herodotus, 5.35.

29 Ibid., 6.1.

30 Ibid., 6.42.

31 *Yasna*, 30.6.

32 Ibid., 32.3.

33 Herodotus, 7.133.

34 Ibid., 6.61.

35 Ibid., 6.95. Six hundred triremes were marshaled for the expedition, but Herodotus does not tell us how many troops were sent. Six thousand four hundred Persians were killed at Marathon, mostly from the center. Since the center of an army was conventionally a third of its total, and since not all of the troops sent on the expedition were present for the battle, a total of 25,000 seems a reasonable estimate.

36 Ibid., 6.94.

37 Ibid., 6.97.

38 The chronology has to be worked out from assorted scattered clues. The key question is whether the Battle of Marathon was fought in August or September—nowhere are we specifically told. The balance of probability is overwhelmingly in favor of August: if the battle was fought in September, as

some scholars argue, then Datis must have spent an unfeasibly long time in crossing the Aegean.

39 Pausanias, 7.10.1.

40 Plutarch, *Spartan Sayings*. The aphorism is attributed to Demaratus.

41 Aristotle, *Rhetoric*, 3.10.

42 Herodotus, 6. 106.

43 The tradition that Philippides hurried back to Athens from Sparta was recorded by the second-century AD essayist Lucian in his article "On Mistakes in Greeting" (3). Rationalist that he generally was, Lucian showed himself merciless toward the more far-fetched claims made about Marathon, scoffing, for instance, in another essay, at the very notion that Pan might have taken part in the battle. This surely suggests that Philippides' return to Athens was taken for granted by the ancients, and although it has been doubted by Lazenby (1993, p. 52), it is hard to see why. The news of Spartan plans was of pressing importance to the Athenians (as it was to the Persians, too, of course), and Philippides would hardly have been in any mood to hang around in Sparta and enjoy the fun of the Carneia. Of course, that the run back to Athens would have been gruelling for the already exhausted runner is not doubted—that he may have pushed himself to the point of hallucinating wildly surely implies that he had his vision of Pan on the return, rather than the outward, leg of his journey.

44 A phrase so celebrated that it ultimately came to serve the Greeks as a proverb. It was quoted as such in a Byzantine encyclopedia, the so-called *Suda*, together with an explanation of its origin in the Marathon campaign. Although the *Suda* was compiled in the tenth century AD, almost 1500 years after Marathon, the fact that it transcribes a saying so obviously traditional and widely known has led most historians to accept its accuracy (although by no means all: see, for instance, Shrimpton). A further clincher—albeit an argument from omission—is the failure of Herodotus to make any mention of cavalry in his account of the famous battle. Clearly, although some horsemen must have been left behind by Datis, there were not enough to influence the result.

45 An alternative theory, that the cavalry were away on a foraging expedition or being watered, makes little sense. Why would *all* the cavalry have been sent away on such a mission in the middle of the night?

46 Herodotus, 6.112.

47 That Themistocles was one of the ten generals is nowhere directly stated, but it is strongly implied by a passage in Plutarch's life of Aristeides (5), in which the two men are described as fighting as equals at Marathon—and Aristeides, we know for certain, was the general of his tribe. Since Themistocles was a recent archon, and a man strongly associated with an anti-Persian policy, it is hard to know whom his tribe might have voted for in preference to him.

48 Aristides, 3.566.
49 Plutarch, *Aristeides*, 18. The phrase quoted is a description of the Spartan phalanx at the later Battle of Plataea.
50 Pausanias, 1.32.6.
51 Herodotus claims that a shield was used, but since the shields used by the Greeks were convex, and a flat surface is needed to catch the sun, this seems improbable. That the signal was sent from Mount Pentelikon is an assumption based on the local topography.
52 Herodotus, 6.116.
53 Ibid., 6.109.
54 Ibid., 8.105.
55 Pausanias, 1.29.4.

VI *The Gathering Storm*

1 From Plato's epigram "On the Eretrian Exiles in Persia."
2 The exact date of Demaratus' flight from Sparta is uncertain. It was most likely some time between September 490 BC and the following September, although it could have been later.
3 Herodotus, 1.136.
4 Plato, *Alcibiades*, 121d. Herodotus (1.136) and Strabo (15.3.18) claim that Persian boys began their full-time education at the age of five; Plato, immediately after the passage quoted, says seven.
5 Ctesias, 54.
6 Although Herodotus (7.2–5) claims that Xerxes was not proclaimed heir until Darius was preparing to depart for Egypt, a frieze dating from much earlier in his reign (at least before 490 BC) shows Darius with Xerxes as crown prince standing behind him.
7 Cicero, 1.41.90.
8 Strabo, 15.3.21.
9 Herodotus, 7.187.
10 Xerxes, inscription at Persepolis (XPf).
11 Plutarch, *Artaxerxes*, 3.
12 Xerxes, inscription at Persepolis (XPh).
13 Ibid. (XPf).
14 Herodotus, 7.6.
15 Herodotus, as ever our principal source, gives us a detailed account of the debate, complete with speeches from Xerxes, Mardonius and Xerxes' uncle Artabanus, a prominent dove—all of which he claims to have derived directly from Persian sources (7.12). Even if the speeches are not the verbatim transcripts that Herodotus implies, the division of opinion which they reflect does seem authentic. The characterization of Mardonius,

bearing in mind what would subsequently happen, appears particularly suggestive.

16 Such, at any rate, is the implication of the comments that Herodotus gives Mardonius after the Battle of Salamis (7.100).

17 To be specific, the southern end of the so-called Apadana Staircase, the sculptures of which have been dated to the beginning of Xerxes' reign.

18 Xenophon, *Economics*, 4.8.

19 Aelian, 1.33.

20 Strabo, 25.3.18.

21 Herodotus, 7.5.

22 "*Paradaida*" is a reconstruction, based on the evidence of the Greek loanword. An exact synonym, the Elamite word "*partetash*," has been found in the Persepolis tablets. See Briant (2002), pp. 442–3.

23 Xenophon, *Household Management*, 4.21.

24 Athenaeus, 9.51. The assertion was originally made by Charon of Lampsacus, a contemporary of Herodotus.

25 An anonymous philosopher of the fifth century—perhaps Democritus. Quoted by Cartledge (1997), p. 12.

26 Plutarch, *Themistocles*, 2.

27 Aristotle, *Politics*, 1302b15.

28 Aristotle (*The Constitution of the Athenians*, 22.1 and 4) specifically states that it was Cleisthenes who was responsible for the law on ostracism. Historians have sometimes doubted whether it would have remained unused for twenty years, but skepticism on the matter ignores the peculiar circumstances of Miltiades' trial, and its aftermath.

29 A title not semi-formalized until 478 BC, a year after the end of the Persian Wars, but evidently in the air long before that (cf. Plutarch, *Aristeides*, 7).

30 Plutarch, *Aristeides*, 2.

31 Pausanias, 1.26.5.

32 The earliest reference to the contest between Athena and Poseidon occurs in Herodotus (8.55), and this has led some scholars (most notably Shapiro) to suggest that it is a fifth-century invention. Certainty on the matter is impossible, but the confusions and inconsistencies in the various versions of the myth suggest a much older origin.

33 Homer, *Odyssey*, 3.278.

34 Aeschylus, *Persians*, 238.

35 Plutarch, *Themistocles*, 4.

36 Plutarch, *Aristeides*, 7.

37 Plutarch, *Cimon*, 12.

38 Xenophon, *Household Management*, 8.8.

39 Thucydides, 142.

40 Plato, *Laws*, 4.706.

41 Herodotus, 7.239.

42 For this explanation of the contradictory stories about Demaratus' paternity found in Herodotus, see Burkert (1965).

43 Pausanias, 3.12.6. It has generally been assumed that the meeting took place at Corinth, where all subsequent meetings were held, but since the earliest source for this is a historian of the first century BC, Diodorus Siculus (9.3), who in turn used Herodotus as his ultimate source of information, I see no reason to dismiss the evidence of Pausanias, as most scholars do; indeed, it makes perfect sense, for the reason I give.

44 Plutarch, *Themistocles*, 6.

45 Herodotus, 7.132.

46 Ezekiel, 27.4.

47 Plato, *The Republic*, 4.436a.

48 *The Odyssey*, 15.416–17.

49 Herodotus, 1.1.

50 Ibid., 3.19.

51 The figure comes from Herodotus (7.89), and is echoed—with some ambiguity—in Aeschylus' play *The Persians* (341–3). The earliness and consistency of the tradition suggest that the Greeks themselves believed it was accurate; but that in itself, of course, is not proof. All the historian can say with any certainty is that the Persian fleet was on a mammoth scale; and that probably—at the outset of its voyage, at any rate—it outnumbered the Greeks by as much as four to one. For the best discussion, see Lazenby (1993), pp. 92–4.

52 Quintus Curtius, 3.3.8. The description is of the banner of Darius III, the last King of Persia, who was overthrown by Alexander the Great. Veneration of the sun, however, was a constant throughout Persian history, and it seems reasonable to suppose that the Great Kings would have preserved it as an emblem of their might. Xenophon (*Anabasis* 1.10) records that the imperial battle standards bore eagles. See also Nylander.

53 Herodotus, 7.83.

54 See, for instance, Cook (1983, pp. 113-15), who settles on a figure of 300,000 for Xerxes' land forces; Hammond (*Cambridge Ancient History*, 1988, p. 534), who goes for 242,000; Green (pp. 58–9), who opts for 210,000; and Lazenby (1993, pp. 90–2), who wavers between 210,000 and 360,000, before finally choosing 90,000. In short, as this range of opinions eloquently suggests, we will never know. The best discussion, although not necessarily the most convincing conclusion, is in Lazenby.

55 Xerxes, inscription at Persepolis (XPh).

56 Herodotus, 7.40.

57 Xenophon, *Cyropaedia*, 8.2.8.

58 Xerxes, inscription at Persepolis (XPl).

59 Herodotus, 7.38.

60 Ibid., 7.39.

61 Ibid., 7.40.

62 Ibid., 7.44–5.

63 Ibid., 7.56.

64 Ibid., 9.37.

65 Ibid., 7.149.

66 Ibid., 7.148.

67 Ibid., 7.220. It is conceivable, of course, that the priests at Delphi and the Spartans might have put their heads together after the war and faked this prophecy, but most improbable. Herodotus quotes it from well within living memory; and it might have been expected, had the Spartans faked it, that they would have hyped their own role in the war a good deal more. As Burn puts it, referring not merely to this, but to all the prophecies recorded by Herodotus: "That the oracular responses, and the stories attached to them, may have been 'improved' in transmission certainly cannot be excluded; that they were asked for and given, it seems unreasonable to disbelieve." (pp. 347–8).

68 Herodotus, 7.162.

69 The date of late May presumes that Xerxes left Sardis in mid-April: it would have taken him a month to reach the Hellespont.

70 Herodotus, to whom we owe the two oracular responses given to the Athenians, gives no indication as to when the fateful consultation may have occurred. Since he does tell us that the Spartans obtained their prophecy the previous year (7.220), some scholars have dated the Athenian prophecies to the same period; but this seems improbable. True, the Athenians almost certainly would have visited Delphi in 481 BC; but the record of any early consultations would have been blotted out by the later, and infinitely more sensational, oracles. So explosive was their message and so transformative their influence that it makes most sense to explain the relationship between them and Athenian policy in the summer of 480 BC as one of instantaneous cause and effect. In which case, the Athenian embassy to Delphi in the early summer of 480 BC is most likely to have been prompted by the news of Xerxes' crossing of the Hellespont—which, as we know from Herodotus (7.147), reached Athens shortly after the return of the expedition to Tempe.

71 Herodotus, 7.140.

72 Ibid., 7.141.

73 From lines 4 and 5 of the so-called "Troezen decree," a stone stele found in 1959, which appears to provide a third-century BC copy of the motion put forward by Themistocles. Its authenticity has been much debated ever since its discovery. Lazenby, cussedly skeptical as ever, dismisses it as "a patriotic fabrication," but most other scholars of the Persian Wars—Green, Frost and Podlecki, *inter alios*—accept that it does indeed, in Green's words, "give us something very close to Themistocles' actual proposals, though it may

possibly run together several motions passed on different days" (p. 98). The best and most nuanced discussion is in Podlecki, pp. 147–67.

74 Thucydides, 1.138.
75 The Troezen decree, 44–5.
76 Plutarch, *Cimon*, 5.
77 Herodotus, 7.178.
78 Ibid., 8.1.
79 Ibid., 7.205.

VII At Bay

1 Tyrtaeus, 12.
2 *The Iliad*, 7.59–62.
3 Herodotus, 7.176.
4 For the implication that each Spartan brought a single helot with him, see ibid., 7.229.
5 Diodorus Siculus, 11.4.7.
6 *The Iliad*, 7.553-6.
7 Such, at any rate, seems the only plausible explanation for the fact that the Greek patrol on Sciathos was so comprehensively ambushed. That their assailants were Sidonian is deducible from Herodotus' description of them as being "the fastest ships" (7.179) in Xerxes' fleet.
8 Plutarch, *Themistocles*, 7.
9 *The Odyssey*, 13.296–9.
10 Quoted by Burkert (1985), p. 141.
11 Plutarch, *Lycurgus*, 22.
12 Diodorus Siculus, 11.5.4.
13 Plutarch, *Spartan Sayings*, Leonidas 11.
14 Herodotus, 7.226.
15 For this last meteorological detail, see the admittedly contested reference in Polyaenus, 1.32.2.
16 Herodotus, 7.188.
17 Ibid., 7.192.
18 Plutarch, *Moralia*, 217 E.
19 Herodotus, 7.211.
20 The chronology here follows that of Lazenby, whose squaring of the numerous circles in Herodotus' account of the twin battles of Thermopylae and Artemisium is by far the most cogent of the many attempts that have been made. See *The Defence of Greece*, pp. 119–23.
21 Herodotus, 8.9.
22 Ibid., 8.12.
23 Ibid., 8.13. The precise location of the shipwreck has resulted in many a

scholarly headache. Herodotus says that it took place off the "Hollows," which later geographers—although not Herodotus himself—place in the south of Euboea. Yet this seems impossible: no fleet setting off from Sciathos in the afternoon could possibly have reached so far before midnight. As Lazenby has pointed out, there is a small island still called "Hollow" ("Koile") to this day: since it is only halfway down Euboea, this seems by far the likeliest site for the disaster.

24 Plutarch, *Themistocles*, 8.
25 Herodotus, 8.15.
26 Athenaeus, 2.48d.
27 Quintus Curtius, 3.4.2.
28 Herodotus, 7.104.
29 Ibid., 7.105.
30 Ibid., 7.236.
31 Ibid., 7.119.
32 Ibid., 7.120.
33 Athenaeus, 14.652b.
34 Ibid., 4.145e.
35 Herodotus, 7.213.
36 Presuming, as most historians now do, that the path taken by the Immortals began at the modern-day village of Ayios Vardates. For the best analysis of the various alternative routes, and the one that I certainly found most helpful during the course of my own walking of them, see Paul Wallace (1980).
37 Herodotus (7.222) claims that Leonidas kept the Thebans against their will, as hostages, but this is one of those occasions where the bias of his—almost certainly Athenian—sources is palpable. As Plutarch, a proud Boeotian, indignantly pointed out, why, if Leonidas regarded the Thebans as hostages, did he not hand them over to the retreating Peloponnesians? The astounding courage and principle shown by the loyalist Thebans at Thermopylae deserved a better memorial than Athenian calumny.
38 Three hundred Spartans marched to Thermopylae, along with perhaps 300 helots, 700 Thespians and 400 Thebans, making a total of 1700 men. Casualties over the previous two days' fighting must have reduced the total to nearer 1500.
39 Diodorus Siculus, 11.9.4.
40 *The Iliad*, 4.450.
41 Herodotus, 8.24.
42 Ibid., 7.238.
43 Aristophanes, *Acharnians*, 1090–3.
44 See Burkert (1983), p. 226.
45 Herodotus, 7.99.
46 Xenophon, *Economics*, 7.5.

47 Demosthenes, *Against Neaera*, 67.
48 Herodotus, 8.71.
49 Plutarch, *Themistocles*, 10.
50 Plutarch, *Themistocles*, 10. Pet-lovers may be relieved to know that Xanthippus' dog was reported by Aelian (12.35) to have survived the crossing.
51 Plutarch, *Themistocles*, 11.
52 Herodotus, 8.49.
53 The figure is Aeschylus' (*Persians*, 339–40). Herodotus (8.48) puts the total of the Greek fleet at 380. On this occasion, Aeschylus is almost certainly more accurate. After all, he fought in the Battle of Salamis.
54 Herodotus, 8.60.
55 Ibid. As they appear in Herodotus, these words were spoken in the debate that followed the burning of the Acropolis. They are not, however, a verbatim record of what Themistocles said, but rather expressive of the gist of his general argument, which he pressed from the beginning.
56 Ibid., 8.50.
57 Ibid., 8.61.
58 The Troezen decree, 11–12.
59 Herodotus, 8.52.
60 Ibid., 8.54.

VIII Nemesis

1 From the letter of Darius to Gadatas. See Meiggs and Lewis, p. 20.
2 Herodotus, 7.235.
3 Ibid., 8.68β.
4 Ibid., 8.59.
5 Ibid., 8.70.
6 Ibid., 8.70–1.
7 We know from Herodotus (8.70) that the Persian fleet had put to sea in the late afternoon; we know from Aeschylus (374–6) that it was back in port in time for supper.
8 Darius, inscription at Naqsh-i-Rustam (Dnb 8c).
9 Ibid.
10 According to Plutarch, he was actually a Persian prisoner of war.
11 Herodotus, 8.75.
12 Aeschylus, 380–1.
13 Herodotus, 8.76.
14 This, at any rate, seems the only explanation for Sicinnus' release that makes sense. Some historians have proposed that he yelled his message from his boat without ever leaving it, but this is not only inherently implausible—

surely the Persians could easily have sent a vessel to capture him—but
directly contradicts what Herodotus (8.75) says.

15 Herodotus, 8.78.

16 Ibid., 8.80.

17 Ibid., 8.83.

18 Ibid., 8.65.

19 Aeschylus, 369–71.

20 Since Salamis was not merely the most momentous battle ever fought, but
also one perilously difficult to reconstruct from the existing sources, the
literature on it is unsurprisingly vast. Indeed, there are almost as many
interpretations of what happened as there are historians who have written
about it. For the best defense of the orthodoxy that the Persian fleet entered
the straits by night, see Lazenby (1993), and his typically trenchant chapter,
"Divine Salamis." The most convincing counterargument can be found in
Green's chapter, "The Wooden Wall," in *The Greco-Persian Wars*. The killer
detail that surely disproves the theory that the Persians entered the straits
by night is the fact that the imperial battle fleet, if it had indeed lined up
directly opposite the allied triremes before dawn, would have swooped
down on their positions the moment that the light permitted, giving the
Greek oarsmen little time to get to their benches, let alone allowing
Themistocles to indulge in an oration, as Herodotus clearly tells us he did.
The theory also makes a nonsense of the Persians' attempt to keep their
maneuvers a secret.

21 Aeschylus, 367.

22 Ibid., 388–90.

23 Herodotus, 8.84.

24 Aeschylus, 399–400.

25 Herodotus, 8.88.

26 Aeschylus, 415–16.

27 Ibid., 426–8.

28 Ibid., 462–4.

29 Herodotus, 8.100.

30 Herodotus, 8.100. Literally "300,000 men whom I will personally choose to
finish off the job," but the figure is an obvious exaggeration.

31 In forty-five days, according to Herodotus (8.115)—although not from
Athens, as is generally assumed, but almost certainly from Thessaly.

32 Ibid., 8.110.

33 Ibid., 8.114.

34 Ibid., 8.109.

35 Ibid., 8.124.

36 Ibid., 9.12.

37 It is hard to believe that Themistocles was removed entirely from the board
of ten generals, but definite evidence is lacking.

38 Herodotus, 8.141.

39 Ibid., 8.142.

40 Ibid., 8.143.

41 Ibid., 8.144. That it was Aristeides who spoke this parting injunction is a detail recorded by Plutarch.

42 Again, according to Plutarch, this embassy was led by Aristeides. Bearing in mind that he was the commander in chief of his city's land forces, however, and that the Persians were occupying Attica at the time, this seems improbable. Even Plutarch himself admits that his information was dubious.

43 Herodotus, 9.12.

44 Ibid., 9.13.

45 Herodotus (9.29) says that there were seven helots for every Spartan—35,000 in all. This seems excessive.

46 Xenophon, *The Constitution of the Spartans*, 9.6

47 Herodotus, 9.16.

48 If Herodotus' figures (9.29) are to be trusted, there were precisely 38,100 hoplites in the allied army. This is certainly more convincing than the total of 69,500 lightly armed troops which he also gives, and which he appears to have arrived at by a series of random calculations. If there were lightly armed troops at Plataea, then their impact on the battle was negligible.

49 Herodotus (9.32) claims that Mardonius' army included 300,000 infantry and 50,000 Boeotian and Thessalian hoplites, to say nothing of cavalry. Since these figures are clearly an exaggeration, the only way to estimate the true size of the Persian forces at Plataea is to calculate how many men might have fitted into the stockade, which, Herodotus tells us, was 2000 square meters. Anything between 70,000 and 120,000 might have been possible. See Lazenby (1993), p. 228.

50 Plutarch, *Aristeides*, 13. The story is often dismissed as a fabrication, partly because it does not appear in Herodotus, and partly because Plutarch's chronology is undoubtedly muddled. Yet it is, as one of the rare glimpses we have been afforded into the Persians' espionage war, an invaluable piece of evidence, and seems convincing when placed in context.

51 Herodotus, 9.41. A claim to the contrary is made a few paragraphs later (9.45), but it comes as part of a message from the inveterately untrustworthy Alexander of Macedon. The king is supposed to have crossed no man's land in person, alone and by dead of night, in order to reveal the Persian battle plans to Aristeides: a hugely implausible story. The whiff of self-exculpation from a man who had been a notorious medizer is palpable.

52 Ibid., 9.39.

53 Ibid., 9.49.

54 Plutarch, *Aristeides*, 17.

55 Herodotus, 9.62.

56 Aeschylus, 816–17.

57 Herodotus, 9.71.

58 Ibid., 9.82.

59 Euripides, *The Phoenician Women*, 184.

60 Herodotus, 1.34.

61 Aristotle, *Rhetoric*, 2.2.6.

62 Herodotus, 8.109.

63 As Green (p. 281) points out, this is the only explanation that can make sense of the claim, asserted unequivocally by the ancient sources, that the battles of Plataea and Mycale were fought on the same day.

64 Herodotus, 9.100.

65 Ibid. Literally, ". . . which prove the hand of things that are divine."

66 Diodorus Siculus, 11.36.

67 Lycurgus, *Against Leocrates*, 81.

68 See Broneer.

69 Aeschylus, 584–90.

70 Ibid., 1024.

71 Xerxes, inscription at Persepolis (XPc).

72 It is all too depressingly typical of the general murk of Near Eastern history in this period that the revolt has also been dated to 482 BC.

73 Herodotus, 9.106.

74 Plutarch, *Themistocles*, 29.

75 Pindar, fragment 64.

76 It is unlikely—although controversy over the matter is endless—that this peace was formalized by treaty: the Great King was not in the habit of signing treaties with foreigners.

77 For this date, and indeed the authenticity of the whole story, see Stadter, pp. 201–4.

78 Plutarch, *Pericles*, 17.

79 Herodotus, 8.144.

80 Ibid., 7.228.

81 Thucydides, 2.41.

82 Plato, *Menexenus*, 240e.

83 Pausanias, 1.33.2.

Envoi

1   *Palatine Anthology*, 7.253.

Bibliography

ABSA: Annual of the British School at Athens
AJA: American Journal of Archaeology
CJ: Classical Journal
JCS: Journal of Cuneiform Studies
JHS: Journal of Hellenic Studies
TAPA: Transactions of the American Philological Association

Anderson, Greg: *The Athenian Experiment: Building an Imagined Political Community in Ancient Attica, 508–490 BC* (Ann Arbor, 2003)

Anderson, J. K.: "The Battle of Sardis" (*California Studies in Classical Antiquity* 7, 1975)

Andrewes, A.: "Kleisthenes' Reform Bill" (*Classic Quarterly* 27, 1977)

Austin, M. M.: "Greek Tyrants and the Persians, 546–479 BC" (*Classic Quarterly* 40, 1990)

Badian, E.: "Back to Kleisthenic Chronology" in *Polis and Politics: Studies in Ancient Greek History*, ed. Pernille Flensted-Jensen, Thomas Heien Nielsen and Lene Rubenstein (Copenhagen, 2000)

Bakker, Egbert J., de Jong, Irene J. F. and van Wees, Hans: *Brill's Companion to Herodotus* (Leiden, 2002)

Balcer, Jack Martin: "Athenian Politics: The Ten Years after Marathon" in *Panathenaia: Studies in Athenian Life and Thought in the Classical Age*, ed. T. E. Gregory and A. J. Podlecki (Lawrence, Kansas, 1979)

——"The Greeks and the Persians: The Processes of Acculturation" (*Historia* 32, 1983)

——*Sparda by the Bitter Sea: Imperial Interaction in Western Anatolia* (Chicago, 1984)

——*Herodotus and Bisitun: Problems in Ancient Persian Historiography* (Stuttgart, 1987)

——"The Persian Wars against Greece: A Reassessment" (*Historia* 38, 1989)

——*A Prosopographical Study of the Ancient Persians Royal and Noble c. 550–450 BC* (Lewiston, Wales, 1993)

Barnett, R. D.: "Xenophon and the Wall of Media" (*JHS* 83, 1963)

Basirov, Oric: "Zoroaster's Time and Place" (*Circle of Ancient Iranian Studies at the School of Oriental and African Studies*, 1998)

Beaulieu, Paul-Alain: *The Reign of Nabonidus, King of Babylon 556–539 BC* (New Haven, 1989)

Bichler, Reinhold: "Some Observations on the Image of the Assyrian and Babylonian Kingdoms within the Greek Tradition" in *Melammu Symposia V: Commerce and Monetary Systems in the Ancient World*, ed. R. Rollinger (Stuttgart, 2004)

Bickerman, E. J. and Tadmor, H.: "Darius I, Pseudo-Smerdis and the Magi" (*Athenaeum* 56, 1978)

Bigwood, J. M.: "Ctesias as Historian of the Persian Wars" (*Phoenix* 32, 1978)

——"Ctesias' Description of Babylon" (*American Journal of Ancient History* 3, 1978)

Boardman, John: "Artemis Orthia and Chronology" (*ABSA* 58, 1963)

——*Persia and the West: An Archaeological Investigation of the Genesis of Achaemenid Art* (London, 2000)

Boedeker, Deborah: "The Two Faces of Demaratus" (*Arethusa* 20, 1987)

——"Protesilaos and the End of Herodotus' *Histories*" (*Classical Association* 7, 1988)

Boegehold, Alan L. and Scafuro, Adele C.: *Athenian Identity and Civic Ideology* (Baltimore, 1994)

Borgeaud, Philippe: *The Cult of Pan in Ancient Greece*, tr. Kathleen Atlass and James Redfield (Chicago, 1988)

Boyce, Mary: *A History of Zoroastrianism*, Vols. 1 and 2 (Leiden, 1975)

——*Zoroastrians: Their Religious Beliefs and Practices* (London and New York, 1979)

Bradford, Ernle: *The Year of Thermopylae* (London, 1980)

Briant, Pierre: *Bulletin d'Histoire Achéménide I* (Paris, 1997)

——*Bulletin d'Histoire Achéménide II* (Paris, 2001)

——*From Cyrus to Alexander: A History of the Persian Empire*, tr. Peter T. Daniels (Winona Lake, 2002)

Broneer, Oscar: "The Tent of Xerxes and the Greek Theater" (*University of California Publications in Classical Archaeology* 1, 1944)

Brosius, Maria: *Women in Ancient Persia (559–331 BC)* (Oxford, 1996)

Brown, S.: "Media and Secondary State Formation in the Neo-Assyrian Zagros: An Anthropological Approach to an Assyriological Problem" (*JCS* 38, 1986)

Brunt, P. A.: "The Hellenic League against Persia" (*Historia* 2, 1953)

Budge, E. A. Wallis and King, L. W.: *Annals of the Kings of Assyria* (London, 1902)

Burke, Jason: *Al-Qaeda: The True Story of Radical Islam* (London, 2004)

Burkert, Walter: "Damaratos, Astrabakos und Herakles: Königsmythos und Politik" (*Muesum Helveticum* 22, 1965)

——*Homo Necans*, tr. Peter Bing (Berkeley and Los Angeles, 1983)

——*Greek Religion*, tr. John Raffan (Oxford, 1985)

——*Babylon, Memphis, Persepolis: Eastern Contexts of Greek Culture* (Cambridge, Mass., 2004)

Burn, A. R.: *Persia and the Greeks: The Defence of the West* (London, 1984)

Byron, Robert: *The Road to Oxiana* (London, 1992)

Cambridge Ancient History: The Expansion of the Greek World, Eighth to Sixth Centuries BC, ed. John Boardman and N. G. L. Hammond (Cambridge, 1982)

Cambridge Ancient History: Persia, Greece and the Western Mediterranean, c. 525–479 BC, ed. John Boardman, N. G. L. Hammond, D. M. Lewis and M. Ostwald (Cambridge, 1988)

Cambridge History of Iran: The Median and Achaemenian Periods, ed. Ilya Gershevitch (Cambridge, 1985)

Cameron, G. G.: *History of Early Iran* (New York, 1936)

Carter, Jane Burr: "The Masks of Ortheia" (*AJA* 91, 1987)

Cartledge, Paul: *Sparta and Lakonia: A Regional History 1300 to 362 BC* (London, 1979)

——"Herodotus and 'The Other': A Meditation on Empire" (*Echos du Monde Classique* 34, 1990)

——" 'Deep Plays': Theatre as Process in Greek Civic Life," in *The Cambridge Companion to Greek Tragedy*, ed. P. E. Easterling (Cambridge, 1997)

——*Spartan Reflections* (London, 2001)

——*The Spartans* (London, 2002)

——"What Have the Spartans Done for Us?: Sparta's Contribution to Western Civilization" (*Greece and Rome* 52 (2), 2004)

Cawkwell, George: *The Greek Wars: The Failure of Persia* (Oxford, 2005)

Champdor, Albert: *Babylon*, tr. Elsa Coult (London, 1958)

Clemen, C. (ed.): *Fontes Historiae Religionis Persicae* (Bonn, 1920)

Cohen, Edward E.: *The Athenian Nation* (Princeton, 2000)

Coldstream, J. N.: *Geometric Greece* (London, 1977)

Coleman, John E. and Walz, Clark A.: *Greeks and Barbarians: Essays on the Interactions between Greeks and Non-Greeks in Antiquity and the Consequences for Eurocentrism* (Bethseda, 1997)

Connolly, Peter: *Greece and Rome at War* (London, 1998)

Connor, W. R.: "Tribes, Festivals, and Processions: Civic Ceremonial and Political Manipulation in Archaic Greece" (*JHS* 107, 1987)

Cook, J. M.: *The Greeks in Ionia and the East* (London, 1962)

——*The Persian Empire* (London, 1983)

Curtis, John (ed.): *Mesopotamia and Iran in the Persian Period: Conquest and Imperialism 539–331 BC* (London, 1997)

Curzon, George N.: *Persia and the Persian Question*, 2 vols. (London, 1892)

Dabrowa, E. (ed.): *Ancient Iran and the Mediterranean World* (Krakow, 1998)

Dandamaev, M. A.: *A Political History of the Achaemenid Empire*, tr. W. J. Vogelsang (Leiden, 1989)

David, Saul: *Military Blunders: The How and Why of Military Failure* (London, 1997)

Davidson, James: *Courtesans and Fishcakes: The Consuming Passions of Classical Athens* (London, 1997)

——"Versailles with Panthers" (*London Review of Books* 13 (23), 2003)

De Jong, Albert: *Traditions of the Magi: Zoroastrianism in Greek and Latin Literature* (Leiden, 1997)

Derow, Peter and Parker, Robert: *Herodotus and His World: Essays from a Conference in Memory of George Forrest* (Oxford, 2003)

De Souza, Philip: *The Greek and Persian Wars 499–386 BC* (Oxford, 2003)

De Souza, Philip, Heckel, Waldemar and Llewellyn-Jones, Lloyd: *The Greeks at War: From Athens to Alexander* (Oxford, 2004)

De Ste Croix, G. E. M.: *The Origins of the Peloponnesian War* (London, 1972)

——*Athenian Democratic Origins*, ed. David Harvey and Robert Parker (Oxford, 2004)

Dillery, J.: "Reconfiguring the Past: Thyrea, Thermopylae and Narrative Patterns in Herodotus" (*American Journal of Philology* 117, 1996)

Dinsmoor, W. B.: "The Hekatompedon on the Athenian Akropolis" (*AJA* 51, 1947)

Donlan, W. and Thompson, J. G.: "The Charge at Marathon: Herodotus 6.112" (*CJ* 71, 1976)

—— "The Charge at Marathon Again" (*Classical World* 72, 1979)

Dontas, G.: "The True Aglaurion" (*Hesperia* 52, 1983)

Dougherty, Carol and Kurke, Leslie (eds.): *Cultural Poetics in Archaic Greece* (Cambridge, 1993)

Drews, Robert: "The First Tyrants in Greece" (*Historia* 21, 1972)

——*The Greek Accounts of Eastern History* (Washington, D.C., 1973)

Ducat, Jean: "Le Mépris des Hilotes" (*Annales* 6, 1974)

Dusinberre, Elspeth R. M.: *Aspects of Empire in Achaemenid Sardis* (Cambridge, 2003)

Ehrenberg, Victor: *From Solon to Socrates: Greek History and Civilization during the Sixth and Fifth Centuries BC* (London, 1973)

Evans, J. A. S.: "Notes on Thermopylae and Artemision" (*Historia* 18, 1969)

——"The Oracle of the 'Wooden Wall' " (*CJ* 78, 1982)

——"Herodotus and Marathon" (*Florilegium* 6, 1984)

Fehling, Detlev: *Herodotus and His "Sources": Citation, Invention and Narrative Art*, tr. J. G. Howie (Leeds, 1989)

Felton, D.: *Haunted Greece and Rome: Ghost Stories from Classical Antiquity* (Austin, 1999)

Fisher, N. R. E.: *Hybris: A Study in the Values of Honor and Shame in Ancient Greece* (Warminster, 1992)

Flower, M.: "Simonides, Ephorus, and Herodotus on the Battle of Thermopylae" (*Classical Quarterly* 48, 1998)

Fornara, C. W.: "The Hoplite Achievement at Psyttaleia" (*JHS* 86, 1966)

——*Herodotus: An Interpretative Essay* (Oxford, 1971)

Forrest, W. G.: "Herodotus and Athens" (*Phoenix* 38, 1984)

Francis, E. D.: "Greeks and Persians: The Art of Hazard and Triumph" in *Ancient Persia: The Art of an Empire*, ed. D. Schmandt-Bessarat (Malibu, 1980)

Francis, E. D. and Vickers, M.: "The Agora Revisited: Athenian Chronology c. 500–450 BC" (*ABSA* 83, 1988)

French, D. H.: "The Persian Royal Road" (*Iran* 36, 1998)

Frost, Frank J.: "A Note on Xerxes at Salamis" (*Historia* 22, 1973)

——*Plutarch's Themistocles: A Historical Commentary* (Princeton, 1980)

——"The Athenian Military before Cleisthenes" (*Historia* 33, 1984)

——"Toward a History of Peisistratid Athens" in *The Craft of the Ancient Historian: Essays in Honor of Chester G. Starr*, ed. J. W. Eadie and J. Ober (Lanham, 1985)

Frye, Richard N.: "The Charisma of Kingship in Ancient Iran" (*Iranica Antiquita* 4, 1964)

——*The Heritage of Persia* (London, 1976)

405

Gentili, Bruno: *Poetry and Its Public in Ancient Greece*, tr. Thomas Cole (Baltimore, 1988)

George, A.: *Babylonian Topographical Texts* (Leuven, 1992)

Georges, Pericles: *Barbarian Asia and the Greek Experience: From the Archaic Period to the Age of Xenophon* (Baltimore, 1994)

Gershevitch, I.: "The False Smerdis" (*Acta Antiqua* 27, 1979)

Ghirshman, Roman: *Persia: From the Origins to Alexander*, tr. Stuart Gilbert and James Emmons (London, 1964)

Gibbon, Edward: *The History of the Decline and Fall of the Roman Empire*, 3 vols., ed. David Womersley (London, 1994)

Gnoli, Gherardo: *Zoroaster in History* (New York, 1997)

Golding, William: *The Hot Gates* (London, 1965)

Gould, John: *Herodotus* (New York, 1989)

Graf, David: "Greek Tyrants and Achaemenid Politics" in *The Craft of the Ancient Historian: Essays in Honor of Chester G. Starr*, ed. J. W. Eadie and J. Ober (Lanham, 1985)

Grant, John R.: "Leonidas' Last Stand" (*Phoenix* 15, 1961)

Grayson, A. K.: *Assyrian and Babylonian Chronicles* (New York, 1975)

Green, Peter: *The Greco-Persian Wars* (Berkeley and Los Angeles, 1996)

Hall, Edith: *Inventing the Barbarian: Greek Self-Definition through Tragedy* (Oxford, 1989)

Hallock, R. T.: *The Evidence of the Persepolis Tablets* (Cambridge, 1972)

Hamilton, Richard: *Choes and Anthestria: Athenian Iconography and Ritual* (Ann Arbor, 1992)

Hansen, M. H.: "The Origins of the Term *Demokratia*" (*Liverpool Classical Monthly 2*, 1986)

——"The 2500th Anniversary of Cleisthenes' Reforms and the Tradition of Athenian Democracy" in *Ritual, Politics, Finance: Athenian Democractic Accounts Presented to David Lewis*, ed. R. Osborne and S. Hornblower (Oxford, 1994)

Hanson, Victor Davis: *The Western Way of War: Infantry Battle in Classical Greece* (Berkeley and Los Angeles, 1989)

——*Warfare and Agriculture in Classical Greece* (Berkeley and Los Angeles, 1998)

——*The Wars of the Ancient Greeks* (London, 1999)

——"No Glory That Was Greece: The Persians Win at Salamis, 480 BC" in *What If?: Military Historians Imagine What Might Have Been*, ed. Robert Cowley (New York, 1999)

Harrison, Thomas: *Divinity and History: The Religion of Herodotus* (Oxford, 2000)

——*The Emptiness of Asia: Aeschylus' "Persians" and the History of the Fifth Century* (London, 2000)

——(ed.): *Greeks and Barbarians* (Edinburgh, 2002)

Hartog, François: *Le Miroir d'Hérodote: Essai sur la Représentation de l'Autre* (Paris, 1980)

Hegel, G. W. F.: *The Philosophy of History*, tr. J. Sibree (New York, 1956)

Herzfeld, Ernst: *The Persian Empire: Studies in Geography and Ethnograpy of the Ancient Near East* (Wiesbaden, 1968)

Hignett, C.: *Xerxes' Invasion of Greece* (Oxford, 1963)

Hodge, A. Trevor: "Marathon: The Persians' Voyage" (*TAPA* 105, 1975)

——"Reflections on the Shield at Marathon" (*ABSA* 91, 2001)

Hodkinson, Stephen: *Property and Wealth in Classical Sparta* (Swansea, 2000)

Hodkinson, Stephen and Powell, Anton (eds.): *Sparta: New Perspectives* (Swansea, 1999)

Hope Simpson, R.: "Leonidas' Decision" (*Phoenix* 26, 1972)

Huxley, G. L.: *Early Sparta* (London, 1962)

——*The Early Ionians* (London, 1966)

——"The Medism of Caryae" (*Greek, Roman and Byzantine Studies* 8, 1967)

Immerwhar, H. R.: *Form and Thought in Herodotus* (Cleveland, 1966)

Jameson, M.: "A Decree of Themistokles from Troizen" (*Hesperia* 29, 1960)

——"Provisions for Mobilization in the Decree of Themistokles" (*Historia* 12, 1963)

Jeffery, L. H.: *Archaic Greece: The City-States c. 700–500 BC* (London, 1976)

Kakavoyannis, Evangelos: "The Silver Ore-Processing Workshops of the Lavrion Region" (*ABSA* 91, 2001)

Karavites, Peter: "Realities and Appearances, 490–480 BC" (*Historia* 26, 1977)

Kellens, Jean: *Essays on Zarathustra and Zoroastrianism*, tr. and ed. Prods Oktor Skjvaerø (Costa Mesa, 2000)

——(ed.): *La Religion Iranienne à l'Époque Achéménide* (Ghent, 1991)

Kennell, Nigel M.: *The Gymnasium of Virtue: Education and Culture in Ancient Sparta* (Chapel Hill, 1995)

Kent, Roland G.: *Old Persian: Grammar, Texts, Lexicon* (New Haven, 1953)

Kimball Armayor, O.: "Herodotus' Catalogues of the Persian Empire in the Light of the Monuments and the Greek Literary Tradition" (*TAPA* 108, 1978)

Kingsley, Peter: "Meetings with Magi: Iranian Themes among the Greeks, from Xanthus of Lydia to Plato's Academy" (*Journal of the Royal Asiatic Society* 3 (5), 1995)

Konstan, David: "Persians, Greeks and Empire" (*Arethusa* 20, 1987)

Kraay, C. M.: *Archaic and Classical Greek Coins* (London, 1976)

Kuhrt, Amélie: "The Cyrus Cylinder and Achaemenid Imperial Policy" (*Journal for the Study of the Old Testament* 25, 1983)

——"Usurpation, Conquest and Ceremonial: from Babylon to Persia" in *Rituals of Royalty: Power and Ceremonial in Traditional Societies*, ed. David Cannadine and Simon Price (Cambridge, 1987)

——*The Ancient Near East, c. 3000–330 BC*, Vols. 1 and 2 (London, 1995)

Kurke, Leslie: *Coins, Bodies, Games, and Gold: The Politics of Meaning in Archaic Greece* (Princeton, 1999)

Lane Fox, Robin: "Cleisthenes and His Reforms" in *The Good Idea: Democracy in Ancient Greece*, ed. John A. Koumoulides (New Rochelle, 1995)

Langdon, M. K.: "The Territorial Basis of the Attic Demes" (*Symbolae Osloenses* 60, 1985)

Lateiner, Donald: *The Historical Method of Herodotus* (Toronto, 1989)

Lavelle, B. M.: *The Sorrow and the Pity: A Prolegomenon to a History of Athens under the Peisistratids, c. 560–510 BC* (Stuttgart, 1993)

Lazenby, J. F.: "The Strategy of the Greeks in the Opening Campaign of the Persian War" (*Hermes* 92, 1964)

——*The Spartan Army* (Warminster, 1985)

——"Aischylos and Salamis" (*Hermes* 116, 1988)

——*The Defence of Greece 490–479 BC* (Warminster, 1993)

Leick, Gwendolyn: *Mesopotamia: The Invention of the City* (London, 2001)

Lenardon, R. J.: *The Saga of Themistocles* (London, 1978)

Lévêque, P. and Vidal-Naquet, P.: *Clisthène l'Athénien: Essai sur la Représentation de l'Espace et du Temps dans la Pensée Politique Grecque de la Fin du VIe Siècle à la Mort de Platon* (Paris, 1964)

Levine, Louis D.: "Geographical Studies in the Neo-Assyrian Zagros" (*Iran* 11 and 12, 1973–4)

Lewis, D. M.: "Cleisthenes and Attica" (*Historia* 12, 1963)

——*Sparta and Persia* (Leiden, 1977)

——"Datis the Mede" (*JHS* 100, 1980)

Loraux, Nicole: *The Invention of Athens: The Funeral Oration in the Classical City*, tr. Alan Sheridan (Cambridge, Mass., 1986)

——*The Experience of Tiresias: The Feminine and the Greek Man*, tr. Paula Wissing (Princeton, 1995)

——*Born of the Earth: Myth & Politics in Athens*, tr. Selina Stewart (Ithaca, 2000)

MacGinnis, J. D. A.: "Herodotus' Description of Babylon" (*Bulletin of the Institute of Classical Studies* 33, 1986)

Mallowan, Max: "Cyrus the Great (558–529 BC)" (*Iran* 10, 1972)

Manville, P. B.: *The Origins of Citizenship in Ancient Athens* (Princeton, 1990)

Matheson, Sylvia A.: *Persia: An Archaeological Guide* (London, 1972)

Mee, Christopher and Spawforth, Antony: *Greece: An Oxford Archaeological Guide* (Oxford, 2001)

Meier, Christian: "Historical Answers to Historical Questions: The Origins of History in Ancient Greece" (*Arethusa* 20, 1987)

——*The Greek Discovery of Politics*, tr. David McLintock (Cambridge, Mass., 1990)

——*Athens: A Portrait of the City in Its Golden Age*, tr. Robert Kimber and Rita Kimber (New York, 1993)

Meiggs, R. and Lewis, D.: *A Selection of Greek Historical Inscriptions to the End of the Fifth Century BC* (Oxford, 1969)

Mill, John Stuart: *Discussions and Dissertations*, Vol. 2 (London, 1859)

Miller, Margaret C.: *Athens and Persia in the Fifth Century BC: A Study in Cultural Receptivity* (Cambridge, 1997)

Miroschedji, P. de: "La Fin du Royaume d'Anshan et de Suse et la Naissance de l'Empire Perse" (*Zeitschrift für Assyriologie* 75, 1985)

Moles, J.: "Herodotus Warns the Athenians" (*Papers of the Leeds International Latin Seminar* 9, 1996)

Momigliano, Arnaldo: "The Place of Herodotus in the History of Historiography" (*History* 43, 1958)

Momigliano, Arnaldo: *Alien Wisdom: The Limits of Hellenization* (Cambridge, 1975)

Montaigne, Michel de: *The Complete Essays*, tr. M. A. Screech (London, 1991)

Morris, Ian: *Burial and Society: The Rise of the Greek City State* (Cambridge, 1987)

———"The Early Polis as City and State" in *City and Country in the Ancient World*, ed. J. Rich and A. Wallace-Hadrill (London, 1991)

Morris, Ian and Raaflaub, Kurt A. (eds.): *Democracy 2500?: Questions and Challenges* (Dubuque, 1998)

Morrison, J. S., Coates, J. F. and Rankov, N. B.: *The Athenian Trireme: The History and Reconstruction of an Ancient Greek Warship* (Cambridge, 2000)

Moscati, Sabatino: *The World of the Phoenicians*, tr. Alastair Hamilton (London, 1968)

———(ed.): *The Phoenicians* (London, 1997)

Munson, Rosaria Vignolo: *Telling Wonders: Ethnographic and Political Discourse in the Work of Herodotus* (Ann Arbor, 2002)

Murdoch, Iris: *The Nice and the Good* (London, 1968)

Nylander, Carl: "The Standard of the Great King—A Problem in the Alexander Mosaic" (*Opuscula Romana* 14, 1983)

Oates, Joan: *Babylon* (London, 1986)

Ober, Josiah: *Mass and Elite in Democratic Athens: Rhetoric, Ideology, and the Power of the People* (Princeton, 1989)

———*The Athenian Revolution: Essays on Ancient Greek Democracy and Political Theory* (Princeton, 1996)

Ober, Josiah and Hedrick, Charles (eds.): *Demokratia: A Conversation on Democracies, Ancient and Modern* (Princeton, 1996)

Ollier, François: *Le Mirage Spartiate: Étude sur l'Idéalisation de Sparte dans l'Antiquité Grecque*, 2 vols. (Paris, 1933 and 1945)

Olmstead, A. T.: "Darius and His Behistun Inscription" (*American Journal of Semitic Languages and Literatures* 55, 1938)

———*History of the Persian Empire* (Chicago, 1948)

Osborne, Robin: *Greece in the Making: 1200–479 BC* (London, 1996)

Ostwald, Martin: *Nomos and the Beginnings of the Athenian Democracy* (Oxford, 1969)

Parke, H. W.: *A History of the Delphic Oracle* (Oxford, 1939)

———*Festivals of the Athenians* (London, 1977)

Patterson, O.: *Freedom in the Making of Western Culture* (New York, 1991)

Pedley, J.: *Sardis in the Age of Croesus* (Norman, 1968)

Pelling, Christopher: "East is East and West is West—or Are They? National Stereotypes in Herodotus" (*Histos* 1, 1997)

———(ed.): *Greek Tragedy and the Historian* (Oxford, 1997)

Petit, Thierry: *Satrapes et Satrapies dans l'Empire Achéménide de Cyrus le Grand à Xerxés Ier* (Paris, 1990)

Podlecki, A. J.: *The Life of Themistocles: A Critical Survey of the Literary and Archaeological Evidence* (Montreal, 1975)

Pomeroy, Sarah B.: *Spartan Women* (New York, 2002)

Powell, Anton (ed.): *Classical Sparta: Techniques Behind Her Success* (London, 1989)

Powell, Anton and Hodkinson, Stephen (eds.): *The Shadow of Sparta* (Swansea, 1994)

——(eds.): *Sparta: Beyond the Mirage* (Swansea, 2002)

Pritchett, W. K.: "New Light on Thermopylae" (*AJA* 62, 1958)

——*The Greek State at War*, Vols. 1–5 (Berkeley and Los Angeles, 1971–91)

Rawson, Elizabeth: *The Spartan Tradition in European Thought* (Oxford, 1969)

Redfield, J.: "Herodotus the Tourist" (*Classical Philology* 80, 1985)

Rhodes, P.: "Peisistratid Chronology Again" (*Phoenix* 30, 1976)

——*A Commentary on the Aristoteleian "Athenaion Politeia"* (Oxford, 1981)

——*Ancient Democracy and Modern Ideology* (London, 2003)

Robertson, Noel: "Solon's Axones and Kyrbeis, and the Sixth-Century Background" (*Historia* 35, 1986)

Root, Margaret Cool: *The King and Kingship in Achaemenid Art: Essays on the Creation of an Iconography of Empire* (Leiden, 1979)

Roux, Georges: *Ancient Iraq* (London, 1992)

Sancisi-Weerdenberg, Heleen: "The Personality of Xerxes, King of Kings" in *Archeologia Iranica et Orientalis: Miscellanea in Honorem L. Vanden Berghe*, Vol. 1, eds. L. de Meyer and E. Haerinck (Ghent, 1989)

——*Peisistratos and the Tyranny: A Reappraisal of the Evidence* (Amsterdam, 2000)

——(ed.): *Achaemenid History 1: Sources, Structures, Synthesis* (Leiden, 1987)

Sancisi-Weerdenberg, Heleen and Kuhrt, Amélie (eds.): *Achaemenid History 2: The Greek Sources* (Leiden, 1987)

——(eds.): *Achaemenid History 3: Method and Theory* (Leiden, 1988)

——(eds.): *Achaemenid History 4: Centre and Periphery* (Leiden, 1990)

——(eds.): *Achaemenid History 5: The Roots of the European Tradition* (Leiden, 1990)

——(eds.): *Achaemenid History 6: Asia Minor and Egypt: Old Cultures in a New Empire* (Leiden, 1991)

Sancisi-Weerdenberg, Heleen, Kuhrt, Amélie and Root, Margaret Cool (eds.): *Achaemenid History 8: Continuity and Change* (Leiden, 1991)

Schoff, Wilfred H. (tr. and ed.): *"Parthian Stations" by Isidore of Charax* (London, 1914)

Sealey, Raphael: "Again the Siege of the Acropolis, 480 BC" (*California Studies in Classical Antiquity* 5, 1972)

——"The Pit and the Well: The Persian Heralds of 491 BC" (*CJ* 72, 1976)

Sekunda, N.: *The Spartan Army* (Oxford, 1998)

——"Greek Swords and Swordsmanship" (*The International Review of Military History* 3 (1), 2001)

Sekunda, N. and Chew, S.: *The Persian Army 560–330 BC* (Oxford, 1992)

Shapiro, Harvey A.: *Art and Cult under the Tyrants in Athens* (Mainz, 1989)

Shrimpton, Gordon: "The Persian Cavalry at Marathon" (*Phoenix* 34, 1980)

Smith, J. A.: *Athens under the Tyrants* (Bristol, 1989)

Smith, Sidney: *Babylonian Historical Texts Relating to the Capture and Downfall of Babylon* (London, 1924)

Snodgrass, A. N.: *Arms and Armor of the Greeks* (Baltimore, 1967)

——*Archaic Greece: The Age of Experiment* (London, 1980)

Stadter, P. A.: *A Commentary on Plutarch's Pericles* (Chapel Hill, 1989)

Starr, Chester G.: *The Origins of Greek Civilization, 1100–650 BC* (New York, 1961)

——"The Credibility of Early Spartan History" (*Historia* 14, 1965)

——*The Economic and Social Growth of Early Greece, 800–500 BC* (Oxford, 1977)

——"Why Did the Greeks Defeat the Persians?" in *Essays on Ancient History*, eds. Arthur Ferrill and Thomas Kelly (Leiden, 1979)

Stoyanov, Yuri: *The Other God: Dualist Religions from Antiquity to the Cathar Heresy* (New Haven, 2000)

Strauss, Barry: *Salamis: The Greatest Naval Battle of the Ancient World, 480 BC* (New York, 2004)

Szemler, G. J., Cherf, W. J. and Kraft, J. C.: *Thermopylai: Myth and Reality in 480 BC* (Chicago, 1996)

Tadmor, H.: "The Campaigns of Sargon II of Assur" (*JCS* 12, 1958)

Tuplin, Christopher: *Achaemenid Studies* (Stuttgart, 1996)

——"The Seasonal Migration of Achaemenid Kings: A Report on Old and New Evidence" in *Studies in Persian History: Essays in Memory of David M. Lewis*, ed. Maria Brosius and Amélie Kuhrt (Leiden, 1998)

——"The Persian Empire" in *The Long March: Xenophon and the Ten Thousand*, ed. Robin Lane Fox (New Haven, 2004)

Van der Veer, J. A. G.: "The Battle of Marathon: A Topographical Survey" (*Mnemosyne* 35, 1982)

Vanderpool, E.: "A Monument to the Battle of Marathon" (*Hesperia* 35, 1966)

Van Wees, Hans: *Greek Warfare: Myths and Realities* (London, 2004)

Vernant, Jean-Pierre: *Mortals and Immortals: Collected Essays*, ed. Froma I. Zeitlin (Princeton, 1991)

Wallace, Paul W.: "Psyttaleia and the Trophies of the Battle of Salamis" (*AJA* 73, 1969)

——"The Anopaia Path at Thermopylae" (*AJA* 84, 1980)

——"Aphetai and the Battle of Artemision" (*Greek, Roman and Byzantine Monographs* 10, 1984)

Wallace, R.: "The Date of Solon's Reforms" (*American Journal of Ancient History* 8, 1983)

Wallinga, H. T.: "The Ionian Revolt" (*Mnemosyne* 37, 1984)

——"The Trireme and History" (*Mnemosyne* 43, 1990)

——*Ships and Sea-Power before the Great Persian War: The Ancestry of the Ancient Trireme* (Leiden, 1993)

West, S. R.: "Herodotus' Portrait of Hecataeus" (*JHS* 111, 1991)

Whatley, N.: "On the Possibility of Reconstructing Marathon and Other Ancient Battles" (*JHS* 84, 1964)

Whitby, Michael (ed.): *Sparta* (Edinburgh, 2002)

Wiesehöfer, Josef: *Ancient Persia*, tr. Azizeh Azodi (London, 2001)

Wycherley, R. E.: *The Stones of Athens* (Princeton, 1978)

Young, T. C. Jnr.: "480/79 BC—a Persian Perspective" (*Iranica Antiqua* 15, 1980)

Zadok, Ron: "On the Connections between Iran and Babylonia in the Sixth Century BC" (*Iran* 14, 1976)

Index

Tom Holland gained the top degree at Cambridge before earning his Ph.D. at Oxford. An accomplished radio personality in Britain, he has written a highly acclaimed series of adaptations for Radio 4 of Herodotus's *Histories*, Virgil's *Aeneid*, and Homer's *Iliad* and *Odyssey*. He is the author of the critically acclaimed history of the fall of the Roman Republic, *Rubicon*, and the novels *The Bone Hunter*, *Slave of My Thirst*, and *Lord of the Dead*.